STERLING PUBLISHING CO., INC.

NEW YORK

• • •

The GOODLY SPELLBOOK

Olde Spells for Modern Problems

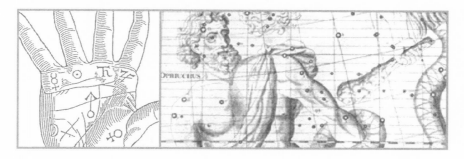

DIXIE DEERMAN
Lady Passion△☆, High Priestess

AND

STEVEN RASMUSSEN
Diuvei△☆, High Priest,
COVEN OLDENWILDE

Library of Congress Cataloging-in-Publication Data Available

2 4 6 8 10 9 7 5 3 1

Published by Sterling Publishing Co., Inc.
387 Park Avenue South, New York, NY 10016
© 2004 by Dixie Deerman and Steve Rasmussen
Distributed in Canada by Sterling Publishing
^{c}/o Canadian Manda Group, 165 Dufferin Street
Toronto, Ontario, Canada M6K 3H6
Distributed in Great Britain by Chrysalis Books Group PLC
The Chrysalis Building, Bramley Road, London W10 6SP, England
Distributed in Australia by Capricorn Link (Australia) Pty. Ltd.
P.O. Box 704, Windsor, NSW 2756, Australia

Illustration credits appear on page 476 and
constitute an extension of this copyright page.

Sterling ISBN 1-4027-0083-0

For information about custom editions, special sales, premium and
corporate purchases, please contact Sterling Special Sales
Department at 800-805-5489 or specialsales@sterlingpub.com.

BOOK DESIGN BY DEBORAH KERNER / DANCING BEARS DESIGN

Dedication

Originally, *dedicate* meant
"to proclaim as sacred — to devote to the Divine."

In that spirit,

we dedicate *The Goodly Spellbook*

to the olde Gods and the Olde Religion.

May the Gods preserve the Craft!

CONTENTS

GLOSSARIES   449

The GOODLY SPELLBOOK

PREFACE

"Let none stop you, or turn you aside."
— ARADIA
MEDIEVAL WITCH

You're not alone—the majority of the world's people believe that it's neither men nor money that rules the earth but magic. Millions continue the age-old tradition of casting goodly spells to achieve health, wealth, peace, strength, and joy in their lives. Folks who do such spellwork are justifiably proud. Blessed with both common sense and conscience, they need never waver in the certainty of what is and always has been. Many still wish on stars, plant by the Moon, and bid the rain to "go away—come again some other day." They still glory in the innate power of their wind-swept hair and become enchanted when a balefire meshes with the shadows like well-woven cloth. Some of us, ecstatic few, delight that by our own rites, we make the seasons turn and the corn grow tall. We take away colic and lullaby the world to sleep with whispered songs we remember fondly from childhood. Sparkling eyes that mirror moonlight are our most common feature. Like innumerable midwives, Gypsies, and granny doctors who preceded us, spellworkers still thrive, devotedly working hand in hand with the powers of nature.

Some things change: Cars replace horses, villages succumb to suburbs, and quills acquiesce to computers. But some things are eternal—such as our yen for freedom and fulfillment, our urge to succor the sick, and our ferocious need to protect our young. For thousands of years, while the rich and the mighty have sought to fulfill these needs through money and armies, the common folk have relied on their own wits and spells.

Magic works—it always has and always will. Olde spells "work like a charm" in modern times because they are based on universal patterns and principles that transcend any particular time or place. Our ancestors phrased these principles in simple, straightforward terms that everyone can understand and use, such as:

- *Like attracts like*—to acquire something, use a spell ingredient that resembles your goal
- *Opposites repel*—to avert a problem, use a spell object that epitomizes its reverse
- *As above, so below*—all things in the universe are interconnected parts of a whole

This perennial wisdom is a source of great power—not for the greedy and the arrogant, but for sensitive, caring people who yearn for a means to truly help themselves, nurture their loved ones, and aid the ecological recovery of their besieged planet.

Spellcraft remains an unbroken, ancestral line of rites celebrating individuals' peaceful, creative means to thrive. Practicing magic is thrilling beyond compare: The siren lure to sacred power and the pleasure spelling evokes in the human heart are as irresistibly magnetic as the attraction kids have to mud puddles! Proving to yourself that your spells can cut through walls and prison bars; suspend time, space, and the conventional laws of physics; and change your life for the better is extremely empowering. After all, who needs a prince, pope, or preacher when you can privately manifest your utmost desires through spellwork?

Spellcraft is applied spirituality—a soul-stirring mental and physical art that inspires its practitioners to operate by no less than their very highest ideals. Two thousand years of propaganda denying the efficacy of spells have failed to obliterate the people's innate desire for, and reliance on, magical fixes for life's daily dilemmas. Spellworkers know, not through blind faith but by their own, direct magical experience, that the Goddesses and Gods of ancient lore are far from being mythical, evil, or dead. They are very real—few spells succeed without their aid, insight, or favor. The magical techniques in this book are presented neither as entertainment nor solely for educational purposes. Magic is an authentic spiritual practice, best used in tandem with medical, legal, and other reasonable measures.

Our ancestors were practical folk. They demanded demonstrable results from their spellwork—as should you. Thousands of their tried-and-true spells still exist, fairly glittering beneath the scholarly library dust of disuse. These antique treasures are just waiting for you to discover, activate, and use them to further your best interests! Many are simple, requiring only one or a handful of easily obtainable ingredients, such as pebbles, eggs, string, fruit peels, and similar items routinely found close at hand. The truth is, you don't need to spend a small fortune on magic—most of the time, you can find or make everything you will need.

There is, however, one secret ingredient in the recipe of every spell. Without it, you cannot unlock the spell's power. That ingredient is knowledge— magical knowledge. Where can you find such knowledge? Unfortunately—as most seekers soon discover—bookstore shelves are littered with flashy titles. They purport to teach magical techniques but actually provide little within but a smattering of New Age clichés and a jumble of spell recipes requiring obscure or unexplained ingredients. Such books are replete with lists and tables but void of insight and experience.

As experienced practitioners and teachers of spellcraft, we think such books dilute magic from a state of firewater to the status of stale ale. We're appalled that such tomes do little but relegate beginners to an unnecessarily superficial knowledge level.

That's why we've filled *The Goodly Spellbook* with authentic spells and practical anecdotes from our own magical experiences. This book does more than merely reproduce recipes—it clearly and vividly teaches you how to create your own spells so that you can tailor your magic to your own individual needs and circumstances. From thought to word to hand to deed, *The Goodly Spellbook* shows you how to cast effective spells anywhere, anytime. We've compiled tried-and-true spell recipes, both ancient and modern, from our many years of experience and our extensive magical library.

The Goodly Spellbook provides the best kind of spells. They are ancient charms based on traditional folk magic, oldies-but-goodies full of spirit-lifting lyrics and thrilling Barbarous Words of Power, simple spells all people can learn to instantly help themselves, their loved ones, and the planet. The spells apply to life today because they address perpetual human desires for love, luck, health, family, friends, prosperity, protection, harmony, fulfillment, intimacy, insight, courage, strength, peace, and joy.

Because human needs are many, spells are very diverse in nature. Anyone, either alone or with others, regardless of age or sexual orientation, can work most of the spells we offer; some, however, are traditionally gender specific. We present them all as they have come down to us through time.

Delightfully simple to do, these spells grant you the satisfaction that comes from getting goodly, reliable results from your magical efforts. By actively practicing the spell variations in *The Goodly Spellbook*, you'll learn to use multiple forms of magic to rectify present-day problems and won't be confined to one magical method.

We've arranged *The Goodly Spellbook* into three easy-to-use parts. If need be, you can turn directly to the **Spells** section, where we've provided hundreds of authentic olde formulas and new ones we've designed and used based on olde ways. They're organized according to persistent, prevalent human needs:

- to heal
- to protect
- to attract something for personal gain or the common good
- to discern past events, present influences, and future probabilities
- to conceal things that should remain secret or safe from harm
- to repel negative onslaught

These recipes redress timeless difficulties, such as how to become fertile, how to mute a riotous party, how to ensure that your computer never crashes, how to keep your phone from being tapped, and how to prevent your car from going kaput at the least opportune moment.

To ensure maximum success in your spellwork, however, we recommend that you provide yourself with a solid foundation in how and why magic works by reading the first two parts of the book. The **Scope** section relates the history of spellcraft, the secrets of how spells work, and the ethical application of them in daily life. The **Skills** section teaches traditional spellwork basics and ways to create your own spells to remedy modern conundrums. It also explains such things as the secret language of Witches, ancient alphabets, ways to make magical music, and ways to convert your desires from words into powerful picture glyphs.

We list our sources at the end of the book so that you may delve more deeply into your magical researches. There you'll also find a helpful glossary listing the magical and medicinal herbs required in the **Spells** section and a glossary of common Craft terms. If you read an unfamiliar word, simply consult it or the Glossary of Ancient Witch Words, page 177.

Liberally spiced throughout with Coven Oldenwilde's magical experiences, *The Goodly Spellbook* confers a penetrating comprehension of how modern spellcrafters continue to work with the immutable powers of nature to effect our celebrated feats.

Spellworkers should approach practicing magic with the patience they'd display while learning any other intricate skill, such as gardening, beading, or loom weaving. Consistent, replicable magical ability requires daily practice. Core principles can be taught, but individual flair must be sought. Your magical intention and urgent desire to master the Craft are more crucial to your success than possessing certain Craft tools or expensive spell supplies.

Reject any initial urge to memorize the spell ingredient lists, recipes, or arcane Craft words we provide. Instead, absorb the ways spells are caressed into being from intangible thought forms into physical reality through a mental/physical alchemy that has been practiced successfully since the dawn of time.

Once you've learned how simple and easy magic is to do, you'll be amazed at the wondrous world that opens for you. You may also feel more than a bit chagrined that you dallied so long in claiming your magical birthright. *The Goodly Spellbook* helps you master core spellwork basics and expand your magical potential in limitless ways without becoming overwhelmed or getting bogged down in superfluous trivia. Soon, you'll swiftly work spells that you once considered complicated—ever perfecting your ability to effect a desired change in your circumstances as the need arises.

Ultimately, *The Goodly Spellbook* imparts not only magical lore and spell skills but also the enchanting, lyrical mysticism so rare in spellbooks these days. Immersed in the very real world of magic, you'll learn to understand spellcraft intuitively rather than remaining frustrated or at the mercy of some local charlatan.

The spellworkers of the world are many, and each person is electric with potential, promise, and wisdom. Our task is, as always, to perpetuate the Olde Ways—proven means by which you can nurture yourself, others, and the planet.

LADY PASSION, HIGH PRIESTESS
and
*DIUVEI, HIGH PRIEST
COVEN OLDENWILDE

PART I

SCOPE

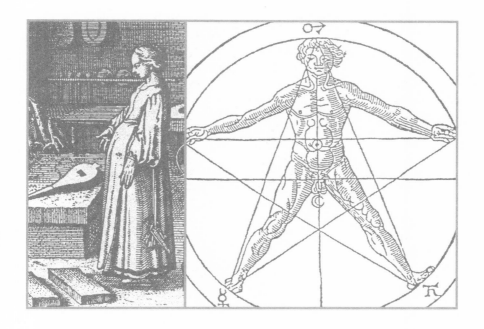

*"Of all cultural expressions, magic passes most
rapidly from people to people."*

J.H.G. GRATTEN AND CHARLES SINGER
Anglo-Saxon Magic and Medicine

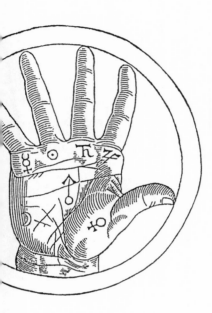 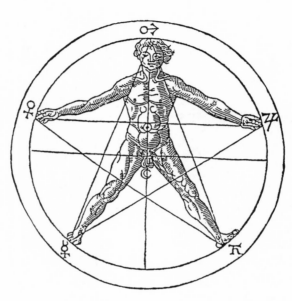

SPELLCRAFT

THE NATURAL AND ANCIENT ART
OF APPLIED SPIRITUALITY

*"Civilized People who read about Red Indian sorcerers and gypsy
witches very promptly conclude that they are mere humbugs or
lunatics—they do not realize how these people, who pass half their lives
in wild places watching waving grass and falling waters, and listening
to the brook until its cadence speaks in real song, believe in their
inspirations, and feel that there is the same mystical feeling and presence
in all things that live and move and murmur as well as in themselves.*

*But nature is eternal, and while grass grows and rivers run man is
ever likely to fall again into the eternal enchantments."*

—CHARLES GODFREY LELAND
Gypsy Sorcery and Fortune Telling

If you've ever hung a horseshoe over your door to attract goodly
luck, knocked on wood to avert ill luck, displayed the first dollar
your business earned to increase its prosperity, wished on a shooting star, tossed a coin into a fountain, pulled apart a wishbone, or
blown out birthday candles, you've cast a spell. Whenever you perform actions
that symbolically express your intent but have no direct physical connection
between the action and its result, you participate in practices that are older than
the Stone Age. Such ritual acts that we routinely laugh off as silly superstitions
(but perform anyway, just in case) have a mighty ancestry in hundreds of thousands of years of human culture.

On every continent and in every age, people have respected or feared shamans, priest/esses,[1] Witches, druids, wise women, and medicine men for their ability to calm tempests or conjure rain, bless crops and herds, or curse an invading army. However, in cultures that rely on magic as an essential tool for daily living—which includes practically every human culture in history, with the sole exception of Western industrial countries' modern dominant culture—spellcraft isn't the monopoly of such specialists. The farmer, the fisher, the midwife, and the milkmaid know that magic is the birthright of every human being. They hang a shiny charm on a baby's crib or horse's bridle, or paint eyes on the prow of a boat to deflect the Evil Eye. They top a newly built house or barn with an evergreen tree to help it stand for many years or beat the boundaries of their property with switches to ward away ill luck. These are examples of traditional European and early-American folk spells that your own great-grandparents might have practiced.

The Hidden History of Spellcraft

"The study of Magic, which has now fallen into disrepute was, among the Egyptians, regarded with a veneration hardly accorded to the highest Philosophy in modern times. To the Ancient Egyptians the most eminent man was he who had by hard training gained supremacy over the Elements, from which his own body and the Manifested World were alike formed; one whose Will had risen Phoenix-like from the ashes of his desires; one whose Intuition, cleansed from the stains of material illusion, was a clear mirror in which he could perceive the Past, the Present and the Future."

—Florence Farr
Egyptian Magic

The worldwide history of spellcraft fills thousands of books and ranges across hundreds of magical cultures and religions, from the Chinese

---

[1] *We use the terms* priest/ess *and* God/dess *to mean "priest and priestess" and "God and Goddess."*

Taoists to the Tibetan Bön and from the African Yoruba to the Meso-American Maya. It's useful and enlightening to study the magical history of somebody else's culture; it's also relatively easy and non-threatening. It's more controversial, but ultimately more empowering, to study your own. If you are from a traditional culture, you know how dominant Western culture has endangered traditional magical practices by denying their validity.

What happened in our culture to drive spellcraft underground? Why do many contemporary people feel publicly compelled to denounce spellcasting as evil or deride it as wishful thinking—even while they privately continue to practice it?

If you have an understanding of how and why things came to be this way, you will feel much more confident—more firmly rooted—as you undertake to study spellcraft. Knowing your own history, you won't feel so isolated, always wondering whether it's you who is crazy for knowing that magic is real, or the world around you for denying it. More than that, you will begin to feel the urgency of reclaiming this birthright, not only for your own sake, but also for the sake of a planet whose very survival has been put at risk by the centuries-long suppression of the natural art of magic.

What follows is a brief account of magic and spellcraft in the West, from ancient Roman times to the present day. Although we have based it entirely on reliable, accessible sources, it's nevertheless a hidden history. Magic has long been viewed as a threat to the dominance of religion and, later, of science—although it is the parent of both of them and the bridge between them. Its practitioners have for centuries been mostly reviled and scorned by the writers of history, who have too often focused on lurid accusations and official slanders at the expense of the truth. Fortunately, starting in the late twentieth century, an increasing number of researchers and academics have pulled off the old blinders and begun taking a detailed new look at the occult history of Western culture.

Although women have preserved and perpetuated much of spellcraft and magic through the ages, the chroniclers of history have usually, until very recently, been men. Because such historical sources are extremely gender-biased, the preponderance of male names you'll see in this account reflects the prejudices and cultural assumptions of those who wrote the histories. Only recently have women been allowed to tell future generations their side of the story.

The story that follows is controversial, even subversive in many people's eyes, not because it's untrue—the facts described here are well documented—but for the very reason that it *is* true. The history of magic in the West reveals a shadow side of our orthodox institutions of religion, science, and politics—the crypts and dungeons hidden in their foundations that the defenders of those powerful citadels strive to keep locked away from public view.

ANTIQUITY

The writings of Roman historians are replete with references to magic's all-pervading role in ancient life. The emperors and generals of Rome—just like the rulers of Greece, Persia, Egypt, Babylon, India, and the other great civilizations that preceded and influenced the Roman Empire—consulted oracles, observed and heeded omens, and interpreted dreams before commencing wars or other complex affairs of state.[2] Merchants did the same before beginning a risky voyage or caravan journey.

In those days, nearly everyone performed prayers and spells as occasions arose. But when people needed powerful magic to be done—an incurable illness healed, bad weather abated, a petition granted or lawsuit won—they turned, as their ancestors had always done, to their society's specialists in spellcraft: the priest/esses[2] and magicians among them, who devoted their lives to mastering the hidden powers of nature. They considered this as normal as we consider consulting a doctor for help with a medical problem. In fact, spells and incantations were an integral part of ancient physicians' repertoire, along with herbal medications and surgery.

In the marble temples whose ruins still grace such sacred mounds as the Acropolis of Athens and the Seven Hills of Rome, schools of priest/esses conducted prayers, divinations, public rituals, and rites to attract and sustain the people's prosperity, fertility, victory, healing, and peace. In the streets and marketplaces below, freelance magicians could be quietly, if illegally, hired to curse an enemy or cast a love spell. Do-it-yourselfers consulted *grimoires,* or manuals of spells, such as the *Papyri Graecae Magicae,* the source of many of the spells in this book. This Hellenistic grimoire's polyglot title reflects the three cultures

[2] *Read throughout the works of Herodotus, Thucydides, Plutarch, Tacitus, and so on.*

that the Romans revered as the most magical they knew—the Egyptians (*papyri*), the Greeks (*graecae*), and the Persians (*magicae,* after the Magi). Temple priest/esses, marketplace magicians, and spellbooks all relied on and called for the divine aid of a panoply of God/desses and spirits as varied and diverse as nature and humanity themselves.

In this pluralistic atmosphere, no one was beholden to any overarching religious hierarchy. For example, a priestess of Isis in Alexandria or of Diana in Ephesus owed no allegiance to the *flamen dialis,* the chief priest of Rome, but simply to her own primary Goddess and temple. Yet the priest/esses routinely acknowledged and harmoniously co-existed with one another's cults, much as modern university professors generally acknowledge the validity of one another's academic disciplines.

In theory, anyone with a grudge could use magic to harm as well as help, so it was perceived as a double-edged sword in Roman times, in the same way many view technology today. Laws forbade certain kinds of magic that were perceived as too manipulative or harmful, such as *necromancy,* raising the spirit of someone dead in order to foretell the future. An account of a second-century Roman lawsuit survives in which the family of a rich widow accused her new and much-younger husband, Lucius Apuleius of Madaura, of casting a love spell to gain her hand—and her estate. Apuleius, the author of *The Golden Ass* (*The Transformations of Lucius*), wittily refuted the charge in a four-hour oration, his *Discourse on Magic.* The wealthy and powerful often worried that those whom they'd impoverished or disenfranchised would retaliate and ruin them with a curse—to the point that the Emperor Augustus ordered the burning of some 2,000 spellbooks he deemed dangerous.

One group of people in the ancient world distinguished good magic from bad—not according to the healing or hurtful intent or effect of the spell, but solely according to the Deity in whose name the magic was performed. In their eyes, even a curse was inherently good if it was uttered in the name of their God, and even a blessing was innately evil if it was uttered in the name of any other Goddess, God, or spirit.

The Christian Bible contains vehement denunciations of sorcerers, magicians, soothsayers, and so on, as well as of priest/esses of Pagan religions. It is equally rife with stories about magical feats termed *miracles,* such as wonder-workings, healings, and curses. Pagan contemporaries of the early Christians expressed difficulty in seeing any difference between the marvels accorded to Moses and those performed by the pharaoh's magicians, or the healings attributed to Jesus versus those done by wandering Pagan philosophers, such as Jesus' contemporary Apollonius of Tyana. Typical of the paradoxes that puzzled—and still puzzle—non-Christians is the first miracle performed by the apostle Paul. He cursed with blindness a magician named Bar-Jesus, who was trying to dissuade a proconsul of Cyprus from converting to Christianity (Acts 13:6–11). This was the very kind of vindictive spell that ancient law and ethics routinely condemned.

To Christians who perceived themselves as a saved elite, however, the distinction was a simple matter of Them *vs.* Us. They deemed justifiable and saintly grave crimes and atrocities committed at the behest of their God, but labeled as evil such life-affirming Pagan miracles as the healings of incurable diseases in the shrines of Asclepius, which numerous surviving inscriptions by grateful sufferers record. Although the polytheistic Pagans included such Judeo-Christian words as *Tetragrammaton* and *Adonai* among the other names in their spell invocations, the early Church fathers and gospel authors demonized Pagan magic because it called on God/desses they reviled as rivals to their one and only Deity.

The Jewish priests who authored the books included in the Old Testament focused their attack on spellcraft and magic from a slightly different angle than the gospel writers did. Instead of battling magic to convert outsiders, they were intent on stamping out the magical practices that flourished within their own community.

When confronted by an injustice, an illness, a lack, or another problem that could not be redressed by conventional physical means, folk magicians and spellcrafters took matters into their own hands. They actively used their will to manifest solutions to their problems. To end a prolonged drought, for example, they would perform magical actions and invoke spiritual entities or elemental powers that bring rain. Then, as now, spellcrafters took a direct role—though in an indirect way.

The stern patriarchs of the Old Testament condemned the spellcrafter's spiritual activism as contradicting the will of God. If a drought afflicted the people, it was a sign of the Lord's anger at the Israelites' backsliding ways or one of the tribulations that the chosen people needed to undergo to purify them.

Casting a spell to counteract Jehovah's will (especially if it included propitiating some other, less harshly inclined divinity, as polytheists are wont to do) could incite their jealous God to rain down divine vengeance upon the people. Like abused children, they were expected to implore their Father to spare his rod of punishment, promise to repent and mend their sinful ways, and find a scapegoat in their midst to blame and persecute for their troubles.

To add insult to injury, although the patriarchs condemned Pagan practices, much of the Torah and the Old Testament have been proven to derive from the Pagan beliefs and mythoi of the cultures the Hebrews conquered or absorbed, such as the Edomites and Canaanites.[3] The cross as a Pagan symbol depicting the Four Directions that define our earthly cosmos far predates its use as a New Testament icon.

Most people are accustomed to hearing about the Roman Empire's persecution of Christians and its razing of the Jewish Temple. We often don't realize that the monotheism of Judeo-Christianity and the monarchy of the Roman Empire had far more in common with each other than either did with polytheistic, anarchic Pagan religion. They were both centralized authorities, demanding obedience and sacrifice by everyone under their sway to one single Being—the one God, Jehovah, or the one emperor, Caesar. Jehovah sought monopoly over people's spiritual lives; Caesar sought monopoly over their political lives. When the declining imperial power and the rising ecclesiastical power recognized their common interest and merged as one under Constantine, catastrophe loomed for Pagan philosophers, priest/esses, and magicians. No longer did the Christian patriarchs have to argue and compete with them for influence. Now, they simply began wiping them out.

Numerically, far more Pagans were martyred in the years after Constantine's conversion to monotheism than Christians had ever been under any of the polytheistic emperors. The Christians used methods at least as brutal as any the Romans had employed, such as boiling Pagans in oil, roasting them in crucible ovens, or peeling their skin off inch by inch. The new state religion systematically burned every book of magic and spellcraft it could lay hands on and fined, imprisoned, or summarily executed their owners. Bands of fanatical monks and lay people destroyed magnificent temples, such as those of Zeus in Pergamon

---

[3] *Richard Elliott Friedman,* Who Wrote the Bible? *(New York: Harper and Row, 1989).*

and Serapis in Alexandria. They murdered famous philosophers, such as the beautiful and learned Hypatia, whom they hacked to death with sharp oyster shells and broken tiles in the streets of Alexandria. The new Church of Rome even stamped out other Christian sects and scriptures that dissented from its authority, such as the Gnostics. Their often mystical, even feminist gospels were lost until 1945, when copies hidden by persecuted monks were discovered in the Egyptian desert at Nag Hammadi.

Especially singled out for persecution were the staunchest intellectual holdouts for Pagan magical philosophy—the followers of such Platonist philosophers as Plotinus and Iamblichus (now called neo-Platonists in a misguided scholarly effort to distance these late-Roman-era metaphysical thinkers from the father of philosophy). Plato and his successors championed the philosophical principles that underlie spellcraft, and Plato's writings contain many discussions of such specifics as the magical correspondences of vowels and consonants and of the musical modes.

Plato attributed much of his philosophy to Pythagoras, the philosopher whom the Greeks credited with introducing the mathematical arts of the Egyptians, Babylonians, and Asian Indians. In his *Symposium,* however, Plato made his teacher, Socrates, admit that he'd learned his famous method of seeking the truth through questioning from a Witch named Diotima of Mantinea, who had once used her powers to prevent a plague from striking Athens. From the very beginnings of Western culture to the present day, Pythagorean and Platonic philosophy have provided an intellectual and logical rationale for magic.

THE MEDIEVAL UNDERGROUND

As the old empire broke up, the Church spread its "one true way" by sending missionaries to the barbarian Celtic, Germanic, and Slavic tribes of Europe. Ambitious chieftains seeking to centralize power in their own realms took a page from Constantine, renouncing the God/desses of their fathers and mothers and converting to the monotheist religion. Fellow tribes that refused to follow suit risked being demonized as evil heathens and made the target of a genocidal holy war. Charlemagne put the people of Saxony to the sword in the eighth century, and the crusading Order of Teutonic Knights hunted down the Balts like game in the thirteenth and fourteenth centuries.

In most of early medieval Christendom, however, magic and spellcraft simply shape-shifted its outward appearance to fit the new religion, and continued to be practiced as pervasively as ever. Although it mattered tremendously to doctrinaire Church councils whether the microcosm and macrocosm were bound together by the cross of Jesus Christ or by Yggdrasil, the World Tree, most people didn't really care which theological entity got credit for curing their diseases or blessing their crops, as long as he, she, or it got the job done. In popular devotion, the saints of the new religion assumed the myths, attributes, and functions of the Deities of the Olde Religion, enabling the needed magic to continue. The same process of changing the label while preserving the contents took place centuries later when missionaries converted Native Americans and African slaves in the Americas, as exemplified by religions such as Santeria.

The many written spells and systems of magic in the grimoires that survive from this period differ from Pagan magic only in that they substitute Jewish and, occasionally, Christian Deities and myths for Pagan ones. Just as Pagan magical writings were often attributed to Hermes Trismegistus as the father of magic, Jewish spellbooks were attributed to wise King Solomon. Mystical Judaism, in fact, became a refuge for magic. The very influential occult tradition of Kabbalah originated in these early centuries C.E.

A traditional English charm ritual that present-day scholars often point to as an example of the blurry medieval line between the old magic and the new religion is the Anglo-Saxon Æcerbot rite. Until relatively recent times, it was still celebrated annually on Plow Monday, the first Monday after Twelfth Night. To protect cropland from sorcery—that is, from being cursed by someone with ill intent—a piece of turf was cut from each of the four corners of the land. The turfs were anointed with farm products, such as fruit, milk, honey, and herbs, as well as holy water. "Commanding" words in Latin, such as *grow* and *multiply,* were spoken over them, as was the Our Father. The anointed turfs were taken to the church and placed under the altar, where a priest said four masses over them. Then, before the sun set, the turfs were replaced in the ground from which they had been dug. Four crosses marked with the names of the authors of the four gospels as well as other sacred words and prayers were placed there. One special prayer called on the Lord, the Heavens, and Earth to bring forth the virtues of the land to grow and multiply. The participant ended this rite by turning three times and reciting a number of Christian prayers. Following this ritual was a similar but even more Pagan-infused one for blessing the plow that used herbs and prayers that called on Mother Earth as well as the Lord.[4]

Change nothing but the names and the prayers and this would be a thoroughly Pagan spell for protection and fertility, particularly if the altar had been erected atop a pre-Christian sacred site, as was common in the Middle Ages. Often, the priest himself would double as the passer-on of traditional Pagan lore.

At the core upper levels of its hierarchy, the Church was, like all bureaucracies, a rigid enforcer of doctrinal conformity. However, as religious orthodoxy radiated outward and downward, magical people, both lay and ordained, diluted and adapted it to fit more realistically with human beings' natural needs and innate abilities. Church council decrees could not stop the olde God/desses from aiding humanity. Devotees might have addressed the Queen of Heaven as Mary, but she continued—and continues—to appear in the visions of mystics and artists wearing the starry blue robe and the crescent Moon of her predecessor, Diana.

Among some hard-to-conquer peoples, Paganism continued to be practiced fairly openly—in many cases even until modern times—such as in the Basque uplands between France and Spain and in the wilder Celtic reaches of Wales. In the remoter villages and hamlets of the Christian kingdoms, the old wizards, seers, shamans, and cunning men and women—now labeled as wicked *Witches, sorcieres,* and *hexen*—continued to pass their rites and spells on to succeeding generations. In the rugged hills of Tuscany, the old lands of the Etruscans, the people from whom the Romans first learned divination and magic—Italian *Strega,* or "Witches," blessed and cursed in the names of Diana and Aradia, practically in the pope's backyard.

In the late nineteenth century, a Tuscan Witch named Maddalena introduced the American scholar Charles Godfrey Leland to her collection of *Strega* lore and writings, which he translated and published as *Aradia: Gospel of the Witches.* One legend depicts Aradia as a daughter of Diana, who came to Earth to teach spells of healing to the poor and to help them resist their oppression by

---

[4] *Karen Louise Jolly, "Magic, Miracle, and Popular Practice in the Early Medieval West: Anglo-Saxon England," in* Religion, Science and Magic, *ed. Jacob Neusner et al. (Oxford: Oxford University Press, 1989), 175–6.*

wealthy landlords. Another story describes a young woman called *la Bella Pellegrina,* or "the Beautiful Pilgrim," who threw off the authority of the Church and her parents and converted to the Witches' religion. Dressed in pilgrim's garb, ". . . she traveled far and wide, teaching and preaching the religion of old times, the religion of Diana, the Queen of the Fairies and of the Moon, the goddess of the poor and the oppressed."[5] Raven Grimassi[6] suggests that Aradia and *la Bella Pellegrina* were the same, a historical personage in the fourteenth century who incited the northern Italian resurgence of Witchcraft to which Renaissance Church historians attributed the Inquisition against Witches.

When Gypsies first wandered into Europe in the fourteenth and fifteenth centuries, they brought their rich, unabashedly Pagan trove of spellcraft with them, which they continue to employ today. Even in the settled lowlands of Europe, secret traditions of spellcraft flourished among the farmers, blacksmiths, midwives, tinkers, thieves, and other common folk up through the Middle Ages and the Renaissance and, in many cases, up to the present day.

A magical tradition somewhat different from the folk tradition evolved among the aristocratic and learned classes of Christendom. They had access to the surviving writings of the Greeks and Romans—especially after they came into renewed contact with ancient Pagan philosophy through their interactions, in Spain, Constantinople, and the Holy Land, with the more religiously tolerant Islamic cultures, which preserved much more of the ancient learning than the cultures of Western Europe did. Ceremonial magic, a term that dates from the Renaissance, followed a path that often intersected creatively with folk magic, but was generally more systematic and formal. Folk magic tended to emphasize the principles of sympathy—like attracts like—and contagion—once in contact, always in contact. Ceremonial magic focused on summoning and controlling hierarchies of spirit Beings, which appealed to nobles accustomed to commanding ranks and files of soldiers, and drawing on the overarching science of astrological correspondences. The learned recognized these correspondences as a key to the fundamental workings of the universe.

---

[5] *Charles Godfrey Leland,* Aradia: Gospel of the Witches *(1890; reprint Blaine, Wash.: Phoenix Publishing, 1990), 68. The name* Aradia *probably derives from Herodias, an ancient, oft-preached-against Goddess of Witchcraft.*

[6] *Raven Grimassi,* Ways of the Strega: Italian Witchcraft: Its Lore, Magick, and Spells *(Los Angeles: Llewellyn Publications, 1995).*

According to the introduction of the famous thirteenth-century ceremonial-magic grimoire the *Sworn Book of Honorius* (*Liber Juratus*), a general council of 811 (some sources say 89) magicians from Naples, Athens, and Toledo gathered to discuss what to do about their persecution by the pope and his cardinals. Church officials had determined to persecute the magicians, the book relates, because they were influencing too many people to follow their Art. Certain that they were marked for death, the magicians chose one of their number, Honorius of Thebes, to preserve the kernel of their Art in the *Sworn Book*. Master magicians would pass the book on at their deaths only to carefully chosen disciples who would swear an oath to do the same at their deaths—hence its name. Honorius also wrote a superficial version of the book that was publicly distributed as a blind for the persecutors to gather up and burn, thus being fooled into thinking they had destroyed all the magicians' works.

The cities the *Sworn Book* mentions were hotbeds of spellcraft. Toledo, in Moorish Spain, was a famous center of magic in the Middle Ages (Chaucer mentions it), as was southern Italy, where the ancient cult of Dionysus never truly died out. Athens still preserved much of Greek learning. Thebes is the Egyptian city where the much earlier author of the *Papyri Graecae Magicae* is believed to have lived.

All over Europe, a Pagan underground of initiatory traditions; worship of Pagan Deities; and *Sabbats,* celebratory seasonal gatherings in groups that came to be called *covens,* continued to be active from ancient times until the present day—often practically under the noses of hostile ecclesiastical and secular authorities.[7] The traditions of what came to be called *Witchcraft* in the Middle Ages were often passed down in secrecy for generations among the close-knit circles of village, guild, and kin—typically from grandparent to grandchild, lover to lover, master to apprentice, or experienced elder to carefully selected seeker.

Such traditions were not confined to any one social class, however. Ceremonial and folk magic, gentry and peasants mingled freely in the covens, which, standing as they did outside the sanctioned social order, provided people a rare oasis of equality in a desert of rigid class stratification. To this day, many Witches meet *skyclad,* or naked, wearing neither silk nor rags to distinguish rich

---

[7] *Doreen Valiente's* An ABC of Witchcraft *and* The Rebirth of Witchcraft *are among the best sources of scholarship on this subject.*

from poor or highborn from lowborn—just as covens are depicted as meeting in fifteenth-century paintings and engravings by Albrecht Dürer and others.

The evidence for this vibrant underground survival of Pagan magic is abundant. Many of the spellbooks these practitioners used survive in private collections and in rare-book sections of libraries. Some are still in use by initiatory Witch traditions in the present day, such as our own Gardnerian practice, having been copied and re-copied, annotated, and added to by preceding generations of Witches. Unfortunately, most popular historians of Witchcraft usually neglect these authentic but often hard-to-obtain documentary sources. The Gardnerian *Book of Shadows,* for example, is oath bound to secrecy and not allowed to be published. Chroniclers focus instead on lurid and distorted descriptions of Witches and their practices that were written and widely published by their enemies and persecutors.

THE MAGICAL RENAISSANCE

An alchemist is hired by a greedy king to seek the Philosopher's Stone, which can transmute lead into gold. A wizard in symbol-spangled robes, high atop a lonely tower, waves his wand to conjure a spirit. A witch in buckled hat and shoes rides a broomstick across the Moon. There is a reason such images have become cartoon clichés for "magic." During the Renaissance, Pagan magic became so popular and pervasive in courtly intellectual life that it became the unofficial religion of the aristocracy. Then, in a nightmare of blood and fire, the magical worldview was suppressed from Western public life so completely and swiftly that these fossilized stereotypes from the sixteenth and seventeenth centuries are all that most people now know of it.

Historians conventionally tell us that the Renaissance dawned in the middle to late 1400s with the rediscovery and translation of the works of Plato and other ancient authors by Marsilio Ficino and Pico della Mirandola, at the behest of the Florentine merchant-prince Cosimo dé Medici. The part of the story they usually leave out is that Ficino and Pico were seeking to recover the magical philosophy they knew pervaded the ancients' writings. Pico, a scholar of Hebrew, was a noted Kabbalist, and Ficino practiced Pagan rituals and wrote a popular book on healing magic, *The Book of Life,* that was suppressed by Church censors.

Ficino's writings on Platonic theology set the fifteenth-century intellectual world on fire. A deeply schismatic and money-corrupted Church had been losing its grip on European culture and politics for well over a century. The secular courts of the princes and kings who ruled such increasingly powerful nation-states and city-states as France, England, Spain, Florence, and Venice were becoming the cultural centers of Europe as nobles and scholars flocked to the new capitals of political and economic power. The spiritual activism of Pagan spellcraft appealed to the humanist heart of this bold and vigorous age of New World explorers and vernacular poets and playwrights. Pagan God/desses and myths and magical themes inspired and permeated the visual and literary arts in a rebirth of ancient learning.

In 1509 and 1510, a 23-year-old German nobleman named Heinrich Cornelius Agrippa of Nettesheim compiled the most influential work on magic and spellcraft ever written. The source for nearly every spellbook written since, Agrippa's *Three Books of Occult Philosophy (De occulta philosophia)* organize spellcraft into ceremonial, celestial, and natural magic. This threefold schema is the essence of the magical philosophy of the Renaissance—and reveals the fault lines along which it would soon shatter so violently.

Ceremonial magic—so called because it derived from the traditional and, in essence, universal ceremonies priest/esses used to communicate with the divine—was the religious aspect of magic. Agrippa and his contemporaries insisted it was profoundly and piously Christian. It was based, they claimed, on the worship of God and the Kabbalistic power of the name of Jesus Christ. Almost every Renaissance-era grimoire begins with elaborate invocations of God, Jesus, the Holy Spirit, and other Judeo-Christian divinities.

The Church censors didn't buy it. After all, once you get past the orthodox pieties, the most obvious feature you see running through the rites and spells of ceremonial magic is their summoning of a vast variety of spirits and Deities. Church authorities categorically classified all of these as devils—with no regard whatsoever to their actual natures, which were and are no less diversely benevolent and malevolent than human souls.

The middle element, celestial magic, was the keystone of Renaissance magic, the hinge that bound the spiritual and the physical elements together. It embraced the arts/sciences of number, geometry, music, and—above all—

astrology. In ancient times, those four interrelated disciplines had been linked together as the *quadrivium,* or four-way crossroads, and were considered the very core from which all other paths of knowledge branched. To the occult polymaths we still remember as Renaissance men, the quadrivial arts revealed the system of correspondences that orders all things and ideas in the universe. They are the basis of the Art of Correspondences, the skeleton key that unlocks all spellcraft.

Natural magic was the down-to-earth aspect—the direct forerunner of what we now call science. It focused on understanding and manipulating the properties of physical things, such as herbs, stones, incenses, animals, weather, the Four Elements, and so on.

Legendary occultists flourished during the courtly Renaissance of magic. In France, Michel de Nostradamus spent his nights in a magic circle, communing with spirits to predict the future, and his days confirming his revelations with astrology and recording them in cryptic quatrains. In Italy, Giordano Bruno wrote inspired treatises on magic, the art of memory, and the ways magicians—and politicians—used images to enchain and manipulate people's minds and wills, foretelling the techniques of modern advertising.

The brilliant and tragic figure of John Dee is inseparable from the romantic history of Elizabethan and Shakespearean England. Many know about his evocations of spirits through a *shewstone,* a type of crystal ball, with the aid of the psychic William Kelly, but few are aware that he was also an international secret agent for Queen Elizabeth I. Dee went by the code name 007 and originated the idea of an Empire of Great Britain.[8] Dee's countryman, the freethinking explorer Sir Francis Drake, is said to have led a Witches' coven in raising the sudden storm that destroyed the Spanish Armada. To this day, people hear "Drake's Drum" beating along the coast whenever England is threatened with invasion.

At the sunset of the Elizabethan era, Robert Fludd's gloriously illustrated writings on occult philosophy helped promulgate the Rosicrucian Enlightenment. Alchemists and a Bohemian king who believed that magical philosophy

---

[8] *Valiente,* An ABC of Witchcraft, *(Blaine, Wash.: Phoenix Publishing, 1988), 79; and Frances Amelia Yates,* The Occult Philosophy in the Elizabethan Age, *(London: Routledge and Kegan Paul, 1979), 85.*

could reform and heal the world led this brief but extremely influential political and intellectual movement.

The Renaissance mages—whose core belief was that Man is a microcosm of the divine macrocosm, that every individual contains the entire universe reflected within himself or herself—posed a powerful challenge to the Church's monopoly of the spirit. They were the vanguard of *humanism,* the assertion that people need not be enslaved by dogmas of sin and conformity. The mages believed that each of us is innately divine, carrying a spark of freedom, creativity, and will that—once emboldened—can change the world we inhabit for the better.

Witches and mages were not Rome's greatest threat, however, nor was the Catholic Church magic's only enemy. The spellcrafters' optimistic hope that human beings could improve the world's lot with magic would be twisted by their heirs into an obsession with shackling nature to the service of Man.

THE BURNING TIMES

The renaissance of magic ran tragically afoul of the Protestant Reformation. During the course of the sixteenth century, religion became a bloody battleground for politics as merchants and monarchs in the increasingly urbanized and independent northern European nation-states joined Martin Luther's rebellion against spiritual domination by Rome. Conflicts between Protestants and Catholics engulfed France, England, the German states, Sweden, and eventually almost all the nations of Europe. Violence and mutual persecution escalated through the 1500s and early 1600s until it exploded in the Thirty Years War—the bloodiest conflict in all of European history before World War II.

As the "one true faith" splintered into opposing factions, a kind of collective schizophrenia seized Christendom. The monotheist religion was now at war, not against such rival faiths as Islam or Judaism or Paganism, but against itself. French Catholics burned Huguenots while English Puritans beheaded Papists. Armies of mercenaries scourged German and Italian towns and villages at the behest of the highest bidders, be they Protestant or Catholic. It seemed to the faithful as if God's covenant was self-destructing. Just as in Old Testament times, a scapegoat had to be found on whose head the blame for these traumas and terrors could be laid.

The Witch Hysteria, or Craze, that ensued resulted in the deaths of some 500,000 people.[9] It got its start in the mid-1400s with the publication of several books—including the notorious *Malleus Maleficarum*—that described Witchcraft in a way it had never been perceived before. From ancient times through the Middle Ages, those in authority, whether Pagan or Christian, had made a distinction between harmful and beneficent spellcasting. Cursing your neighbor's cattle was condemned and punished as an anti-social act, whereas healing them through charms or prayers to Pagan Deities was, if not overlooked, at worst treated as a misguided superstition.

The new Christian ideologues, however, presented magic as the exclusive product of a pact with the Devil. Regardless of intent, they insisted, anyone who practiced unauthorized magic was by definition in league with Satan. Manuals such as the *Malleus* presented detailed "proofs" of the supposed reality and pervasiveness of Satanic witch cults. The male writers of such books claimed that women, because of their "lustful nature," were particularly prone to practicing Witchcraft, and filled their books with the morbid "confessions" made by women under torture to having had bizarre sexual relations with a male devil. The newly invented printing press made distributing the books easy, and the zealots succeeded in convincing many people of the falsehood that people could learn and practice magic only by making a pact with the Devil.

There were probably more active covens of Witches in the freethinking ferment of the Renaissance than at any other time between Roman antiquity and the present day. Then, as now, they followed not only the Goddess of the Moon, whom they called Diana, Herodias, or Hecate, but also the Horned God, whom some called by the Christianized names Lucifer, Old Nick, or the Devil. This male divinity, however, was not the biblical Prince of Darkness. Satan is a Christian Deity, the evil counterpart to a good God that is necessitated by that religion's dualistic theology. Witches have always followed the Horned God of the animals and forests—an ancient Deity honored in every culture around the world and known in various parts of pre-Christian Europe as Pan, Dionysus, Cernunnos, Hermes, and Herne. He was, and is, the divine protector of the untamed wild places that Pagans loved and Christians feared. The Greeks

---

[9] *Estimates vary widely, from a couple hundred thousand to several million victims, of whom an estimated 85 percent were women.*

depicted Pan as bearing horns, hooves, and a tail—and often a very erect member—to symbolize his closeness to the animal kingdom and the fertility of the Earth. The Christian ideologues of the Renaissance took this image from the ancient Pagan sculptures and mosaics and re-framed it as a figure of ultimate evil—the icon of the "fleshly nature" that the preachers insisted was a source not of joy, ecstasy, and beauty, as Pagans saw it, but of suffering and spiritual corruption.

These ancient seals depict a God and Goddess much beloved by Witches. *Pashupati,* Lord of the Animals, the Horned God depicted on this 4,000-year-old seal from the Indus Valley, is the same deity as Shiva, Pan, Cernunnos, and Herne. Hecate Triformis, in this seal from the Roman era, wields magical tools representing her triple nature: a knife of midwifery (birth), a scourge of purification (life), and a torch to guide souls through the Underworld (death).

The reaction against Renaissance magic grew in tandem with the religious wars, which accelerated as attitudes on both sides of the Christian schism hardened in the Counter-Reformation that followed the Council of Trent in 1565. The Witch Craze was worst, scholars point out, where the old ecclesiastical order was weakest and most threatened—in Germany, Switzerland, and France, for example. They also point out that Protestants were just as eager to burn Witches as Catholics. One of the few things Christians from both sides could agree on was their mutual hatred of Paganism.

In this, as in all subsequent witch hunts—Hitler's Holocaust, McCarthy's Red Scare, assorted wars on drugs and terror—ideological fanatics controlled a mechanism of state repression. The spread of the Witch Craze, scholars note, coincided with the spread of secular courts. As political power became increasingly centralized in the capitals of the monarchies, rulers began cementing their control over their far-flung domains. They replaced local barons' traditional power to settle disputes and punish criminals with regional courts in which appointed judges dispensed the king's justice. Because ecclesiastical authorities were forbidden by canon law to torture and execute criminals, accused Witches were remanded to secular courts for trial and punishment. The accused often rotted in prison for months while awaiting the arrival of an appointed circuit judge who knew nothing and cared less about the local intrigues that prompted neighbor to lie about neighbor. Academia was dragged into service of the hunt, as well: Various universities were founded to educate inquisitors.

The Witch Craze was a much deeper phenomenon than just a war on women by celibate men, a property grab by poor neighbors against rich, or a mass hallucination caused by moldy wheat—all theories propounded by various authors grasping for the reason behind this profoundly irrational event. It was no less than a wholesale war against magic, waged by religious reactionaries. Women were targeted because the persecutors—who not infrequently were ex-dabblers in spellcraft themselves—recognized that women are generally more intuitive and more instinctively talented in the Art Magical than most men are. The persecutors were most intent on wiping out an entire way of thinking—the very belief in and practice of occultism. They hounded prominent magical men, such as the Renaissance mages, with no less zeal than they hounded the women.

Agrippa was chased out of every country he tried to settle in. By the time Christopher Marlowe damned him for the ages as the model for the power-seeking necromancer in his extremely influential play *Doctor Faustus,* Agrippa's enemies had already tarred him with the unshakable rumor that the Devil followed him everywhere in the form of a huge black dog. Christian vandals burned John Dee's vast library of magical and classical texts, and after the Witch-hating King James I succeeded Elizabeth on the throne, England's latter-day Merlin spent the last of his days in poverty and disgrace. Giordano Bruno fared worst of all—an Italian nobleman lured him to his palace with a request for healing and then denounced him to Church officials, who burned him at the stake.

The terror of the Burning Times pervades the text dating from that period in the spellbook passed down for many generations in the Gardnerian tradition, today known as the *Book of Shadows.*

One passage in the section called the *Ardanes,* traditional Witchcraft laws, instructs newly initiated Witches to make all their magical tools of wax so that they can be tossed quickly into the fire if the Witch is found out. A series of heartrendingly practical instructions on how to survive torture poignantly concludes:

"If the worst comes, and you go to the pyre, wait until the flames and smoke spring up, bend your head over, & breathe in with long breaths; you choke and die swiftly, & wake in the arms of the Goddess."

The last public upsurge of magic took place in the early 1600s. An "invisible fraternity" of alchemists and doctors calling themselves the Rosicrucians published an anonymous invitation to the intelligentsia of Europe to arise and join them in transforming and healing the suffering realm of Christendom through magical philosophy.

But these well-intentioned mystics who hoped to usher in a new age of spirituality tragically underestimated the degree of spiritual perversity, paranoia, and hatred that filled the air around them. Like a candle lit in a methane-filled swamp, their announcement that a secret society of magicians existed in the very midst of Christian society sparked an explosive furor that caused exactly the opposite of what the Rosicrucians intended. In 1620, armies of the reactionary Catholic powers attacked and defeated the liberal Protestant kingdom of Bohemia, in whose capital of Prague the Rosicrucian movement was secretly centered, and instituted the worst purge of the entire Counter-Reformation. That battle initiated the murderously destructive Thirty Years War—which in turn brought an all-time peak of witch burnings.

THE AGE OF (SELECTIVE) REASON

The fascination with nature that the magical renaissance had inspired could not be suppressed. When at last the orgy of violence subsided, around 1648, the students of the alchemists and Rosicrucians of the previous generation came out of hiding in London to found the Royal Society—the opening salvo of the Scientific Revolution. However, most of these explorers of what their elders had called natural magic took a different and superficially safer tack than the Dees and Agrippas. Rather than risk further violent persecution and censorship from religious zealots, they declared that their studies of the workings of the cosmos would focus strictly on the physical realm, with no consideration whatsoever of the spiritual or religious. To pursue their studies of nature unhindered, these new scientists consciously detached themselves from the magicians of olde.

This new rationalist reaction caught on quickly all over Europe. In revolt-

ing against both religion and magic, however, the philosophers of the new science, such as Descartes, Mersenne, Locke, and Hobbes, swung to the opposite
extreme. They aggressively rejected the reality of magic and denied that the
soul or spirit exists. The new materialist regime became just as virulently fundamentalist as the old spiritual regime it opposed. For orthodox followers of science, attacking magic was—and still is—a roundabout way of attacking their
chief rival paradigm, religion. For science, magic is merely a more pernicious
form of the same superstition of spirituality on which religion is based.

The age of Swift and Voltaire found that ridiculing magicians was far
more effective in suppressing their philosophy than burning them had been.
The rationalists began making fun of the Renaissance mages as pointy-hatted
wizards, lampooning the alchemists as seekers after fool's gold, and caricaturing
Witches as deluded, wart-nosed old women. In the centuries-long attempt by
the powers-that-be to marginalize practitioners of magic, science accomplished
far more with a sneer than religion had done with a stake.

Science was one of the new powers in this modern world, advancing side
by side with the merchants and manufacturers who were taking over the reins
of power from the crestfallen, war-exhausted aristocrats. The new philosophy
of matter served to rationalize the moneymen's materialism. It adopted from
Renaissance magical philosophy the belief in the infinite potential of humans,
but stripped it of the ethical constraints on the human will that the spiritual
component of magic imposes. The philosophy of matter proclaimed that matter
and Earth are soulless, inert, and useless until exploited and developed by
humans. Nature is not a God/dess nor a living Being, it insisted, but a mere
mechanism that can be dissected and analyzed like a corpse on a laboratory
table—then rebuilt, like Frankenstein's monster, to serve nature's master, Man.

For the new men of business, this proved to be a far more utilitarian philosophy than the old Christian doctrine that the material world was fallen from
its creator's grace. It denied the forests and mountains not only the life force and
spirit that Pagans believed inhabited them, but even the respect and steward-
ship Christians believed they were due as God's handiwork. This allowed
profit-seekers to cut them down for timber and dig them up for mines without
suffering any twinge of conscience or compassion.

As the Scientific Revolution paved the way for the Industrial Age, natural
magic was reduced to laboratory science. Alchemy, stripped of its metaphors for

the transmutation of the soul, became chemistry; and metaphysics, merely physics. Herbs were distilled into pharmaceuticals, stones milled into minerals, and the body of Nature was, in a metaphor that recurs in writings of the early scientists, racked and tortured to make her confess her secrets. In place of the respectful and compassionate cooperation with Nature that the mages and Witches practiced, the new, soulless wizardry would enslave her under the dominion of Man—one doctrine the new priests of technology shared with their ecclesiastical predecessors.

Accompanying the new materialism in science was a new literalism in religion. As the human imaginative faculties once nourished by magic now withered, fundamentalist Christian sects began insisting on the word-for-word literal truth of the Bible. This put religion in open conflict with science over such discoveries as evolution and the age of Earth. Ironically, by shutting themselves off from magic—the bridge that connects the realm of the spirit with the realm of matter—religion and science separated themselves with an uncrossable chasm.

Nevertheless, magic survived. Many magicians simply went underground once more, and formed secret societies to preserve and pass on occult lore. The most notorious and influential of these was the Freemasons. Their documented history begins in Britain in the 1640s, when Robert Moray and the famous bibliophile and astrologer Elias Ashmole were initiated into lodges.[10] Both men later became founding members of the Royal Society, the very wellspring of the Scientific Revolution.

Freemasonry flourished just beneath the surface of eighteenth-century society as a haven for occultists and freethinkers. Few magicians during this time dared step out from the shadows and openly expose themselves to the kind of public scorn heaped upon figures such as Count Cagliostro and the semi-legendary Comte de Saint-Germain, who were derided as charlatans and frauds. Within the lodges of the Freemasons, however, the positive aspects of the magic-based ideals of Renaissance humanism continued to blossom—soon to bear fruit as the political ideals of the American and French Revolutions.

If, as the Renaissance magicians believed, the individual human soul is innately divine (a microcosm of the universe) and the individual human will is

[10] Frances A. Yates, The Rosicrucian Enlightenment *(Boston: Shambhala Publications, 1978), 210.*

capable of effecting change and altering destiny (the premise of magic and spell-craft), then it stands to reason that the individual human being can share in the freedom and the power of the Divine, which transcends all limitations of time and space. In their occult Fraternities, the tradesmen and gentlemen farmers of the magical enlightenment took this ideal of Liberty from the aristocrats of the magical renaissance and added to it the democratic ideal of Equality, which was actively practiced in covens. They believed all people are endowed by nature with inalienable rights to determine their own destiny and to express themselves as free individuals. Because all human beings are born with this capacity to participate in divinity, then popes and kings, churches and governments rule not by divine right, as they pretend, but only by arbitrary convention.

The Masons symbolized the continuity of the magical tradition by inscribing in the center of the floors of their temples the same symbol that magicians had used since at least the time of Pythagoras. The five-pointed pentagram, or the "Eastern Star," as Masons call it, represented the head and four limbs of the archetypal human being.

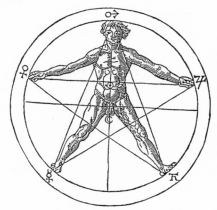

The Pentagram patterns the human body.

In the early 1800s, a few decades after Masons such as George Washington and Benjamin Franklin helped lead the American Revolution and found a new nation on the ideals of religious freedom and political equality, the five-pointed star began appearing everywhere on the flags, seals, and other insignia of the United States. The pentagram replaced the traditional six- or eight-pointed stars used on the earliest versions of the American flag and seal. This identification of the Eastern Star with the American star took place at the same time as a national explosion in popularity of Freemasonry.

There are ironies aplenty here. Today, flags around the world bear the Witches' five-pointed star, even those of Communist and Islamic nations, as an American-inspired symbol of aspiration toward freedom. Very few of the citizens who patriotically salute their national flag realize that they are paying homage to a pre-Christian magical sign.

MAGIC'S MODERN REVIVAL

During the nineteenth and twentieth centuries, while magic's prodigal child, science, legitimized the Industrial Age, spellcraft continued to survive underground. In 1801, Frances Barrett's *The Magus*—a spellbook derived principally from Agrippa—sparked a wave of grimoires, some of which showed up in unusual places. For example, Joseph Smith, the founder of the Church of Jesus Christ of Latter Day Saints (Mormons), and his father were avid practitioners of magic; some of their sigil-covered manuscripts still survive. Smith was a newly initiated Mason when, according to his earliest accounts to friends, a white salamander—an elemental Fire spirit summoned through spellcraft—led him to the Indian mound where he dug up the inscribed plates that he later claimed contained the Book of Mormon. Later, the Angel Moroni replaced the salamander in Smith's story.

In the New World, Native Americans and African Americans defended themselves against spiritual colonization by the white invaders and slave-owners by preserving their magical traditions through religions such as Voudon, Santeria, Candomble, and Umbanda. These practices variously combined indigenous spells, Deities, and natural lore with Christianity, European Witchcraft, and other influences into unique but interrelated magical systems. The principles and techniques of magic in these systems are fundamentally the same as in Western magic. As with spellcraft everywhere, the tools and terminology were simply adapted to the environment and culture within which the magicians practiced.

Some indigenous spellcrafters fought back against the whites through magic. The famous Shawnee warrior Tecumseh, who sought valiantly but vainly to organize the Native American tribes of the Southeast against white invasion in the early 1800s, told the Creeks that he would signal the start of a holy war against the whites by stamping his foot on the ground and causing the earth to tremble. From December 1811 to February 1812, a series of mighty earthquakes hit the frontier with such force that the town of New Madrid, Missouri, was destroyed, and the Mississippi River ran backward for a time.[11] To this day, geologists are hard put to explain the New Madrid fault line. It is an isolated anomaly in an otherwise stable zone of the North American continental plate, and shows no evidence of activity before or since the 1811–12 earthquakes—the most powerful recorded in North America since the arrival of Europeans.

Most European settlers, thoroughly indoctrinated by religious intolerance or scientific skepticism, viewed the Native Americans' ancient and powerful magical lore with loathing, and tried to convert them to the beliefs of Christian civilization. A few, however, sought out the wisdom of the indigenous shamans and medicine men. Among these were a band of German mystics calling themselves the Society of Woman in the Wilderness, after the figure in Revelations, who fled religious persecution at home in the early 1700s to settle in Pennsylvania. The hex signs still painted on houses and barns in Pennsylvania sprang from their folk-magic tradition, as well as the Pow Wow tradition of European–Native American magic that still thrives in that region.

In Europe and around the world, scholars such as the Brothers Grimm; James G. Frazer, author of *The Golden Bough;* and Charles Godfrey Leland worked to gather and chronicle folk-magic traditions before they disappeared under the rapidly advancing steamrollers of colonialism and industrialism. Their efforts helped lay the groundwork for the new science of anthropology, whose practitioners, even if they couldn't understand the magical practices they witnessed in traditional cultures, at least recorded them for the benefit of future generations. Today, those records are invaluable as the children of lost cultures around the world work to revive the wisdom of their ancestors.

In the mid-1800s, in the United States and Europe, spiritualist séances with the spirits of the dead—necromancy, although its practitioners understandably avoided using the pejorative term—inspired a new wave of intellectual interest in the occult. In England, this interest crystallized on the eve of the twentieth century into the extremely influential Order of the Golden Dawn, which opened the door for the reintroduction of ceremonial magic into aboveground Western culture. Its luminaries included MacGregor and Moina Mathers, who

---

[11] *Ronald N. Satz,* Tennessee's Indian Peoples, *(Knoxville: University of Tennessee Press, 1979), 39.*

translated the *Greater Key of Solomon* and other important grimoires, and explored ancient Egyptian magic and ritual; the poet William Butler Yeats; and the renegade occultist and skilled theorist and practitioner of magic Aleister Crowley.

In 1940, as flying machines rained the acrid fruits of Nazi scientists' alchemy of war on the cities of Great Britain, Drake's Drum beat once more along the English coastline. A coven of English Witches led by a High Priestess named "Old Dorothy" Clutterbuck gathered in the New Forest to cast a spell to repel Adolf Hitler's imminent invasion of the island. Dancing skyclad in the winter chill, they raised a magical Cone of Power, a vortex of magical energy. They then rushed in a line again and again and again in the direction of Germany to push the invader back with sheer force of magical will. Almost all of them were elderly, and several gave up their lives during the next few days as a result of their tremendous expenditure of vital energy.

One recent initiate to the New Forest Coven, whose life was changed by what he witnessed that night, was a world-traveling British civil servant named Gerald B. Gardner. Moved by the antiquity and beauty of the spells and rituals he was learning from this secretive but aging band of spellcrafters, he resolved to keep their tradition from dying out by whatever means necessary. When the British government liberalized its old laws against Witchcraft in the early 1950s, Gardner published several books describing the Witch tradition into which he had been initiated, and began openly initiating new members. The explosion of publicity that followed horrified his reclusive elders, but Gardner succeeded in spawning a worldwide resurgence of interest in and renewed practice of Witchcraft that is still growing by leaps and bounds.

The psychedelic movement that started in the 1960s further stoked people's interest in alternative spirituality, and the rise of feminism and environmentalism beginning in the early 1970s opened more people's eyes to the intuitive, Earth-based arts of magic. As the twenty-first century dawned, the phenomenal popularity of the Harry Potter books—fiction closely based on authentic magical tradition—revealed a new generation's voracious appetite for spellcraft.

After 2,000 years of repression by monotheistic religion and dismissal by materialistic science, magic is experiencing a rebirth as the spiritually starved inhabitants of an ecologically devastated Earth search for ways to heal themselves and the planet. Wicca is one of the fastest-growing religions in the world today. Even many Jews, Christians, and Muslims are rediscovering the mysticism hidden in the Pagan foundations of their own religions. Many scientists—astonished by the paradoxical implications of quantum physics and disturbed by the ravaging effects of the technological Frankenstein's monster they have helped create—are turning away from the old materialist orthodoxy and developing an understanding of the universe that is practically indistinguishable from magic.

The history of spellcraft in the West reveals wisdom's defiant survival in the face of aggressive ignorance. Like nature, magic has often been fenced from view or forced underground, but never successfully suppressed. Now, Earth's urgent environmental crisis makes the magical revival we are currently undergoing all the more important. It's not enough to talk about holism and the interconnection of all things—we have to live it.

Canny and strong in the knowledge and courage bequeathed us by the spellcrafters and Witches of yore, we can use our magical wisdom and will to survive, flourish, and heal ourselves, our communities, and our planet.

How the Art Magical Works

"The world is not a machine. Everything in it is force, life, thought."
—G. W. von Leibnitz
German philosopher

Everything is interconnected in patterns—including you. Every object, every person, every being is a part of one vast universe, like the individual cells that compose a living body. All these parts, from quarks to galaxies, from the infinitesimally small to the infinitely vast, are webbed together in universal patterns of order, like the meshed gears of a clock or nested repetitions of fractal geometry. You can learn and use these patterns because you, too, are an active part of the whole.

This cosmic order is neither random, nor meaningless. It isn't a soulless machine grinding impersonally toward a pointless eternity, as many scientists claim. It's not a deluded dream state or drama you create to attain personal enlightenment, as some New Agers assert. Nor is it all just a cosmic wrestling match for your soul between a God and a devil, as certain religions preach. Magic isn't about such constraining creeds.

The philosophy behind spellcraft is the very oldest of human beliefs. Plato and Pythagoras are this philosophy's best-known proponents from ancient times, although it far pre-dates them, as they themselves pointed out. Such quantum physicists as David Bohm and Fritjof Capra advocate its basic tenets today. Trace any particular religion or branch of science through its intricate patchwork of dogmas and beliefs to its origin, and you'll find a scrap torn from the robe of this philosophy. It has gone by countless names, but the only truly accurate one is "the perennial philosophy." In traditional cultures, it is viewed as the most precious heritage of the human race, routinely given to the first people of any culture by a divine Being, such as Elegba in Africa, the Yellow Emperor in China, Votan or White Buffalo Woman in Native America, and Hermes Trismegistus in Europe.

The essential premise of the perennial philosophy is that between the unimaginably vast and eternal whole of the universe and the familiar little corner of the here-and-now that you inhabit lies an apparent gulf. On one shore of this abyss is the timeless, spaceless realm of spirit—the immortal inner world of thoughts and dreams where your consciousness and will reside in the invisible company of divine and semi-divine Beings, God/desses, and spirits. On the other shore is the temporal, limited realm of matter—the observable world of birth, death, and reincarnation that your body, your belongings, and all things physical inhabit.

This gulf is bridged by the patterns that pervade every level of existence. There are many names for these universal patterns. Plato called them *ideas* or *forms*. Jung called them *archetypes*. Tibetan Buddhists call them *mind*. The physicist Bohm called them *the implicate order*. Spellcrafters know and interact with them through the Art of Correspondences. These patterns are the very thoughts and dreams of the God/desses, the very bones and blood of the Earth.

Your soul—the awareness that calls itself "I," a reincarnating wanderer that sojourns in and out of bodily form—is both perceiver of and participant within these patterns. They exist simultaneously within you, in the realm of the spirit, and outside you, in the realm of matter.

Your soul possesses both receptive and active properties. The receptive side is wisdom, and the active side is will. You gather wisdom as you learn from and experience the world as it exists and has existed until now. You project will as you act on and alter the world from the way it is now toward the way you want it to be. In the central moment, right here and now, the point at which wisdom and will ecstatically join together, magic is born.

Just as there are three levels to the universe—the spiritual, the material, and the consciousness that moves between—so there are three components to a spell: prayer, means, and intention, which unites prayer with means.

Contrary to some misconceptions, therefore, there's no way to separate spellcraft from spirituality. Depending on your religious preference, you may call on a God, a Goddess, a spirit, or the particular Deity or spiritual Being whose attributes are most appropriate to your need. In one form or another, however, you will need to work hand-in-hand with higher powers to cast an effective spell. This is not mere religious piety—magic depends on the spiritual force of life itself.

We are Wiccans and use the words *spellcrafter, Crafter,* and *Witch* more or less interchangeably throughout. However, don't infer that only people who belong to our religion can practice the Arts we describe here. As spells from around the world and throughout history show plainly, magic is adaptable to any religion, even Christianity. The principles of magic are universal—the main changes from one religion to another are the names of the divinities to whom spellcrafters pray.

But spellcrafters don't confine themselves to prayer—they use means, as well. They actively manipulate physical symbols—objects, words, letters, gestures, etc.—to make ideas manifest themselves within time and space. After all, to make music, you need an instrument. To paint a picture, you need brushes and pigments. Just as there's reason behind every note of a composition and every color of a painting, so there's reason behind every ingredient of a spell, based on the Art of Correspondences.

Finally, there's the central component: you. Your intention is everything—your will, guided by your wisdom, is what unites spirit with matter and makes a spell work. The energy you pour into it powers your spell.

To understand in your heart as well as your mind how magic works, you must understand life force, energy, and patterns of connections.

LIFE FORCE

All the universe is alive, infused with spiritual life force. Nature is sacred and has innate power. Spirits inhabit each tree, mountain, river, cloud, stone, and star, and each has unique powers that the wise can cultivate and tap but that the ignorant ignore or abuse.

Traditional peoples on every continent know that everything in nature, including inanimate objects, is ensouled and animated. Anthropologists call this belief *animism, vitalism,* or even *hylozoism.* If you've spent more than a few hours away from other humans, in the company of a tree, a mountain, a river, or even the soil, plants, and insects in your backyard, you've undoubtedly sensed this living, pervasive presence.

There is, in reality, no separation between dead matter and living spirit. In nature, the egg and the fossil, the leafing tree and the rotting log are simply opposite elements of an unbroken continuum.

The impenetrable wall we're indoctrinated to believe separates matter and spirit is but a new and arbitrary construct of civilization—city making, that process by which modern people set themselves apart from Nature and enclose themselves in an entirely artificial world. The foundations of this wall are laid when missionaries and preachers declare off-limits all spirituality except that which is boxed into their church. The wall is bricked up when schools and laws ridicule and persecute the traditional practices and substances that help humans perceive the invisible Beings and magical virtues embodied in the natural world. It closes in to suffocate us all when the sacred mountains are strip-mined and the healing groves are clear-cut merely to be transmuted into arbitrary money.

Yet behind and between and through the cracks in the wall, life force surges—even through the heart of the urban jungle. It runs not only on the surface, in the frantic pulse of human activity, but also secretly, in the buried rivers that flow as sewers under the ground-up stones of our streets, in the wires bearing currents of fire to animate our lights and machines. Abandoned buildings are often inhabited not only by rats and pigeons but also by ghosts—human spirits who have lost their bodies but still cling, confused and unresolved, to the material realm. Cars, ships, and household appliances—even computers— typically become animated with their own primitive personalities and souls, especially if the machines are old and have seen much use.

Everywhere around you, there is Life, unseen only because you've forgotten—or been made to forget—how to look. Just because you can't see something doesn't mean it's unreal—it may mean only that it exists outside the very narrow range of ordinary human perception.

Most modern adults try to laugh off the occasions when they've been startled by a Green Man's face looking out at them from the gnarls of an old oak, or a nymph's voice singing in the babbling of a stream. But young children are natural animists who recognize the Life in the objects around them. Indeed, parents know that a child's attention gives Life to the crudest doll or the raggediest blanket, and grandparents know that the very presence of children enlivens everyone around them like the warmth of the springtime Sun coaxing sprouts from the frozen ground. Like a child, the more you recognize and cultivate the spirit that lives just under the surface of matter, the more it makes its presence felt and seen.

Up until a few hundred years ago, artists depicted the Sun, the Moon, and the planets with faces, as you can see in olde astronomical engravings. Until very recently, artists decorated books, buildings, and household objects with vines and leaves and animals. They animated these objects, transferring the life force of the tree or the stone into their wood, paper, or metal creations. Only when so-called progress and efficiency took craftsmanship away from human hands and assigned it to mass-production machines did our household objects begin to look sterile and inert—and our lives begin to feel as cold and impersonal as our surroundings.

Where there is no Life, there is no spirit—where there is no spirit, magic is impossible. Spellcasting almost always involves a prayer, an invocation, an offering, or some other form of intentional connection

> HERE IS PLATO'S INFLUENTIAL VIEW on the nature of spirits. In the course of a discussion on the nature of love, Socrates recounts the words of his teacher, the Witch Diotima of Mantinea:
>
> "'. . . Spirits, you know, are halfway between god and man.'
> 'What powers have they, then?' I asked.
> 'They are the envoys and interpreters that ply between heaven and earth, flying upward with our worship and our prayers, and descending with the heavenly answers and commandments, and since they are between the two estates they weld both sides together and merge them into one great whole. They form the medium of the prophetic arts, of the priestly arts of sacrifice, initiation, and incantation, of divination and of sorcery, for the divine will not mingle directly with the human, and it is only through the mediation of the spirit world that man can have any intercourse, whether waking or sleeping, with the gods. And the man who is versed in such matters is said to have spiritual powers, as opposed to the mechanical powers of the man who is expert in the more mundane arts. There are many spirits, and many kinds of spirits, too, and Love is one of them.'"
>
> "Symposium," 202d–203a, trans. Michael Joyce, from Plato: The Collected Dialogues, eds. Edith Hamilton and Huntington Cairns (Princeton: Princeton University Press, 1961).

with a Deity or other spiritual Being. A love spell, for instance, usually includes calling on the aid of a Goddess of love, such as Venus—also known as Aphrodite, as Oshun, and by many other names. This divine ruler of all things amorous will have no desire to help you—and your spell won't work—if you treat her merely as an abstract name or symbol, as if she is nothing but an arbitrary, inanimate mental construct or a human creation. She also won't help you if you approach her in fear.

Gods and Goddesses are real Beings. Ditch your anthropocentric assumptions—Gods and Goddesses are not evil demons (the religious prejudice)—or mere psychological projections (the scientific prejudice). They are powerful, independently conscious Beings that reside largely in the spirit realm. But don't take their existence on faith—experience them for yourself. Learn all you can about a Deity from books. Then call on them—offer them a stick of incense or a few drops of wine, write their name and symbol on a piece of paper and place it under your pillow, or pray for them to appear in a dream or vision. The Deity will choose their own method or time in which to contact you, but if you summon them with proper sincerity, they *will* manifest in a form that you'll find profoundly touching or meaningful.

Remembering that Life is everywhere makes you naturally compassionate, and helps prevent you from abusing the magical powers you attain. If you respect other things and entities as being as alive in their own fashion as you are, you are far less likely to harm them by exploiting them for selfish ends. You will bless rather than curse, and heal rather than harm others. Honor the bits of spirit that animate even the ingredients and tools you use in your spells—your herbs, wands, gems, feathers, etc. In the words of the Wiccan Rede, "An [if] it harm none, do as ye will."

CONCERNING SACRIFICE AND BLOOD

Such considerations bring us to an extremely sensitive subject: sacrifice. It never ceases to amaze us that many people believe Witchcraft is synonymous with blood sacrifice. The truth is that the real sacrifices involved with magic consist mainly of having to deal with others' criticism or ostracism when you admit you're working to become an adept; pressures they impose to get you to quit—

"Give up the Craft or I'm leaving"; the positive but difficult internal changes you make along the way—being highly ethical in an unconscionable world isn't easy; and the time and effort required to master the occult.

Respect for Life should prevent you from murdering a cat or a toad or a bat or another sentient life-form just to serve as an ingredient in a spell. No spell-crafter we know would ever want to do such a thing—we love animals too much to harm them intentionally. Yet it's undeniable that some olde spells call for just such ingredients.

Often, such spell recipes simply used gruesome terms as code words for herbal ingredients. (See Chants and Charms—The Power of Words, page 153.) That doesn't account for *all* the olde spells, though. Some *do* call for sacrificing an animal. Don't use those spells. Find or create an alternative that doesn't require that kind of sacrifice.

There's always a reason for every part of a spell. If you understand the reasons behind required spell ingredients, you'll be able to use correspondences, which we explain later, to find humane substitutes. For instance, a love spell that calls for the heart of a dove can rely instead on the seeds of an apple because doves and apples are both sacred to Venus.

Still, the issue deserves deeper thought. Why wouldn't the original recipe have called for an apple? Why a sentient animal? Why, for that matter, do priest/esses in many traditional religions, such as Santeria, continue to sacrifice animals such as chickens and goats to the God/desses?

One answer is that in traditional agricultural subsistence societies, people's diet is primarily vegetarian. Animals are too valuable to kill routinely—they're needed for pulling plows, hauling burdens, giving wool and milk, fertilizing fields, and so forth. Moreover, they are recognized as sentient beings with feelings and souls of their own. Unlike industrial societies, which slaughter animals in assembly-line fashion for the sake of cheeseburgers and chicken wings, traditional societies take their animals' lives on the most sacred occasions—for religious feast days or to augment important magic. Even then, nothing of the animal goes to waste. Its meat will be shared with the community, its skin tanned for leather, its fur felted into cloth, its bones burned for lime. Neither is its life force wasted—it is offered back to the spirit world whence it came.

Roadkill happens, too. Many spellcrafters we know who happen upon such an adventitious sacrifice can't bear to let it go to waste. They will stop to gather beaks, feathers, claws, or tails to preserve for future spells or to use as magical tools, then bury the remains with a suitable prayer or offering.

Many people feel a natural and legitimate revulsion for animal sacrifice while paradoxically glorifying the human sacrifice that is war. Political leaders exhort people to sacrifice themselves to their cause and praise the resultant victims for the sacrifice of their lives. This illustrates how, when torn from its spiritual and ethical constraints, a once-magical concept such as sacrifice can be manipulated into a perverse form of spell with the power to transform millions into cannon fodder.

This is not to rule out the sacrifice that some spellcrafters occasionally practice—offering a drop or two of their own blood to empower a spell. Life force inheres in blood. It is a viscous carrier of vitality throughout the physical body. So, also, is breath—the words *spirit* and *respiration* come from the same root—from the newborn's first cry until the final death rattle. Blood and breath bridge the realms of spirit and matter, and therefore have always been perceived as powerful vehicles of magic. But they are not the only, and by no means the primary, magical substances.

ENERGY

There is an animating current that sometimes flows like water, sinuous and serpentine, and sometimes flashes arrow-straight like light. It accumulates and resonates in circles of stone and mounds of earth, whether natural mountains or constructed pyramids. It pools and condenses at intersections, such as crossroads, thresholds, and the geometrical centers and axes of things, such as your spine or the obelisk or steeple in the center of your town. It rides in the tides of water, blood, and saliva, on the billows of wind and breath, and along lines of electromagnetism, the physical force most closely related to it. This power shines like the radiant upper air on a beautiful day, yet it's invisible to ordinary sight. You can sense it intuitively—and you can raise it, channel it, charge objects with it, and heal with it. You can even kill with it—which is not a good idea, because it moves in circles and tends to return to its sender. It is the bearer of the life force, the vehicle that vivifies mortal matter with immortal spirit.

Chinese Taoists call it *chi;* Hindu yogis, *prana;* Sufi dervishes, *baraka;* and Polynesian kahunas, *mana.* To ancient Egyptian priest/esses, it was *ka;* to Roman diviners, it was *numen;* to Norse seers, it was *megin,* akin to our word *might.* Medieval scholars honored it as the Quintessence, or Fifth Element, that both generates and transcends the other four. In Renaissance Europe, magical philosophers such as Giordano Bruno and Robert Fludd termed it *pneuma, ether,* or simply *spirit.*

In modern languages, such as English, people call it . . . well, we really don't have a unique name for it any longer. It is one of the many concepts of magic purged from so-called respectable intellectual discourse following the Scientific Revolution—and down the memory-hole with the idea went the words to describe it. Only poets and occultists remembered its existence. They kept the adjectives that derived from the olde magical terms—*numinous, ethereal, quintessential,* and *pneumatic*—and used them romantically and symbolically to describe an elusive quality that hovers just beyond the borders of the mundane.

Today, the idea of a universal, all-pervading medium is reappearing in many languages as both metaphysical seekers and theoretical physicists converge on it anew. Although many new terms have cropped up—such as *kundalini, light,* and *the force* from the metaphysical side, and *flux, field,* and the recently resuscitated *ether* from the scientific side[12]—there seems to be only one broad, though vague, term that everyone agrees on: *energy.*

Matter, physicists explain, is not really solid—it is composed of vibrating waves of energy. Occultists agree; if you could see things as they truly are, the reality beyond the mundane world (as can happen in an altered state or out-of-body experience), you would see that each physical object is actually the condensed, crystallized core of what resembles a streaming, emanating fountain of many-colored light.

Sensing, raising, and directing energy is primarily what magic is all about. Circles, altars, temples, standing stones, groves, wells, and the tops of mountains

---

[12] *In recent decades, quantum physics and unified-field theory have led notable physicists, such as the late Paul Dirac, back to the pre-twentieth century idea of an all-pervading field, variously termed* ether, flux, *or* zero-point energy, *in which electromagnetic waves and atomic particles can be explained as localized perturbations. The resurgence of this idea parallels the rise of ecological thinking, which views humans as interconnected with and interdependent on the whole web of life.*

or pyramids, obelisks, pagodas, and steeples are just a few of the sacred structures that concentrate and focus energy. Casting a spell in a place where energy accumulates enhances the potency of the working tremendously.

Feng Shui, the Oriental art of placement, is a highly sophisticated science of recognizing places where energy is focused, and arranging objects in such a way that it flows unimpeded. Its Western equivalent, often called *geomancy,* is the study of Earth energies as they flow and intersect along *ley lines,* which are invisible, pulsating lines of force stretching across the landscape. Students of these arts point out that energy is not uniformly good or healthful. When it is disharmonious, stagnant, or moving too fast, it can create very harmful effects. That is why when spellcrafters consecrate a magical tool, a ritual space, a new home, or a place of business, they first cleanse it of all unwanted energies, usually by spurging it with salt water, then censing it with a pungent incense, such as white sage.

Energy is often experienced as light or Fire, that one of the Four Elements with which it is most closely akin. You may find it more helpful to consider energy as behaving like "higher fire"—electromagnetic fields and charges. As with electricity, some materials conduct spiritual energy more readily than others. Quartz crystal, for instance, is a far better natural conductor of energy than glass, which in turn is far superior to plastic.

Spellcrafters raise energy during rituals by intentionally generating a magical electric potential. We direct the energy we raise through our hands, a wand, or a blade, much as a beam of light or an electrical current is aimed and channeled. When we charge an object, such as a talisman or magical tool, we infuse the object with this energy, which the object then stores, like a battery, until we need to use it.

Nevertheless, the energy of spellcraft is not the same as physical electromagnetic energy. It's a living fire that flows much more readily through materials that are organic and natural than through those that are artificial and manufactured. However, as synthetic materials age, rust, and dent, and take on character over time, they become capable of carrying this energy, like the rickety old car that seems to run on its owner's daily prayers.

Energy whirls. From our spiral galaxy, to our spinning planet, to the circling of the Sun and the Moon, to the cycling power of an electromagnetic generator or motor, energy tends to rotate and revolve. This is why Buddhists spin prayer wheels and circumambulate sacred mountains. It is also why Witches primarily move in the same direction as the Sun in their ritual rooms—to keep the vortex of energy we raise in spellwork whirling consistently in a direction that's most harmonious with the cosmos. We move against the Sun only when doing magic to oppose or diminish something.

The human body is a powerful generator of energy. Many medical traditions, such as acupuncture, are devoted entirely to diagnosing and rectifying bodily energy imbalances which are seen as being the principal source of every illness. In rituals, Witches often use their bodies to raise energy for spells: We dance ecstatically, chant, pound drums, and even make love to raise energy for our magic.

When people mass in groups—such as at a rock concert, political demonstration, or public ritual or gathering—their collective energy amplifies and seems to take on a life of its own. People acknowledge this when they talk about sensing good or bad "vibes" or vibrational feelings from a person, place, or crowd.

Heeding such nuances of energy can save you from harm, as *Diuvei experienced in Berkeley during one of the second-generation People's Park riots in the late 1980s. He was walking by himself at night a few blocks from his home, listening warily to the far-off sirens and helicopters. When he rounded a corner onto a main street, he suddenly felt a wave of violent and frightening energy sweeping toward him. He peered down the street but didn't see or hear anything unusual. Still, he decided to heed the invisible warning and turned down a side street. He hadn't gotten more than a block when he heard a terrible din moving swiftly along the main street he'd just left. He turned to see a mob of rioters running down the road, hotly pursued by a phalanx of armored cops swinging batons and firing rubber bullets. If he'd ignored the energy surge, he would have been overrun and beaten.

Although energy touches and inhabits, shapes and guides the physical world, it isn't physical in and of itself. It exists at the boundary between mind and body, the intersection of spirit with matter. This is why it is most strongly affected and stirred by that part of your mind which is closest to your body— your feelings. Powerful emotions can raise so much energy that it acts on matter without a physical intermediary. For example, poltergeist activities—the most frequent kind of haunting, where doors slam, TVs go on and off, and furniture is rearranged by invisible hands—are commonly associated with a house inhabited by a hormone-wracked teenager or the soul of a suicide or murder victim trapped by anger, guilt, or fear between this world and the next.

INTENTION

To cast a successful spell, you must be aroused, impassioned, enflamed by your desire or need—whether it is love or terror or ecstasy or fury matters less than that you strongly express your will. This can come from within you, in the force of urgency that prompted the spell in the first place. It can also come from without, such as when you absorb the heightened emotions of others around you. The best spellcrafters are those who deeply explore their passionate selves—as folklore acknowledges in the archetype of the untamed Gypsy and the wild Witch, and in spellcrafters of romantic legend such as Circe and Cagliostro.

It doesn't do, though, to just flare off emotion in a fit of rage or joy. Instead, like a skilled rider of a spirited horse, you must wisely use your will to transform your emotions into magical energy, then channel it via spellwork to effect your desire. You must be focused and certain of what you intend. As the oft-quoted saying goes, "Be careful what you wish for—you're likely to get it." As we say, "Intention is everything." Once, a student of ours cast a spell in which he purposefully broke a gold chain in order to break an addiction. Afterward, anytime he felt that someone or something was holding him back, other things similarly broke, such as the vacuum cleaner his wife wanted him to use. He hadn't realized that he unconsciously viewed chores as chains, too. Worse, the physical chain he'd broken during the spell was a piece of his wife's jewelry, so his marital bonds didn't last much longer, either.

PATTERNS OF CONNECTIONS

Because everything in the universe is composed of life force and energy, nothing is static. Everything vibrates, rotates, resonates, ebbs and flows, comes and goes, changes. Nothing and no one in this perpetual flux is an island—all affect one another. For spellcrafters, the question isn't whether everything is interconnected, but in what ways, and how best to work with these patterns of connections in order to help ourselves and heal our world.

Spellcrafters observe that the following principles of connection permeate our lives, and so we apply them in our magic. Both individually and as a group, these natural laws explain the basic workings of the cosmos.

• **MACROCOSM = MICROCOSM:** As above, so below.[13]

Every level of the cosmos shares the same fundamental patterns, from the infinitely large to the infinitesimally small. Planetary systems, human societies, and atomic structures all operate by similar principles of order, just as a fractal's whole shape can be seen in every one of its parts. This understanding that every part reflects the whole is the basis of the Art of Correspondences, which categorizes things by how they function in the cosmic order.

Many spells, amulets, and talismans work because of this principle. For example, a medallion inscribed with all 12 signs of the zodiac or all 24 letters of the runes in their correct order has healing and protective power because it contains the power of the whole to set right disordered parts.

• **SYMPATHY/ANTIPATHY:** Like attracts like, and opposites repel.

You can produce an effect by imitating it (a principle also called the Law of Similarity), or prevent or dispel something by opposing it with something it loathes.

This principle of using symbolic correspondences to induce action from a distance is by far the most commonly used in magic. One simple spell to induce two people to fall in love involves inscribing their names on two candles, then moving the candles closer and closer together until they touch. Then the candles are bound together with honeysuckle vine. To break up, you'd gradually move the candles farther and farther apart.

---

[13] *"As above, so below" derives from the Emerald Tablet of Hermes Trismegistus, which begins: "It is true, without falsehood, and most certain. What is below is like that which is above; and what is above is like that which is below: to accomplish the miracle of the one thing."*

- **CONTAGION:** Once in contact, always in contact.

A part represents its whole. Many spells depend on contact or proximity to work; for example, carry an amulet for safe travel with you—don't leave it in a drawer at home. The candle spell described above is certain to be effective if you have a hair from each target person and attach it to the candle that represents the person. A poppet or voodoo doll works because it contains a nail paring, a bit of hair, a picture, or some similar thing that has been in close contact with the person the poppet represents.

- **INVERSION:** Any polarity can be reversed.

What can kill can also cure, such as a vaccine, which introduces a toxin into the body to stimulate immunity. The famous wound salve of the Middle Ages was a balm applied to a sword that had inflicted a wound in order to heal the wound itself. A mirror can reflect a curse back on the curse-caster; an image of an eye can repel the Evil Eye.

Similia similibus curantur (like things can be cured by like): Imitating an undesirable phenomenon or using an ingredient's typical attribute to cause an opposite effect can avert or negate a problem or peril. A variation of this principle is "Murphy's magic," or preventing the worst by preparing for it in advance. (See "Murphy's Magic"—Mastering the Art of Opposites, page 149.)

- **REPETITION:** Repeating a spell over and over increases its power—often exponentially.

Ancient spells are more innately powerful than modern ones because they've been perfected by repeated use through the ages.

The rhythm of a spell chant is an essential part of its power. There are Witches who cast spells by rocking in a chair or swinging in a swing and impressing their will with every cycle. The genius inventor Nikola Tesla once attached a tiny clockwork hammer to a girder of a skyscraper under construction. Before long, the tiny taps of the hammer had built up such resonance in the structure that the huge building began swaying and would have toppled over had he not removed his device.

If you do a spell but don't get fairly immediate results, you may need to mentally re-impress your will upon it or reiterate the spell.

- **BETWEEN THE WORLDS:** Boundaries, thresholds, and centers are inherently magical places.

This is a very important secret that will empower your magic no matter where you are—a temple courtyard or a prison cell. Because a structure's boundaries and centers are the basis of its archetypal geometric Form, they are the places where matter intersects with spirit. They are the joints or cracks in visible matter, which hidden spirit shines through. Doorways, windowsills, chimneys—all such parts of buildings are places that lie between inside and outside. The exact center of a room, courtyard, or plaza; or the central beam of a roof—these are the axes around which energy whirls. If you cast a spell in such a place, you can alter energy your way, like tipping a gyroscope.

This applies to time as well as space. The "joints" of the day are times of power—noon and midnight are the centers around which day and night pivot. The two twilights, dawn and dusk, are the thresholds between the world of light and the world of dark. Further, the new, half, and full Moons and the year's solstices and equinoxes are potent turning points of the cycles of the Moon and the Sun. (See Timing Spells for Maximum Efficacy, page 102.)

What Constitutes a Spell?

"Instead of manipulating the physical universe directly, magic uses ritual and spells. . . . The word 'spell' is actually derived from the Anglo-Saxon word meaning 'play.' Casting a spell is a kind of psychic theater in which the intentions of the operator are focused on bringing about a certain kind of result. Here is where the will comes in. The spell can be a ritual, the creating of an amulet or charm, the recitation of magic or ritualistic words or other things as well. It is extremely open-ended in its structure."

—ROB HAND
Astrology by Hand

hen confronted by an injustice, an illness, a lack, or another problem that can't be remedied by conventional physical means, spellcrafters take matters into their own hands and actively use will to manifest a solution. To end a prolonged drought, for example, you may perform magical actions and invoke spiritual entities or elemental powers whose forte is to bring rain. Spellcrafters take a direct role in the outcomes of their lives, only in an indirect way.

A spell is anything you do with magical intention, such as projecting a strident wish, intoning occult words, or doing specific mystical actions that cause your desire to manifest physically. For most spells, the recipes of instructions have been handed down for eons or are based on traditional magical principles or natural, universal laws.

Spells may consist of one or many acts or components, and range from quick and simple "wish" magic to intricate rituals and even spells that come to fruition after many years. For example, you may simply pray a poetic invocation to a God/dess, or formally cast a circle wherein you use multiple tools and ingredients. You can bathe and do a relaxation spell, or banish a curse as the water goes down the drain. You can bury protective Witches' bottles or bury a spell ingredient overnight to charge it with elemental Earth energy. All qualify as spells, and hundreds of variations exist.

SPELLWORK

GOODLY HELP FOR YOU,
YOUR LOVED ONES, AND THE PLANET

". . . the person who ardently desires has the power to attract into his orbit the object of his desire."

—IOAN P. COULIANO
Eros and Magic in the Renaissance

agic links spirit with matter. Because each of us possesses a soul, our own bridge between the two realms, each of us is innately magical. History demonstrates that magic's efficacy is open to anyone who is inclined to use it.

Spells are inclusive by nature; anyone who finds one can work it. Both females and males of any age can do magic because it doesn't depend on such factors to work. We've taught magically gifted kids as young as 7 and 9, who matched their parents' abilities. The Wise accept one and all and encourage everyone to lend their spellcraft to the greater good of the whole—to participate in rites and spells to the utmost of their ability. If you're unable to dance a circle for any reason, the hope is that you'll sing or shake a rattle—anything to augment the ambient energy so the spell will take hold.

There are so many aspects to spellcrafting that there's something within it to appeal to everyone. You can learn how to heal the sick if that's your wont, or how to become invisible. You can protect a pristine grove or psychically communicate with faraway friends.

Few tools are required, and just about anything you'll need is readily available or easily made yourself. Most spells are so inconspicuous or discreet that folks won't even recognize a spell, even if you're doing it in plain sight or in public.

Working magic is wicked fun. You get to dance, write in code, prepare potions, and do all the deliciously Witchy things that give life pizzazz. Afterward, you get the pleasure of seeing your efforts manifest in direct, positive ways. Doing successful spells accords you a satisfaction that few of life's other endeavors provide. Working with spiritual matters will afford you delightful epiphanies and moments of clarity or bliss along the way. It's a continuous, heady thrill in being able to make something out of thin air. Learning *how* to do it is as much fun as *doing* it!

Like any skill, though, the Art Magical necessitates practice. The more you practice, and the more emotion and focused intention you apply to spells, the more powerful your results will be. The more you read about how to apply standard Witchcraft techniques and experiment with doing spells you find, the more you'll be working with immense cosmic forces, whose powers, in turn, help increase your own. The longer you practice magic, the stronger your magical abilities grow.

You Can Live a Magical Life

"Sorcery! We are all sorcerers, and live in a wonderland of marvel and beauty if we did but know it."
— Charles Godfrey Leland
Gypsy Sorcery and Fortune Telling

For many people, fear of being ridiculed or considered strange or crazy by others is the psychic whip that keeps them ever pretending that there's no such thing as magic. Then when they dabble in magic, they often get angry when their spells don't work the way they want them to. They rarely realize it's their fault for approaching magic from a needless and counterproductive basis of fear.

The fact is, your life, your pursuits, your soul, your spirit, are yours alone to do with as you will—no one has the right to dictate your choices or actions.

No one can live your life for you; from beginning to end, each person is a unique individual with immense potential, and an instinctive imperative to be happy, help others, and make the world a better place. If you want to practice magic, do so.

Look beyond the typical, conventional way you've been taught to view the world; instead, see things as they magically exist. Your inner mind already knows how to do this—but unless you were born a psychic or raised in a traditional culture that values magic, you were probably made to deny or forget this understanding at an early age.

It's not hard to find your way back into the magical universe. It's so much the natural and real way things work that suppressing it requires constant effort, just as it requires unending labor to keep a lawn artificially pest and weed free. When you first feel the rush of doing successful spellwork, you may want to swing to the other extreme and abandon conventional reality in favor of more preferable realms—to let go, just as some folks completely let their lawns go. But to do that would be to plunge into non-productive chaos, however. After all, you can't help anyone with your magic if you simply walk out the door and vanish into the wilderness.

Spells always work if you have your material and spiritual acts together before you attempt them. They can fail if you're addicted, lazy, irresponsible, or neglectful in some manner, or if your thoughts or feelings are clouded by negative opinions, assumptions, prejudices, or fears regarding magic. For example, if you blew off a court date and provoked an arrest warrant for failure to appear, it's a bit late in the game to cast a spell for justice, no matter how wrongful the charge against you may be. In such a case, the only spell you *should* consider casting is on yourself—for the courage to face the consequences.

It's important to keep your head in the sky and your feet on the ground. Practice magic from a balanced perspective, and with a steady hand. Don't solely consider universal patterns in your mind or just read, talk, or write about them—see, feel, hear, and intuit them through your senses.

There are various time-honored and effective methods you can use to enhance your sensitivity to invisible natural energies. Meditate; wear an amulet, such as a quartz crystal or sacred symbol; intentionally go barefoot; induce an altered state; fast; spend time alone with plants and animals; and quietly watch whatever is happening around you. Above all, listen to the world around you.

As the great Egyptian sage Ptahhotep wrote:

"When the listening is good, life is good
He who listens is the master of what is beneficial
Listening is beneficial to the listener
Listening is better than anything else
That is how perfect love is born."[14]

Spurn society's suppression of your natural desires and magical capabilities. Instead, mind your inner voice, and free your straining spirit to do as *it* wills. Walk *adoors* (a Witch word meaning "outdoors") and notice that one tree resembles a nude sculpture and another looks like a Goddess's hand rising from below the ground, its limbs her fingers reaching to touch the sky or grasp an invisible sword.

Consider how peaceful you'd feel surrounded by nature's beauty indoors. Then decorate with grasses, twigs, twisted branches, stones, and shells. The more you wean yourself off plastics and machines, the more you'll become attuned to the magic that whirls and pulses around you at any given moment.

Be consciously open—discard your pre-conceived notions, defenses, and emotional walls so that you can begin to experience the hidden world. You'll soon see the true reality beneath the modern blur—the magical matrix that makes the world go around. Occult physics isn't dependent on money. It isn't a pawn of the privileged, and it doesn't dance to the tune of the elite or titled gentry. Its perpetual motion influences people regardless of whether they acknowledge it.

Magic is based not on faith regarding unseen things, but on personal experience. We write about the existence of God/desses, elementals, spirits, entities, and so on because we've *experienced* them. Crafters don't expect anyone else to be able to see or communicate with Deities in exactly the same way they do. Witches don't proselytize because they know that if people practice the Art Magical, their own experiences will prove its efficacy.

Repetitious tasks are excellent vehicles for spellcraft, so don't waste the time and energy you expend doing them—use their rhythms to focus your mag-

---

[14] *Christian Jacq,* L'Enseignement du Sage Aegyptien Ptahhotep *(La Maison de Vie, 1993).*

ical intent. Each dish you rinse repeats your wish for healing your loved one. Each weed you whack clears another chunk of debt from your credit record. As long as your mind's intent corresponds appropriately to the task your body is performing, you will not only feed energy into your spell, but also likely find yourself performing the task much more deftly and skillfully than usual. Appropriateness is important, though—those who curse their enemies while washing the dishes may wind up with a lot of broken crockery!

As a case in point, *Diuvei once worked at a temp-agency job that he considered the most boring but strenuous work he ever remembered doing—sweeping up plastic scraps in a plastic-recycling warehouse. Financially he was trapped in the job, but emotionally he was desperate to leave it. One Friday, he was assigned to heft piles of chunks of plastic molding into big boxes to be discarded. Straining to lift the heavy gobs of congealed goo off the cold gray concrete floor, he decided he'd had enough—he'd reached the lowest point in his career, and he refused to go any lower.

As he cussed and sweated and groaned, he began intentionally focusing the pent-up force of his frustration and resentment into the energy of the task itself. With each chunk of plastic he heaved into the box, he hurled a phrase affirming his will along with it. "I *will* get a job I enjoy!" *(boom!)* "It *will* come swiftly to me!" *(bam!)* "*No more* will I have to do this!" *(ka-blam!)* That day turned out to be his last in the plastic-waste warehouse. On Monday, the temp agency phoned and assigned him to a new job. It marked the beginning of an upward turn in his career that continued until he eventually attained the work he loved—writing and journalism.

Spellcasters typically experience several successive, predictable mental and emotional phases:

- INTELLECTUAL EPIPHANY—You experience an almost overwhelming moment of clarity that occurs when you suddenly realize magic's pervasive sway.

Your initial reaction to this is often "How could I not have seen it before?" quickly followed by "Why doesn't *everyone* see this?"

When you experience this mind-boggling, life-changing revelation, society's rote rejection of magic can feel unsettling and may even spark smoldering anger within you. At this point, you're probably still practicing as a solitary, and are therefore prone to feeling disoriented or alienated.

It's hard and unnecessary to bear such wonder alone, so to dispel your sense of isolation, contact others of like mind and express your newfound enlightenment. They will likely share with you their own, similar past experiences and help eradicate your sense of estrangement from the workaday world.

Avoid regretting having missed magic's obviousness—simply focus on being grateful that at least you know now. Revel in your delicious secret; feel the joy that comes from understanding that the workings of the world have a poetic order that makes sense. Appreciate the comfort such wisdom brings, and remain open to receive more insight.

- CONFUSION—With so much to be learned and done, however should you begin? What kind of magic should you practice?

It's up to you to determine your magical destiny—no one should impose limits regarding what fascinates or intrigues you about Witchcraft. If, on the other hand, the plethora of knowledge to learn overwhelms you, take heart from Albert Einstein's wise words: "The most incomprehensible thing about the universe is that it is comprehensible."

During this time, you'd be well advised to absorb all the information you can find regarding the Craft. We encourage people in this stage to read everything concerning the occult—including pejorative tomes. Doing so tends to strengthen your resolve as well as reveal the existence of countless creative magical methods for you to consider.

Study Craft history. Although reading the *Malleus Malificarum* will make your blood boil with outrage, it's crucial that you get a complete picture of the dichotomy between magic's efficacy and its detractors' demonization of our ways.

Explore your own Witchy lineage—almost every family has a granny who made herbal potions, a great-aunt who foretold the future, or a black-sheep cousin reputed to be a Witch somewhere in the family tree. Feel as one with the long line of magical practitioners who have preceded you. Appreciate their sacrifice, their practical wisdom, and their dignity and perseverance in the face of severe, institutionalized oppression. Your ancestral spirits want you, their descendant, to thrive, and can aid your magical progress if you contact and pro-pitiate them. (See To Relieve Poverty, page 374.)

Read about different Craft traditions. Delve into diverse pantheons of God/desses. Then select one or more cultural mythologies for which you feel an affinity, such as Egyptian, Greek, Celtic, Nordic, Italian, and so on.

Read about the different kinds of Beings. Get to know spirits, entities, and God/desses on an intimate level. Learn their traits, attributes, typical ways of manifesting, and specific powers. Extol their virtues aloud. Invoke their aid as need be. Track how helpful they are, in what ways, and regarding which types of situations.

- OBSESSION WITH DETAIL—You're prone to believe that the only way to master magic is to memorize endless lists of correspondences, spell ingre-dients, and the common and scientific names of stones and herbs.

This daunting task often stops enthusiastic seekers in their tracks. Sure, you should read such lists, but focus on their common generalities, not their specifics. You'll learn far more by directly working spells, recording how you did them, and tracking how you succeeded with each one. Time, patience, and practice will reveal when you're on target, or if you've skipped a crucial step or missed a necessary spell component.

- APPROACH/AVOIDANCE—You have an urgent desire to perform the spells you found while reading coupled with a hesitation to put your new knowledge into actual practice. After all, isn't it a cliché that catastrophic things will occur if you accidentally perform a spell wrong?

Don't let societal conditioning get the better of you—dive into magic with relish! Get your hands dirty transforming wax and clay into powerful Craft tools. Get your feet wet in dew while conjuring rain. Don't hold back—delight in your magical abilities!

- MAGICAL STYLE—You feel compelled to establish your own way of working magic.

You may begin casting circles using all the bells and whistles, such as consecrating your ritual area with salt water, incense, and triple perambulations around the sacred space. This is fine. You may cement your procedures into default with a set practice, or find that your method gradually evolves into simpler ways that are unique to you. Either way, the main thing is to do some kind of spell every day—even if it's only mentally parting clouds or listening to the wind whispering of things to come.

This is a goodly time to plunge into the wider Wiccan world. Attend gatherings, Witch meets, public Craft rituals, and the like. Carefully observe how others work magic. Internalize methods that work, and reject techniques that you see dissipate spells rather than raise appropriate energy.

Learn from powerful, seasoned Witches while approaching with caution boastful posers whose actions fall short of their claims. Be as the former, not the latter. Here's an important piece of advice: When it comes to magical prowess, words are cheap, but deeds are dear.

Remain alert for daily crises that you're in a position to ameliorate or outright solve. When needs arise, drop everything and magically deal with them immediately.

• ENTHUSIASM—You have an insatiable appetite for all things magical.

This is a fun, exhilarating time of exploration and stretching your capabilities. You learn something new every day. You feel expansive, boundless, unrestrained. You're finally finding your true, spiritual self—coming to terms with cosmic matters and plumbing the depths of your soul. Suddenly, modern spells seem pale, and you may quest or conduct research to uncover ancient ways and recipes.

• INTEGRATION—You incorporate the Craft into your daily life.

You've broken down the inner wall between the spiritual and the material, and you see and act on the potential for magic in even the most mundane matters. You have learned to listen to your intuition for magic. You're fully empowered, magically adept, and highly utilized by everyone who knows you.

Trust Your Magical Instincts

"Go by your instincts, your feelings, your intuition."
— RAYMOND BUCKLAND
Buckland's Complete Book of Witchcraft

To some degree, everyone has magical instincts on which goodly spell-work relies. We have an instinct for going quiet to prevent attack or interference. We have an inner sense when things are fair or foul. We know that when something looks too goodly to be true, it usually *isn't* true. And we know that not all may be as it first appears.

Trust yourself to be able to work magic. If you ever feel inadequate to the task, banish the thought. Remind yourself that you have innate magical talent and myriad protective and spiritual instincts waiting to be tapped and sharpened.

If you sense that a chirping bird is singing for your benefit or in some way communicating a message to you, you're probably right. Its song probably *is* an omen telling you the status of present things, or events to come. Pay attention to signs. If you do a rite for a sweetie of your own, then dream that she or he kissed you and feel that's a significant sign, you're right again.

In whatever magic you do, act on your instinctual feelings or urges the moment they arise. For instance, whenever you're in the middle of a spell in which all is going well and you suddenly feel compelled to add a component or express your desire in a different way, you should do so. If you meet people who purport to be Crafters, but make you feel uncomfortable, move on and look for others of like mind with which to circle.

Become attuned to minute changes that occur all around you—subtle shifts in people's moods, weather patterns, neighborhood noises, political climates, and so forth. It pays to keep your wits about you so that you'll be better able to protect yourself and others from numerous avoidable problems. For instance, if you're doing a spell adoors and don't wish to be disturbed, it's vital that you stay alert for telltale twig snaps that could indicate approaching intruders.

Your conscience knows when you want to classify something as a favorable omen, even though it really isn't, and when something happens that truly *is* indicative, even if it bodes ill. Follow your heart in such matters. It is typically on target regarding how your occult studies and spellwork are progressing, and accurately predicts events likely to happen in your future.

If you're initially drawn to one form of magic but, after due practice, find that it's just not working for you, discard it for a while and use a different method. You'll eventually discover numerous methods that click with your personality and afford you reliable results.

Let your primal side empower your spells. For instance, if you want to help family and friends through magic, ensure that the spells you do on their behalf reflect the depth of your love for them—pour a mama bear's intensity into them. If you're outraged about something, express it with a leonine roar, or counter a sly manipulator with secret rites of your own.

If you feel like baying at the Moon and it's appropriate, do so. By the same token, should a spell spark silent reflection within you, go along with it—you will be happily surprised by the wisdom it reveals. Magic works on *you* as you work *it*.

Generally, play magic whatever way feels right to you. Do spells you want to try and feel goodly about. Spurn those you feel uncertain about. With experience, you'll likely discover that spells you initially felt an abhorrence for eventually reveal the reason for their existence, and they may suddenly begin to appeal to you.

When in doubt—don't. For instance, if you're not sure whether you should do a particular spell or you worry that an herb you plan to use in a potion or brew is past its prime, don't do the spell and don't use the plant. If you long to do a spell that seems simple enough, but don't quite understand parts of the recipe, take some time and research the answers to your questions before you attempt it.

Record what happens when you heed your instincts, and what happens when you don't. You'll consistently find that, when you follow them, your instincts are your best ally.

Let Your Talents
and Interests Guide Your Spellcraft

*"If you're a knitter, you could make a healing shawl . . . the sick person
could wear the shawl, and thus directly absorb the healing energy.*

*"A carpenter might create a 'magic table,' with a round top and
runes carved into its legs, or a cabinet specially designed to house herbs
and oils used in magic. A lapidary may create ritual jewelry, utilizing the
proper stones and metals to bring specific influences into her or his life."*
— SCOTT CUNNINGHAM AND DAVID HARRINGTON
Spell Crafts

After you've done several dozen spells, you'll realize that you possess particular magical talents that seem to manifest themselves effortlessly whenever you do specific forms of magic. Some people hone such skills until they choose a magical specialty, such as astrology, divination, kitchen witchery (intentional cooking or making herbal medicines), hedge witchery (magical gardening and outdoor workings), ceremonial magic (stylized rites and practices), or healing (through therapeutic touch, crystals, and so on). Many discover and cultivate the magical aspects of the mundane work or hobbies they practice, or explore the hidden wisdom in their studies at school.

For example, individual members of Coven Oldenwilde practice specialties that make the group magically well rounded. Lady Passion has two specialties—divination and the creation of beautiful, powerful public rituals. The High Priestess employs hundreds of different methods with which to predict the future, including reading tarot cards; practicing chiromancy (reading palms); tasseography (reading tea leaves); and phrenology (noting skull patterns); scrying; and throwing bones, shells, or nut halves. She also excels at transforming mundane places into mysterious realms for Sabbats, and devising new rituals based on traditional rites.

*Diuvei's specialties include astrology and *geomancy,* in which he randomly pulls stones out of a bag or makes random marks with a stick and divines future events from the patterns produced. People rely on his interpretations of their natal charts as well as his ability to determine auspicious times for events. He teaches Wiccan planetary correspondences that make astrology practical and easy to understand. He first began exploring the Art of Correspondences while he was a music-theory major at Princeton University. There, he discovered that both the most ancient texts of metaphysics and the most up-to-date research in particle physics link music to the harmonies of planets and atoms alike.

Another coven member specializes in memorizing traditional texts and Barbarous Words of Power. He can control a crowd through drumming specific beats and serves as a walking reference regarding proper ritual procedures.

Yet another coven member excels in transforming herself into otherworldly beings through costumes, makeup, and accoutrements. She comes up with creative ideas for rites, is a graceful trance and fascination dancer, and plays the sistrum, an ancient musical instrument whose ethereal tinkling pleases the God/desses.

Don't rush into a specialty—take your time exploring things you've always been interested in or secretly wanted to do, such as delving into your past lives, learning Tai Chi, or learning to levitate. Exploring a wide variety of goodly Craft spells and experiences will gently guide you in numerous directions until you find or develop the path that feels right to you and helps others.

Avoid duplicating the specialties of other, well-established Crafters in your community. If your town already has a plethora of established tarot readers, maybe it needs a healer or prophet/ess.

If there's no belly dancer, perhaps you should take up that art of fascination, and then openly teach it to others as something more than just a fun way to lose weight.

If you're musically inclined, what instrument does your area lack? Consider obscure types, such as a shawm, a dulcimer, panpipes, zils, a zither, or a sitar. No matter what you play, you're sure to find fans if you learn to entrance your listeners with the powerful but little-known magic of modal scales and harmonies.

If you're artistic, learn to make your own magical inks, transform common chemicals into colored fires, convert plant matter into fabric dyes, or tint bath salts in numerous hues. Work with decoupage, wood stains, and papier-mâché.

If you're inclined toward guarding or protecting people, study the magic of warding and binding, or practice ways of gently inclining chaotic folks into a state of polite helpfulness. Dance at community gatherings with wands or glow-sticks, or spin fire on a rope or stick.

Cast your net wide in searching for the magical specialty that's right for you. The main thing is to experiment with many methods until you find a naturally fitting niche wherein you're unique in your area, and hence of use to others.

Spell Ingredients Are Everywhere

*"With your left hand
in the night
doings lit by candlelight—
papyrus from a mummy torn,
a shiny stone,
a bit of horn,
string with which to bind it tight—
a prayer on the water's borne . . .*

*"Such normal things
have magic might,
abound,
and set the world aright!"*
—LADY PASSION

Beginning spellcrafters start practicing magic with whatever they have on hand and, over time, steadily build up a stock of herbs, stones, and ritual accoutrements collected in the course of doing magic. At first, you may have only a shelf to use as an altar, with a solitary candle, one essential oil, and, perhaps, a *boleen,* a white-handled utility knife. Not to worry—you could probably do 50 or more spells using only those items.

Don't focus on what you don't have; focus on what you *do* have or can easily acquire. Enjoy going out to collect certain herbs. Comb your kitchen for helpful implements, such as silver spoons or chopsticks to help you stir your potions, spices, and dyes. Make a list of components you can obtain at your local grocer. Scour your house and collect balls of string, pins, broken glass shards, rusty nails, and other ingredients for spells you're interested in eventually doing. Pore through your sewing room for needle and thread and your bathroom for cotton balls, cotton-tipped swabs, and bandages.

Take advantage of fortuitous events to help you gather spellwork ingredients. Although it may take some time, take the trouble to peel off any burrs that stick to your cape—they're extra-magical because of this, and you can use them to reflect back curses sent your way. Don't leave a goodly cookie fortune on the table after you've eaten at a Chinese restaurant; if it says you're coming into money, take it home and immediately put it in your coin purse or wallet.

If you camp outside for Sabbats, search the area with a helpful field guide in hand. If you see an abundance of flora, harvest a tad of jewelweed here, a bit of fairy fern there. Should you come upon a dead blacksnake, consider taking the carcass home and making an athamé (a magical knife) sheath from its beautiful skin.

Frequent thrift stores for diaphanous robes, interesting vests, and black clothing or costumes for Sabbats, gatherings, and mythos reenactments. Stop at yard sales, go to flea markets and bazaars—you'll be thrilled at the Witchy treasures some folks can't wait to get rid of. Keep your eye out for anything magical, such as items made of wicker, rattan, glass, silver, wood, metal, bone, stone, or shells. As you can, pick up things decorated with natural motifs, such as spirals, stars, leaves, or vines.

Let folks know what you need, like, or will accept regarding donations of goods to help your spellcraft. If you don't tell them you're in dire need of a simple component, they won't know to give it to you.

Many people know that Witches work with just about anything, so we are constantly delighted when we receive rare ingredients that really help us help others. Friends offer us bolts of black fabric, wolf hair, arrowheads, stones, and candles of every shape, color, and scent. They know that we have a standing order for them to bring back a bit of water from everywhere they travel, which we then add to our collection of waters of the world.

Spurn synthetic ingredients, and try not to suffer plastic in any ritual space. Although many forms and fibers conduct magical energy well, plastics impede magic's flow. No matter how goodly a Witchy bauble may appear, if it is made

PART I
Scope

of polyresin, filled with foam, or shiny and slimy to the touch, you'd be better off not purchasing it or using it in your spells.

Not having the right ingredient is rarely a good excuse for not doing a spell; appropriate substitutions exist or can be acquired. If a spell calls for a piece of hemp and you have none, substitute common string or a long lamp wick. If it specifies wax and you're out of candles, use clear paraffin instead.

How to Find or Create a Magical Atmosphere

". . . one of the most important secrets of magic is to provide the atmosphere in which the unusual can happen . . .

"The atmosphere created by incense and candlelight, can transform an ordinary room into a cave of mystery, a shrine wherein strange powers can manifest. If you wish to work magic, then you must create an atmosphere, both mental and physical, in which magic can work."

— DOREEN VALIENTE
An ABC of Witchcraft

Although you can work magic anywhere, some atmospheres are more conducive or responsive to spellwork than others. Spirits abound in primordial glades, whereas it's hard to feel magical at all if you're in the middle of a mini-mall.

Notice the effects differing designs in your environment exert on you. Your decor tends to make you feel either calm or chaotic, nonchalant or nervous, the latter usually because of too many busy designs vying with one another for your attention. Often, much of it is clutter that you hate to dust.

When considering mystical atmospheres, it helps to learn the astrological and sacred-geometry principles our ancestors used in determining both what constituted an innately magical place, and how they could work with an existing landscape to add to its power. Read books such as *Secrets of Ancient and Sacred Places* or *At the Center of the World: Polar Symbolism Discovered in Celtic, Norse and Other Ritualized Landscapes.*

Learn about ley lines. Research why the Egyptians' intricate and accurate sacred geometry enabled them to build pyramids that continue to astound the world with their magical depth (*Secrets of the Great Pyramid*). Read about lesser-known pyramid-building cultures (*Mysteries of the Mexican Pyramids*) or about omphali, standing stones that formed the center of ancient towns, or what makes obelisks so powerful (*The Magic of Obelisks*).

Magical places physically exist worldwide. Some are in remote locations, and some are where you'd least expect them to be. Many display such poetic beauty that even the most hardened developer inhales sharply whenever he happens onto one. Some wild places are eerily silent and timeless in a way that's impossible to define, but nonetheless pervades their every inch. Picturesque outdoor areas are often habitats for elementals, fairies, and botanical devas. They may also be the abode of a Deity, such as Herne of the Woods or Flidais, a Goddess of wildlife.

Places with a documented history of having once been a site for Pagan ceremonies retain their sacredness despite the passage of time. Earthen mounds, babbling streams, high waterfalls, stark deserts, old-growth forests, grassy fields, mountaintops, flower-filled meadows, and wetlands are all well-known examples of innately magical places.

To find magical places in your area, research your town library for mention of past mystical events, such as the erection of an obelisk or the dedication of a Masonic temple. Ask a local historian where the notorious haunted places are. Consult a city map and look for remote parks, trails, or abandoned roads or parts of town. Look at a topographical map that shows the high and low places of your surrounding area. Use maps and a pendulum to divine for future locations to scout. (See To Discover Where You Should Relocate, page 386.)

Chances are, however, that if you can find a magical place, others have already used it for magical purposes, or will soon inexplicably discover it at about the same time you do and begin to beat a steady path to it every chance they get. Therefore, if you do find a pristine site, don't tell anyone else about it unless you've gotten an oath not to reveal its location to others.

If you don't have access to a natural magical place or can't travel to one, create a mystical atmosphere indoors. First, lock the door so no one will be able to break your enchantment. Next, turn off any electric lighting and dim the room with shadows cast from a lit candle or two. Light evocative incense and imbue the area with its seductive scent. If your spell requires still concentration, sit atop a plush rug or plump fabric cushion. If it calls for much movement, wear moccasins, slippers, or boots, or go barefoot. Play music conducive to the mood you want to set. If persistent neighborhood noise distracts you, wear earplugs to minimize the problem.

Bring nature inside and decorate with plants, boughs, branches, fresh flowers, grasses, reeds, petrified wood, stones, or driftwood. Bedeck the tops of your windows, doorways, or tabletops. Press and preserve pretty plant specimens; then frame them and showcase nature's beauty as wall art throughout your home or in your ritual room. We've known many young Witches who converted their closets into pretty, serviceable magical areas.

Take a day or two and fashion an outdoor shrine or a meditation area. Collect natural treasures from your property or neighborhood walks, and group them according to their magical correspondences. (See Spellwork Rules of Thumb, page 258.)

Some magical places are created in astral realms or different dimensions, and reflect your heart's desires. Pagans often mentally construct—piece by piece, twig by twig—their conceptions of the ultimate secret retreat. These are non-physical places of refuge where people can go to relax, meditate, recuperate, practice solitary magic, or simply have fun. Some folks people their places, create interesting creatures, or exist there in ways corporeal life prevents.

You can make your own magical place at any time by meditating and mentally fashioning how you'd like to live. Once created, freeze it that way in your mind, and it will be there for you whenever you need it.

No matter where you go, you always have the ability to create magical space around your own body. Witches often call this "casting a protective circle" around themselves. This involves mentally envisioning and then willfully projecting a bubble around yourself that is typically invisible but can glow enough that those who can read auras can see it. It repulses negativity and coalesces your power in case you need to discharge it. It can prevent mugging, kidnapping, and other threats from harming you in any way. Some Witches effect it with a flick of a wrist; others silently pray for it to manifest itself, or envision an athamé drawing it around them.

How to Practice
Ethical Magic in an Unconscionable World

*"So it is Ardane, that none shall use the Art in any way to do ill to any.
how evermuch they have injured us. And for long we have obeyed this
law. 'Harm none' and nowtimes, many believe we exist not. So be it
Ardane. that this Law shall still continue to help us in our plight. No
one, however great an injury or injustice they receive, may use the Art
in any way to do ill or harm any.*

*"But, they may, after great consideration with all, use the Art to prevent
or restrain Christians from harming us and others, but only to let or
constrain them and never to punish."*

EXCERPT FROM THE OLDE ARDANES

*J*t's a cold, cruel world out there, full of suffering caused by humans'
refusal to heed the inner voice of conscience. Some people rationalize suffering as inevitable, and then revel in selfishness—greed is good, they say, and
it's every man for himself in a dog-eat-dog, kill-or-be-killed world. Other people claim to oppose evil while actually perpetrating it. In their zeal to impose a
rigid code of moral commandments on a fallen world, they commit violence in
the name of peace, and practice hatred in the name of love. Still others simply
deny the reality of suffering—it's all good, they claim, and they need do nothing
to alleviate suffering because humanity's evolution is pre-ordained.

Those who succumb to such reactions of nihilism, authoritarianism, or
passivism take their moral cues from without, rather than from their own
innate sense of right and wrong.

By contrast, spellcrafters' ethics derive from within. Independent of fad,
law, or commandment, their conscience provides them with an inner sense of
fairness that considers the whole rather than the self or the moment.

Magic is power, and can be directed for good or ill, depending on the
intention of the user. Just as a knife can save lives through surgery or take lives
through murder, so the tools of magic can be used to bless for the good of all,
or curse for selfish ends. But those who have developed sufficient spiritual dis-

cipline to cast an effective spell usually also have acquired sufficient ethical discipline to strive to harm none. They dedicate their magical efforts to the all-knowing God/desses as an ultimate safety check. If they choose to ignore their conscience, the Law of Threefold Return soon reminds them of it the hard way.

Magicians desperate or amoral enough to cast curses for cash, for kicks, or out of pique have always been far rarer than non-spellcrafters' fears and fantasies have led them to imagine.

The three basic components of a spell—spiritual prayer, personal intention, and physical means—naturally correspond to three essential ethical principles you should always keep in mind:

- **DIVINE EARLY AND OFTEN**—Even if the recipe you're using doesn't specify it, you should precede every spell you cast with a divination. Spells and divinations are the active and passive poles of magic. The spell is a projection of your will into the world. You're only human, though—you can't foresee all the consequences, intended and unintended, that your spell will create. The God/desses, however, are wise beyond time and space and can see all things as if looking down on a landscape from their mountaintop abode. Pray that their will may ultimately supersede yours, and you will obtain what you, and the planet, truly need and desire—although that may be different from what you think you need at the moment.

To communicate with the divine before, after, or even during a rite, learn to do some form of divination. Read cards, runes, stars, or bones, or use one of the methods in Witches Scry Over Spilt Milk—The Art of Divination, page 114, or Discernment Spells, page 383.

- **AN IT HARM NONE, DO AS YE WILL**—"Harm none" is a safety check on your will. This Pagan maxim is essentially the same as many sages' highest ethical principles. Jesus' Golden Rule is "Do unto others as you would have others do unto you." The great philosopher Immanuel Kant's categorical imperative is "Always treat others as an end, never as a means."

Olde spells sometimes used the sacrifice of an animal—or even, in some religions, a person—to obtain that being's vital energy. It bears repeating here that modern spellcrafters, and many traditional ones, don't perform sacrifices, mostly because they believe it's wrong to use a sentient Being as a means to an end. An exception would be an animal that's already bound for slaughter as food, such as the chicken a Santeria priest/ess offers, as long as it is killed as humanely and painlessly as possible.

Cursing is a much trickier subject. There are times when people do such wrong to you, other people, or the planet that a curse may be necessary to stop them. There are better ways to accomplish this than casting a spell to make their heads explode, much as you might think they deserve it. You can bind them to prevent them from doing further harm, or you can mirror their own ill deeds back upon them. Your intent should not be to wreak vengeance—which leads only to more vengeance when somebody sooner or later tracks the scent of hatred back to you, and tries to get even—but simply to stop the harm they are doing.

Because they believe it's manipulative, some spellcrafters insist you should never do healings on people without their permission. It is a good idea to get someone's cooperation before you work a healing spell on them, but that often isn't possible. The person may be unable to talk to you, or be too young or too biased against magic to understand what you're trying to do. Is it better to let people suffer instead of working a secret spell? Of course not—then you would be harming them by omission. Avoid accidentally harming people by commission, however, and invoke the God/desses' aid as well.

- **THE LAW OF THREEFOLD RETURN**—This is the law of karma—what goes around, comes around. Whatever you do has consequences—every action creates a reaction. If magic is involved, the reaction may be magnified—perhaps not literally times three, but certainly with more intensity than normal physical actions. Just remember that there are few straight lines in magic, and many circles.

Most of the time, the karmic return for the magic you do will be positive—but if your motives are amiss, then you will regret the spell's *afterclap,* a Witch word meaning "unintended consequences." Don't, for example, steal your spell ingredients. If you do, the spell may still work, but you'll suffer repercussions, such as losing something you value shortly after you cast it.

The Law of Threefold Return is not only a passive ethic; it's also an active one. Spellcrafters have the capacity and, some say, the obligation, to return three times the harm done to them. That's one way to keep a bully from messing with you again! Still, be careful—the line between justice and vengeance is thin. Not all people who hurt you do so intentionally; you may discover when you talk to them that they were simply being careless or ignorant. Don't waste your curses on people who cut you off in traffic; save them for people who intentionally work to harm you, your loved ones, or the planet.

Some folks say you should never haggle or bargain for magical items. That's a misunderstanding of a traditional rule: Never haggle over the price of something you've obtained through magic—it insults the God/desses. And don't stiff a craftsperson who made you a magical item—give them the full amount you agreed upon, or the item will be forever polluted and unreliable. Whenever possible, barter instead of buy.

In general, money and magic don't mix. Doing spells in exchange for money cheapens the Art Magical and chains you to the bidding of your clients—tempting you to validate their wishes rather than view their situations objectively. In fact, the Ardanes stipulate that Crafters should never charge money for teaching occult techniques. Teachers of magic should accept voluntary donations only, especially of ritual items such as candles or incense. Many of us are so wary of money's degrading and obsession-inducing tendencies that we would rather barter than buy or sell goods and services whenever possible. Money is not a neutral force. It's highly toxic, and should be handled with extreme caution. Money is not found in nature—it's an arbitrary contrivance that enslaves billions of people. Many Pagans consider money a cold, black form of number magic that's ultimately controlled and manipulated for selfish advantage by an elite priesthood of financiers and investors.

Doing a spell to obtain money is a different matter altogether. We live in a world in which money is currently as crucial to survival as food, water, and air. You're not ripping anybody off if you simply ask the God/desses to help bring you your fair share. In Coven Oldenwilde's experience, however, the God/desses find it difficult to understand this uniquely human construct, and are far more forthcoming with a specific thing, such as a house or a car, than with an artificial abstraction, such as a $5,000 check. Money magic is a very unreliable art—don't count on making a living with it.

You can do many things on a daily basis to model Pagan tenets, inspire hope in others, and gently perpetuate the Olde Religion's peaceful ways. As your magical powers increase through practice, folks will either see enough instances of your skill in action, or sense it despite your every effort to keep it private. Soon, people will seek you out for your wisdom or help as problems arise in their lives. When this happens—not *if*—decide on a case-by-case basis whether the cause is just, and the motives pure, and, therefore, whether you should help, and in what ways. If people know nothing of magic and aren't willing to physically do anything magical to help themselves, then provide them with minimal information. If, however, they are in need and seem goodly folk, help them to the degree that their manner suggests they can comprehend.

Occasionally, you'll help people so much that their gratitude mutates into dependence. To avoid being harangued about every hangnail, empower them to learn how to do spells themselves and remain available to answer questions if they then run into any difficulty.

Perhaps the most revolutionary thing you can do is to physically act, in whatever way you can, as the conscience of those in your community who feel nameless, voiceless, disregarded, or forgotten. The more conventional your town seems, the more it *needs* your Witchy wit and wisdom. Write commentaries, letters to the editor, and such—expose to the light of print smoldering city scandals, secret travesties, and ongoing hypocrisies.

A local Witch in our community made it a public point to visit paupers' graves, acknowledge their shameful anonymity and neglect by the community, and honor their passing with typically sweet, Pagan respect. She didn't do it for money or vainglory, but solely because when she became aware of the problem (no Christian minister felt obliged to bother), it touched her heart and compelled her to do something on the paupers' behalf.

Pick your battles carefully so you don't wear out your welcome in the public eye. When an issue crops up on your local news that negatively affects the Pagan community, immediately rally supporters to help you protest or picket the needless injustice. But reserve your ire for important issues that have broad ramifications.

The solution to a problem is often embedded in the nature of the problem itself. Use your spellworking skills to find and craft that solution. For instance, to challenge an unconstitutional law, you may need to activate the magical principle of antipathy—opposites repel—and publicly do the very thing that the law forbids.

For example, several years ago Lady Passion and *Diuvei were made aware that the state in which we reside (North Carolina) kept a law on the books forbidding divination (unless, tellingly, it was for fun purposes during a school festival or took place under the auspices of a church function). Enacted in 1951 as a means to roust transients and Gypsies, the law was one of a slew of antiquated state statutes, including one forbidding dogs to "worry squirrels on the Capitol square," and another prohibiting the erection of a gravestone accusing someone of murder. Because Coven Oldenwilde annually conducts public Sabbat rituals at which we provide free divinations to hundreds of participants, we knew that if such a law could be used against our kind, it inevitably would be. Therefore, Lady Passion wrote a commentary for the local newspaper about the problem, warning area Pagans of the threat and exhorting them to stand firmly in support of Witches' documented history of helping folks with divination. She also appealed to the state and requested that the committee responsible for striking antiquated laws do so in this instance.

Within two years of Lady Passion's warning, cops in a neighboring burg, acting on an anonymous complaint, ran out of town a psychic who had paid for and received a legitimate business license. He had a wife and three children to support and had harmed no one. This outraged Coven Oldenwilde, so members held a protest on the town's courthouse steps, giving free divinations to one and all. When the crackdown spread like a brushfire and police began threatening all psychics, we joined a protest by Asheville's community of Witches wherein we defiantly gave free readings. A pregnant protest leader was arrested, but was so well defended by the ACLU that the case was dismissed. We chronicled the protests on our Web site, urging folks to press state officials to rescind the law, and continued to perform our public divinations despite occasional threats of arrest. Six years after we began targeting the law, state legislators struck it from the books.

These are no small tasks, but little in life is as rewarding as seeing over the years how you and a few others have radically changed your realm for the better. Although magical rivals may accuse you of being publicity seekers, disregard their lack of involvement and act on your own conscience. Do everything you can—and more than you ever thought yourself capable of—to improve the tone of your chosen locale.

It's great to be concerned about how other countries fare, but it's best to start cleaning up your own backyard before you tackle problems on a planetary scale. If you can help your own area to the point where it's common knowledge that you, a Pagan spellcrafter, have been instrumental in its betterment, then you may very well be ready to weigh into the grander scheme of things. As Wisefolk, we see how things are, strive for them to be better, and help others do their best to help make them so.

PART II

SKILLS

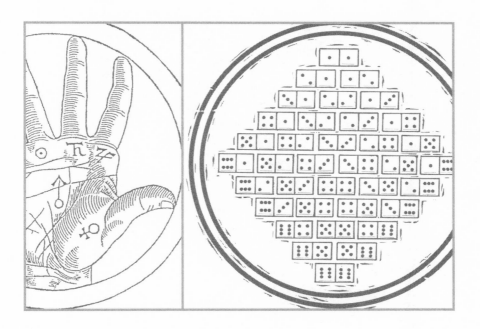

"Magic is a faculty of wonderful virtue, full of most high mysteries, containing the most profound contemplation of most secret things, together with the nature, power, quality, substance, and virtues thereof . . . the most perfect, and chief science, that sacred, and sublimer kind of philosophy, and lastly the most absolute perfection of all most excellent philosophy."

— H. CORNELIUS AGRIPPA
De occulta philosophia, Book I, Chapter II

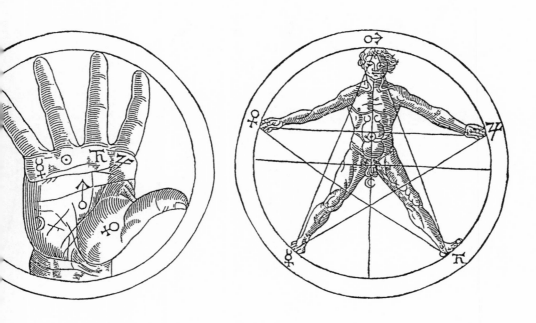

As above, so below

The Art of Correspondences

> *"Now there is a traditional correspondence, which modern experiment has shown to be fairly reliable. There is a certain natural connexion between certain letters, words, numbers, gestures, shapes, perfumes and so on, so that any idea or (as we might call it) 'spirit,' may be composed or called forth by the use of those things which are harmonious with it, and express particular parts of its nature."*
> — ALEISTER CROWLEY
> *Magick in Theory and Practice*

Everything in the physical universe, the world of matter, has a form that takes up space and exists in time. Consider this book you are holding: In space, it occupies a certain length, breadth, depth, and weight. In time, it came to be on the day when these pages were printed and bound, and it will cease to be on the day whenever mold or fire consumes them.

This book's form in space and time isn't random—it has order. The fact that you are able to turn its pages and read its print means that its individual parts and molecules are not chaotically flying all over the room. Its copyright date is good evidence that it didn't disengage itself from the twenty-first century and suddenly appear in the middle of the nineteenth or twenty-fifth centuries. That's not to say such things can't happen—just that they probably won't. No matter how senseless and chaotic the world around you may seem, beneath the turmoil is a fundamental order of things—a pattern. This pattern has meaning, just as the letters you're reading now are not arbitrarily jumbled up, but flow in sequence to create words, sentences, and chapters that convey ideas.

The patterns behind things are not fixed and motionless, as are religious commandments graven in stone, nor can they be reduced and confined to dry scientific formulas chalked on a blackboard. They are just as much alive as the beat of the drums that animate a gathering of Pagan dancers, as the heat of the bonfire they writhe ecstatically around. The same patterns pervade all levels of the cosmos, reaching as far above as the infinite stars, as far below as the infinitesimal atoms.

Imagine yourself as such a dancer, stamping and clapping out a rhythm as you circle. Whether you're alone around a flickering candle or among others in a great crowd around a blazing balefire, as you step around your central fire to the rhythm of your handclaps, the Earth is spinning around the central orb of the Sun to the rhythm of the days and nights. As you circle and salute the Four Directions, from East to South to West to North and back to East again, so the Earth circles through the seasons, from spring to summer to autumn to winter and back to spring again. As you whirl around the fire and the Earth whirls around the Sun, so our star, in one of the four arms of our Milky Way Galaxy, whirls in a similar but far greater cycle, passing through its own stellar seasons on a scale of time spanning millions of years, billions of handclaps. On every level of space and time, from the galactic vast and slow, to the subatomic small and fast, you'll find similar patterns of cyclic motion.

Such patterns pervade all levels of the cosmos. They interconnect—they *correspond* to one another. It is that correspondence that gives them their meanings, which—like letters in some great book of nature—the Wise learn to read and write through divination and spellcasting.

Our culturally ingrained habit of viewing things as separate pieces blinds us to this all-pervading matrix of the universe. Spellcrafters, by contrast, cultivate the holistic habit of reasoning by analogy—a way of thinking that is more poetic and imaginative than concrete, cause-and-effect, scientific rationalism, yet more grounded and logical than abstract, metaphysical speculation. Link by similar link, spellcrafters forge a chain of associations that connects the transcendent with the temporal, the spiritual with the material, the "as above" with the "so below."

Anchoring each of these chains of analogies is an archetype, a fundamental Idea from which correspondences emanate, like branches from a central stem. The specific words and symbols used to express an archetype are not the archetype itself. They are simply material manifestations—facets, aspects, or forms—of a transcendent Idea that exists in the spiritual realm, beyond space and time. The hub of a wheel, as Taoist spellcrafters say, is an empty hole—you can know it only by the spokes that surround it.

Consider the four cardinal directions, for example. We take them for granted as arbitrary letters on a compass dial—E S W N—because we are accustomed to using them merely as a means to get more efficiently from point A to point B.

To the spellcrafter, however, each of the Four Directions is a secret door that opens onto a vast hallway of interconnected meanings. Each direction corresponds to certain times, seasons, elements, colors, plants, stones, and so on.

Correspondences determine the choice of a spell's components. When you create a spell, you seek to stack up correspondences like layers of pancakes. Align with your magical intention an appropriate color, herb, stone, incense, number, planet, direction—everything you can that looks like, seems like, resembles, or evokes whatever you desire or seek to accomplish. These magical tokens focus your will; by gathering them together with intention, you're fashioning a microcosm of the universe as you wish it to be. It is as if the web of correspondences you weave enables your will to reach forth and pluck the vaster, universal web of archetypes. The more artfully you use your wisdom to construct this web, the more effective your spell will be.

For example, we provide a spell variation under To Make Wishes Come True (page 351) that involves making a Japanese wish pot to store your dreams in until they are fulfilled. When it comes time to put the little pot somewhere on your property to let it begin doing its work, on which wall of your house or boundary of your property would you set or bury it near? Your intent is to birth a wish into manifestation, to bring it forth into the light of day, so naturally, you would house the pot in the East, the direction of the rising Sun. If you put it in the West, the direction of the waning Sun, you would be negating your spell's intention, unless the wish involved many correspondences specifically associated with the West.

Generally, the more correspondences you use, the more you amplify your spell's force. This is why the shelves and cabinets of a Witch's house are always overflowing with collections of bizarre objects. That snakeskin, for example, might be just the thing for a spell of healing and renewal, and that dried owl's wing might be needful for invoking the wisdom of Air. Spellcrafters value objects as much for their symbolic correspondences as for their physical properties, which are merely the most tangible parts of their essence.

At the same time, the Art of Correspondences is just that—an art, not merely a rote technique. To create a powerful spell, you don't want to just pile up a lot of miscellaneous junk. Use your sense of beauty, of justice, of rightness to choose the correspondences that most aptly and effectively express your intent. Spellcrafters use correspondences in much the same way poets use words or artists use colors.

Correspondences describe the underlying structure of the universe—even the scientist's periodic table of the elements is a table of atomic correspondences. (See Divine Number—The Magic of Counting, page 135.) It would therefore be possible to write a library's worth of books detailing countless links between letters, colors, numbers, shapes, sounds, planets, herbs, stones, and more. Potentially, every type of thing in the known universe could find its place somewhere in a table of correspondences of sufficient size.

Trusting to tables to look up correspondences for your magic is risky, however. Although every book on magic contains a table of correspondences, you'll soon notice that such tables often contradict one another (and sometimes even themselves), contain errors, or appear arbitrary and confusing.

Instead, study reliable tables, such as ours. (See page 89.) Get a feel for the most important archetypes and correspondences in magic; then set such tables aside and simply practice recognizing the archetype of or behind every thing you encounter and every event that occurs. Consider correspondences as a sheaf of labels you carry around in your head that enable you to mentally categorize items or circumstances. Naturally you'll want to classify people you encounter, too; just avoid doing so obviously—it's insensitive to make others feel as if you're profiling them. By practicing divination, you'll become skilled at recognizing correspondences. By practicing spellcraft—divination's active counterpart—you'll become skilled at using them.

Beginning spellcrafters need to know just a few fundamental archetypes and their correspondences: the Two Polarities, the Four Elements and Four

Quarters, the Seven Planets, and the Ten Numbers. Especially important are the Four Elements and Four Quarters, which are the principal tools spell-crafters use to work with space, and the Seven Planets, which they use to work with time.

Except for the Ten Numbers, which have their own chapter, these fundamental correspondences are illustrated in the accompanying tables. They are laid out for easy study and teaching—they begin with the most basic archetypes, and build from there.

The Two Polarities

"In the pursuit of knowledge, every day something is acquired.
In the pursuit of wisdom, every day something is dropped."
Tao Te Ching

The cosmos is inherently balanced. It provides both light and dark, both life and death, both laughter and tears. For every yang, there is a yin; for every day, there is a night; for every active, outward, or upward action, there is a passive, inward, or downward reaction—and vice versa. Male and female, Sun and Moon, rich and poor, fat and thin, I and you, us and them—there is no one without the other.

Witches know this, and keep their equilibrium in a dizzying world by tempering an excess of one pole with a goodly antidote of its opposite. For instance, it's often unwise to run heedless into battle—often it's preferable to observe and strategize. On the other hand, too much thought can lead to paralysis or pointless inaction.

Polarity is not static, but dynamic. As the well-known yin-yang symbol illustrates, each pole is distinct from, but mirrors, its opposite form. In time, each transforms into its opposite. Dawn gives way to dusk, and dusk yields to dawn again. The wheel of fortune turns, the mighty fall, and the meek inherit the Earth—and then mightily oppress a new set of meek, who will eventually topple them in their turn.

Much of the world's madness stems from people's denial of the interpenetration of opposites. They impose too great an abyss between things, races, genders, ages, beliefs, customs, and so on by arbitrarily denying duality. The young forget that they'll one day be old; the old forget what it was like to be young. Haves and have-nots, whites and blacks, and men and women deny that their fortunes are inextricably linked. The greedy think they can take without giving, and eventually end up sacrificing everything of true value. The violent focus on an action while disregarding its inevitable consequences. The intolerant never consider what it's like to be on the receiving end of their hate.

The most divisive and perverse denial of duality is moral prejudice, or the insistence that one aspect of a polarity is innately good, while its opposite is inherently evil. The "one-way-onlyism" of divided duality is impossible to sustain in the real world: The inevitable shadow side of pretended virtue is practiced vice.

Victorian London, behind its façade of straitlaced sexual morality, had the highest per-capita number of prostitutes in the world. During the cold war, the CIA and the KGB each accused the other side of practicing the very atrocities they themselves were secretly committing.

Spellcrafters appreciate the value of *both* poles of a duality. We use the Moon's waxing phase, sunwise (clockwise) movement, and the right hand for yang magic—spells to create, generate, attract, acquire, and so on. We use the Moon's waning phase, ayenward (counterclockwise) movement, and the left hand for yin magic—spells of binding, banishing, blasting, and dispersing.

Although experienced magical practitioners believe in good and evil, they avoid making the naïve mistake of aligning polarities such as right-hand and left-hand or white and black with the polarity of good and evil. Only the uneducated classify magic in white-and-black terms such as the right-hand path (by which they mean positive, healing practices) and the left-hand path (negative, coercive magic).

There's a time and place for everything. As surely as you believe you'll never have cause to perform left-hand magic, some circumstance will arise that forces you to reconsider when passivity constitutes consent. Should you avoid magically binding a dangerous rapist because the spell would be coercive?

Pagans believe that good and evil is a choice people make in their hearts, then willfully enact. The existence of opposites is not evil; in nature, even predator and prey maintain each other in a symbiotic balance. What's actually the good is the truth that opposites can unite in cooperation and peace. What's actually the evil is the lie that opposites must divide in competition and war.

Witches use the principle of duality in the way they move in circle. For example, in the Northern Hemisphere, sunwise is clockwise (or *deosil*)—East, South, West, North, and back to East again. Ayenward is counterclockwise (or *widdershins)*. In the Southern Hemisphere, sunwise is counterclockwise, and ayenward is clockwise.

In sacred space, Crafters always move sunwise by default, unless we are specifically doing a working to banish, disperse, unwind, or undo something.

Four Elements and Four Quarters

"Witches use the seen world to master the unseen world."
—Lady Passion

THE FOUR ELEMENTS

THE FOUR ELEMENTS—FIRE, AIR, WATER, AND EARTH—are the best-known magical correspondences. They represent all the things and processes of the material realm.

FIRE corresponds to things of spirit and will—to the magic of passion and ecstasy, as well as of violence—and to processes of intensifying, transmuting, and creating or destroying. Fire is like the light and warmth of our souls.

AIR corresponds to things intellectual and to processes of transferring, communicating, and clarifying—as in spells for travel or divinations for knowledge. Air is like our breath, which conveys our words.

WATER corresponds to things emotional and to processes of flowing, adapting, and reflecting—as in spells involving love, friendship, reconciliation, laughter, loss, and grief. Water is like our tears, which express both our sorrow and our joy.

EARTH corresponds to things physical and tangible and to processes of solidifying, stabilizing, and reinforcing—as in spells for healing the body, attracting wealth or a job, or stabilizing a home or family. Earth is like the bones that give strength and structure to our bodies.

The Four Elements are divided into Two Polarities. Fire and Air are yang, masculine, and associated with levity, the tendency to rise upward. Water and Earth are yin, feminine, and associated with gravity, the tendency to fall downward. The traditional alchemical symbols for Fire and Air are based on an upward-pointing triangle; for Water and Earth, on a downward-pointing one. When superimposed, the triangles create a hexagram, often called the Star of David, symbolizing the totality of the cosmos, or As Above, So Below. To remember which symbol goes with which element, notice that the Fire triangle points up like a flame, the line on the Air triangle is like clouds around a mountaintop, the Water triangle resembles a cup, and the Earth triangle looks as if it's stuck into the ground.

Each element is animated by magical creatures called elementals, which live within it. These Beings are often visible if you scry their element long enough.

SALAMANDERS OF THE FIRE often resemble white-hot or red worms or lizards. They are spirit critters that resemble the coals they play in and the flames whose heat they ride as the fire licks the logs. A destructive form of Salamander occasionally manifests itself in especially ferocious fires—a building fire or a wildfire—as a triangular face made of flames.

SYLPHS OF THE AIR are light, fairylike entities who float, fly, and delight in riding wind fronts and air currents. You may see them floating about; they often mimic dandelion wisps or insects.

UNDINES OF THE WATER are slippery, silvery, or iridescent creatures that your eye may catch wherever sun-dappled water flows. Their preferred realm is backwoods creeks and uncharted fathoms, which is why Witches traditionally address them as Undines of the Deep. They ride ocean streams and currents, shooting rapids like reckless kids.

GNOMES OF THE EARTH are troll-like, plodding, protective, treasure-loving elves. They live in—or beneath fallen—trees or stumps, especially those with rotten roots used by animals as shelter. Their skin, clothes, and accoutrements match the flora, fauna, and foliage of the forests they dwell in.

The elementals' favor is crucial in many kinds of spellwork. You can propitiate a specific type in order to attract its beneficence; for example, to lure wealth to your family, give jewelry offerings to Gnomes.

Further, you can request that an elemental manifest itself as an affirmative or a negative omen in answer to a question you pose to the God/desses. You can note one's sudden appearance and heed its meaning as a portent of future events, then take measures to prevent the likely outcome if you consider it undesirable.

In olden times, the Four Elements were especially used in medicine. Before materialistic science taught doctors to dissect the body but discard the soul, they took for granted the connection between psychological disposition and physical health that is nowadays considered the cutting edge of modern medical investigation. Physicians summarized this mind-body dynamic as:

THE FOUR HUMORS OR TEMPERAMENTS

YELLOW BILE (choleric)—fiery: active, excitable, and intemperate
BLOOD (sanguine)—airy: intellectual or whimsical
PHLEGM (phlegmatic)—watery: expressive, emotional, and caring
BLACK BILE (melancholic)—earthy: introspective or depressive

We still use these terms to describe people's overall personalities, and the medical profession acknowledges them in the recognition that hot-tempered, quick-to-anger, choleric persons are especially susceptible to high blood pressure and heart attacks.

If scientific types scoff at your honoring only four elements when "there are more than 100 in the atomic table of elements," explain that they're simply confused by two different meanings of the word *element*. What scientists call elements are irreducible chemical substances, basic patterns of atomic configurations, which are themselves based on an underlying numerological archetype. (See Divine Number—The Magic of Counting, page 135.) What spellcrafters call the Four Elements are no different from what physicists call the four states of matter: plasma, gas, liquid, and solid, which correspond respectively to Fire, Air, Water, and Earth. Both spellcrafter and physicist agree that the application of energy transforms one state of matter into another, as heat applied to ice melts it into water, then boils it into steam.

THE FOUR ELEMENTS
AND THE FOUR STATES OF MATTER

FIRE = plasma
AIR = gas
WATER = liquid
EARTH = solid

Consider the alchemy required to make a cup of tea. You start with Earth in the form of tea leaves, then apply Fire to a pot of Water and bring it to the boiling point—that boundary state at which Water begins to transmute into Air in the form of steam. Finally, you mingle the Four Elements by mixing the boiling liquid with the leaves to produce your magical brew—a stimulating cup of tea.

There is a natural sequence to the Four Elements: from densest to rarest—Earth, Water, Air, and Fire; or from rarest to densest—Fire, Air, Water, then Earth. This is how olde magic books always present them. You can see this in the diagram drawn by Robert Fludd to illustrate the magical cosmos. Rock-solid Earth at the center is surrounded in turn by the fish-filled Water of the oceans and rivers, the cloud-bearing Air of the sky, and the region of Fire where the lights of the aurora borealis are sometimes seen to dance.

THE CONCENTRIC SPHERES OF THE FOUR ELEMENTS

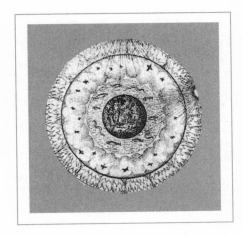

This detail of a cosmological diagram by Robert Fludd shows the Earth at the center and Water, Air, and Fire in successive rings. *Source:* Robert Fludd, *Utriusque Cosmi Maioris*, Vol. I, 1617.

The modern Earth sciences divide our planet into these same concentric spheres. Scientists use four Greek elemental terms to describe the structure of our planet. *Geosphere* designates solid land; *hydrosphere,* the waters that run and pool atop it. *Atmosphere* designates the air that carries winds and rains; and *magnetosphere,* the electromagnetic aura that envelops the planet, a fiery field generated by the interaction between Earth's magnetic field and electrically charged particles emanating from the Sun, or solar wind.

Many modern authors on magic list the Four Elements in an order different from the natural sequence. They reverse Fire and Air, presenting the sequence as Air, Fire, Water, and Earth. The reason for this mix up is that most Witches and magicians in Western culture use the correspondence between the Four Quarters and the Four Elements that was popularized by the Order of the Golden Dawn, in which Air = East and Fire = South.

Although this is a goodly and natural fit—the direction of the Sun's noontide glory is rightly assigned to Fire, not Air—it does confuse folks when they forget that the Quarters and the Elements are not necessarily interchangeable. This order might also have been influenced by the Tibetan Buddhist order of the Elements, which is Wind, Fire, Water, and Earth. Our advice is to use the Air-first order when summoning the Four Quarters before spellwork. In all other contexts, use the Fire-first order.

Many authors also insist on a peculiar correlation between the Four Elements and the four suits of tarot cards. Almost everyone agrees that the tarot suits represent the four basic tools of magic and correspond to the playing-cards suits, which are stylized representations of the tarot symbols.

THE FOUR TAROT SUITS AND FOUR CARD SUITS

SWORDS = spades
WANDS = clubs
CUPS = hearts
PENTACLES = diamonds

Everyone also agrees that pentacles correspond to Earth and cups to Water. Some people, however, assign swords to Air, ignoring the harsh, fiery meaning of the sword suit in tarot, as well as the cutting, stabbing, warlike nature of a sword, and the fact that its steel is forged in Fire. They then assign wands to Fire, ignoring the largely benevolent meaning of this suit, as well as the prevalent use of wands to direct power or communicate, such a conductor's baton, a teacher's pointer, or a writer's pencil. Wands are traditionally made from tree branches, which grow out in the Air and are moved to and fro by the wind while attached to the tree. Because they're made of wood, they could be burned by Fire.

If you consider their actual natures, it's clear that swords should correspond to Fire, and wands to Air. The erroneous reversal may originate with Aleister Crowley, who boasted about inserting "blinds," or intentional magical errors, in his books as a means to mislead naïve readers not initiated into his magical order.

Chinese magicians use five elements: Wood, Fire, Earth, Metal, and Water. Their system doesn't actually contradict the Western way, though. The more you study Chinese astrological philosophy, the more you understand that, in practice, the meanings of the Chinese elements are very closely bound to the planets with which they correspond: Jupiter, Mars, Saturn, Venus, and Mercury, respectively. These are the Seven Planets minus the Two Lights, or the Sun and Moon.[15]

Western magic has its own fifth element, the Quintessence, or Spirit, in the sense of energy, ether, and chi. If the Four Elements correspond to the Four Directions—East, South, West, and North—then the Quintessence is the center or origin, an animating, pervasive element—the most rarified form of life force.

THE ELEMENTAL PENTAGRAM

For Wiccans, the pentagram symbolizes the Four Elements crowned by the Quintessence, Spirit.

[15] *See, for example,* Derek Walters, Chinese Astrology *(Wellingborough, Northamptonshire, England: Aquarian Press, 1987).*

THE FOUR QUARTERS

The Four Quarters are also called the Four Directions, Watchtowers, or Quartergates. So important are these crossroads of the cosmos that almost every culture honors them. They are the universal demarcations of sacred space. They are also closely linked to the turning points of time.

The cross symbolizes the Four Elements, Four Directions, four seasons, and four annual Lesser Sabbats of Yule, Ostara, Litha, and Mabon.

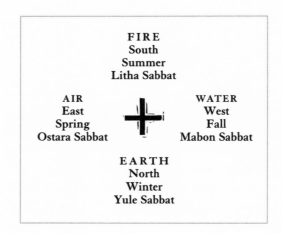

FIRE
South
Summer
Litha Sabbat

AIR   **WATER**
East   **West**
Spring   **Fall**
Ostara Sabbat   **Mabon Sabbat**

EARTH
North
Winter
Yule Sabbat

East, the place of sunrise, represents new life, beginnings, and purity. It corresponds to the time of year when nature's rebirth begins, the spring equinox, which Pagans call *Ostara*. The words *east* and *Easter* come originally from the same root word for *dawn*.

Halfway between dawn and dusk, the Sun reaches his zenith of blazing glory at high noon. As the day, so the year: The longest day of the year, the summer solstice (which Pagans call *Litha*), when the Sun stands as close to the apex of the sky as he reaches all year, is analogous to noon, when the Sun stands at the highest point he reaches all day. (If you live north of the equator, then at noon you see the Sun due south.) This links South with heat, fire, and light. (If you live south of the equator, then at noon you see the Sun due north, and the correspondences given here for South instead apply to North and vice versa.)

Opposing birth is death, and opposing sunrise is sunset—West, the opposite of East. Traditionally, folks bury the dead with their heads toward the West.

West corresponds to the fall equinox, which Pagans call *Mabon,* when warmth starts giving way to cold, and dying leaves fall from the trees like tears.

North is the opposite of South—the direction of midnight, the dark, cold winter of the day. Because the Sun is at his lowest point down below the Earth's horizon, North is linked to earthen depth, secrecy, and solidity—the essence of matter itself. (In the Southern Hemisphere, these associations apply to South.)

Generally, magical main altars and prayers are oriented toward the light-bringing East—the word *orient* originally meant "to turn east." Greek and Roman temples were often built with their main doors facing the East so that they could be thrown open to let the light of dawn illuminate the statue of the God/dess within. North is also often used because it is the direction of the fixed axis of the Pole Star, around which the sky revolves, and so represents stability and eternity. By the same token, most cultures consider the day to begin at dawn and the year, at springtime. Some, however, begin them at other times—modern clock days begin at midnight, for instance, and calendar years in midwinter. Rationales for multiple ways abound, and which you use depends on context, culture, and custom.

The Four Quarters are closely linked with the Four Elements. Today, in Western culture, most spellcrafters use this correspondence:

> EAST = Air
> SOUTH = Fire
> WEST = Water
> NORTH = Earth

Below the equator, South corresponds to Earth and North to Fire.

Most modern Witches associate the Four Quarters with certain colors. (See Regarding Color, page 110.)

THE FOUR QUARTER COLORS

> EAST = yellow
> SOUTH = red
> WEST = blue
> NORTH = green

If you have a ritual room or an outdoor circle, we recommend that you erect an altar in each of the Four Quarters, each dedicated to its corresponding element, and heap them with candles, colors, and magical objects that reflect each direction's times, seasons, and elements. (See Spellwork Rules of Thumb, page 258.)

CASTING A MAGIC CIRCLE

Most spellcrafters, whether they perform their rites in a formal temple, an apartment living room, a forest, or a desert, begin by marking out the sacred space within which they will invoke the divine and make magic happen.

Start by casting a circle. First, visualize the boundary you're going to create—not as a flat circle, but as a three-dimensional bubble that will surround and protect you while you work magic.

Begin and end your circuit(s) in the eastern direction. Walk around in a circle—either sunwise to attract or increase something or ayenward if you plan to banish or dispel something. Use an athamé, a wand, a sword, or a staff to trace the perimeter of a circle in your working space once or three times. You may also demarcate sacred space by laying down a cord, drawing it on the floor with chalk, drawing it on the ground with a stick, or using similar means. Traditionally, the circle is 9 feet in diameter.

Many Witches cast circle thrice: once around with a sharp tool raised to delineate its basic shape, then twice more around to purify the space. The second time around, they spurge the circle's perimeter by sprinkling salt water or scented oil, and the third time around they cense it with incense smoke.

Whether you cast once or thrice, chant or sing the following or something similar as you do so:

I conjure thee,
a space between the worlds,
that ye be
a guardian
of the pow'r
that (I/we) shall raise
in the names of (God's name) and (Goddess's name).

In Coven Oldenwilde, we cast circle in the names of our primary Deities: Herne and Hecate.

Throughout your rite's duration, scrupulously protect your circle's integrity from any breach. If anyone must enter or exit circle before the rite's end, he or she must formally "cut in" or "cut out" of it, using an athamé or index finger to trace an archway opening at the circle's edge. After walking through it, the person must immediately turn around and "seal" the circle closed again by making three horizontal passes across the invisible doorway with the athamé or index finger.

CALLING THE QUARTERS

Follow casting with "calling" the Four Quarters, starting usually with East and proceeding sunwise. Some Crafters also follow the Native American tradition of acknowledging seven directions—East, South, West, North, Above (Father Sky), Below (Mother Earth), and Center (the Source of All).

Honoring the directional elements promotes their favor. You don't always have to formally cast a circle and invoke the Four Quarters and the Four Elements before every spell, but it is a goodly idea to do so before, or in the course of, casting an especially powerful or difficult one.

Traditionally, Witches possess four primal powers: to know (*noscere* in the original Latin), to will (*velle*), to dare (*audere*), and to be silent (*tacere*). These signify a Crafter's ability to discern and boldly act on the truth while also remembering that discretion is the better part of valor. The Four Witch Powers are associated with the Four Quarters and the Four Elements:

AIR (East)—The Power to Know
FIRE (South)—The Power to Will
WATER (West)—The Power to Dare
EARTH (North)—The Power to Be Silent

To summon these powers and the elementals, pause before each direction in turn, raise your athamé (or index and middle fingers) in salute, then sincerely and poetically extol their virtues. Address the elementals by name; then relate their associated powers, manifestations, or correspondences.

For instance, if you wanted to conjure the essence of Water, you'd stand facing the West and lyrically intone something such as:

Hail, Ye Undines of the Deep.
Rain, snow, sleet, and hail
Sorrow's end and Day's farewell,
Favor (me/us)
with the Power to Dare.

When you finish spellworking, dispel your circle by formally dismissing the four elementals in either sunwise or ayenward order. Thank them for any manifestations they displayed, or help they gave. For example:

Hail, Ye Undines of the Deep.
(I/We) thank You for all Your kindness here.
As Ye depart for Your Wat'ry realms,
Go if Ye must, but stay if Ye will.
Hail and farewell!

The Seven Planets and Their Properties

*I*n antiquity, magicians often used the celestial magic of the Seven Planets as a guide for many of their magical correspondences and as the key to timing spells. The Seven Planets are the five planets visible to the naked eye, plus the Sun and the Moon. The system magicians used in considering the arrangement of the Seven Planets is called the Chaldean Order. (The Babylonians, who transmitted this knowledge to the Greeks, were often called Chaldeans.) This runs in the order of the planets' orbital speed around the Sun, from the slowest (Saturn) to the fastest (the Moon).

THE POLARITIES, QUARTERS, AND ELEMENTS

• • •

POLARITIES	YANG OR MALE	YIN OR FEMALE
Lunar Phases	waxing, brightening	waning, darkening
Movements	out, front, up, right	in, back, down, left

QUARTERS	EAST	SOUTH	WEST	NORTH
Time of Day/Night	dawn (sunrise)	noon	dusk (sunset)	midnight
Seasons	spring	summer	autumn	winter
Sabbats	Ostara *(spring equinox)*	Litha *(summer solstice)*	Mabon *(autumn equinox)*	Yule *(winter solstice)*
Colors	yellow or white	red or orange	blue or silver	green or black

ELEMENTS	AIR	FIRE	WATER	EARTH
Elementals	Sylphs	Salamanders	Undines	Gnomes
Matter States	gas	plasma	liquid	solid
Astrological Signs	Libra, Aquarius, Gemini	Aries, Leo, Sagittarius	Cancer, Scorpio, Pisces	Capricorn, Taurus, Virgo
Earth Levels	atmosphere	magnetosphere	hydrosphere	geosphere
Archetypes	intellect, mind	energy, force	emotion, desire	matter, body
Witch Powers	to know	to will	to dare	to be silent
Tarot (Card) Suits	wands (clubs)	swords (spades)	cups (hearts)	pentacles (diamonds)
Craft Tools	bell, wand, incense smoke	sword, athamé, candle	chalice, cauldron, wine	pentacle, altar stone, salt
Human Parts	breath	blood	tears	nails, hair
Humors	sanguine	choleric	phlegmatic	melancholic
Animal Parts	feathers, wings	fangs, claws	shells, fins	bones, hide
Typical Spells	psychism, prophecy, divination	purification, repulsion, love magic, dance	libation offering, conjuring rain, counseling	prosperity, healing, poppetry, banishing, regression
Spell Disposal	scatter (in wind)	burn (in fire)	dissolve (in water)	bury (in ground)

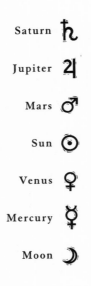

Saturn ♄

Jupiter ♃

Mars ♂

Sun ☉

Venus ♀

Mercury ☿

Moon ☽

THE CHALDEAN ORDER

Try this simple mnemonic to memorize the Chaldean Order:

Sad **Ju**dge **Ma**rtin **Su**ed **Ve**ry **Me**rry **Mo**nica

As you can see, the first two letters of each word are the same as the first two letters of the planets. The order also works in reverse, from the Moon to Saturn. Either way, the Sun's place is always presumed to be in the middle, or "mean," as the ancients put it—the central axis of the system.

In ancient magical cosmology, the planets were depicted in a geocentric way (as we perceive them from Earth), as if they were moving around us through the signs of the zodiac in seven concentric circles that radiated outward into space—the seven heavens we still remember when we describe a state of highest bliss as being "in seventh heaven."

The Moon's orbit appears closest to Earth, and each successive planet seems to be orbiting higher up and farther out than the last, until Saturn, the farthest visible planet. Our terrestrial realm of matter lies below the Moon, which is why the ancients called Earth the "sublunary" world. On Saturn's far side and just beyond the stars lay the ethereal realm of spirit. Together, they composed the threefold division of the universe that olde magicians such as Agrippa described:

Spirit above—*the divinity-invoking object of ceremonial magic*
The planets mediating between the two—*the concern of celestial magic*
Matter below—*within the purview of natural magic*

DIAGRAM OF THE MAGICAL COSMOS

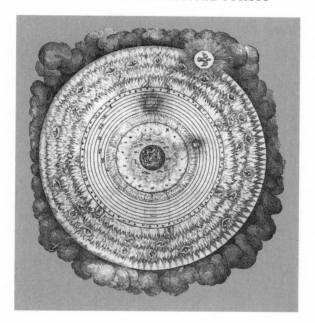

Fludd's full diagram shows the 4 Elements of the realm of Matter in the center, the Divine realm of Spirit around the perimeter (surrounded by the primal void), and the Celestial realm of the 7 Planets mediating between the two.

The olde occultists believed that, as a kind of rainbow bridge between the spiritual and the material worlds, the Seven Planets were among the most important and powerful archetypes that govern correspondences. Through correspondences, they believed, this concentric spectrum of vibrating orbs connected spirit with matter in both directions. It was not only the means through which divinity guided the workings of the sublunary world, but also a means by which mortals could comprehend, predict, and, through magic, even enact the will of the immortals.

Some magicians described their mechanism as the "seven gates of paradise" through which the human soul must descend in order to be incarnated, clothing its spirit in each planet's properties like raiments along the way. When a soul left a body in death and returned to the spirit world, it discarded the "garments of light" as it flew outward past the planets. Others metaphorically described how planetary archetypes mediated between spirit and matter by comparing their cyclical orbits to shuttles on a loom, each weaving its individual thread into the flowing tapestry of time and physical existence, worked by the hands of a divine weaver.

The olde astrological system didn't account for the planets that have been discovered since the invention of the telescope—Uranus, Neptune, and Pluto—but present-day astrologers know that they also have a role to play in the scheme of things. With one or two exceptions, we don't include the outer planets in *The Goodly Spellbook*. In our experience, they are not only unnecessary for most practical spellcraft, but are also magically very difficult to control—even dangerous, like toying with uranium. Learn the Seven thoroughly first; then study the meanings of the outer three in astrology books, and experiment with them very cautiously.

The astrological planets are not just lumps of rock, ice, and gas, as astronomers consider them, any more than humans are simply bags of bone and water. The planets, too, are animated with spirit.

The astrological planets are divine Beings—manifestations of God/desses. They possess attributes, aspects, temperaments, and magical powers. This is why we refer to each of the Seven Planets as *she* or *he* instead of *it*.

The mythological stories attached to their names provide clues to their characters and functions. For example, Mars and Venus are planets of aggression and attraction, respectively, just as they are the Roman God/desses of war and love.

Most of the symbols of the planets reflect attributes of the God/dess associated with each one, as Agrippa noted.[16] Saturn's sign resembles the sickle the planet wields as Father Time or the Grim Reaper. The planetary symbol for Jupiter resembles an imperial scepter. Mars's sign contains a warrior's arrow. Venus's mimics a woman's hand-held looking glass. Mercury's glyph resembles a herald's wand. The symbols of the Sun and the Moon are based on the physi-

---

[16] Agrippa, *"Of characters which are drawn from things themselves by a certain likeness," in* Three Books of Occult Philosophy.

cal appearances of those orbs: The circle with a center dot representing the Sun reflects his round brightness, and the Moon's crescent sign mirrors the horns she grows during her phases.

Don't consider planets as personified entities derived from Greek myths (meddlers in human affairs like Olympian kings and queens) or akin to an Old Testament patriarch, for that matter. Further, don't reduce their interaction with the realm of humans to quasi-scientific cause-and-effect theory, or assume that they could effect their work only by emitting undiscovered "rays" that somehow physically influence us to behave in certain ways.

The planets exist at a higher level of being than humans do, just as we exist at a higher level than the cellular organisms that help compose our bodies, such as mitochondria. We are all parts of a greater Being that is our solar system, in which individual human beings are comparable to individual cells, and the planets are comparable to bodily organs. This isn't simply a mystical metaphor. Even looked at strictly from the point of view of physics, our solar system is a whirling vortex of ripples in the fabric of space-time—a swirling pool of eddying, intersecting gravitational and electromagnetic currents. We, too, are made from space-time, as are all material things. Our essential nature as spirits accords us free will, but the actions we magically will as individuals are constrained by the collective movements of the whole of which we are each a part.

Cooperate with the universe. Harmonize your actions and movements with it throughout life, and your individual efforts will be nourished and supported in both direct and indirect ways—ways you can see, and ways you have yet to imagine. Don't ignore the rhythms and patterns of the whole and act solely by force of your own individual will, or you are liable to end up in the kind of chaotic, self-destructive mess that humankind finds itself in following 300 years of willful contempt for nature.

The Seven Planets fall into natural patterns of harmony and disharmony that you can use in spellwork involving sympathy and antipathy. There is a positive-negative polarity of two pairs of planets with an affinity for each other:

- the benefics—the auspicious, benevolent planets Jupiter and Venus
- neutral—mutable Mercury
- the malefics—the ill-starred, harsh planets Saturn and Mars

Planets that have an antipathy for each other are Venus and Mars, just as love opposes war, and Jupiter and Saturn, just as expansion resists constriction. The Two Lights, the Moon and the Sun, are complementary opposites, as different as night and day.

PLANETARY CORRESPONDENCES

Each planet is associated with certain metals, stones, colors, animals, incenses, and countless other categories of things. The Table of the Seven Planets (page 96) lists examples of some of the most important traditional correspondences Witches use when selecting ingredients for different spells.

Of all the correspondences listed in the table, the planetary metals are among the most useful for making amulets and talismans. From the cradle of metallurgy in the ancient Anatolian city of Harran (peopled by the Sabians, who practiced an astrological religion for thousands of years until the thirteenth century), through the heyday of Renaissance alchemy, to the modern Craft revival, planetary metals have been among the oldest and most-commonly used sets of correspondences. They are keys to unlocking the magic of *smithcraft,* the alchemy of crucible and forge.

THE PLANETARY METALS

SATURN = lead

JUPITER = tin

MARS = iron

SUN = gold

VENUS = copper

MERCURY = mercury or pewter

MOON = silver

The virtues of these metals help illustrate the properties of the planets. Lead is the densest and heaviest metal, and so is associated with the slowest, outermost planet, Saturn. It is poisonous; Saturn is the ruler of death. Tin is plentiful and cheap, just as Jupiter rules generosity and abundance. Tin was formerly used to make religious medals; Jupiter is the ruler of religion. Iron is red in its natural, oxidized state, which gives blood its crimson color, and used to make weapons and tools—appropriate for the red planet of war, Mars. Steel, a metal based on iron, is also ruled by Mars.

Gold is not only traditionally the most valuable, but also the most ductile of all metals, maintaining its integrity even when beaten to a thinness of just a few molecules. It shines brightly like its ruler, the incorruptible Sun. Copper in its natural, oxidized state is green, the color traditionally associated with its ruler, Venus. And what metal could be more appropriate for la Luna than silver, the color of moonbeams?

Mercury, or quicksilver, is so adaptable that it remains liquid at room temperature. It is used in thermometers to indicate temperature and as a catalyst to extract gold, the solar metal, from ore. Adaptability, measurement, catalysis (acting as an alchemical go-between) are all associated with Mercury, the messenger of the God/esses and ruler of communication. But quicksilver is highly toxic, and a liquid metal can't be used for talismans, so mutable Mercury is traditionally associated with mixed metals, or alloys. Anciently, electrum, an alloy of silver and gold, was used to make Mercury talismans, but today the most common Mercurial alloy used is pewter, a gray-colored mixture of copper and tin.

Mercury's adaptability allows it to stand in for any other planet. It's therefore acceptable to use its metal, pewter, as a substitute for any other planetary metal, such as gold or lead, in making talismans. Don't let anyone talk you into substituting brass for gold or aluminum for silver, though. These lesser metals tarnish and cloud over, and do not share any of the properties of gold or silver except superficial appearance.

What makes planet-metal correspondences especially intriguing is that they also operate on a chemical level—which helps prove the fact that science is actually a subset of magic. The ways in which chemists rank these metals correspond to their ranking in the Chaldean Order:

CHEMICAL VALENCE (the propensity of atoms to combine with other atoms)—silver is lowest, lead is highest

THERMAL AND ELECTRICAL CONDUCTIVITY—lead is least conductive, silver is most conductive

LUSTER—lead is lowest, silver is highest, with the anomaly that tin is more lustrous than iron[17]

The atomic-number sequence of these metals follows what you'd obtain if you used the Chaldean Order beginning with Saturn, and moved upward in sequence, skipping every other planet: lead (Pb, 82), mercury (Hg, 80), gold (Au, 79), tin (Su, 50), silver (Ag, 49), copper (Cu, 29), iron (Fe, 26).[18]

The planet-metal correspondences are helpful for making magical jewelry, Craft tools, and other ritual items. Use them singly or in combination. For example, we have seen a Wiccan blacksmith make athamé blades from an alloy of all seven planetary metals. Tibetan singing bowls are traditionally made from this alloy, too.

TABLE OF THE SEVEN PLANETS

Use the following key to the categories in the planetary table:

- **PHYSICAL TRAITS:** Like a doctrine of signatures, the distinctive physical characteristics of each planet express its core meaning.
- **ORBITAL PERIOD:** The span of time the planet takes to circle the Earth or the Sun or to pass through all the signs of the zodiac represents a number closely associated with that planet.
- **KEYWORDS:** words that evoke the planet's properties
- **SIGN(S) AND WEEKDAY RULED:** Each planet rules one or two of the 12 zodiacal signs, and one of the seven weekdays.
- **DEITIES:** a few examples of God/desses and mythological Beings associated with each planet
- **SPELL:** one common example within that planet's magical purview
- **CORRESPONDENCES:** metal(s), stone(s), color(s), body parts, plant (one example), animal (one each, according to Agrippa), and incense(s) (from

[17] Nick Kollerstrom, "The Star Temples of Harran," in History and Astrology, ed. Annabella Kitson (Unwin 1989), 47–60.
[18] Keith Critchlow, Time Stands Still (St. Martin's Press, 1982), 63–64. Critchlow goes into greater detail than Kollerstrom about the valency and conductivity sequences.

the *Sworn Book of Honorius,* a thirteenth-century grimoire that attributes these to Hermes and Solomon)[19]

NOTE: The correspondences given for plant, animal, and incense(s) are only selective examples from among hundreds, if not thousands, that could be included. As you deepen your understanding of the planets' properties, you will be able to compile your own lists of correspondences, under these as well as other categories not mentioned here, that are adapted to your particular needs, special skills, local environment, and so on.

The personifications of the planets are from Giordano Bruno's *Ars Memoriae.* They show each planet's symbol (upper right), signs (lower left and right), and attributes.

• MOON •

PHYSICAL TRAITS: The Earth's satellite reflects the light of the Sun and responds to the ever-changing gravitational tugs of the other planets. The Moon influences the tides of the Earth's oceans and the biological rhythms of Earth's creatures.

ORBITAL PERIOD: The Moon circles the Earth in 27 or 28 days, a cycle called the sidereal period. It was traditionally divided into three groups of nine days or four groups of seven days—the weeks. The tropical period, the cycle from full Moon to full Moon, is about 30 days a month (Moon-th). The Moon circles the Earth 13 times per year; there are 12 or 13 full Moons per year.

KEYWORDS: magic, mystery, intuition, emotion, subconscious, instinct, moods, flow, rhythm, femininity

SIGN AND WEEKDAY RULED: Cancer; Monday

DEITIES: Luna, Selene, Diana

SPELL: fertility

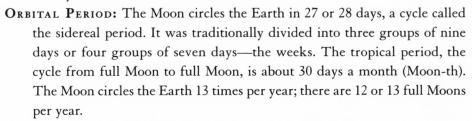

[19] Agrippa, *"The Composition of some Fumes appropriated to the Planets," in* Three Books of Occult Philosophy. *A similar list of planetary incenses.*

CORRESPONDENCES:
>   **METAL:** silver
>   **STONES:** pearl, moonstone
>   **COLORS:** silver, white
>   **BODY PARTS:** stomach, womb
>   **PLANT:** lettuce
>   **ANIMAL:** cat
>   **INCENSES:** leaves, such as myrtle or laurel

• MERCURY •

PHYSICAL TRAITS: Mercury is the planet closest to the Sun and, after the Moon, the swiftest and smallest planet.

ORBITAL PERIOD: Mercury orbits the Sun every 88 days. Its conjunctions with the Sun trace an equilateral triangle on the zodiac. Avoid doing Mercurial spells on the day when Mercury goes retrograde.

KEYWORDS: communication, messages, information, intellect, logic, hermaphroditic

SIGNS AND WEEKDAY RULED: Gemini, Virgo; Wednesday

DEITIES: Hermes Trismegistus (thrice greatest), Anubis, Elegba. Buddha is Mercury's Hindu name.

SPELL: divination

CORRESPONDENCES:
>   **METALS:** quicksilver, alloyed metals
>   **STONE:** agate
>   **COLORS:** mixed, clear
>   **BODY PARTS:** nerves
>   **PLANT:** anise
>   **ANIMAL:** ape
>   **INCENSES:** rinds and sweet seeds, such as cinnamon or cassia

• VENUS •

PHYSICAL TRAITS: Venus is hot and sultry because of a thick blanket of clouds that stores solar heat.

ORBITAL PERIOD: Venus completes five orbits every eight years. Her conjunctions with the Sun trace a perfect pentagram.

KEYWORDS: aesthetics, grace, harmony, romance, attraction, sensuality, ambiance

SIGNS AND WEEKDAY RULED: Taurus, Libra; Friday

DEITIES: Aphrodite, Astarte, Freya

SPELL: love

CORRESPONDENCES:

    METAL: copper

    STONES: emerald, rose quartz, tourmaline

    COLORS: green, pink, pastels

    BODY PARTS: skin (with Saturn), vulva

    PLANT: apple

    ANIMAL: goat

    INCENSES: flowers, such as roses or saffron

• SUN •

PHYSICAL TRAITS: The yellow star at the heart of our solar system, the Sun is our source of light and heat.

ORBITAL PERIOD: The Sun's course through the zodiac takes one year, or 365 days. This is very close to the 360 degrees of a circle.

KEYWORDS: center, ruler, life force, vitality, self, power, ego, masculinity

SIGN AND WEEKDAY RULED: Leo; Sunday

DEITIES: Sol, Apollo, Shango

SPELL: health

CORRESPONDENCES:

    METAL: gold

    STONES: topaz, citrine, amber

COLORS: gold, yellow, orange
BODY PARTS: eyes, heart
PLANT: calendula (pot marigold)
ANIMAL: lion
INCENSES: resinous gums, such as mastic, storax, copal, or amber

• MARS •

PHYSICAL TRAITS: The red planet was once moist, but is now a desert.
ORBITAL PERIOD: Mars's orbit takes 23 months—a whip crack less than
    two years.
KEYWORDS: impulse, boldness, aggression, conflict, brute force, sharp,
    violent, blood
SIGNS AND WEEKDAY RULED: Aries, Scorpio; Tuesday
DEITIES: Ares, Tyr, Ogun—Deities of fire and war
SPELL: assertiveness
CORRESPONDENCES:
    METAL: iron
    STONES: ruby, garnet
    COLOR: red
    BODY PARTS: muscles, penis
    PLANTS: nettle, pine needles
    ANIMAL: wolf
    INCENSES: woods, such as cypress or balsam; sulfur; dragon's blood

• JUPITER •

PHYSICAL TRAITS: Jupiter is the largest planet, almost large enough to
    ignite into a star. He has a powerful electromagnetic field.
ORBITAL PERIOD: Jupiter completes one orbit every 12 years.
KEYWORDS: plenty, generosity, quantity, growth, expansiveness, philoso-
    phy, religion, ideals

SIGNS AND WEEKDAY RULED: Sagittarius, Pisces; Thursday

DEITIES: Zeus, Thor, Santa Claus. Guru is Jupiter's Hindu name.

SPELL: prosperity

CORRESPONDENCES:

    METAL: tin

    STONE: amethyst

    COLORS: royal purple, dark blue

    BODY PARTS: fat, liver

    PLANT: oak

    ANIMAL: hart

    INCENSES: fruits and spices, such as nutmeg, cloves, orange peels

• SATURN •

PHYSICAL TRAITS: The ringed planet is the farthest planet visible to the naked eye.

ORBITAL PERIOD: Saturn takes 29.5 years to orbit the Sun. Two Saturn returns in a person's life equals 59 years.

KEYWORDS: boundaries, constraint, hardness, restriction, discipline, structure, limits, walls, contraction, age

SIGNS AND WEEKDAY RULED: Capricorn, Aquarius; Saturday

DEITIES: Cronus, Baron Samedi, Father Time

SPELL: binding

CORRESPONDENCES:

    METAL: lead

    STONES: onyx, jet

    COLOR: black

    BODY PARTS: bones, skin (with Venus)

    PLANT: horsetail

    ANIMAL: mole

    INCENSES: roots, such as costus and mandrake. (Be cautious—mandrake is toxic.)

Timing Spells for Maximum Efficacy

"Everyone praises a different day but few know their nature."
— HESIOD
Works and Days

*I*t's no secret that the astronomical cycles of the planets time the movements of human and worldly affairs with such accuracy that they can be used to predict events. Clearly, the planets are deeply involved with the workings of time. What few people realize, however, is that astrology can be used for more than divination—spellcrafters who know how to work with planetary correspondances can use them actively, to direct the future magically.

A key aspect of magic is timing—catching and using the pivotal moment, the sweet spot wherein all the forces of the cosmos are aligned in just the right way to influence or manifest our magical need or desire. The planetary correspondences work most effectively in a spell when you cast it at an astrologically appropriate time. Timing a spell by the stars is like boosting its energy with a powerful electrical transformer.

Of course, in spellcraft—as in music or baseball or comedy—goodly timing is as much a matter of intuition as of planning. When you pay close attention to what's happening around you, you can cast your Witchy intent into the moment—whisper the word, make the gesture, think the thought—just when the energy "seems right." But if you follow your forebrain as well as your gut, and select beforehand the days or hours when time's currents are flowing in the same direction as your intent, your spells will speed much more swiftly and effectively toward fulfillment.

Below are the basic kinds of astrological spell timing you can use. (Most of the spell instructions in Part III include their traditional or recommended timing.) As with other correspondences, the more of them you can line up with your spell, the better.

Note that when you're using a precise time, such as the exact moment of sunrise, you won't be able to use a clock or other timepiece to know the exact moment. It's too distracting to have to keep an eye on, it might be a few minutes off, and (as experience proves) it probably won't work right in that warping of space-time that a magic rite creates.

There are two main ways to time your spell precisely. The easier is to begin your working at the right moment, and continue on the assumption that the "power of the hour" carries through until your spell is complete. The more effective way is to begin a bit ahead of time, and let your intuition and the working's flow guide you to sense when the right moment comes to perform your most important spell action.

PHASES OF THE MOON AND THE SUN

Certain times are always conducive for doing goodly spellwork:

- The full Moon helps bring all desires into fruition. The new Moon is good for darker, more introspective magic, especially divination.
- The waxing Moon (from new until full) is good for working increase magic—for creating, generating, acquiring, etc. The waning Moon (from full until new) is good for doing decrease magic—for destroying, banishing, dispersing, and so on.
- The daily and yearly times of change are goodly for scheduling the exact time to perform a spell or prayer, and for ensuring seasonal progression and crop growth. On the daily level, these times of change are twilight (both dawn and dusk), noontide, and the Witching Hour (midnight). On the annual level, they are the seasonal turning points in time of the equinoxes and solstices and the Cross-Quarter Days, or Greater Sabbats, which occur midway through each season.

The Wheel of the Year

"Not the sun or the summer alone, but every hour and season yields its tribute of delight; for every hour and change corresponds to and authorizes a different state of mind, from breathless noon to grimmest midnight."

—RALPH WALDO EMERSON

Nature

From the center outward are the 4 Directions, the 4 turning points of the day, the 8 Sabbats of the year, and the 12 signs of the zodiac. On the periphery are the 4 Elements, which govern the seasons, times of day, and directions.

WHEELS WITHIN WHEELS OF TIME

*T*his diagram shows the correspondences of time—the wheels within wheels that govern the cycles of our lives. Its center depicts the here and now—wherever and in whatever moment you happen to be. You're always surrounded by the Four Directions, which correspond to the four turning points in the Sun's course that quarter the day and the night. These solar pivots are mirrored in the turning points of the Moon. Midnight equates with the new Moon, sunrise with the waxing half Moon, noon with the full Moon, and sunset with the waning half Moon.

As above, so below—the zodiacal signs reflect the attributes of the season they're associated with. The sprouts of early spring burst out of the ground when the Sun is in headstrong Aries. Spring culminates in full flower when the Sun is in sensual Taurus, and spring's flowers transition toward the fruits of summer when the Sun is in mutable Gemini.

As the day, so the year—Earth's morning is spring, her afternoon is summer, her evening is fall, and her late night is winter. Witches mark the turning of this seasonal wheel by celebrating the Lesser and Greater Sabbats.

The outermost symbols of the diagram are those of the Four Elements, bringing you back to the center through their correspondence with the Four Directions.

Sunrise, noon, sunset, and midnight are the turning points of the day. You can find the exact times of sunrise and sunset online or in a local newspaper. The exact time of true noon or midnight almost never coincides with the clock time of 12:00. This is partly due to daylight savings time, which adds an hour when it's in effect, and the Earth's orbital wobble, which usually adds or subtracts a few minutes. You can easily figure it out, though, by counting the hours and minutes between sunrise and sunset, then adding half of the total to the time of sunrise to obtain true noon, or to the time of sunset to obtain true midnight.

The turning points of the year are the equinoxes and solstices. Their exact times and dates vary from year to year; you can find these listed in a farmer's almanac or an astrological calendar.

Halfway between them are the Cross Quarter Days, or what Witches term the Greater Sabbats. These power times are the midpoints, or culminating peaks, of the seasons in which they occur.

Beltane (May Day) occurs halfway between the spring equinox (Ostara) and the summer solstice (Litha), and marks spring's full blossoming. Lammas occurs during the dog days of summer, midway between the summer solstice and the fall equinox (Mabon). Samhain (Halloween) is between the fall equinox and the winter solstice (Yule), and Imbolc (Candlemas, Groundhog Day) is betwixt the winter solstice and the spring equinox.

Contrary to what many people assume, the signs of the zodiac are based not on the stars and constellations, but on the hinges of the year—the equinoxes and solstices. These turning points in the Earth's orbital relationship with the Sun, the Moon, and the planets are the natural pivots of that whirling gyroscope of space-time we and our planet inhabit—the solar system.

TIMING BY THE PLANETS

To refine and target your spell, select the time when the appropriately corresponding planet is most powerful.

Planetary Days and Hours

Each of the seven days of the week is governed by one of the Seven Planets.

SUNDAY = Sun

MONDAY = Moon

TUESDAY = Mars

WEDNESDAY = Mercury

THURSDAY = Jupiter

FRIDAY = Venus

SATURDAY = Saturn

Work your spell on the day when the appropriate planet will best lend his or her energy. Here are some examples of spell purposes appropriate to each weekday:

SUN'S DAY: vitality, self-confidence

MOON'S DAY: fertility, lucid dreaming

MARS'S DAY: protest, self-defense

MERCURY'S DAY: communication, divination

JUPITER'S DAY: wealth, travel

VENUS'S DAY: love, beauty

SATURN'S DAY: protection, binding

PLANETS RULING THE WEEKDAYS

SU = Sunday

MO = Monday

TU = Tuesday

WE = Wednesday

TH = Thursday

FR = Friday

SA = Saturday

Few people realize that this planetary scheme is actually the origin of the names of the seven days. Magicians in Hellenistic Alexandria are thought to have invented the week around the first century, combining the Jewish Sabbath cycle with the Chaldean Order. The system spread swiftly and grew in popularity throughout the Roman Empire. When it reached the provinces bordering the Germanic tribes, the names of four of the Roman planetary Deities were translated into the equivalent Norse Deities, giving us the days of Tiw (God of war—corresponds to Mars), Woden (God of writing—corresponds to Mercury), Thor (God of lightning—corresponds to Jupiter), and Freya (Goddess of love—corresponds to Venus). Saturday was named for the Roman God of time, Saturn, and Sunday and Monday were named for the Sun and the Moon.

You can also use the weekdays very effectively in determining the best and worst times to schedule mundane affairs. For instance, avoid scheduling a job interview for Tuesday—the day of Mars, a malefic. Instead, aim for Wednesday, Thursday, or Friday because Mercury, Jupiter, and Venus are all helpful, benefic planets for business. You can even attune yourself to each day's planetary energies by wearing the planet's color.

TABLE OF THE PLANETARY HOURS

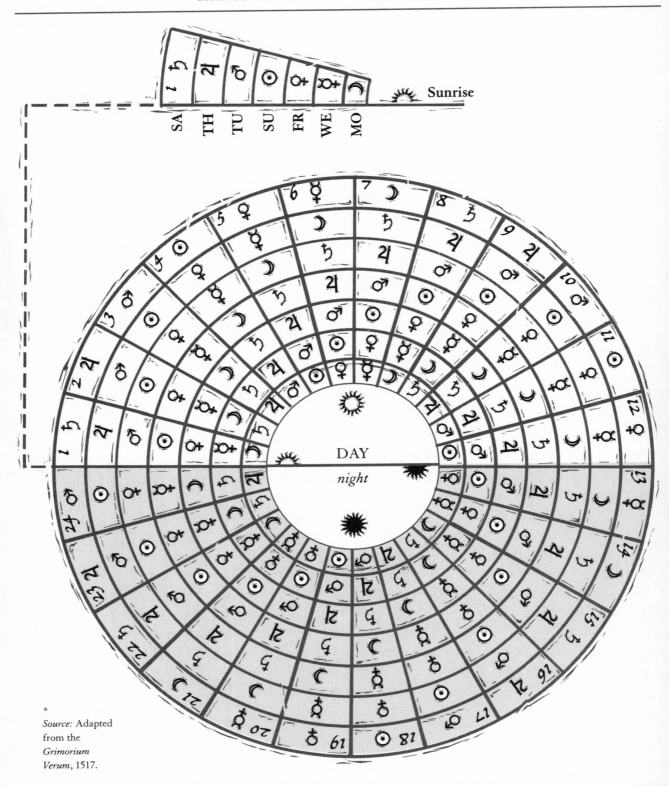

Source: Adapted
from the
*Grimorium
Verum*, 1517.

To further ensure your spell's success, use the table shown here to calculate the daily hours when the planet is most powerful.

The first hour of any planetary day starts with sunrise, not midnight. That first-hour ruler is the basis for the planetary rulerships of the weekdays. As you can see, after the first hour, the planets follow the Chaldean Order sequence, repeating the cycle until the day's hours are complete. For example, Mars rules the 24th and final hour of Saturn's day (Saturday). Because the Sun follows Mars in the Chaldean Order, the Sun rules the first hour of the following day; hence, the day after Saturn's day is the Sun's day (Sunday). This is the real origin of the seemingly arbitrary order of the planetary weekdays.

There are two common ways to match this scheme up with actual time. The simpler, artificial way is based on the clock. Consider 6:00 a.m. the default hour of sunrise, and assume 6:00 to 6:59 as the first hour of the planetary day, 7:00 to 7:59 a.m. as the second hour, and so on. Then you can count the hours and compare them with the Chaldean Order until you find the time that matches the planet you want. (Elias Ashmole, the seventeenth-century bibliophile, astrologer, and magician, used this system.)

Here's a shortcut: Because the planets are seven hours apart, the one that rules the weekday always rules the following hours. On a Monday, the Moon would rule these hours, on a Tuesday, Mars would rule them, and so forth.

6:00 a.m.

1:00 p.m.

8:00 p.m.

3:00 a.m.

The more laborious, natural way—which most magic books recommend—is based on the sundial. If you don't happen to have one handy, divide the time between exact sunrise and exact sunset by 12. This gives you the length of a planetary daytime hour, which is usually either longer or shorter than a clock hour, depending on the season of the year. Add these lengths one by one until you arrive at the clock time for the planetary hour you want. For a nighttime hour, divide the total time between sunset and sunrise by 12, then continue as above.

Are sundial hours more powerful than clock hours, or are the two systems equally valid? Experiment with both and decide for yourself.

In our experience, the most potent spell time is the moment when the appropriate planet is rising, setting, or at its highest or lowest position—when it is at one of the turning points in its daily cycle around Earth.

The Moon's Aspect or Sign

If you're familiar enough with basic astrology that you can read an astrological calendar, you can align your spell with the appropriate planet by choosing a day when the Moon is in a good aspect (angular relationship) with that planet, or passing through a sign ruled by that planet. The best aspects to use are those astrologers term *soft*:

CONJUNCTION—Moon in same sign as planet
SEXTILE—Moon two signs away from planet
TRINE—Moon four signs away from planet

Beginning spellcrafters should avoid the *hard* aspects:
SQUARE—Moon three signs away from planet
OPPOSITION—Moon six signs away from planet

To work astrologically with a particular element, conduct your spell on a day when the Moon is in a sign belonging to the element you're working with, such as a Fire, an Air, a Water, or an Earth sign.

Another traditional method of Moon magic, once widely practiced but now underutilized, is to use the Moon's own 28-sign zodiac, the Lunar Mansions. In Book II of his *Three Books of Occult Philosophy,* Agrippa describes this fascinating magical system that the ancients used to time the casting of spells and the making of talismans.

Regarding Color

"Generally speaking, colour is power which directly influences the soul. Colour is the key-board, the eyes are the hammers, the soul is the piano with many strings. . . . It is therefore evident that colour harmony must rest only on a corresponding vibration in the human soul."

— KANDINSKY

*A*s without, so within: Like music, sculpture, graphic design, or any other art, the Art of Correspondences is partly objective, based on conforming to the laws of Nature; and partly subjective, based on evoking psychological associations. The Four Quarters are examples of the objective, natural side of things, while color is an example of the subjective, cultural, and personal side.

When you compare the magical correspondences of different cultures and time lines, you find that although all consider the Four Quarters central to their cosmology, not one of them uses the same four color correspondences for the Quarters.

Druids used:

EAST = red
SOUTH = white
WEST = gray
NORTH = black

Cherokee use:

EAST = red
SOUTH = white
WEST = black
NORTH = blue

Tibetan Buddhists use:

EAST = black
SOUTH = red
WEST = yellow
NORTH = white

Those are just a few examples from around the world.

Most Witches use:

EAST = yellow
SOUTH = red
WEST = blue
NORTH = green

These differences aren't arbitrary. Every color scheme has cultural reasons behind it that make sense to the spellcrafters who use it. The colors are evocative of certain qualities. To Witches, yellow evokes the rising Sun, and the rest evoke the element associated with each Quarter: Fire—hot red, Water—deep blue, and Earth—fertile green.

Coven Oldenwilde uses a range of colors for each of the Four Quarters. Clear and white things go to Air in the East, connecting the transparency of Air with mental clarity and the whiteness of clouds. The warm colors gold, orange, and red increase energy, spark passion, and ignite the Fire of the South. Blue, silver, and pearl in the West mirror the Watery depths of lakes and seas, the cooling mist of evening, and the glint of teardrops. West is a good direction to cry in whene'er you feel "blue." North is established not only by its traditional Earth greens, mud browns, and beige flotsam colors of wheat fields, but also by the black of a mountain winter night during the new Moon at the Witching Hour.

The color correspondences of the Seven Planets are less variable than those of the elements.

SUN = gold, yellow
MOON = silver, white
MARS = red (like oxidized iron)
SATURN = black
VENUS = green (like verdigris copper)
JUPITER = royal purple, dark blue
MERCURY = gray, mixed colors, transparent

Most are well fixed by tradition, though by no means arbitrarily so. The Sun's color correspondence is gold or yellow, the Moon's is silver or white, and Mars's is red, based directly on their physical appearances. Other correspondences evoke the planets' attributes: Saturn, black as a boundary line; Venus, green as a lush garden; commanding Jupiter, royal purple or rich blue; and communicative Mercury . . . well, some say this adaptable planet takes on the color of its surroundings, as a chameleon does. Some people assign it mixed colors; others accord it transparency. Still others assign it brown, orange, or light blue. There is little agreement or consistency on Mercury's correspondence color, so the choice is up to you. Perhaps the simplest color to use is that nondescript, yet infinitely variable one, the color a pencil communicates in—gray.

In the Oldenwilde way, the planetary colors harmonize well with the appropriate elements. The Moon rules silvery waters; Mercury can be clear as the morning air. Venus and Saturn rule earthy colors, fertile green and midnight black; the Sun and Mars are fiery-colored orbs. Jupiter traditionally corresponds to Air (the blue of the sky), but it could also correspond to the blue of the West because Jupiter rules the water sign Pisces.

As you grow more advanced in the Art of Correspondences, you'll become fascinated with creating your own tables of interconnections, This is a very healthy urge. Now that you've read this chapter, you should begin thinking about how the craft, science, or skill you're most familiar with fits with the correspondences demonstrated here.

Do you like to cook? Most scientists say there are four basic flavors: salty, sweet, sour, and bitter. How would you classify them according to the Four Elements?

Do you like to work on cars? Which element would you associate with the carburetor? the electrical system? the hydraulics? the frame?

Are you an artist, a seamstress, or a carpenter? Square, blocky shapes belong to Earth, silk-textured cloth to Water, and redwood to Fire. No doubt you can think of other examples.

All arts and sciences are interconnected through correspondences, but schools organize them into different departments, which then separate themselves further by developing specialized technical languages. This prevents us from seeing their similarities. If you're a student in school, studying many different subjects, you are especially fortunate to be learning the Art of Correspondences now—it will help you find the connections between such seemingly diverse disciplines as math and music, history and poetry, and geology and dance.

Remember, though, the measure of the Art of Correspondences is not only its beauty, but also its usefulness. Don't simply map these connections on paper—use them in your daily life to help create a more magical, holistic, and organically functioning life.

Witches Scry over Spilt Milk

The Art of Divination

"When people come to a fork, they must choose exactly where they want to go. It is a place of choice. Usually they have foreknowledge of the way to go. Everyone has such knowledge. But the diviner goes between the paths to a secret place. He knows more than other people. He has secret knowledge."

—Victor W. Turner
"Muchona the Hornet, Interpreter of Religion"[20]

To know what's to come is a divine art—a skill that helps Witches chart their course. Everyone is born with some degree of natural intuition, an ability to sense the right path to take at the times when it really matters. Spellcrafters learn to augment their own still, small inner voice by observing omens and portents—age-old signs that reflect the present status of things, or predict future events.

Witches believe that to be forewarned is to be forearmed—we prefer to brace ourselves for hardship rather than be caught unprepared to handle inevitable difficulties. Many beginning magical practitioners are skittish about knowing the future because they don't want to see anything negative. However, life rarely resembles a comfortable feather bed, so we encourage everyone to divine

[20] *Philip M. Peek, ed.,* African Divination Systems: Ways of Knowing *(Bloomington: Indiana University Press, 1991).*

early and often. The fact is, no one ever avoids ill luck by refusing to see it coming—your best hope is to anticipate it in time to take magical measures to avert it.

You can use practically anything to predict the future. Thousands of different divinatory methods flourish in countries throughout the world; all, however, are based on archetypal correspondences and apply similar formulas to achieve their astounding results. Some techniques involve applying set meanings to shapes or patterns they produce, such as tea-leaf reading or fire scrying. Others require the reader to interpret the meanings of a number of symbolic objects, as with runes or tarot cards. Many Crafters rely on astrology to plot short-term personal influences and long-term societal phases, or use palmistry to get to know friends' pasts and paths. Whatever method you use, respect the integrity of that system's rules. For example, don't arbitrarily rearrange a card-spread simply because you consider its message too negative.

Divinatory techniques derive from ancient practices, but modern equipment may be employed . For example, you can use playing cards to read tarot. Some rune sets are plastic and sold in arbitrary or incomplete form, so study up on the subject before you plunk your money down for a set. You can always make your own sets from natural ingredients, using bone, stone, or clay, for example; just ensure that you *bigrave,* or inscribe, them with the traditional symbols associated with the divinatory method you've chosen.

Avoid memorizing the descriptive pamphlets included in such rune sets or tarot decks; instead, focus on one rune, one card, or one divinatory symbol within your chosen system per day to learn its meaning. Admire its design and note how the rune resembles the meaning it's known for, or how the figures on tarot cards form triangles, ovals, or boxes that fill the entire card. This helps clue you in to its basic nature. Next, notice any color(s) that may convey nuances of meaning. If you're mastering Tarot, for example, see which directions the figures face, where they're standing in relation to other objects, what they hold, how they're dressed, and what they're doing.

Consider the differences between runes, cards, or symbols that appear right side up to you when you lay them down, and those that appear reversed. In general, upside-down glyphs portend setbacks or reversals of fortune. Finally, synthesize all your observations into one basic concept; that is, what the rune or card portends. Only then should you double-check your intuition with the pamphlet to help you fine-tune your understanding.

After almost 30 years of doing readings for all and sundry, Lady Passion has found that most people want to know about prosperity or love matters. But her divinations also often reveal mean people in their midst working at cross purposes against them, an upcoming move, a vacation abroad, career changes, painful or pleasurable events to come, and so forth.

Reassure yourself of any divinatory system's merit by initially posing questions to which you already know the definitive answers. Test the system until you consistently achieve accurate results about things you *do* know—then you can rely on it for things you *don't* know. For instance, whenever you acquire a new tarot deck, shuffle thrice and ask it if you're female or male. If the deck is working with you, your first pull should be a face card or one of the Major Arcana that depicts a woman or a man who resembles you.

When you get negative readings, or feel uncomfortable with the results, first simply accept the answer as given. Although you can re-cast for validation of your initial reading, it usually only reiterates the original message. If you still feel iffy about it, you can always do spellwork to try to avert or negate the future that you've been warned about.

At times you'll be successful in so avoiding ill luck; at other times, you won't be able to prevent reversals, for beyond our own desires is the God/desses' design (fate). Sometimes their will and the universe's needs prevail no matter what you attempt.

DIVINING FOR OTHERS

Divine for your family, friends, co-workers, and strangers. You'll soon intuit people's secret concerns, regardless of what questions they initially pose aloud, and feel properly empowered by your growing uncanny accuracy. Doing readings for folks is a nurturing act that prepares them for life's inevitable challenges.

Don't quibble or dissemble about negative aspects in your readings—tell the *querent,* the person asking the divinatory question, the absolute truth as you see it. Soften the blow with exhortations for the querent to physically or magically do things to minimize future damage. Don't accentuate the positive when you know the person will have to endure some hardship—simply offer a spell to minimize impact, or outright avert the setback.

Keep divinatory readings utterly confidential between you and querents—

remember that you're literally peeking into their private lives, inner doubts, and bad pasts. Such information should be considered sacrosanct and classified. The better you get at divination, and the better you are at keeping information confidential, the more word will spread, and folks will duly flock to your door desirous of your expertise. Don't be surprised when even fundamentalist Christians come knocking after sundown, or politicians sheepishly utilize your services. Treat every needy querent with the same delicate consideration.

Never reveal how you know what it is you see. People who come to you for readings are relying on expertise that took you hard work and long hours to develop—therefore, you have a right to your mystery. For example, if someone asks, "How did you know my son trashed his room yesterday?" don't point to the Knight of Swords and explain; instead, say, "The cards lever lie," or some such.

Folks who don't practice divination rarely understand its intricacies, and telling querents how you know all about their lives only robs them of the mystic thrill that is vital in a goodly reading. If they truly desire to know how you know, they can always study the method at their leisure.

Practice will help you become attuned to the multiple layers of magic within divinatory methods. Tarot, for instance, has layers of color, planetary symbols, archetypal shapes, female and male figures, astrological animals, yin-yang and right-left dichotomies, and more. Each layer is an important level regarding the querent's existence and can help you home in on aspects that are unique to their circumstances.

Elemental Scrying

"Every divinatory rite, however simple it may be, rests on a preexisting sympathy between certain beings, and on a traditionally admitted kinship between a certain sign and a certain future event. Further, a divinatory rite is generally not isolated; it is part of an organized whole. The science of the diviners, therefore, does not form isolated groups of things, but binds these groups to each other. At the basis of a system of divination there is thus, at least implicitly, a system of classification."

—EMILE DURKHEIM AND MARCEL MAUSS
Primitive Classification

ise folk find meaning in minutia—it's not that Witches see things that *aren't* there, but rather that we see everything that *is* there. One way Pagans prognosticate the future is by scrying natural phenomena, such as a flowing stream or crackling fire, and observing their intricate movements and sounds—the stream's ripples, the fire's pops—to deduce events their qualities foretell.

To scry something, stare at it intently in a relaxed, but alert, manner. Note the patterns, pictures, or glyphs it forms. Consider how it seems or feels to you—energetic or lethargic, for instance. It's fine if your eyes blur or cloud a bit. Trance out and see visions of things to be.

A goodly way to begin divining is to match your method to the element with which your query corresponds. If your reading concerns an issue involving communication, use an "airy" technique. If you want to know whether money is coming in, choose an earthy means, and so on.

The following are some select ways you can begin exploring divination from an elemental perspective:

FIRE—Listen to the pop and crackle of a balefire. A popping fire portends strife; green flame implies that someone present is inwardly seething with jealousy. Blue flame connotes the presence of Spirit, the God/desses, or goodly company. Red or orange corresponds with strength, courage, force, or health.

Allow yourself to be hypnotized by the fire's flickering flames. Relax and scry the pictures that appear in the hot coals, for they form recognizable faces of those you know, love, or are destined to encounter.

Witches often ask questions about the future, either aloud or mentally, and then note how the fire answers by crackling or sputtering accordingly. We often do the same with fireworks—ask a question and then wait to see and hear whether the next display is grand, or fizzles. A beautiful explosion means *yes;* a dud means *no.*

Harness the power of Fire by scrying a candle flame and drippings, a balefire, or hot coals, and noting their color and intensity. A fire that lights with difficulty bodes ill. A candle that hisses portends rain or treachery.

AIR—Sense the quality of the air around you—the various ways it feels connote different divinatory meanings. At different times, it can seem stagnant, humid, foggy, chilly, electric, dry, or alive with insect activity.

Listen to the whisper of the wind. At times, Air moans. Sometimes it almost seems to breathe itself, as if at peace. At other times it howls, foretelling storm fronts or bad luck on the rise. Sometimes it rings with the songs of crickets, bees, mosquitoes, or birds.

Note the wind's direction of origin. A wind from the East implies that someone is thinking about you, or that a message, a letter, or an e-mail is on the way. A South wind portends an argument or slander; a West wind, joy, sadness, or resentment; a North wind, prosperity or hardship.

Look at the effect of the wind around you. Is it quick and blustery, or is it steady? How the air seems and feels to you are important determiners.

Scry incense smoke for patterns and pictures. Does it whirl sunwise, which equates with *yes* for questions? Does it move ayenward, which means *no*? Does it form a face or figure that seems animated or alive? If so, you wouldn't be the first Witch to note this with delight.

Use the same scrying technique with clouds. The God/desses use clouds like paint on canvas—to warn us on a grand scale with portentous symbols of future events. Another airy-cloud skill to become goodly at is parting a cloud at will, or merging two to form one.

We routinely check out ritual sites before hosting large gatherings, particularly noting the current wind and weather. We find that the rite will have the same weather we experienced while initially scoping out the site.

WATER—Listen to the pitter-patter of falling rain, to fountains, mighty waterfalls, and coursing rivers. What sweet music they make!

Watch the ripples form glyphs, validating your current status, or foretelling things to come. Pools and puddles are a tad more difficult to scry because they're still, but the amoeba-like shapes of splashed or spilled liquid often point in portentous directions, and are therefore easier to interpret.

Learn the ebb and flow of things through the power of Water. See how it dances, sparkles, diverts itself, whirls in vortexes, runs rapidly, trickles, and patiently waits until it has enough weight to drip.

Cast river pebbles or seashells on the sand, close your eyes, and move the shells around. Then open your eyes and contemplate the arrangement and its meaning for you.

EARTH—Lie on your back on the ground and scry the sun-dappled or shadowy tree leaves above—their movements form pictures that have meaning regarding your life.

Scry constellations, stars, and waving tree limbs.

Observe the movements of your pet or familiar animal, or of wild animals. Heed as omens their moods, vocalizations, and actions.

Conjure the power of Earth by throwing bones, stones, nutshells, gems, sticks, or string on the ground, and studying the glyphs or patterns they form.

Omens and Portents

"Coming Events cast their shadow Before."
— THOMAS CAMPBELL
SCOTTISH POET

*O*mens and portents are physical clues that foretell upcoming events and guide Witches' daily decisions. Often obvious, but occasionally cryptic, omens are a divine language of symbols that the God/esses employ to communicate with, or warn, mortals. Omens accurately predict spellwork results because omens are predicated on ancestral experience and timeless natural laws.

Omens and portents come in all shapes and guises, and manifest themselves in diverse ways. Pagans particularly heed directional or formational warnings:

Directional omens involve animals, such as birds in flight; natural phenomena, such as wind origin, weather patterns, or smoke spin; or people, such as someone approaching from your right, which portends force or anger.

Formational omens are phenomena that appear different from their norm—as when clouds paint portraits, mist forms rainbows, or sea chop resembles pyramids on the horizon.

Study nature, people, and inanimate objects to learn what constitutes their typical and unusual forms and behaviors. There are reasons things are the way they normally are—and, conversely, there is some principle at play whenever they deviate from the norm.

Look up, down, and all around as you traipse hither and yon on your Crafty adventures. Notice when something appears unusual, such as when feathery flotsam or grassy detritus takes the form of letters that have meaning to you.

Investigate the origins of "silly" superstitions—they often have magical reasons behind their seeming naïveté. For example, breaking a mirror presages bad luck because a mirror reflects your image, and therefore is a representation of you. In the same vein, it's a bad omen for a loved one whose picture hangs on your wall, if it suddenly crashes to the ground.

Although individual omens are as numerous as the stars in the sky, they often manifest themselves in discernible patterns like constellations. Memorize many different omens and portents, but also notice when similar omens reiterate a single meaning or message. For example, sometimes an omen comes as a single, one-time-only sign. At other times, omens of a similar nature synchronistically repeat themselves within a small amount of time, obviously reiterating the same theme.

In general, the more an omen or similar omens recur, the more urgent the God/desses' message is to you. For instance, narrowly avoiding a car crash is one thing, but if it happens the same day a hearse passes you, a black dog tails you, and an emphatic crow screeches at you, you'd better take heed of your peril. However much you may prefer to dismiss your near wreck as a fortuitous close call, such a string of death portents represents a strident, ominous pattern you'd be foolish to ignore.

Although *anything* can be portentous, not everything that happens *is*. When you first become aware that the universe teems with cosmic signs, you may be tempted to go overboard and label everything as indicative. Sometimes, however, a black cat is just a black cat. Avoid paranoia by focusing on blatant, undeniable omens that affect you on a deep level—especially those that occur at the moment you start thinking or talking about the matter in question. In time, practice will perfect your ability to differentiate.

Many omens have opposite connotations for Witches because we appreciate things others fear or deem suspect. Far from being sinister, left is lucky for Witches. We appreciate black cats crossing our paths and the number *13,* and we don't view nighttime signs as being more innately ominous than daytime omens.

Omens frequently validate or forewarn against whatever you were doing, saying, or thinking when you got the sign, but their meaning isn't always immediately obvious. Magical correspondences are often the key to unlocking a sign's mysterious meaning. Another way to interpret a puzzling omen is to consider the meaning of the element of which it is composed. Burning your finger on a hot stove is a Fire omen. A sudden blast of wind on a still day is an Air omen. Other factors to consider include when the omen occurred (its planetary hour or day, the current astrological alignments); its size, color, and texture (soft or hard, smooth or sharp, and so on); its proximity to you when it appeared; and how it made you feel. Portents are more difficult to interpret accurately the day or two before and after Mercury, the Messenger of the Gods, turns retrograde in his orbit.

The universe and the God/esses send out a steady stream of omens unbidden, but you can also request one at will. The ancients called the spontaneous type *oblative* omens, and the asked-for variety, *impetrative.* Oblative omens are direct and personal. They usually involve out-of-the-ordinary events, and their meanings are usually hard to miss unless you start talking yourself out of it. (If you were watching yourself in a movie, you'd be shouting at the screen: "Pay attention to that sign! Can't you see what will happen if you go that way?") Impetrative portents are signs that you request to answer a question or prayer, or as a way to deduce the effectiveness of a spell. They are frequently more archetypal than personal in nature, and must generally be interpreted according to their correspondences—the Quarters they come from, their numbers, colors, and so on.

Although omens most often manifest themselves spontaneously, you can verbally request an omen whenever you need help making a choice. Stand at a threshold or in an open doorway during a pivotal time, such as twilight, noon, dusk, or midnight; during the solstices and equinoxes; after love making; while in a swoon, trance, or daydream; or when you're sleepy. Close your eyes, formally whisper your plea, and wait several seconds or minutes. Take as your sign the first thing you see when you open your eyes.

Another olde Greek way to get an impetrative portent is to ask the Gods for an audible sign, or *kle'do'n.* Think of a question, and then prevent yourself from hearing for a while (wear earplugs or some such). When you are ready, listen intently, and then heed the significance of the first thing you hear. For instance, if you ask whether you'll soon marry, and then hear words associated with nuptials, such as *flowers, ring,* or *cake,* you've received an auspicious *kle'-do'n;* hearing *one, single,* or *miss* would be inauspicious.

To receive omens regarding events that will occur throughout an entire year, perform *ambulomancy,* divination while walking. Circumnavigate the area around your home at the time when the Wheel of the Year is aligned with the direction your front door faces. Use the diagram below as a template to denote the time frames during which important happenings will occur.

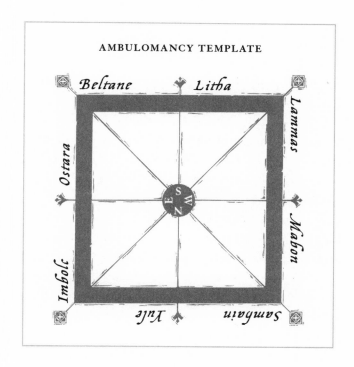

AMBULOMANCY TEMPLATE

The shaded strip represents the route you will walk. Draw a box on the template, representing your home, on the side or corner of the square that corresponds most closely to the direction your front door faces. For instance, if your front door faces approximately east, you'll draw the box by Ostara and perform the divination on or close to Ostara. If your door faces more toward the southeast, you'd draw the box and do the divination at Beltane.

On the night of (or very near to) the designated date, use a copy of your template and a pencil to document or draw indicative designs that you notice. Walk straight out your front door, turn sunwise, and begin observing for omens. The first omens you observe represent events closest to the present time. Subsequent omens represent events that will occur during the time of the year associated with the point on your route at which you observe them. To give one real-life example, if you come upon police cars with lights flashing when you pass the point of Yule, you or a loved one may be on the run from the law come late December.

Sketch cracks in the road that resemble shapes, flotsam that's curled into letters or the initials of folks who will impact your life, and evocative tree limbs—their positions, whether they seem to be beckoning you or barring you with their "arms," and so on. Note anything unusual, such as homes where people are arguing, a dog barking at you, or someone who closes the door as you approach or, conversely, turns on a bright light because the person suspects your motives.

When you return indoors, plot on the template where the omens appeared. Periodically consult it, and check off omens that prove correct in their own time. For instance, hearing a door slam around the point of Litha may prove to have warned that around midsummer, someone would sever a relationship with you. A coin found just before you reached the point of Lammas might have presaged an influx of funds before August.

The efficacy of this exercise can't be overstressed. Coven Oldenwilde routinely does this each Imbolc (benefiting from every watchful eye of our covenmates so we won't miss clues), but one recent circuit was particularly impressive. We encountered a mysterious letter *J* several times during the walk, made of curled twigs and grasses. Our consensus was that it was the first name of someone we would get to know in the coming year. Sure enough, precisely at the time predicted, a woman began studying with us after Lady Passion counseled her when she phoned complaining about being plagued by an incubus named Jay.

Paper Ball Toss

*T*he following divinatory technique is largely inconspicuous and can therefore be performed practically anywhere, at any time. Practice this technique often to sharpen your psychic skills.

Form a question in your mind and either concentrate on it or say it aloud as you wad a piece of paper into a ball with both hands. Any kind of paper or foil will do, even a candy wrapper. When the time feels right, toss the ball directly in front of you.

If your orb oracle bounces off something before landing, it implies that your wish will encounter an obstacle or opposition. If the ball sails to the right, your answer is an emphatic *yes*. A left landing is a resounding *no*. Should the paper plop between the two sides, in the middle, it means *maybe,* and you may elect to redo the reading at another time when the universe may provide a more decisive response.

Another version of this technique is to toss the paper ball toward the nearest wastebasket, but not directly into it—bounce it off a wall or a vertical surface next to it. If the wad bounces directly into the basket, the answer is *yes*. If it misses and lands on the floor, the answer is *no*. If it hits the wastebasket's rim first but still makes it in, expect a positive outcome after a close call!

How to Read the Past, Present, and Future with Three Pebbles

*F*ind three pretty pebbles—one white, clear, or yellowish; one black; and one reddish. Sit and face the North (the Quarter of secrets). Close your eyes, consider your question, shake the pebbles in your cupped hands, and toss them in front of you. Where do the colored stones land in relation to you?

Walk to them, scoop them up, take them back to your sitting place, and replace them before you in their original positions. Study them at length.

The pebble to the left represents the past. The middle pebble represents the present, and the pebble to the right represents the future. The white pebble equates with *yes,* the black represents *no,* and the red connotes that your wish may require additional physical measures in order to manifest itself—in other words, *maybe,* or *yes* but after some delay.

For instance, if your toss yields (from left to right) black, red, and white, your situation is improving, and you'll likely get your wish. In this case, black on the left indicates the problem, or previous hardship. Red in the central, present position shows that your magical will and strength currently match your desire, which is always goodly. (Folks with conflicting motives and actions rarely succeed in achieving their stated aspirations.) The white pebble in the future position portends lightness and happiness as long as you continue to do whatever you've been doing about the matter.

Tree Divination Using Three Nutshell Halves

To determine when and how your or another querent's wish will be fulfilled, employ *cleromancy,* an ancient form of lot divination based on the principle of polarity, such as the concepts of up-down, rough-smooth, and yes-no. Part masculinely linear and part femininely spherical, this God/dess-feedback method requires few tools and little practice to master.

Walk into a greenwood and collect three dried walnut shell halves or shell halves of another species of nut that have a similar heft, shape, and consistency. Choose specimens that match one another in size, texture, and color. Use a stick to scratch the following tree design in the dirt. If you're reading for yourself, make the longest horizontal line closest to you; if you're reading for another querent, have the person sit opposite you in front of the top of the tree.

Squat, kneel, or sit cross-legged before the base of the tree. Hold all three walnut shell halves in both cupped hands. Close your eyes, ponder the question, and cast the halves over the tree template.

QUERENT

READER

The tree's vertical trunk divides answers into terms of left, or magical influences, such as secrets, artistry, dreams, and spiritual reality, and right, or mundane matters, such as jobs, bills, commitments, and physical reality. The horizontal lines demarcate time at three-month intervals. The longest horizontal line shows events that will occur within three months of the divination. The central horizontal line shows events that will happen six months in advance. The third, shortest line shows things nine months hence, and the treetop concerns the culmination or outcome regarding the question a full year after the reading. The farther away from you that the shells land, the more distantly in time the wish will be fulfilled.

Shells that land cup up generally signify success—they're collecting goodly luck. Those that land flat side down typically portend setback—luck is running out. For the querent's wish to succeed, the person must use magical measures or physical labor or change the current plan. The more halves that balance cup up, the more auspicious the reading; the more shells that land flat side down, the more ill-omened the answer.

Cup-up halves that land right of the vertical line signify progress regarding the querent's will, and urge staying the present course; those that land on the right but flat part down signify that the querent should exercise more or different physical actions to ensure attainment of the wish.

Shells that land left of the tree trunk indicate that unseen influences are at work regarding the wish. Again, cup-up castings imply divine favor, but flat side–down halves reflect negative aspects regarding the matter, such as treacherous opposition to the wish. In the case of the latter, the querent would be well advised to take magical countermeasures to ensure the project's success.

For example, a cast that produces one cup-up shell to the left of the six-month line and two flat-side-down halves to the right of the nine-month line indicates that a current plan will succeed only if the querent does a spell in six months. If the querent does the spell, the wish may be fulfilled three months later (nine months after the divination). Because two shells are flat side down on the right (the realm of physical form), the wish probably won't manifest itself if the querent forgets to follow up by doing magic for it six months hence.

Of course, these are only the basic, traditional correspondences. By practicing the method, you'll learn the intricacies of each variation and how they apply in your and other folks' lives. Rely on the default guidelines summarized below so you can relax and intuit more meanings.

A GUIDE TO SPARK FURTHER INTUITION

LEFT OF CENTER—magical influences; the spiritual realm

RIGHT OF CENTER—mundane matters; the physical realm

TREE TRUNK BASE AREA NEAR READER—near-future event(s) that will happen one to three months hence

LONG HORIZONTAL LINE—wish-affecting event(s) that will occur three months from the time of the divination

CENTRAL HORIZONTAL LINE—event(s) that will happen within six months' time

SHORT HORIZONTAL LINE—event(s) that will happen within nine months of the reading

TREETOP—the status of the question as it will stand a year from now; the final outcome

CUP-UP LANDINGS—yes; progress; positive

    LEFT OF CENTER—the magical universe favors the desire

    RIGHT OF CENTER—the tangible universe favors the desire

FLAT SIDE–DOWN LANDINGS—no; setback; negative

    LEFT OF CENTER—magical measures are required for the wish to come to fruition

    RIGHT OF CENTER—physical actions are required to ensure success

Random Mark Making—Geomancy

Chance allows the God/desses to speak. The random element in any divination—the shuffling of the cards, the casting of the shells, whatever means the divination may employ—disengages the process from any influence by the reader's or querent's personal will, and places it in the hands of the divine. Randomness allows a higher order to communicate a message that the diviner interprets by recognizing the particular archetypes it reveals.

Many cultures and Witches around the world have used and continue to use geomancy. Although the first documented evidence regarding its use dates to around 800 (in the Arabic *ilm al-raml,* meaning "sand science"), legend credits Hermes Trismegistus with the invention of the practice. Highly sophisticated versions of geomancy are practiced by West African Yoruba diviners and their descendants in the United States, who call it *ifa,* and by diviners in Madagascar, who call it *sikidy.*

Oracular geomancy relies on a random process to construct one of 16 possible figures, each of which represents a distinct meaning. It's an easy technique to perform almost anywhere, and the 16 figures it depends on are few enough to memorize readily, but numerous enough to reflect a wide range of phenomena.

The 16 geomantic figures are each associated with numerous magical correspondences, including the Seven Planets. Some sigils, or signs, are utterly auspicious or positive (+); some are altogether inauspicious or negative (-); and some have both positive and negative aspects. The figures group themselves into eight complementary pairs, each member of which is the geometric inverse of the other. Some have an affinity for each other; for example, Puella and Puer are, respectively, the archetypal girl and boy. Others display an antipathy against their opposites: Acquisitio equals acquiring, and its partner, Amissio, equals losing. Other pairs show that every goodly thing has a potential downside—Conjunctio represents a happy marriage, whereas Carcer symbolizes the prison of an unhappy one. The duality that pervades geomancy, based on twos, fours, eights, and 16s, reflects the power of polarity, which generates the material realm's ever-fluctuating cycles of change.

The geomantic figures pictorially display their magical meanings. Populus resembles a full room or packed vehicle. Via looks like a road or path—a way or a way out—an arrow pointing in the right direction. Carcer evokes a feeling of confinement—as if others are trying to reach you, but are barred entrance into your cell. Acquisitio looks like an upright goblet of wine (your cup runneth over), whereas Amissio resembles an overturned goblet (your wine, or luck, is spilling out onto the ground, lost). Puella looks like a girl with breasts; Puer, like an erect sword. The dragon's head is practically visible in Caput Draconis.

The following illustrates, from left to right, each geomantic figure; its traditional Latin name; the meaning of its name; whether it's considered positive (+), negative (-), or both (+ and -); its interpretation; and the planet to which it corresponds. Complementary pairs are grouped together.

THE 16 GEOMANTIC FIGURES

POPULUS *The People and Their Assembly* (+ and -): Society is concerned with the issue or may influence its outcome; a judge may rule on the situation; news or rumor (MOON)

VIA *The Way and the Wanderer* (+ and -): Path, road, way, journey, direction, route, language; auspicious for travel or loners (MOON)

CARCER *The Prison* (- or +): Constraint, cell, servitude, binding, delay, despair, lies, resistance to your plan or idea; protective secret keeper (SATURN)

CONJUNCTIO *Union and Marriage* (+): Bonding friendship; couple love; connection; opposites conjoined in common cause; auspicious regarding contracts, weights and measures, and communication (MERCURY)

FORTUNA MAJOR *The Great Fortune* (most +): Luck, success, victory, fertility, loyalty, health, safe and sound, goodly return for efforts, achievement, recognition, fame (SUN)

FORTUNA MINOR *The Lesser Fortune* (+): Goodly fortune to a lesser extent than F. Major; aid from others; protection for lone exploits or travels; voyage; dispersion (SUN)

ACQUISITIO *Acquiring* (very +): Gain; profit; seizing riches or property; rise to power; a successful coven or group; wounds healed (JUPITER)

AMISSIO *Losing* (-): Missing, loss; plan/idea doomed to failure; illness; stranger; deception by a loved one; minimal personal power/maximum external forces at work regarding question; escape; auspicious for prisoners (VENUS)

LAETITIA *Joy* (very +): Bliss, balance, beauty; liberation, release; concord, peace; positive regarding marriage, foundations, or forming things (JUPITER)

TRISTITIA *Sadness* (very –): Suffering, humiliation, devastation, grief; death, shadows, toiling in obscurity; inflexibility (SATURN)

ALBUS *The White One* (definitely +): Epiphany, wisdom, clarity of reasoning; fairness, purity; spiritual revelation; auspicious for business and when commencing a project (MERCURY)

RUBEUS *The Red One* (–): Stop what you're doing! Destruction, violence, corruption; vice, war, blood, chaos, killing, fire; anger, rage, oppression (MARS)

PUELLA *The Girl* (mildly +): Sweet, kindly wife, newlywed, daughter, or nurse; auspicious regarding love affairs and purchasing; can warn of deception or hypocrisy (VENUS)

PUER *The Boy* (–): Impulsive, combative young man, son, servant, employee; unknown enemy or taker; rival; clueless opposition to plan or idea; a dangerous sign unless it concerns a lover or imminent combat (MARS)

CAPUT DRACONIS *The Dragon's Head* (+): Fate; the Heavens, astrological influences regarding query; depth; mystic development; auspicious for taking leaps of faith, crossing thresholds, and so forth (MOON'S NORTH NODE)

CAUDA DRACONIS *The Dragon's Tail* (–): Karma; the Underworld; a way out of embroilment; calamity, fraud, danger, curse; change your direction or strategy or you'll lose something (MOON'S SOUTH NODE)

To perform geomantic divination, mentally focus intently on your question, then make four rows of random marks with a stick in the sand or dirt, or with a pen or pencil on paper. Taking pains not to consciously count during the exercise, make a series of at least half a dozen marks in each row—traditionally, from right to left. Stop marking in each row whenever it feels right to do so; then proceed downward on the dirt or paper to begin a new row. When you've made four rows, total the number of marks in each one. When the marks in a row add up to an odd number, place one dot beside it; when a row's marks add up to an even number, place two dots beside it. Together, the four groups of single or double dots will yield a magical symbol—a geomantic sign.

For instance, if you want to know whether to buy a house with which you're enchanted, make four random rows of marks, such as these:

/	/	/	/	/	/	/	/	/	/	/	11	=	•
	/	/	/	/	/	/	/	/	/	/	10	=	• •
		/	/	/	/	/	/	/	/	/	9	=	•
/	/	/	/	/	/	/	/	/	/	/	11	=	•

The answer in this example is Puella, the Girl. Although Puella can be auspicious regarding purchases, such as a home, the Girl also warns of things with false appearances, or sly deception. Based on such a reading, you'd do well to hire a perfectionistic inspector to ensure that the property isn't termite infested, that it doesn't have a cracked foundation or poor roof, or that the owners aren't actively hiding other costly problems.

When you've mastered this method, go adoors and select at least 17 small, rounded pebbles or similar natural items such as acorn caps (or use gem chips). Place them in a bag. Pull one out and set it in front of you as a spirit stone to guide the rest. Then, instead of making rows of marks to determine each single or double dot, reach into the bag and grab a small handful of stones. Count them to see whether you've grabbed an odd number or an even number. Lay down one stone (if odd) or two (if even). Repeat this for a total of four times to construct your geomantic figure.

After you've gotten a feel for the figures, you can cast them in pairs. Decide ahead of time what each of the two figures you cast will represent. For example, the first figure could represent the present and the second figure, the future. You might interpret the first figure as a verb and the second one as a noun. Acquisitio followed by Albus would mean "acquire wisdom"—or "catch a clue." You can pursue this further with the aid of a book on geomancy, which will teach you the classical technique of deriving a full spread of interrelated figures called mothers, daughters, nephews, witnesses, and judges.

You can also use four successive coin tosses or dice rolls to generate a geomantic figure. Assign one side of the coin or odd-numbered dice rolls to stand for one dot, and the flip side or even-numbered rolls for two dots.

You can even divine a figure by applying an olde Russian geomantic method to this very book. Open *The Goodly Spellbook* at random four separate times. Each time, note the first letter of the text on the left page, and give it the numerical value of its sequence in the alphabet—A equals 1, B equals 2, C equals 3, and so on. An odd value generates a single dot, an even value two dots.

The 16 geomantic figures can be used actively for spellcraft. Draw or bigrave them anywhere, alone or in combinations, as simple dots or elaborated glyphs, to reinforce your spell intent. (See To Lure People to Your Web Site, page 358.)

Digital Divination—Chronomancy

Finally, here is an ultra new, utterly non-traditional technique that nevertheless demonstrates just how "timeless" the principles of divination truly are! Nowadays, if you live in a urban environment, there's a digital clock everywhere you look—on your microwave, your DVD, your computer, your car's dashboard. You can use the numbers on the clock for divination, either to gauge whether the time is right for an action you're about to take, or to judge whether something you're wondering about is true or untrue, wise or unwise, and so on.

Think of a question or say it aloud, then glance at the clock and note the time. Notice the pattern or relationship between the number for the hour and the number for the minute. Do they repeat, as in 1:11, 12:12, 2:02, 5:55, or 11:33?

Are they in sequence, as with 3:45 or 4:56? All such times are very positive—
they signify *yes,* act now, it is true, etc.

Times that are symmetrical are mildly positive, such as 1:41, 12:21, or 9:19.
So are exact hours, such as 12:00, 3:00, or 10:00. Times in which the minute is
a multiple or division of the hour are positive, as in 12:24, 9:36, 12:06, 8:04, 9:03,
or 4:20.

Pattern-less, random-looking times are negative, such as 1:05, 6:01, 12:17,
or 7:41. They mean *no,* not true, and so forth.

You can interpret the patterns you see in the numbers. The exact hour
(12:00, 6:00) means you are heading in the right direction, but the minute before
the hour (11:59, 5:59) is decisively telling you it's too soon or your timing is a little off. Times such as 12:34 signify increase, as of luck; 3:21, decrease, as of
income. The time 5:54 means too soon, whereas 5:56 means too late, because
these are respectively one minute before and one minute after the auspicious
time of 5:55.

A variation on the system is to consider the hour as representing the present, and the minute as representing the future. In this version, odd numbers are
more auspicious than even ones. In this case, 11:33 would mean your situation is
positive now and will remain positive; 11:22 would mean it is positive now but
will turn negative in the future.

If certain numbers are lucky in your life, then it's very fortunate when they
appear. For example, Lady Passion's lucky time is 3:13.

If you use a 24-hour clock, the same principles apply, but you have more
potential patterns to work with.

You can take chronomancy (a term we revised from the Greek words for
"time" and "divination") even further by interpreting the times according to the
numerological qualities of the numbers, which are explained in the next chapter, Divine Number—The Magic of Counting.

The divination you get from chronomancy is surprisingly effective because
it is instantaneous—it shows you an immediate correspondence in the form of
the moment whenever you ask a question. Chronomancy should not be used to
answer weighty questions, of course, which should be considered by employing
a more sophisticated form of divination. However, for divining on the fly, when
you don't have time to pull out a deck of cards or bag of stones, chronomancy
can be well worth your while.

DIVINE NUMBER

THE MAGIC OF COUNTING

"For the harmony of the world is made manifest in Form and Number, and the heart and soul and all the poetry of Natural Philosophy are embodied in the concept of mathematical beauty."
— SIR D'ARCY WENTWORTH THOMPSON
On Growth and Form

Witches have always used numerology in myriad ways, such as in determining the most auspicious time to cast a spell or in interpreting tarot cards and other divinatory systems' answers. Spellcrafters often reduce names, a problem, or key words to their lowest numerical equivalents before fashioning magical seals. We compare numbers when divining whether we're compatible with an intended mate. Numbers are crucial components when making astrological calculations to plot future events. As in everything related to magic, to know a thing intimately is to master it; therefore, knowing the number(s) that manifest an object or a force affords you the ability to create, nullify, or control that object or force at will.

The Qualities of Quantities

"It is a shame that children are exposed to numbers merely as quantities instead of qualities and characters with distinct personalities relating to each other in various patterns. If only they could see numbers and shapes as the ancients did, as symbols of principles available to teach us about the natural structure and processes of the universe and to give us perspective on human nature."

— MICHAEL S. SCHNEIDER

MATHEMATICIAN[21]

Numbers' magical qualities derive from their unique characteristics— individual personalities that they innately possess. The number *1* often seems lonely. The number *2,* on the other hand, can be amenable, suggesting companionship, or contentious, creating rivalry or sparking a quarrel. The number *3* seems happy, lucky, complete, which is why folks append phrases with an anchoring, third word, as in "on your mark, get set, *go!*" or "hip, hip, *hooray!*"

A number, or set of numbers, may even seem to follow you around throughout life—as if it's trying to tell you something or feels a particular affinity for you. Lady Passion is followed by *1*'s, *3*'s, and *13*'s; a friend swears he routinely encounters *128* in such things as bills, prices, phone numbers, and addresses.

Numbers have innate intention like that of our own DNA programming. They bring order to the universe. The shape, depth, composition, proportion, texture, and movement of tangible objects and life-forms are all defined by, and normally limited to, the number(s) that rule them. Even natural phenomena, such as wind configuration, the visual spectrum, and molecular structure, owe their consistency to numerical influences. Numbers serve as templates for both macrocosmic and microcosmic mechanisms. For instance, the Golden Mean or the Fibonacci series embodied in the pentagram is responsible for both a tornado's whirl and the spiral growth pattern of leaves around a plant stalk. The

---

[21] *Michael S. Schneider,* A Beginner's Guide to Constructing the Universe: The Mathematical Archetypes of Nature, Art, and Science *(New York: HarperCollins, 1994).*

structure of atoms as laid out in the periodic table of the elements is based directly on the number *2* applied to the counting numbers *1, 2, 3,* and so on. Genealogy, geomancy, and even computer memory capacity are similarly based on powers of *2.* The intervals of the musical scale are heard numbers: Each is based on a

THE MODERN PERIODIC TABLE of the elements confirms the ancient Pythagorean belief that number is the foundation of the universe. The table's ranks represent successive vibrational levels of electrons surrounding an atomic nucleus. These levels can be conceived of as concentric spheres or shells. Each successive shell is saturated by a certain maximum number of electrons in the sequence 2, 8, 18, and so on. The formula expressing this is $2n^2$, where n represents the shell's number of succession (first shell = 1, second shell = 2, and so forth). This formula is very dualistic—the numbers are both doubled and squared. The first shell is saturated by two electrons, or $2 = 2(1)^2$; the second by eight electrons, or $8 = 2(2)^2$; the third by 18 electrons, or $18 = 2(3)^2$; and so on. *(Thanks to Dr. Dean Kahl, Department of Chemistry, Warren Wilson College, for expert consultation.)*

numerical ratio between vibrational frequencies. For example, tripling the frequency of a note raises it by the interval that musicians call a "perfect fifth."

The ancient Pythagoreans employed mathematics to comprehend the workings of the universe and viewed the first ten numbers as its seed-patterns—the fundamental creative principles of the cosmos. The Pythagoreans laid the foundations for numerology and mathematics in present times.

Here are the basic Craft correspondences for the numbers *1* through *10.* Use their meanings to help you target your magic or devise appropriate spells to relieve daily problems.

1 • THE MONAD

Pictured as a dot, a circle, or a circle with a center dot.
Unity or independence; the interconnection of all things.
Cyclicity; perimeter; center; rotary motion; introspection.
An Egyptian glyph for *light* as the origin of life.
The astrological symbol for the Sun.
Asar—the Egyptian Goddess of cycles.
The occult symbol *ouroboros,* a circular snake that swallows its tail, representing timeless eternity.
The first parent number that contains all numbers within itself, and hence generates all other numbers.
Geometrically, the circle accommodates all shapes within itself.

1
The Monad

2

The Dyad

2 • THE DYAD

Pictured as a line or as two overlapping circles. *Vesica piscis* is the name of the almond shape produced where the two circles overlap.

Polarity or duality. As above, so below.

Kindred spirits, binding link, and balance; conversely, opposition and dichotomy.

In Wicca, the Perfect Couple,[22] who work magic together.

The two poles of the equinoxes and solstices.

The second parent number that begins the Many as opposed to the One.

Magnetic fields; cell division; genealogy.

3

The Triad

3 • THE TRIAD

Pictured as a triangle.

Cooperation, harmony. Spirit.

In the Craft, the Triad equates with plurality. For example, three people are necessary to form a coven. The Triad also equates with triplicity: the waxing, full, and waning Moons; the three phases of being—birth, death, and rebirth; the three phases of womanhood—Maiden, Mother, and Crone; and the three Fates, who spin, weave, and cut the fabric of our lives.

The three traditional types of magical practice: celestial, ceremonial, and natural.

Creation, maintenance, and destruction; beginning, middle, and end; light, energy, and mass (as in $E=mc^2$); length, width, and height; fight, fly, or fortify.

[22] *The Perfect Couple, usually a Priestess who represents the Goddess and a Priest who represents the God, expresses the Wiccan cosmology of balanced polarities.*

4 • THE TETRAD

Pictured as a square, cross, or cube.

Duality squared. Grid, matrix. Matter.

Solidity; conformity; the establishment.

The square is an ancient symbol for Earth that Witches still use. In
   Wicca, *4* corresponds to the Four Elements (Fire, Air, Water,
   Earth), the four states of matter (plasma, gas, liquid, solid), the Four
   Elementals (Salamanders, Sylphs, Undines, Gnomes), the Four
   Quarters (East, South, West, North), and the four outwardly
   spiraling arms of the Milky Way Galaxy.

5 • THE PENTAD

Pictured as a pentagon or pentagram (a five-pointed star).

Will; growth; regeneration.

The generative numerical pattern of life.

Visible whenever you slice an edible fruit on its equator.

In magic, the Pentad symbolizes the Four Elements plus Spirit (the
   Quintessence); the body's five fingers and toes or four limbs and
   head, and the Golden Mean proportion manifested in fetal
   formation, plants' growth structures, musical compositions, and the
   dimensions of the swirl patterns in seashells, whirlpools, tornadoes,
   and spiral galaxies.

6 • THE HEXAD

Pictured as a hexagon or hexagram (an upright triangle conjoined with
   an inverse triangle).

Efficient organization with flexibility; family; group bond.

The shape of snowflakes and honeycombs.

Sacred to Witches because the Hexad is the structure of quartz crystals,
   the true number of colors in a rainbow, the basis of many

4

The Tetrad

5

The Pentad

6

The Hexad

Pennsylvania Dutch hex signs, the same as the occult Seal of
Solomon (or Star of David symbol), and a symbol for the Great Rite,
a ceremony enacting or representing the sexual union of the God
and Goddess.

All true insects have six legs.

7

The Heptad

𝒿 • THE HEPTAD

Pictured as a heptagon or heptagram (sometimes called a "fairy star").
Lucky; blessed; whole.

Sacred to the Egyptian Goddess Seshat, whose name means "seven."

Corresponds to the Seven Planets, the seven notes of the diatonic music
scale, the seven liberal arts, the seven weekdays, the Seven Wonders
of the World, and the seven seas.

8

The Octad

𝟪 • THE OCTAD

Pictured as an octagon or two conjoined squares.

Reinforcement; strength; quadruple opposition.

Witches revere the Octad as representing the traditional Eightfold
Path to Enlightenment, the eight annual Sabbats, the eight feng shui
trigrams, and the Moon's main monthly phases: new, waxing
crescent, first quarter, waxing gibbous, full, waning gibbous, last
quarter, and waning crescent.

There are eight stages of cell division.

Turtle shell segments are octagonal, and spiders have eight legs.

In music, male and female voices are an octave (eight diatonic notes)
apart.

9 • **THE ENNEAD**

Pictured as a nonagon or enneagram.

Spirituality; creativity; hidden influences; joy.

Witches demarcate a 9-foot circle when casting.

There are nine Muses of inspiration.

Human gestation requires nine months.

Nine is the highest single number.

The resulting digits of any number multiplied by *9* always add up to *9*.

10 • **THE DECAD**

Pictured as a decagon or the Pythagorean dot triangle, the Tetractys.

Completion; perfection, as in a "perfect ten"; law; order; systems; rules.

Ten equates with totality (ten fingers and ten toes) and the two perfect
    pentacles (the hands) that work in tandem to do magic.

All other numbers stem from *1* through *10*.

Certain numbers beyond *10* are especially important in magic. The numbers *12* and *24* represent the cosmos—as in the 12 months of a year, 12 signs of the zodiac, and 24 hours of a day. The number *13* is 12 plus *1*—a dozen apostles plus an avatar, a dozen Witches plus a High Priestess, 12 full Moons in a normal year plus a 13th "blue" Moon every few years. A default period of time for potions to steep is *21* days, or thrice *7*. The number *40* is a number of penance and purification (40 lashes, 40 days and 40 nights of rain). The number *60* is the ground of all being, the basis for compass, calendar, and clock, as well as for the proportions that create musical harmony.

Occult authors have published many idiosyncratic schemes for associating numbers with astrological planets, but the most magically effective correspondence is, as usual, the most direct and natural one. Use the numbers that relate directly to their orbital periods, as given in the Table of the Seven Planets. (See page 97.) For instance, *29* is an especially Saturnian number because it is the number of years in a Saturn return, the time Saturn takes to complete one circuit around the zodiac.

Witches typically use odd numbers in magic because they display a certain forward momentum or generative impulse. On the other hand, the oppositional quality of even numbers often impedes spell objectives (although love magic often involves the number 2). When a spell recipe instructs you to reiterate actions in a spell, such as striking, stirring, measuring out, or verbally repeating something, it usually specifies three, seven, or nine times. In the Craft, three is the minimum number of people needed to establish a proper coven; the Olde Religion's sacred symbol is the five-pointed star, or pentagram; and a coven can't exceed 13 members.

Before using numbers in magical applications, first observe how they manifest themselves in your everyday life, such as in dream imagery, the number of times or ways in which omens and portents appear, the repeated patterns of problems, or the numbers that inexplicably recur within a 24-hour period. Ponder why you're attracted by specific number(s), but feel repulsed by others. Notice how different musical rhythms make you feel, based on their number of beats. Consider the meaning of number patterns embedded in Craft myths, such as the Goddess Demeter's eight-day search for her daughter, Persephone, who was found on the magically auspicious ninth day.

One way to use numbers in magic is to convert them into an ancient sigil or write them in a magical script. (See Magical Alphabets, page 193.)

SACRED PROPORTIONS: NUMBERS OF LIFE

Like a community of Beings, numbers express their creative potential through the relationships they form with other numbers. The Pythagoreans recognized the generative power of the first ten numbers in the oath they swore by the Tetractys:

> *"By Him that gave to our generation the Tetractys, which contains the fount and root of eternal Nature."*

The three-sided Tetractys (1+2+3+4 = 10) denotes the four increasing densities of matter (Fire=1, Air=2, Water=3, Earth=4) and also incorporates the hexagon in its center. The Tetractys gives rise to one of the most important patterns of relationships in numerology, the Pythagorean Lambda, which Plato described as the first division of the original soul-stuff God made in order to create the universe.[23] (*Lambda* is the name of the Greek letter it resembles.)

$$
\begin{array}{ccc}
& 1 & \\
2 & & 3 \\
4 & & 9 \\
8 & & 27
\end{array}
$$

At the top of the Lambda is a triangle of the numbers *1, 2,* and *3.* From there, the numbers fork like the two legs of the Divine Geometer's compass, then continue down separate paths.

The Powers of Two proceed along one leg:

$$2^1 = 2$$
$$2^2 = 4$$
$$2^3 = 8$$

The Powers of Three move along the other:

$$3^1 = 3$$
$$3^2 = 9$$
$$3^3 = 27$$

One side is the twices, the other the thrices.

Plato also pointed out that the Lambda's four stacked layers represent the manifestation of the physical world—emanating from the Same (1); then to the Different (2) and its linking with the Same as Being (3); then to the level of squares (4 and 9), representing existence in two dimensions; and then to the level of cubes (8 and 27), representing existence in three dimensions.

The number *2* is the first even number, and *3* is the first odd number. To Wiccans, *2* is the number of the Horned God, who is the Oak King during the

[23] *Plato,* Timaeus and Critias, *trans. Desmond Lee (London: Penguin UK, 1971) 35b. Ancient and medieval philosophers revered the "Timaeus" for its elucidation of the metaphysical origins of the cosmos.*

waxing part of the year, from Yule to Litha, and the Holly King during the waning part (from Litha to Yule). Three is the number of the Triple Goddess, who is Maiden, Mother, and Crone, corresponding with the waxing, full, and waning phases of the Moon. Duality is the Horned God's numerology, and triplicity is the Triple Goddess's.

The Pythagorean Lambda expresses many other correspondences that help reveal the underpinnings of the universe. In music, doubling a note's frequency—its vibration rate measured in cycles per second—raises its pitch by an octave each time; for example, from C to c to c' to c''. Tripling the frequency raises the pitch each time by the interval called a fifth (it spans five notes in the musical scale); for example, from C to G to d. In astrology, two planets separated by one-half or one-fourth of the zodiac (opposition or square) are in a tense relationship (hard aspect). When they are separated by one-third of the zodiac (trine) or a multiple of a third, they are in an easy relationship (soft aspect). In geometry, this is the polarity of a rectilinear versus a triangular figure. These correspondences among the four branches of the quadrivium—that unifying source and meeting point of all arts and sciences—are illustrated here.

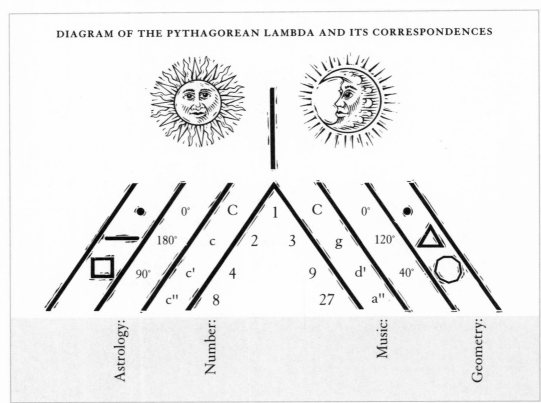

DIAGRAM OF THE PYTHAGOREAN LAMBDA AND ITS CORRESPONDENCES

The two limbs of the Lambda correspond to cycles of time. The double side belongs to the Sun because there are four seasons and eight Sabbats in the solar year. The triple side belongs to the Moon because la Luna completes a full circle around Earth every 27 days (more exactly, 27.3 days)—meaning that if she passes the Pleiades tonight, she will pass them again in 27 days.

			1				
SUN		2	3			**MOON**	
Seasons =		4			9	**= Months of Pregnancy**	
Sabbats =	8				27	**= Days of Moon's Orbit**	

There are many other fruitful correspondences, both magical and mundane, that are generated between the two legs of the Lambda. To find them, just keep putting two and two together . . . then three and three.

The Golden Mean proportion is a series of number relationships famous for its appearance in the graceful forms of classical sculpture and architecture, in the proportions of natural structures such as a nautilus shell or a human body, and in many, many other places throughout art and in nature. It begins the same way as the Lambda, with *1, 2,* and *3,* but then proceeds along a different track. The Golden Mean ratio, which mathematicians call *phi* (the Greek letter Φ), is an irrational number that, like perfection itself, can never be exactly achieved, but only approximated. You can approach it through the Fibonacci series, which you obtain by adding $0+1 = 1, 1+1 = 2, 2+1 = 3$, and then continue by adding each successive sum to its predecessor to obtain the next sum: $3+2 = 5$, $5+3 = 8, 8+5 = 13$, and so on. The pairs of numbers you obtain this way, when arranged as fractions, get closer and closer to Φ (whose value is 1.6180339 . . .) as they get higher and higher.

$$\frac{1}{0} \quad \frac{1}{1} \quad \frac{2}{1} \quad \frac{3}{2} \quad \frac{5}{3} \quad \frac{8}{5} \quad \frac{13}{8} \quad \frac{21}{13} \quad \frac{34}{21} \quad \frac{55}{34} \quad \frac{89}{55}$$

Its numerical series "grows by accruing terms that come from *within* itself, from its immediate past, taking nothing from outside the sequence for its growth. Each term may be traced back to its beginning as unity in the Monad, which itself arose from the incomprehensible mystery of zero."[24]

The pentagram, as the Pythagoreans discovered, is based on the Golden Mean. It illustrates one of the most vital properties of the Golden Mean, its hologrammic nature. Each part reflects its whole; each whole is part of a greater whole. The infinitely self-reproducing pattern called the Lute of Pythagoras is based on this property.

In antiquity, number canons or conventional formulas such as the Golden Mean were used as a sacred basis for artistic creation. Such canons or conventions explain the beauty of Egyptian hieroglyphic art. Cheat lines composed of 19 or 22 squares were initially cut into rock, and the proportions of figures were based on their confines. The guidelines, which remain visible in crypts, helped carvers standardize body proportions throughout the kingdoms and encode sacred geometry in their designs.

Shrines and temples were based on the numerical archetype of the Deity they hoped to honor. For example, Athena's temple was a heptagon because her number is *7*, long associated with virginity because no number below it can divide it, and it can't reproduce, or make another number, before *10*. The Greek letters of her name add up to 77, and the Greek letters in her epithet *Pallas* (Maiden) add up to 343 (7 x 7 x 7). Her appellation *Parthenos* equals 515, with 51.5 degrees per angle, making a near-perfect seven-sided geometric shape.

The ancients knew that by using these generative proportions of life in creating carvings and sculptures of their God/desses, they could animate matter with spirit. These sacred number ratios enabled mere clay or marble to be inhabited by Deities—a secret that monotheists who condemned those whom they called "idol-worshiping Pagans" never understood but that fascinated Renaissance magicians, notably Ficino and Agrippa. Ficino's famous discoveries in Greek texts of the secrets of the Egyptian art of animating statues inspired Renaissance painters and sculptors to explore ancient canons such as the Golden Mean. That was how they learned to create the dynamic, vivid works of art that even today take our breath away with their lifelike proportions and perspectives.

[24]*Schneider,* A Beginner's Guide, *117.*

THE LUTE OF PYTHAGORAS

The interlacing proportions of the pentagram illustrate the infinitely self-generating property of the Golden Mean.

ARITHMOMANCY: NUMBER DIVINATION

Although you can magically use the power of numbers in many ways, the following are two fascinating, easy examples. The first method involves practicing Gypsy-style fortune telling by using any common card deck. (The Romany technique is based on the numbers *4*, as in suits, and *13*—four sets of *1* through *10* plus four sets of three jacks, queens, and kings.)

Shuffle thrice a deck of playing cards, think about or say aloud a question or quandary that you have, and then remove one card at random. Its meaning has bearing on the situation's future outcome. Positive interpretations presage imminent goodly luck. If the reading seems negative, accept the warning, then strive to avert the undesirable outcome by changing the way you'd normally handle the problem.

Here are key meanings of the cards:

CARD	SPADES	CLUBS	HEARTS	DIAMONDS
ACE	change	dream; opinion	love; goal	drive; poverty
2	treachery	concord or conflict	rendezvous	money trouble
3	estrangement	shared beliefs	friendship	group activities
4	funeral	quarrel	loyalty	legacy
5	setback	epiphany	infatuation	good luck; travel
6	reversal	doubt; lawsuit	camaraderie	destitution
7	deception	good news	charity	inheritance
8	resignation	denial	popularity	prosperity
9	suffering	wish granted	bliss; grief	loss of money or property
10	deprivation	comprehension	contentment	success; financial gain
JACK	sinister youth; probable rival	flattering fellow; braggart	charming boy, but often fickle	materialistic lad; entrepreneur
QUEEN	mysterious temptress	eloquent wise woman	nurturing seductress	wealthy, cultured matron
KING	forceful	philosophical professor	generous aristocrat	accomplished tycoon

Another numerical way to predict future events involves determining the kinds of challenges or pleasures a person has in store in the current year. Add the person's birth month plus their birth date plus the current year's digits. Reduce the numbers to their smallest expression. For example, during the year 2006, someone whose birthday is April 14 would be rendered thus: 4 + 14 + 2006.

Keep adding the digits until they yield one number:

$$4 + 14 + 2006 = 2024$$

$$2 + 0 + 2 + 4 = 8$$

In this case, the result is *8*. Using the chart below, which is based on nine-year cycles, you'd know that the person you're divining about will likely have a lucrative year that includes winning money unexpectedly, inheriting wealth, or getting a job promotion. If nothing of the sort happens within several months, the person would be well advised to ask for a raise (their boss will probably grant it).

1 = independence or isolation; new beginnings or projects; possible relocation

2 = couplehood; increased security and stability; settling down

3 = joining or teaming up with a small group; expanding plans and efforts

4 = hard work; solidity or restriction; building and maintaining

5 = time of change; magical surprises; unexpected travel; adventure

6 = marriage, family, and friends; giving time and effort to large groups

7 = time of reflection; spiritual questing; personal doubts or yearnings

8 = high-money year—a promotion, raise, inheritance, or winning a lottery

9 = time of endings—a relationship, job, and so on; psychic phenomena

If you are ever stumped by a problem involving numbers, appeal for divine aid from Numeria, the Roman Goddess of numbers.

"Murphy's Magic"—Mastering the Art of Opposites

*I*f you carry an umbrella, it's sure not to rain; if you wash your car, it surely will. If you prepare for the worst, you prevent it from happening.

We call intentionally using the power of paradox "Murphy's Magic," based on Murphy's Law—"If anything can go wrong, it will." Instead of fatalistically bemoaning this fact of life, pragmatically turn it to your advantage.

The occult principle of inversion—any polarity can be reversed—implies that everything has equal and opposite aspects or qualities, both of which are striving at any given moment for the opportunity to manifest themselves. Knowing this, spellcasters avoid many needless problems by extrapolating the negative possibilities in a situation. To people who believe in always looking on the sunny side of life, it may seem cynical and pessimistic to always be on the lookout for what can go wrong. In real life, though, pretending to ignore the specter of trouble rarely makes it go away—in fact, shutting your eyes to a problem practically dares it to show up. If you acknowledge and arm yourself against it, the worst that can happen is that you'll be prepared if it does come.

There are many ways to use Murphy's Magic. If you have to go to court, take a toothbrush to ensure that you won't spend the night in jail—because that's one thing you'll want if they do lock you up. If you're going camping,

> THIS IS ALSO CALLED "Sod's Law" or "Finagle's Law." The Murphy whose name was, somewhat unfairly, appropriated to this law was an aerospace engineer, Captain Edward A. Murphy. In 1949, while consulting on a project at Edwards Air Force Base to test how much sudden deceleration a person can stand in a crash, he discovered that all the sensors in the test pilot's suit had been installed backward. He redesigned them so that they could be installed only one way. "If there are two or more ways to do something and one of those results in a catastrophe, then someone will do it that way" was the useful principle he drew from this experience, which engineers still rely on to make new technology designs "dummy-proof."

pack a snakebite kit—because if you're prepared, you won't encounter any snakes. Make out your last will and testament as a magical action to prolong your life.

To work with the principle of paradox, consider first your need or desire, then what constitutes its opposite—the outcome you want to avert. Do something concrete to prepare for that outcome, even simply speaking it aloud. By confronting what you fear, bringing it into the light of your consciousness, you banish it—like turning around to face the bogeyman that pursues you in a nightmare.

Use Murphy's Magic on a daily basis to help smooth out the rough corners of life, as well as before important or risky events.

Three Times' the Charm

Crafters' cosmology contains many triplicities:

> matter, magic, spirit
> natural, celestial, and ceremonial magic
> Goddess, God, and spellcrafter
> Maiden, Mother, Crone
> seeker, initiate, elder
> virginity, fertility, wisdom
> male, female, hermaphrodite
> birth, life, death
> past, present, future
> beginning, middle, end
> up, down, around
> in, out, throughout
> and so on . . .

Patterns of three occur throughout magic and spellwork. In the Craft, when Witches cast a circle to create a cleansed, protected, sacred space for ritual, we trace it not once, but generally thrice. The ideal width of a circle is 9 feet (thrice *3*). Among covens, at least three members must attend a circle or it doesn't qualify as a legitimate coven meeting. It pays to intone, chant, spell, wish, or pray thrice for desires—we alert the God/desses to our needs with each successive repetition. Covens often have three female designees to play parts in myth reenactments, which correspond to the Moon's major phases (waxing, full, and waning) and the Goddess Hecate's aspects (Maiden, Mother, and Crone). The ancients called Hecate *Triformis,* (three-formed), and she is depicted facing in three directions, wearing a three-tiered skirt to symbolize her sway over Heaven, Earth, and the Underworld. Hermes *Trismegistus* (thrice-greatest) is Hermes as the God of magic and giver of the Emerald Tablet, whose precept, "as above, so below," bridges spirit and matter through magic. Three represents a third way out of a dilemma, the mediating alternative that can bring conflicting opposites into harmony.

Traditionally trained Witches can earn three degrees over the course of no less than three years and three days' study. The degrees are bestowed in three separate ceremonies. The First Degree rite is called Initiation, wherein the candidate is validated as knowing basic Craft tenets and practices. The candidate is officially taken into the Olde Religion, and afterward can rightly call herself or himself a Witch. Both the Second Degree and the Third Degree rituals are called Elevations. In the Second Degree ceremony, the High Priest/ess passes to the candidate the power transmitted from the beginning of the tradition's foundation and exercised by all its practitioners up to the present day. The Sublime and Ultimate Third Degree Elevation involves the Great Rite, or the spiritual and sexual union of the Perfect Couple.

Our list of Craft threes could go on for quite some time, but we trust that we've shown how much spellcrafters rely on the magical principle of triplicity.

DIVINE TRIPLICITY:
Hecate Triformis (Three-formed), the Maiden, Mother, and Crone, exemplifies the reverence spellcrafters accord to threeness.

The Cymric Count or "Shepherd's Score"

Away of counting that survives in the Celtic Cymric tongue was used until recent times by Lincolnshire shepherds to help them keep track of their sheep.[25] Gardnerian Witches still employ the "Shepherd's Score."

Use the Cymric Count when you write secret communiqués or need to count something during spellwork.

1	= yan	**11**	= yan-a-dik
2	= tan	**12**	= tan-a-dik
3	= tethera	**13**	= tethera-dik
4	= pethera	**14**	= pethera-dik
5	= pimp	**15**	= bumfit
6	= sethera	**16**	= yan-a-bumfit
7	= lethera	**17**	= tan-a-bumfit
8	= hovera	**18**	= tethera-bumfit
9	= dovera	**19**	= pethera-bumfit
10	= dik	**20**	= figgit

An olde Witch trick for counting during spellwork is to count your heartbeats. Track your pulse at your wrist, using the tips of your forefinger and middle finger.

[25] *Charles Francis Potter, "Shepherd's Score,"* Funk & Wagnalls Standard Dictionary of Folklore, Mythology, and Legend, *ed. Maria Leach (Funk & Wagnalls, Harper & Row, 1949/1972), 1006–7. According to Potter, Henry Bett suggested the "Shepherd's Score" as the source of the childhood rhyme "Hickory, Dickory, Dock" in his* Nursery Rhymes and Tales: Their Origin and History.

CHANTS AND CHARMS

THE POWER OF WORDS

"They say that the power of enchantments and verses is so great, that it is believed they are able to subvert almost all nature . . . that with a magical whispering, swift rivers are turned back, the slow sea is bound, the winds are breathed out with one accord, the Sun is stopped, the Moon is clarified, the stars are pulled out, the day is kept back, the night is prolonged.

. . . Moreover all poets sing, and philosophers do not deny, that by verses many wonderful things may be done, as corn to be removed, lightnings to be commanded, diseases cured, and such like."

—HEINRICH CORNELIUS AGRIPPA
"OF THE WONDERFUL POWER OF ENCHANTMENTS"
Three Books of Occult Philosophy

Words are the middle ground between thoughts and things—your first tangible expression of your will into the physical world. Our ancestors knew well the magic in the spoken word, as you'll soon discover if you investigate the origins of many English words for magic and healing. For example, *leech* originally meant not "a blood-sucking parasite," but "a physician who healed with magic words" (from the same root as *lecture*). Similarly, *grimoire,* or "book of spells," was once the same word as *grammar.*

In modern times, TVs, radios, and telephones subject people to such a constant bombardment of babble that many are tempted to take words for granted, treating them as little more than the world's cheapest commodity. How many people do you know who chatter nonstop, though their words reveal nothing of substance? This litter of language makes it all too easy to minimize the power words actually have over us. What are laws but collections of words? What effect can TV ad pitches have on you when you mute the sound? Crusades are fought over books of holy words and nations roused to war by such fighting words as *tyranny* and *terrorism*. Millions of women and men have lost their lives because of a single word—*Witch*.

In spellcraft, carefully chosen or intoned words articulate, contain, and project your intent. Using words, you tell the universe what you want, why you want it, exactly how you want it to manifest itself, and so on. But herein lies a mystery: There's a world of difference between rotely reciting "I am consciously affirming my intention to open my being to manifesting my visualization," and ecstatically chanting "Wind and Water, Earth and Fire, Bring to me what I desire!"

Plodding prose cannot free you from your head—from the constriction of petty thoughts, prejudices, and doubts. To cast a goodly spell, you must enflame your passions into poetic frenzy. You must speak your spell with "vehement affection," as Agrippa declared—chanting each word as if you were ringing a bell to awaken the Gods.

Words are living Beings. A word's meaning is its spirit; its sound is its body. Ignore either, and you weaken its innate power. In a spell, sound is as important as sense. Often—as with seemingly nonsensical Barbarous Words of Power—the sound *is* the meaning of the words. The rhythm of the syllables, the repetition of certain consonants and vowels, the rhymes that bind the ends of each line—these reverberate your intention into other realms, and all the more powerfully if the sounds are artfully selected for their magical correspondences. A skilled spellworker knows their spell is truly taking hold when the words seem to flow freely from their tongue and dance together of their own accord.

Many spellcrafters believe that it's best to chant in the ancient languages of people known for their magic—Sanskrit, Egyptian, Hebrew, Gaelic, Greek, and Latin. Such "dead" languages live powerfully in spirit: The spells and prayers intoned in those tongues in the temples, pyramids, and caves by generation upon generation of Priest/esses still echo in the ears of the Gods.

Yet every language has its own magical dialects, running like pre-urban streams under the pedantic pavement of modern parlance. Spellcrafters often use archaic verb forms, such as *so mote it be,* and distinct types of poetic meters—*by* all *the* pow'r *of* Moon *and* Sun—in their spells. Our own British tradition of Witchcraft has passed down to us a rich trove of secret magical words, some of which we reveal in this chapter in the glossary of Ancient Witch Words (see page 177). Other magically derived words surface occasionally in everyday talk like the flash of a rare fish through the flood of mundane verbiage. For example, *inaugurate* originally meant "to interpret the omens" accompanying the coronation of a new leader, and *monster* originally meant a "showing" of divine wrath (from the same root as *demonstrate*).

Everyone works with words—if not as a writer or poet, then as a reader or listener. The word skills you'll learn through spellcraft need not be practiced only in the confines of a ritual room. By using them everywhere, you will find your eyes and ears opened and your speech ever better attuned to multiple layers of meaning. You'll also recognize more clearly that the *way* something is said often packs a bigger punch than *what* is said, as with a preacher's rhythmic cadences or a politician's alliterating slogans. Finally, you will begin to appreciate the limits of words, and the vast amount of information that can be conveyed by knowing looks and prolonged silences—like the hidden dark matter that fills the universe between stars.

As Howard Rheingold noted in *They Have a Word for It,* "If there is one thing that all the world's different spiritual traditions agree upon, it is the necessity of both using words, and then abandoning them when they have served their purpose."

The Magic in Consonants and Vowels

"SOCRATES: Again, is there not an essence of each thing, just as there is a
color, or sound? And is there not an essence of color and sound as
well as of anything else which may be said to have an essence?
HERMOGENES: I should think so.
SOCRATES: Well, and if anyone could express the essence of each thing in
letters and syllables, would he not express the nature of each thing?
HERMOGENES: Quite so."

— PLATO
Cratylus

Spoken spells are strings of sounds. Each sound—like a uniquely colored
bead—has its own innate form and meaning. Poets and spellcrafters—
kindred artists since the days of bards and griots—use similar tools of Art to
weave these sound-beads into entrancing webs of words. Rhyme and rhythm
are two of those tools (which we'll detail in the next chapter). Two others are
called by the rather unpoetic names *assonance* and *alliteration*.

All of these tongue tools work by the magical principle of repetition—that
simple "tap, tap, tap . . ." that, when knowingly applied, has the power to
shake a skyscraper. Assonance is the repetition of vowel sounds; alliteration, of
consonants.

Alliterating and assonating phrases abound throughout English. Since
Anglo-Saxon times, speakers of English have loved to link words in this way.
We tell *tall tales,* praise *sweet sixteen,* feel *right as rain,* and sign off *over and
out.* Echoing a particular sound emphasizes it, making it stand out from all
the rest.

You may be tempted to think that the sounds are arbitrary, that it's only the
repetition that counts. Spellcrafters know, however, that nothing is truly random. Everything in our interconnected, animated universe has pattern and
purpose—even when we're not consciously aware of it. The sounds we speak
aren't just haphazard vocalizations; each has a quality that's more than subjective—what the olde magicians called its "virtue." Respect and befriend these
virtues, and the sounds of language will leap like elemental spirits to help you.

"Flags, flax, fodder and frigg" is an olde Witches' blessing that wishes one the basic essentials of life: shelter (flagstones), clothing (flax yields linen), food (fodder), and sex (Frigga is an Anglo-Saxon Goddess of fertility). It's also a classic example of magical alliteration, repeating the sound *f* as if the blesser was blowing on coals to make a hearth fire alight.

Abracadabra, on the other hand, assonates. The *a* sound—pronounced *ah,* like a sigh of relief—is a key to this olde anti-fever charm.

Embedded in ancient charms such as these are clues to what once was a sophisticated and powerful lore of the voice. Back in the days before *grammar* split off from *grimoire,* when magic was taught alongside poetry, and rhetoric was an application of philosophy, Priest/esses and bards passed along to their initiates the correspondences between their languages' particles of sound and the parts and patterns of the world around them. Tragically, as cultures were conquered by new religions and their old wisdom-keepers persecuted, most of this oral soundlore was lost—forcibly forgotten, or buried beneath the new priesthood's patter and Babel.

It is very difficult to reconstruct this lore from the bits and scraps that survive. Many of the efforts to do so (such as Robert Graves's writings about the Druidic alphabet) are beautiful and poetic, but speculative. Other attempts are based on the letters of written alphabets, such as the Norse runes, which aren't necessarily the same as spoken sounds—as anyone who has competed in a spelling bee knows.

Scientists, however, have now given us the keys to unlock this long-shut wizard's tower, through their investigations of the relationships between acoustics and linguistics. *Psycholinguistics,* the study of sound symbolism in language, is a rapidly growing field, impelled partly, as it happens, by the demands of advertisers for expressive product names.

If sentences are the molecules of language, then words are its atoms, and their component sounds—which linguists call phonemes—are their quantum particles. Languages evolve and mutate, divide themselves into dialects and relate back to their mother tongues, on this quantum dimension of vowels and consonants. (Compare *fire* in English, *feuer* in its cousin German, *pyr* in its more distant relative Greek, and *pür* in Indo-European, the ancestor of all those tongues.) Systematic patterns of phonemes also govern grammatical inflections in languages. The verb-endings and noun-endings that students of a foreign language are usually forced to learn by rote memorization can be acquired far more effectively when students are taught to recognize these controlling patterns.

The human voice is the prototypical musical instrument. Your lungs blow air, as bagpipes do, past your vocal cords—an arrangement of folds of cartilage and muscle that vibrates like a double reed, and can tune itself up and down a wide range of tones, like a string being tightened or loosened by a tuning peg. Your chest and nasal cavities resonate and amplify these tones like the body of a violin or an acoustic guitar. Your mouth—using tongue, teeth and gums, lips, palate, and throat—alters the timbre of the tones, as a brass-player's hand does over the bell of a trumpet.

Uttering vowels and uttering consonants are the two ways of playing this vocal instrument. You produce vowels by sending a steady stream of air through your open mouth; you produce consonants by closing parts of the mouth and constricting or interrupting the stream.

Vowels equate with spirit, whose energy flows free and unfettered, like uninterrupted breath. Consonants correspond to matter, which is energy constricted and congealed, like blocked breath. The two are complementary; words need both consonants and vowels to exist, just as creatures need both body and spirit to live.

VOWELS TO SING THE NAMES DIVINE . . .

Inhale deeply. As you slowly release your breath, pronounce this sequence of sounds: *ee, eh, ah, oh, oo.* Now do it again, but this time merge the sounds into each other: *ee-ih-eh-aa-ah-aw-oh-oo.* Exaggerate the movements of your mouth, grinning for *ee,* gaping for *ah,* and puckering for *oo.* Finally, relax your mouth into a neutral position and say the sound *uh.*

There are some 6,000 languages spoken around the world today, and countless thousands more that thrived, then vanished, in the past. Underlying every one is the series of sounds you just pronounced. This is called the vowel spectrum—the full sequence of vowel sounds that the human mouth can physically form. It's like running your finger along all the keys on the piano. Just as a song will require only some of the keys and leave others silent, so particular languages and dialects use some of the parts of the vowel spectrum but leave others out. Linguists illustrate the way the mouth forms this sequence with

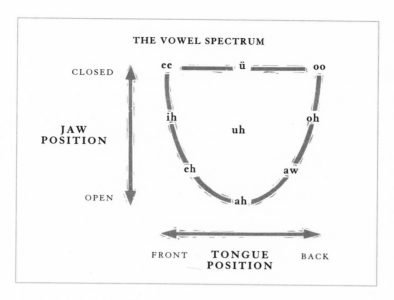

THE VOWEL SPECTRUM

CLOSED

ee   ü   oo

ih   oh

uh

JAW
POSITION

eh   aw

OPEN   ah

FRONT   **TONGUE
POSITION**   BACK

maps such as the one above.

At the top left and right are the extremes: the brightest, sharpest vowel sound, *ee,* and the darkest, narrowest vowel sound, *oo.* At the bottom middle is the broadest vowel sound, *ah.* In the center is the neutral vowel sound, *uh*—the *schwa* sound into which unaccented vowels in such languages as English and Russian tend to degenerate. (The *schwa* requires the least effort to pronounce.) The sequence you practiced doesn't include every possible vowel sound—for instance, it doesn't include the French *u* or the German *ü,* shown at the top center of the graph—but it does outline the overall shape of the spectrum.

In magic, the whole empowers its parts. It's no surprise, then, that the vowel spectrum is also a divine name—and, for many religions, the basis of the name of the Supreme Being. The ancient Gnostics addressed the Sun God as **IAO** or **IAU** (*ee-ah-oh* or *ee-ah-oo*)—selecting from the vowel spectrum the two extremes and the middle, as if to encompass all creation by denoting its beginning, middle, and end. For Jews, the name of the Infinite is considered ultimately unpronounceable—after all, no human tongue can utter all the sounds of every word—but is written as **YHWH** (using the Hebrew letters *yod he vau he*). Y is pronounced as the bright extreme, *ee,* and *W* as the dark extreme, *oo.* Ancient Roman writers reported that contemporary Jews, like the Gnostics, pronounced this approximation of the name as **IAO**, reproducing it in Greek letters as *iota, alpha, omega:*

$$IA\Omega$$

This *ee-oo* sequence—the two vowel sounds that are formed highest in the mouth—is incorporated into the root word for *to shine* (in the sense of "the shining heavens" or "the bright sky") in Indo-European, the long-dead, never-written language that was the prehistoric parent of English, Spanish, German, Latin, Russian, Greek, Sanskrit, Gaelic, and many other tongues. This root word, *deiw-*, begat many sky God/dess names and words, such as *Iacchus* (later *Bacchus*), *Jove, Jupiter, Dianus* (later *Janus*) and *Diana, Dios, Deus, Tyr, divine, day* and, of course, **Diuvei.*

The broad, deep sound *ah,* however, appears in many names of the mother Goddess—such as *Ma, Mater, Ma'at, Mary, Inanna,* and *Asherah.*

Triplicity is traditionally associated with spirit, so it's appropriate that the three sounds *ee-ah-oo* that outline the boundaries of the spectrum stand for the whole of vowels. Witches hear in *ee* the excited shriek of the Maiden; in *ah* the broad, comforting sigh of the Mother; in *oo* the spooky foretelling of the Crone.

Plato also gives meanings for these vowel sounds. In the dialogue *Cratylus,* Socrates describes the thin sound of *ee* as expressing the subtle elements that pass through all things. Broad *ah,* he says, is an expression of size, and *eh* connotes length; he characterizes both as "great" letters. *Oh* signifies roundness.

Other classical writers reported that worshippers of Hecate, the Goddess of Witches, invoked her by wordlessly chanting vowels. Egyptian priests used vowel incantations in their rites of magic and healing. The *Greek Magical Papyri,*[26] which come from Thebes, in Hellenistic Egypt, are full of vowel chants, such as in the following spell:

SPELL TO CATCH A THIEF

Take a Plant Chelkbei[27] and Bugloss,[28] strain them, burn what you strain out, mix well with Juice, and write CHOO' with it on a Wall. Take Gallows Wood

---

[26] Hans Dieter Betz, ed., Greek Magical Papyri in Translation: Including the Demotic Spells *(The University of Chicago Press, 1986),* Papyri Graecae Magicae (PGM) *V. 70–95.*
[27] John Gerard, *The Herbal or General History of Plants (1633; revised and enlarged by Thomas Johnson, Mineola, N.Y.: Dover Publications, 1975), 816. Considering Witches' penchant for marking thieves so they physically reveal themselves to others, chelkbei is possibly* Chelidonium minus *(small celandine), which blisters skin and makes fingernails and toenails fall off. Mixed with honey and snorted, it "purgeth the head of foule and filthie humors," that is, removes bad thoughts or ill intention.*
[28] *Probably* Echium vulgare *(viper's bugloss), which, appropriately, repels serpents and cures snakebite. If you want to use this spell, you may wish to substitute* Borago officinalis *(borage) for bugloss.*

and carve a Hammer.[29] With the Hammer strike the Eye (see below) while saying the formula:

> *I conjure You by the Holy Names!*
> *Hand over the Thief who made off with it!*
> *CHALCHAK CHALKOUM*
> *CHIAM CHARCHROUM*
> *ZBAR BE'RI ZBARKOM*
> *CHRE' KARIO'B PHARIBOU,*
> *and by the Shudderful Names:*
> *A EE E'E'E' IIII OOOOO YYYYYY O'O'O'O'O'O'O'!*

While saying this, Strike with the Hammer:

> *Hand over the Thief who Stole it!*
> *As long as I strike the Eye with this Hammer,*
> *let the Eye of the Thief be struck,*
> *and let it Swell Up until it betrays him!*

This is the figure to strike:

The Shudderful Names are the seven vowel letters of the Greek alphabet: *alpha, epsilon, eta, iota, omicron, upsilon,* and *omega.* They are written:

$$A \; E \; H \; I \; O \; Y \; \Omega$$

and pronounced *ah, eh, ay, ee, oh, ü,* and *ooh* (prolonged *o,* the closest equivalent in Greek to the English *oo*). Ancient magicians correlated these vowels with the Seven Planets: respectively, Moon, Mercury, Venus, Sun, Mars, Jupiter, and Saturn. Their secret name for the solar Supreme Being,

$$I A \Omega$$

is composed of the middle, first, and last vowels of the sequence, starting with *I,* the vowel they correlated with the Sun.

The invocation of the Shudderful Names combines the vowels with magical number. The first vowel, *A,* is repeated once, the second vowel, *E,* is repeated twice, and so on up to the seventh vowel, *O'* (representing Ω), which is repeated seven times. This incantation appears frequently in ancient magical and philosophical texts.

As effective as this incantation is in its native language, it's nevertheless based on the arbitrary order of the letters in the Greek alphabet, and so would not be very idiomatic for other languages. A more holistic approach is to work with the acoustical qualities of vowels—the vowel spectrum. With the vowels, as with all systems of correspondences, your spells will be most powerful if you take the ecological tack—respect the integrity of whole systems, and view their components together as a microcosmic universe that reflects the macrocosm.[30]

. . . CONSONANTS FOR MORTAL RHYMES

Say these sounds: *b—b—b—b, p—p—p—p, d—d—d—d, q—q—q—q,* and *g—g—g—g.* Don't they all share an explosive quality? Now repeat this sequence several times: *b, v, f, p; b, v, f, p.* Don't they seem to blend and mutate into each other, as if in a circular fashion?

Like the vowels, the consonants also arrange themselves into natural patterns, according to the ways the human mouth produces them. Linguists have

---

[30] *The best reference for exploring these traditions is* The Mystery of the Seven Vowels: In Theory and Practice, *by Joscelyn Godwin (York Beach, Maine: Red Wheel/Weiser, Phanes Press, 1991).*

discovered that these patterns govern the way languages evolve and change through the passage of time and with the movement of peoples. These same patterns reveal to spellcrafters the magical correspondences of the consonant sounds.

In questing for magical correspondences, it's always best to start with the most basic: the principle of polarity. First divide the dark from the light—the yin from the yang, the female from the male. Since Plato's time, students of language have noticed the dualism between sounded, or voiced, consonants, and mute, or voiceless, ones.

Say these phrases aloud: *pat the bat, dip the tip, gore the core.* (To avoid double entendre, just don't say these in a crowded bar or while walking down the street in a raincoat.) Next, try whispering the phrases *without* using your voice; you can barely tell the difference between the pairs of sounds *b* and *p; d* and *t; g* and *k,* or hard *c.*

In the explosive sequence you pronounced earlier (linguists in fact, term such sounds *plosives*), the voiced consonants were *b, d,* and *g.* The voiceless consonants were *p* and the sound *k,* which we spelled as *q.* We did this not only to remind you that the written characters of the alphabet and the spoken sounds of the language aren't always neatly matched, but also to see whether you happened to notice that all those plosive sounds can be written with letters that are inversions and reversals of one another. You'll find such patterns useful later in this book, when you learn about making written sigils and talismans.

Other voiced/voiceless pairs in the English language are *v* and *f, z* and *s,* and a pair that exemplifies the discordance between the written alphabet and the spoken word: *dh* and *th.*

Dh is the hard *th* of *breathe; th* is the soft *th* of *breath.* In Old and Middle English, *dh* and *th* were spelled with the runic *eth* ð and *thorn* þ.

Next time you see a sign such as Ye Olde Laundromat, you'll really be able to impress your friends by pointing out that *Ye* is the same as *The.* When they make jest of thee, explain that the old *Y* was actually a misread *thorn,* the ghost that the medieval letter left behind when it died out from modern English.

Here's a charm *Diuvei composed that illustrates how you can employ voiced/voiceless consonant pairs to apply the magical principle of polarity:

Sweet the female, bad the boy,
Lady, find a nicer toy.

The first phrase describes the problem in the present—one of those prom-queen-flirts-with-crack-dealer infatuations that has turned nasty and abusive—and conveys it magically by according only one voiceless consonant (*f* in *female*) to the girl, but two voiced consonants (*b* in *bad* and *boy*) to the guy, showing his initial dominance. The second phrase declares your will for the future—bust out and find a better beau, girlfriend!—by reversing the relationship: the girl now gets two voiced consonants (*d* in *Lady* and *find*) and the guy only one of the voiceless variety (*t* in *toy*). In both phrases, pairs of voiced/voiceless consonants express the link between the girl and the boy. The stronger person in each phrase gets more, voiced consonants; the weaker gets fewer, voiceless ones. Because the female ends up with two voiced consonants in the last line (the final say, so to speak), she will grow stronger than the bad boy, thereby overcoming her negative situation.

Obstruents, which "obstruct" your breath, are consonants that come in voiced/voiceless, yang/yin pairs. But their duality doesn't stop there. Like the seasons, the structure of DNA, and matter itself, obstruents are fourfold in nature: Each pair of voiced/voiceless consonants is itself closely linked to another pair.

For example, all of the four sounds in the cycle you pronounced at the start of this section (*b, v, f, p*) are made at the very front of the mouth, using your lips. The voiced/voiceless pairs are *b* and *p,* and *v* and *f.* Linguists studying the evolution of languages have found that *b* and *v* are practically interchangeable, as are *f* and *p* (recall *fire* and *pyr*).

There are four such foursomes—for a total of 16 obstruents. Because 16 is divisible by 4, it's obvious to spellcrafters that obstruents correspond with the Four Elements: Fire, Air, Water, and Earth. The most natural way to find the correspondences between the obstruents and the Four Elements is to resp-ect the system of linguistic classification itself, which is based on how far for-ward or how far back in the mouth the groups of consonants are formed.

Fire, the lightest, most yang element, corresponds to the farthest for-ward—the sounds you make with your lips. Earth, the densest, or most yin ele-ment, corresponds to the farthest back—the sounds you make with your throat. In between these two are the sounds you make with the tip of your tongue and your palate.

Here is a table of correspondences between the consonants and the Four

Elements, followed by some comments and a list of sample words for each element. Add your own by purusing a dictionary and gathering appropriate words.

THE 16 OBSTRUENT SOUNDS = THE FOUR ELEMENTS

LIPS: *b* and *p,* and *v* and *f* = Fire
TONGUE: *d* and *t,* and *dh* and *th* = Air
PALATE: *z* and *s,* and *zh* and *sh* = Water
THROAT: *g* and *k,* and *gh* and *h* = Earth

• **LIPS:** *b* and *p,* and *v* and *f* = Fire

The same part of the body that creates kisses also creates the Fiery consonants. Linguists call *b* and *p* labials, referring to the lips, and *v* and *f* labiodentals, because they involve the front teeth as well.

Fiery word examples include:

b—burn, bright, bonfire, begin, break, bust, but, abrupt
p—pyre, point, prick, playful
v—very, vivid, vital, vibrant, violent, devour, revolt
f—fire, fiery, flame, fist

• **TONGUE:** *d* and *t,* and *dh* and *th* = Air

These are made a bit farther back in your mouth, using the tip of your tongue against your gums and teeth. If you play a flute or other wind instrument, you know that *t* is the sound you make to articulate musical notes.

D and *t* are termed alveolars, referring to the gums, which the tongue strikes to make these sounds.[31] *Dh* and *th* are called dentals, because the tongue touches the teeth. (In English, the sound *dh* is always spelled *th.*)

Airy word examples include:

d—drive, discuss, dissipate, deliberate, delude
t—talk, travel, transport, transitory, article
dh—these, those, thither, breathe
th—think, throw, through, breath

[31] *The Four Elements aren't the only consonantal correspondences you can use. For Plato, the alveolars contained a Saturnine component: "He [the original namer of things] seems to have thought that the closing and pressure of the tongue in the utterance of 'd' and 't' were expressive of binding and rest in a place." Cratylus, 427b.*

- **PALATE:** *z* and *s*, and *zh* and *sh* = Water

Pronounced even farther back in the mouth, involving your palate and gums, are the four hissing consonants that linguists call sibilants. *Zh* is pronounced as in *azure*; it and its voiceless partner, *sh,* are also called hushings.

Watery word examples include:

> z—sizzle, misery
>
> s—stream, slurry, steam, slake, sorrow, glisten
>
> zh—pleasure, leisure
>
> sh—shush, hush, slush, wash, fresh, fish

Z has exceptional qualities. It's often associated with jaggedness and electricity, which are aspects of Fire (zap, zigzag, buzz).

- **THROAT:** *g* and *k*, and *gh* and *h* = Earth

At the back of the mouth, practically in your throat, are the gutturals, which you make with your soft palate and glottis. *G* and *k* have a solid, grounded sound. *Gh* is a sound extinct in English—its last lingering shade is in the spelling of the word *ghost.* As for *h,* in most other languages it is pronounced more heavily as *kh,* as in the Scottish *ch* in *Loch Ness*.

Earthy word examples include:

> g—get, good, glob, gunk, gourd, grave, grove, goddess
>
> k—keep, contain, cauldron, close, claim, crunch, crush, rock,
>   block, cash, cattle, kin, kill
>
> h—hunk, hack, hold, hard, heft

There are two other obstruent consonants in English, which are actually combinations of others: the voiced *dzh* (spelled *j* as in *jade* or *g* as in *Gypsy*) and its voiceless partner *tsh* (spelled *ch* as in *change*). These obstruents occur in the very center of the correspondence table, combining Air (*t* and *d*) with Water (*sh* and *zh*).

You can use these sounds in spellwork to signify centrality, neutrality, or even impartiality—as in the word *judge,* whose central sound is the neutral vowel sound *uh.*

One consonant sound is so deep and primal that letters of the alphabet can't represent it: the glottal stop. This is the click of the glottal valve in your throat that you make when you begin a sentence with a vowel sound. Listen for it at the beginning of *afterward, elsewhere,* or *otherwise.* You will also hear it frequently in certain working-class British dialects. (Imagine John Lennon exclaiming in his Liverpool accent, "'Ello, what's the ma'er with Paul?") The glottal stop is represented in writing by an apostrophe. Paradoxically, this most guttural of consonants can be followed only by a vowel; it's so yin that it would be absorbed into any other consonant.

Polarity can be shocking, in language no less than in electricity. An extreme duality links the sounds of the most sacred word with those of the most profane. One of these words is traditionally unpronounceable, and the other, conventionally unprintable: the Deity name described earlier that contains the vowel sounds *ee-oo,* and the curse word *f**k*. Just as the vowel sounds of the Deity name begin and end at the two extremes of the vowel spectrum, so the consonant sounds of the curse word begin at the very front of the mouth and end at the very back, with the neutral *uh* vowel sound in the middle. Both of the consonants in the curse word are voiceless, so this olde Anglo-Saxon word is thoroughly yin. Another intriguing coincidence here is that the vowel sounds of the word *you,* which all too often follows this expletive, are the same as those of the sacred Deity name.

Most Earthy four-letter words rely on plosives for their expressive force. That's what makes you instinctively shout them after you've hit your thumb with a hammer. In spellwork, that same quality makes plosives particularly effective for forcefully expressing your magical will. For example, when you cement an incantation with "As I will it, so mote it be!" strongly emphasize the concluding *b*. Plosive consonant pairs are *b* and *p, d* and *t,* and *g* and *k*.

Complementary to plosives are the fricative consonants, which include *v* and *f, dh* and *th,* and *h,* as well as all four of the sibilants: *z, s, zh,* and *sh*. Plato characterized fricatives as "imitating what is windy" because "their pronunciation is accompanied by great expenditure of breath."

Using this correspondence magically, spellcrafters could use fricatives when weather-working to "blow away" an approaching storm that imperils their rite.

Resonants are words that hum like *m,* whir like *r,* or ring like *ng*. Although you make them with your mouth almost or completely closed (as with obstruents), resonants aren't dual in nature—they don't come as voiced/voiceless pairs, as obstruents do. Whereas obstruents are formed with a single puff of breath, resonants are formed as a continuous sound, like vowels.

They are not singable as the vowels are, but they *are* hummable. To put it meta-physically, resonants—like the Seven Planets—are the middle realm between the fourfold material realm of the obstruents, and the threefold spiritual realm of the vowels.

Here is a table showing how the seven resonant consonants correspond to the Seven Planets, followed by a few comments and examples of corresponding words you can employ while composing charms or during spellwork.

THE SEVEN RESONANTS = THE SEVEN PLANETS

LIQUIDS:
l = Moon
r = Mercury
SEMI-VOWELS:
w = Venus
y = Sun
NASAL RESONANTS:
ng = Mars
n = Jupiter
m = Saturn

Floating on top of the resonants—closest to the realm of vowels—are the mellifluous liquids *l* and *r.*

In a middle zone are the semi-vowels: *y* (as in *yes*) and *w,* which are constricted versions of the vowel sounds *ee* and *oo.*

Darkest and closest to the obstruents are the nasal resonants *ng, n,* and *m,* which are pronounced with the mouth completely closed.

In English (among other languages), there are seven resonants. The number 7 automatically suggests a corresponding connection with the Seven Planets. Therefore, the most natural correspondence to infer is that between the sequence of resonants from the most vowel-like to the most consonantal, and the Chaldean Order of the planets from the swiftest-orbiting to the slowest.

- *l* = Moon

Your mouth makes la Luna's crescent around your tongue when you pronounce this sound.

Lunar words include *lolling, dwelling, lingering, mellow, lovely, silver, lady.*

Plato noted that earthy *g* or *k* and liquid *l* together (*gl* or *cl*) "[create] the notion of a glutinous clammy nature." Examples of such gelatinous words are *globular, cluster,* and *cling.*

- *r* = Mercury

R is "an excellent instrument for the expression of motion," wrote Plato, because "the tongue [is] most agitated and least at rest." In Greek, as in most other languages (including the English of Chaucer's time), *r* is often spoken with a trill—fluttering like a card in the spokes of a bicycle wheel. Interestingly, the runic letter for the *r* sound (*raidho*) symbolizes forward, wheel-like motion and equates with travel.

Mercurial words include *ride, run, rapid, roll, race, wriggle.*

- *w* = Venus

The Romans began the name of the Goddess of love and fertility with this sound, pronouncing *Venus* as "WAY-noos."

Venereal words include *women, wave, warmth, welcome, with, wealth.*

- *y* = Sun

Y is the first consonant in the written Hebrew name for the supreme Deity, YHWH, which is a variation on the solar name IAU.

Solar words include *yes, yellow, youth, yolk, yesterday.*

- *ng* = Mars

Impatient Mars is the appropriate correspondence for English's present participle—the *-ing* ending, as in "I'm leaving!"

Martial words include *sting, string, sling, bang, clang.*

- *n* = Jupiter

According to Plato, *n* is the sound of inwardness, which suggests the philosophical and spiritual side of Jupiter rather than the expansiveness that the planet is better known for bestowing.

Jovial words include *nine, now, nexus, number, nose, nirvana.*

- *m* = Saturn

The darkest, most yin sound is appropriate for the slowest-moving planet.

Saturnine words include *melancholy, malefic, miscreant, mortal, Om, mire, mute, moot.*

Just as the ancient Alexandrian magicians intoned the Shudderful Names of the seven Greek vowels to invoke the powers of the Seven Planets, so you can intone the seven resonants in sequence to conjure all the planets' energies to aid your spell: *l-r-r-w-w-w-y-y-y-y-ng-ng-ng-ng-ng-n-n-n-n-n-n-m-m-m-m-m-m-m.*

To remember the sequence of the resonants, devise a mnemonic from planetary words containing them. One memorable example is:

Lady *r*unning *w*ith *y*ouths ba*ng*s *n*ine *m*ortals.

We trust it's clear by now that the sounds of your voice potentially contain the power of the spirit above, the elements below, and the planets between. Understanding these correspondences gives you a set of skeleton keys you can use to unlock the magic hidden within any word or phrase.

On the next page is a pictorial table of vowel, resonant, and obstruent correspondences. At the top is the archetypal Word, the divine name $IA\Omega$, depicted as an Idea in the spiritual realm. Below it, the spellcrafter's tongue transmutes this Idea into the vowel spectrum, giving voice to their inner spirit. Resonants emanate from the spellcrafter's mouth outward through the seven orbits of the planets—like ripples spreading out in a pond or the concentric emanations of the human aura. The elemental obstruents are spoken with voiced or—deepest in the material realm—mute, voiceless consonants. The spellcrafter's speech has the stability of Earth's bedrock, the depth of unplumbed oceans, the force of gale winds, and the fiery crackle of conviction. Summoned by such sounds, the very stars support their magical endeavors. Their every utterance has the power to affect all realms.

A goodly exercise is to let your eyes rove over the corresponding connections in the pictorial. Consider their deep implications, and allow your mind to form other sound and word examples over time. Experiment by speaking the vowels and consonants slowly, fast, staccato, and languorously.

Skeptics might say that it's easy to choose words from a dictionary that fit this scheme of correspondences and ignore the many that don't. We're asserting, for instance, that *b* is an abrupt, Firey sound and that you can emphasize this correspondence through alliteration. But what about a phrase such as "bland and boring"?

One answer is that the Art of Correspondences is just that—an art. Like a

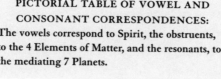

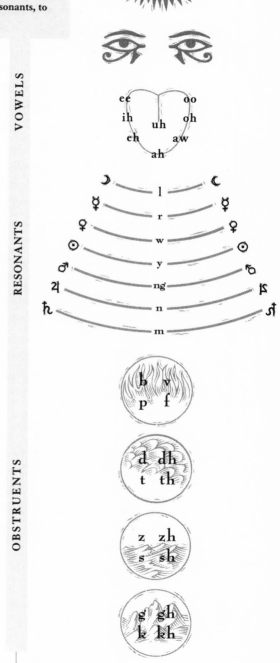

painter who selects colors from a palette, you'll choose the words and highlight the sounds that are best suited to projecting your spell's particular intention. You are not trying to prove that all words in every language fit into this correspondence scheme; obviously, a great many don't. Spellcraft is a practical art—you focus on the words that work.

Another explanation is that word sounds don't exist in a laboratory vacuum. The meaning of the word and the context in which you use it will attract certain sounds to the forefront, and de-emphasize the rest. Sure, *bland* and *boring* both begin with the plosive *b,* but like a movie whose previews promise more action than it delivers, the words' sounds move on to the lulling resonants *l, n, r, ng.* (Picture a film critic yelling "Boooring!" from the back of the theater—dragging out the *oh* as if they were moaning about being stuck in traffic during rush hour.)

Languages are the channels that carry the streams of human culture.

Different languages tend to favor certain kinds of sounds while neglecting others. The sound qualities of these phonetic preferences reflect not only the histories of the peoples speaking them, but also the cultural values they developed along the way. Consider the differences that grew up among the Indo-Europeans as they fanned out across Europe. The tribes that settled in northern climes developed the consonant-rich Germanic tongues: Modern German, for example, reflects a liking for gutturals; and, to foreigners, English sounds saturated with sibilants. In contrast, the tribes that moved south to the warm Mediterranean evolved vowel-laden Romance languages, such as Italian and Spanish. Further, consider also how weak in earthy obstruents modern English is; the dominant language of the Industrial Age sacrificed *gh* and *kh* when its native speakers left the soil and abandoned herds and farms in favor of factories.

Finally, there's proof in the pudding: the mystical effects you obtain when you practice this voice-lore. For example, what unbidden images do the sounds evoke in your mind's eye when you pronounce the vowel spectrum, starting with the glottal stop and ending with the neutral schwa—',*ee, ih, eh, ah, aw, oh, oo,* and *uh?*

Some words of caution: In chants you compose, never force-fit word sounds together to the point where you sacrifice the meaning and the impact of the words.

Ultimately, remember that you don't have to use any of these vocal correspondences. Whatever system(s) of correspondences you employ, the important thing is that in understanding the power of sounds, you perfect an ear for word magic.

"*I forged in the fire of utterances
Shards from the speech of song
And wielding my weapons of wordcraft
Set forth in the writing of wrongs. . . .*"
— *Diuvei

And Better It Be in Rhyme

"The exact words matter little if the intent is clear and you raise the
Power. Always in rhyme they are. There is something queer about
rhyme. When tried, the same words seem to lose Power if ye miss the
rhyme. Also in rhyme, the words seem to say themselves. You do not
have to pause and think about what comes next. Doing so takes away
much of your intent."

—UNKNOWN AUTHOR
TRADITIONAL SOURCE

Rhymes are correspondences—little *as above, so below*s. Like the twists
in Celtic knot-work, they turn the lines of a spell back in on itself in
an enchanting, yet orderly, fashion—tying the words together in a net to capture what you seek.

Rhymes are an ancient memory tool—a means for folks to transform mundane thoughts into memorable rhythms. Many olde Craft rites, rituals, and
recipes revolve around the recitation of rhymed chants at precise moments.
Some appear deceptively simple but prove fascinating when intoned in the right
place at the right time. Some are more magically complex, while others are so
artfully descriptive, they read like epics in their breadth and scope.

Rhymes are psychologically potent. The late defense attorney Johnnie
Cochran relied on rhyme to persuade a jury to acquit O. J. Simpson of murder:
"If the glove doesn't fit, you must acquit!" The sermons of Pentecostal preachers and the songs of rap artists entrance their audiences through lengthy streams
of rhymes.

Noting this power of rhymes to sway the masses, Matthew McGlone,
Ph.D., recently determined[32] that "our reaction to any phrase is a response to
both what it *says* and how it *sounds*." McGlone, a psychologist at Lafayette
College in Pennsylvania, offered test subjects lists of rhyming aphorisms, such
as "woes unite foes," and, separately, their non-rhyming translations: "misfor-

---

[32] *Annie Murphy Paul, "Sounds True to Me,"* Psychology Today *(September–October 1998). "Research*
shows that rhyme has power to influence, as evidenced in political campaigns."

tunes unite foes." The subjects were asked to rate how accurately they felt that the aphorisms described human behavior. Almost invariably, they rated the rhymed aphorisms as more accurate than the non-rhymed translations. Further, they routinely disagreed with non-rhyming sentiments, but sympathetically considered similar, rhymed versions. For example, they denied that "monetary success makes people healthier," but agreed that "wealth makes health." McGlone labeled this psychological effect the "rhyme as reason" response. Rhymes, he concluded, swayed folks best whenever their words and meter pleased both the intellect and the ear in equal measure.

The rhythm of a chant or spell is its meter. Spells that are rhymed and metered (as most are) very commonly rely on pairs of seven-syllable lines in which the odd-numbered syllables are accented: *one* two *three* four *five* six *seven,* *one* two *three* four *five* six *seven.* (Sometimes an eighth, unaccented, syllable is added to either the beginning or the end of a line.)

In *Gypsy Sorcery and Fortune-Telling,* the nineteenth-century scholar Charles Godfrey Leland termed these "staff-rhymes":

> *"All of the sagas, or legends, of the Algonkin-Wabanaki were till within even fifty years chants or songs, and if they are now rapidly losing that character it is because they are no longer recited with the interest and accuracy which was once observed in the narrators. But it was simply because all things often repeated were thus intoned that the exorcisms became metrical. It is remarkable that among the Aryan races it assumed what is called the staff-rhyme, like that which Shakespeare, and Ben Jonson, and Byron, and many more employ, as it would seem, instinctively, whenever witches speak or spells or charms are uttered. It will not escape the reader that, in the Hungarian gypsy incantations in this work, the same measure is used as that which occurs in the Norse sagas, or in the scenes of Macbeth. It is also common in Italy. This is intelligible—that its short, bold, deeply-marked movement has in itself something mysterious and terrible."*

These staff-rhymes, with their two-fold beats, are magically effective because they are forceful—like a repeated knock on a door. Consider the infamous charm intoned by the Witches in "the Scottish play":

"Dou-*ble,* dou-*ble,* toil *and* trou-*ble,*
Fi-*re* burn *and* caul-*dron* bub-*ble!*"

In contrast, a triple-beat meter (*one*-two-three, *two*-two-three, *three*-two-three, *four*) evokes a dancing, skittering feeling, as in these lines from "'Twas the Night Before Christmas":

"*A*-way *to the* win-*dow I* flew *like a* flash,
Tore o-*pen the* shut-*ters and* threw *up the* sash."

Composing a beautiful and evocative rhymed chant is not always easy—as proven by the plethora of clunky, clichéd poetry with off-meter, forced rhymes common in Pagan periodicals. However, there *is* a cure for a tin ear.

First, don't let yourself be rushed by publication deadlines or the imminent arrival of friends. Second, whenever you're composing spell rhymes, begin by listing your magical goal(s). Third, duly consider the correspondences that apply to your dilemma, as well as your word options. Then devise the most lyrical rhyme that conveys your spell intention. Goodly poetry necessitates a certain amount of contemplation, inspiration, exploration, and experimentation. Creating potent, captivating rhymes requires practice and nuance. Rhyme takes time.

When you master composing couplets (two-line poems), strive to excel in the more intricate realms of triplets (three lines) and quatrains (four-line rhymes). Triplets encourage bonding, so they are good to use whenever you're involved in disagreements of the he said/she said/I say variety. A quatrain's four-fold, boxy nature can help solidify a tenuous relationship.

Some Crafters begin composing a rhyme by considering the type of drum-beat that would best accompany its recitation. Imagining a primal, heartbeat rhythm or picturing Gypsies dancing around a fire to a wild three-beat will help spark your poetic muse, and free you to be able to write mystical spellwork rhymes.

AN ALL-PURPOSE RHYMING SPELL

Chant this during any spellwork to aid your magical focus and to summon the Four Elements, the Moon, and the Sun to support your desires.

I summon Earth to seal my spell.
And Air, to speed its travel well.
Bright as Fire make it glow . . .
Deep as Water may it flow.

Mind the Elements, four-fold—
With the Spirit—fifth—take hold.

By all the pow'r of Moon and Sun—
This is my spell. Let it be spun!
This is my Will. Let it be done!

Lingua Arcana—
The Secret Language of Witchcraft

"Adoors, and allantum
Arready the besom
Anés casé prest the assay?
Infere ibonde—
La boyten ifandé—
A wheel and a day . . .

"(In woods, we make merry
The broom, bedeck fairly
Art ready for come what may?
Hand to hand, side by side—
This pair as one would bide—
Twelve Moons and a day . . .)"

—LADY PASSION, EXCERPT FROM "THE HANDFASTING SONG"

The first verse of the song above contains some of the many arcane Witch words we inherited from our initiatory tradition. Witches have used such words for centuries to talk secretly amongst themselves.

Witch words surface in surprising places. Each July, our own beloved city of Asheville (North Carolina) hosts a popular, weekend-long downtown street festival called *Bele Chere*. No one remembers any longer who gave the festival its unusual name, or why, or even what it means, but our collection of olde Witch words reveals that *bele chere* means "good company."

We provide hundreds of examples of ancient Witch words below. Our selection includes spellcrafting terms for which there are no mundane equivalents, such as *afterclap* and *afterwit*. To the best of our knowledge, this is the first time they have ever been published. We present them to inspire you with a venerable, lyrical way to communicate with others of like mind. We recommend that you *ack* (take heed of) such olde Craft words for use in your *cantrips* (magical spells) and amongst your *coven* (a group that practices magic together).

ANCIENT WITCH WORDS

The following are selected words from an arcane collection we possess of terms that olde Crafters used when talking about magic:

A

ack—*to take heed of; to notice*

adoubed—*armed, having all the tools*

adoors—*outside*

affy—*to confide in or trust*

afterclap—*a disagreeable consequence*

afterwit—*corrective measures taken after damage is done*

a-lore—*hidden; hide; a hiding place; in hiding*

ambry—*a hiding place for Craft tools*

apece—*Witch ciphers or writings; any magical alphabet*

apprest—*a preparation; mixture; potion*

arede—*to advise, explain, or counsel*

arraught—*seized by the government; legal theft (for example, asset forfeiture)*

aryoles—*fortune-tellers*

aspergilum—*a magical tool (typically a tree bough) used to spurge Crafters, the circle, and so forth preparatory to spellwork*

astart—*to escape; to run away*

astringe—*to bind; to compel; to have strings on, as in a binding spell or poppet*

at-wirch—*to work against (physically or via magic)*

aver—*to strip (for example, to get skyclad)*

azen-risina—*reincarnation*

azles—*fearless; willing to fight against anybody or anything*

B

bacbearand—*caught in the act*

baetylus—*altar stone*

bareand—*to assist (for instance, a brother or sister of the Art Magical)*

bate-breeding—*anything that causes argument or strife*

batten—*to thrive on or grow fat by unjust means (as the Roman Catholic Church and Witch finders did during the Burning Times)*

bavishness—*mockery; ridicule*

beard—*to oppose; to face in a daring manner*

bedoled—*stupefied from pain*

bele chere—*good company*

bening—*kind*

bichaunt—*to enchant; to weave a spell; to use the wand*

bigrave—*to engrave (for example, candles for spellwork)*

bishop—*to do anything to cheat; to force; to drug*

blemmel—*to mix anything by stirring in water or other fluids*

boggle—*a ghost; a goblin*

bosky—*a heavily wooded area, such as a grove site*

bougy—*a candle; a light*

broke—*to enjoy; to use; to keep*

byde—*where you live (a town or home)*

by-gols—*anything gilded or plated with gold (in other words, fake)*

by-layen—*to sleep with someone*

C

cagmag—*bad food*

cantrip—*a magical spell*

caoine—*a mourning song honoring someone who has crossed over into the Summerlands*

ceruse—*cosmetics; face powder; rouge*

clamjamfry—*a mob; a rabble*

clish-ma-claver—*foolish gossip*

coalishangi—*a fight, quarrel, or row*

cob—*a wealthy miser*

conjun—*a coward*

copatin—*a Witch's tall, black, pointed hat (initially, a primitive helmet)*

covendom—*an area where Witches exercise their secret sway regarding events; traditionally, it spans a league (3 miles around a covenstead)*

cowan—*initially, any non-initiate; in modern times, one who may not practice magic, but treats the Wise as friends*

D

dawnten—*to tame by kindness*

decantate—*to sing or chant a charm*

delator—*an accuser of Witches, such as*

a neighbor, magical rival, or
   fundamentalist detractor

dern—*a secret*

desterine—*to trouble; to annoy*

deze—*to die; dead*

dirge-ales—*funeral toasts honoring one
   who has crossed over to the
   Summerlands*

dole—*sorrow; pain; disaster; misfortune*

douter—*a candlesnuffer*

dree—*to endure; to suffer*

dwale—*nightshade; poison potion or
   drug—what warders were bribed to
   convey to Witches in prison to enable
   them to withstand torture or commit
   suicide during the Burning Times*

E

eem—*leisure; spare time*

envoutement—*casting a spell using a
   picture or image of a person or an
   object*

F

fand—*to try out, prove, or experiment
   (as with spells)*

fennyere—*in former times; in your last
   incarnation*

fone—*foes; enemies*

frem, fren—*strangers (introducing
   anyone as a frem or fren warns others
   to be wary—the newcomer typically
   believes you referred to them as a
   friend)*

G

gabel—*a tax or regular payment*

gamp—*a midwife*

God-pays—*anyone who obtains credit
   with no intention to eliminate the
   debt Priests used to buy goods, then
   claims they had no money but that
   God would pay.*

H

hele—*to hide; to preserve; to conceal; to
   keep secret*

hidel—*a hiding place, secret storage
   space, or refuge*

hwyl—*a very emotional invocation to
   the God/desses*

hyght—*vowed; promised*

I

invultuation—*using wax images in
   spellwork*

J

jauk—*to trifle with or mislead another*

jossa—*a standstill*

K

ka-me, ka-thee—*"Do me a favor, and
   I'll do one for you"*

kittle-kattle—*dangerous; ticklish, as in
   a tricky problem*

kokum—*false sympathy*

L

leasynge—*lying*
liche—*the body*
ligge—*play*
lin—*to stop; to stay*
lown—*villain*

M

masar—*a goblet as used in magic or during Cakes and Wine*
meacock—*a cowardly man*
mickle—*much; great; very*
muckle-ganging—*walking much*

N

natterjack—*a toad (traditional Witch familiar)*

P

pawky—*shrewd, cunning; astute*
pollrumptious—*noisy; violent*
provulge—*to publish; to make public, such as admitting you work magic to friends and family*

Q

qualtagh—*the first person you meet after leaving the covenstead—their sex, demeanor, hair color, and course portend the spell's outcome*

R

raith—*a quarter-year or season of three months*

R

rapper—*an enormous lie or a strong oath taken to confirm a lie*
reuth—*pity*

S

sark—*a shirt*
scafe—*to wander; to camp out*
scoper—*the last meal of the day*
shewing—*a warning; images seen in a shewstone, crystal ball, or dream*
(a) simple—*a medicinal potion made up of a single herb and an alcoholic liquid that extracts its properties*
skere—*to escape; to get clear*
snast—*a candlewick*
so-gates—*"Do it in this manner, this way"*
stravage—*to wander boldly*
sweaven—*a dream*

T

tapinige—*to skulk; to initiate intrigue*
tene—*grief*
tentie—*careful*
thingus—*a noble man; royalty or one who acts with genteel aplomb*
toledo—*originally, a magician who studied at Tollet, or Toledo, Spain; more recently, a Witchy password*
tout—*buttocks*
tray—*anger*
truckle—*to submit under pressure*

𝒱
verdugo—*a tormentor*

𝒲
wale—*to cause misery; to damage; to massacre*

wanchancy—*unlucky; uncertain; bad to attempt*

weathersacting—*prophesying what the weather will be*

wede, wode—*mad; wild; berserk*

welkin—*the sky*

𝒴
yeuling—*dancing around fruit trees to ensure a good crop*

yill-caup—*an ale mug*

OLDE SPELL INGREDIENT NAMES

You may feel confused or even a tad horrified when you read spells that call for snake's blood, a man's bile, or a pig's tail. Don't despair, however—the ancients didn't necessarily mandate that you use those types of ingredients. Such ghastly names frequently derived from descriptions of a spell ingredient's appearance, or how an herb worked according to the olde Doctrine of Signatures, the observed fact that many plants physically resemble the bodily organ or system they can either harm or cure.

Snake's blood, for example, is really only another name for the semi-precious stone hematite. You can understand why spellcrafters applied such a nickname to it when you recall that hematite is iron and, therefore, red on the inside, resembling blood. When hematite is polished, it's also silvery black on the outside, a color long associated with the night and, therefore, magic. Furthermore, snakes are nocturnal and prefer to hunt after dark. Therefore, *snake's blood* is an excellent name for a gem that imbues wearers with the strength of iron from within, and the silvery stealth of a moonlit night from without.

Many lists of folk names for plants and spell components exist. As usual, we caution you not to stress over memorizing their contents. Rather, take them under advisement in their entirety.

The following table translating olde spell ingredient names comes from the *Greek Magical Papyri in Translation: Including the Demotic Spells.*

blood from a head—*lupine; wolf's blood or hair*

blood from a shoulder/bear's breach—*the plant hellebore, probably* Acanthus mollis L. *or* Helleborus foetidus L.

blood of a goose—*mulberry tree milk (sap)*

blood of an eye—*a tamarisk's gall*

blood of Ares—*the purslane plant*

blood of a snake—*hematite*

blood of Hephaistos—*wormwood*

blood of Hestia—*chamomile*

bone of an ibis—*the buckthorn plant*

bull's semen—*the egg of a blister beetle*

crocodile dung—*Ethiopian soil or dirt from Africa*

eagle—*wild garlic, possibly* Trigonella foenumgraecum

from the belly—*Earth apple*

from the foot—*the herb houseleek*

from the loins—*chamomile*

hairs of a Hamadryas baboon—*dill seed*

hawk's heart—*heart (fleshy, inner pith) of the wormwood plant*

Kronos's blood—*cedar*

Kronos's spice—*piglet's milk*

lion semen—*a human male's sperm*

lion's hairs—*tongue of a turnip (the leaves of a turnip's taproot)*

man's bile—*turnip sap, probably* Brassica napus L.

physician's bone—*sandstone*

pig's tail—*the plant leopard's bane, probably a variety of the genus* boronicum, *or one of the heliotropes (sunlike plants*)

semen of Ammon—*the herb houseleek*

semen of Ares—*clover*

semen of Helios—*white hellebore*

semen of Hephaistos—*the herb fleabane*

semen of Herakles (Hercules)—*mustard-rocket (probably* Eruca sativa)

semen of Hermes (Mercury)—*dill*

snake's ball of thread—*soapstone*

snake's head—*a leech*

tears (or sleep sand) of a Hamadryas baboon—*dill juice*

Titan's blood—*wild lettuce*

From *Abracadabra* to *Zomelak*
Barbarous Words of Power

"Shall we write about the things not to be spoken of?
Shall we divulge the things not to be divulged?
Shall we pronounce the things not to be pronounced?"
—EMPEROR JULIAN THE APOSTATE
"HYMN TO THE MOTHER OF THE GODS"

itches have always used Barbarous Words to add power to spells. Barbarous Words are usually ancient. Every country had its own particularly preferred Barbarous Words of Power, but they all shared certain commonalities, such as being spoken only during spellwork, or in times of dire emergency. They were words whose efficacy spellcrafters had reached consensus about; through millennia of use, the words grew mighty in and of themselves.

The author and magical practitioner Dion Fortune well knew the importance of employing Barbarous Words of Power "in the operation of transforming the forces of one plane, into their correspondences on a lower and denser level."

In her book *Esoteric Orders & Their Works,* Fortune explained:

"Upon the subtler planes are many different types of force, each with its own vibration-rhythm; if the rate of that rhythm can be discovered, and either its root or prime factors be ascertained, and sounds be formulated which have the vibration-rate of the several factors, and these be enunciated in sequence, they will evoke the complementary vibration in the subtle body which corresponds to the plane of the potency it is intended to evoke, just as the musical tone causes the color to which it bears a ratio to rise in consciousness. This is the rationale of the use of Sacred Names and Words of Power."

Through experience, Crafters learn that certain sacred Deity names and ancient words are as inherently powerful as the colors red, blue, green, and yellow, or the fixed musical tones everyone takes for granted. Because Barbarous Words of Power have been used in rites, rituals, and spells for eons, they naturally contain their own inherent power. By using them during spellwork, you can coax them to expend this energy on your behalf.

If you want to make your spells more potent, just chant, sing, or repeat the following Barbarous Words of Power. Note that pronunciations given are approximate; accented syllables are indicated where known. *R* should be trilled.

THE EPHESIA GRAMMATA

Known to 4th century B.C.E. Cretans and Greeks as "the Ephesian vengeance," the *ephesia grammata* (Ephesian letters) was a magical formula of six words famous in the ancient world for imbuing a possessor or speaker "with great power, both defensive and aggressive":[33]

Askion
Kataskion
Lix
Tetrax
Damnameneus
Aision

(AH-skee-on,
kah-TAH-skee-on,
LEEKS,
teh-TRAKS,
DAHM-nah-meh-NEH-oos,
AY-see-on)

One of the many ancient uses of this formula was to provide magical protection for newlyweds. Another was in sports—ancient Greek writers told of an Ephesian wrestler who wore the words inscribed on an amulet during a match with a Milesian. At first the Milesian could not wrestle at all; but after the amulet was discovered and removed, he threw the Ephesian thirty times.

For a protective spell that employs the first two words in the form *Askei Kataskei,* see To Avert Imminent, Life-threatening Peril, page 447.

[33] John G. Gager, *Curse Tablets and Binding Spells from the Ancient World* (Oxford: Oxford University Press, 1992), 6.

ANAZAPTA
(an-ah-ZAP-tah)

Anazapta is an ancient God of healing. The olde Anazapta rhyme below would make a fine chant whenever you're healing someone.

> *For Anazapta slayeth Death*
> *where'er an He may be,*
> *Thrice each day*
> *Anazapta say*
> *and Death will fly from thee.*

Chant Anazapta throughout a healing or during similar spellwork.

NEPHERIE'RI
(Neh-feh-ree-EH-ree)

Possibly Old Coptic, from the ancient *Papyri Graecae Magicae* (*PGM*, IV. 1265–74), Nepherie'ri is an olde Egyptian name for the Goddess Hathor. It means "[She of] the beautiful eye." Nepherie'ri is an epithet of the Great Mother in an aspect similar to Aphrodite, the Greek Goddess of love.

Chant Nepherie'ri throughout your spell whenever you want to imbue it with the kind of tender care mothers and doting girlfriends shower on those they love.

"If you wish to win a woman who is beautiful," says the PGM, chant the name over an offering of frankincense to Aphrodite, then "say it seven times in your soul" when you approach the woman, and do so for seven days.

EKO, EKO

The word *eko* is probably from the same root as the Latin *ecce*, "behold," as in *Ecce homo*, "Behold the man." Chant or sing Eko, Eko with these God/dess names to summon the power of each of the Four Quarters.

East	*Eko, Eko Azarak*
South	*Eko, Eko Zomelak*
West	*Eko, Eko Cernunnos*
North	*Eko, Eko Aradia*

*(EH-koh, EH-koh AH-zah-rahk
EH-koh, EH-koh ZOH-meh-lahk
EH-koh, EH-koh kehr-NOO-nohs
EH-koh, EH-koh ah-RAH-dee-ah)*

MERTALIA, MUSALIA, DOPHALIA, ONEMALIA, ZITANSEIA

*(mehr-TAH-lee-ah, moo-SAH-lee-ah, doh-FAH-lee-ah,
oh-neh-MAH-lee-ah, zih-TAHN-say-ah)*

Recite when you magically purify or consecrate water to use in spellwork.

YAMENTON, YARON, TATONON, ZARMESITON, TILEON, TIXMION

*(yah-MEN-ton, YAR-on, TAHT-oh-non, zar-MEH-sit-on,
TEE-leh-on, TEEKS-mee-on)*

Say when you add consecrated salt to consecrated water, typically done at the beginning of magic rites or spellwork.

THAZI N EPIBATHA CHEOUCH CHA
(THAH-zee neh-PIH-bah-thah KHEH-ookh KHAH)

This love charm is from the *Papyri Graecae Magicae,* VII. 405–6. While kissing someone passionately, whisper:

*I am Thazi N Epibatha Cheouch Cha.
I am
I am
Chariemouth Lailam.
(KHAH-ree-eh-mooth LAH-ee-lahm)*

Add your wish for love at this point.

THE BAGAHI RUNE

Chant the Bagahi numerous times to empower your spells with primal masculine strength and energy.

*Bagahi Laca Bachahe
Lamac Cahi Achabahe.
Karrelyos!*

*Lamac Lamec Bachalyos.
Cabahagi Sabalyos,
Baryolas!!*

*Lagozatha Cabyolas.
Samahac et famyolas,
Harrahya!!!*

*(bah-GAH-hee LAH-ka BAH-khah-hey
lah-MAHK kah-HEE ah-KHAH-bah-hey.
kah-RREL-yohs!*

*lah-MAHK lah-MEHK bah-KHAH-lee-ohs.
kah-BAH-hah-GEE sah-BAH-lee-ohs,
bah-RREE-oh-lahs!!*

*lah-GOH-zah-THAH kah-BEE-oh-lahs
Sah-MAH-HAHK EHT fah-MEE-oh-lahs,
Hah-RRAH-hee-yah!!!)*

THE HE-GOAT ABOVE, THE HE-GOAT BELOW

*Akkera Goiti,
Akkera Beiti!
(ahk-KEH-rah goh-EE-tee,
ahk-KEH-rah beh-EE-tee!)*

Repeat as needed to praise and evoke balanced masculine strength and energies.

EURUS
(YOO-ruhs)

Chant this Barbarous Word of Power to summon the East Wind.

NOTUS
(NOH-tuhs)

Chant to summon the South Wind.

ZEPHYRUS
(ZEHF-ur-uhs)

Chant to summon the West Wind.

BOREAS
(BOHR-ee-ahs)

Chant to summon the North Wind.

IO EVO HE
(EE-oh EH-voh hay)

Io Evo He was originally an ecstatic cry of worshippers of Dionysus. Modern Witches now chant Io Evo He as an aid to meditation, as a call to begin ritual, or as a way of raising energy. This chant can induce a magical trance state during spellwork. If many people intone it indoors in a circle, it quickly sets up such a powerful resonance that the very walls may shake!

Similar ancient calling words, some of them derived from Io Evo He, are listed on following pages.

Eheie
Iehoua
Evoe Evoe
Emen Haten
Ab hur, Ab hus
Ho! Ho! Ho!, Ise! Ise! Ise!
Ieo Veo Veo Veo, Veov Orov, Ov Ovovo

You may elect to chant the Ieo Veo as a spell in and of itself, but it is best employed to summon folks to begin a ritual.

ABRACADABRA
(AH-brah-kah-DAH-brah)

This most famous of all Barbarous Words of Power first appears in recorded history as a charm to cure fever. (See To Break a Fever, p. 268.) Although theories about its origin abound, *abracadabra* likely derives from the Chaldean words *abbâdâ ke dâbrâ,* which mean "perish like the word."[34]

APHEIBOE'O'
(ah-feh-ee-boh-EH-oh)

This heartfelt and powerful prayer for help from the Moon is from *PGM*, VII. 756–94. In the concluding invocation, pronounce vowels that are followed by an apostrophe as long vowels, and *ch* as *kh*.

I call upon You
who have All Forms and Many Names.

Double-Horned Goddess, Mene, whose Form no one knows
except Him who made the entire World, IAU,

---

[34] *Sir E. A. Wallis Budge,* Amulets and Talismans *(University Books, 1961). Cited by Raymond Buckland,* The Witch Book: The Encyclopedia of Witchcraft, Wicca, and Neo-paganism *(Canton, Mich.: Visible Ink Press, 2002), 2.*

the One who shaped You into Twenty-Eight Shapes of the World
so that they might complete every Figure and distribute Breath
to every Animal and Plant, that it might Flourish.

You who grow from Obscurity into Light
and leave Light for Darkness.

And the First Companion of Your Name is silence.
The second, a popping sound.
The third, groaning.
The fourth, hissing.
The fifth, a cry of joy.
The sixth, moaning.
The seventh, barking.
The eighth, bellowing.
The ninth, neighing.
The tenth, a musical sound.
The eleventh, a sounding wind.
The twelfth, a wind-creating sound.
The thirteenth, a coercive sound.
The fourteenth, a coercive emanation from perfection.

Ox, Vulture, Bull, Beetle, Falcon, Crab, Dog, Wolf,
Serpent, Horse, She-Goat, Asp, Goat, He-Goat, Baboon,
Cat, Lion, Leopard, Field-Mouse, Deer, Multi-Form,
Virgin, Torch, Lightning, Garland, a Herald's Wand, Child, Key.

I have said Your Signs and Symbols of Your Name
so that You might hear me, because I pray to You.

Mistress of the Whole World, Hear me,
You the Stable One, the Mighty One!

APHEIBOE'O' MINTE'R OCHAO'
PIZEPHYDO'R CHANTHAR CHADE'ROZO

*MOCHTHION EOT- NEU PHE'RZON
AINDE'S LACHABOO' PITTO'
RIPHTHAMER ZMOMOCHO'LEIE
TIE'DRANTEIA OISOZOCHABE'DO'PHRA.*

State your prayer desire at this point, and then listen and watch for one of la Luna's sounds or symbols; if one does occur, it is a goodly omen that your need will be met.

**THOATHOE'THATHO-
OYTHAETHO'USTHOAITHITHE'THOINTHO'**
(*THOH-ah-THOH-eh-THAH-thoh
ohü-THAH-eh-thoh-oos-thoh-ah-EE-thee-theh-THOH-een-THOH*)

From *PGM*, XCII. 1-16:

*Everyone fears Your Great Might.
Grant me the Good Things:*

*The Strength of AKRYSKYLOS,
the Speech of EUO'NOS,
the Eyes of Solomon,
the Voice of ABRASAX,
the Grace of ADO'NIOS, the God.*

*Come to me, Kypris, every day!
The Hidden Name bestowed to You:
Thoathoe'Thatho-Oythaetho'Usthoaithithe'Thointho'
Grant me Victory, Repute, Beauty toward all Men and all Women!*

Intone this invocation whenever you need abundant magical favor.

UTPA, TPAU, PAUT, AUTP

Following are examples of Enochian angel names divined in the 1500s by magician John Dee and seer Edward Kelly. Pronounce them as you see fit. Most of them are acrostics, or rearrangements of four letters, as here:

U	T
A	P

To protect yourself from mishap and prevent breakage, theft, or loss of goods while traveling or moving, chant the Enochian name of God (shown in capital letters) and the four angels who correspond to the direction toward which you're going:

East	*EUTPA*
	Utpa, Tpau, Paut, Autp
South	*EPHRA*
	Phra, Hrap, Raph, Aphr
West	*ATDIM*
	Tdim, Dimt, Imtd, Mtdi
North	*AANAA*
	Anaa, Naaa, Aaan, Aana

Need to learn UNIX fast to qualify for a promotion? Chant the names **Cnbr, Nbrc, Brcn, Rcnb** during spellwork to evoke aid in understanding computers and other complex machinery.

This Enochian chant will compel your cranky, old, electrically shorting household appliances to start working: **Roan, Oanr, Anro, Nroa**.

Repeat the names **Ziza, Izaz, Zazi, Aziz** to learn the Craft secrets other Witches know.

Do you want your spell to be as solid as a rock? Wish you had help learning the magical powers of diverse metals and gems? Then chant the names of angels skilled in geology and metallurgy: **Gmnm, Ecop, Amox, Brap**.

Secret Writing

Letters, Glyphs, and Runes

"All things are full of signs, and it is a wise man who can learn about one thing from another."

—Plotinus

Whereas spoken spells convey your thought through ephemeral sound, written spells transform thought into tangible matter.

Writing has always been a sacred art. The very word for a mystical working—*spell*—reminds us that letters were originally the province of Priest/esses.

Modern Crafters perpetuate this hallowed tradition by converting mundane words that describe our needs into a magical script or sigil that helps us magically manifest them.

Magical Alphabets

Witches use magical alphabets to encode spells that they want to remain secret, to increase the efficacy of their workings, and to connect with spirits and God/desses in a sacred manner. Furthermore, it's simply prudent to develop cryptic writing skills in case you ever require a discreet mode of communication.

An alphabet is esteemed as magical if it is:

- *ancient,* such as Sanskrit
- *picturesque,* such as hieroglyphs, runes, or Celestial letters
- *obscure,* such as Cymry and Ogham
- *known traditionally to be effective,* such as Theban,[35] Enochian, and *Transitus Fluvii,* or Passing the River[36]

Hundreds of magical alphabets exist, ranging in style from primitively powerful to hauntingly beautiful.

Other lovely, fascinating magical scripts include Phoenician, Canaanite, Appolonian,[37] Etruscan, Friesian, Rose Cross Cipher, and Libyan Tifnagh. The more arcane and little known your choice of alphabet, the safer your mystical encryptions will be.

Crafters first convert utilitarian letters or numbers into a divine alphabet, then arrange the encrypted signs in numerous ways to confuse prying eyes further. For instance, Witches often repeat, delete, shuffle, or anagrammatize such letters, and even insert arbitrary characters as an intentional blind to mislead unauthorized readers.

Another traditional way to protect your magical writings is to append tiny circles randomly to the ends of your letter strokes. For example, a capital *A* would have a circle atop it and two anchoring circles for feet and resemble an overview of a triangular fort with three turrets. Although magically meaningless, such circles are nonetheless successfully distracting.

Witches routinely add extra power to their encryptions by drawing them with a magical ink. Examples include invisible ink (lemon juice), sepia ink (coffee liquid), and a royal-purple ink called dragon's blood ink (which we make by pressing, straining, and fermenting pokeweed berries; you may elect to make the ink from the plant bearing its name [see Glossary: Magical and Medical

---

[35] *Theban is said to be named for Honorius of Thebes, a 13th-century magician who helped preserve the secrets of the Art Magical from papal persecution in* The Sworn Book of Honorius.

[36] *The version of Passing the River illustrated opposite is Raymond Buckland's English-language adaptation. The older version found in Agrippa's* Three Books of Occult Philosophy, *which is based on the Hebrew alphabet, lacks too many letters to be useful for encoding non-Hebraic words.*

[37] *A medieval script attributed to the famous Pagan Appolonius of Tyana recorded in 1586 by B. de Vignere in* Traicte' des Chiffres, ou Secretes Manieres d'Escrire.

MAGICAL ALPHABETS

THEBAN

A	B	C	D	E	F	G	H
I/J	K	L	M	N	O	P	Q
R	S	T	U/V/W	X	Y	Z	PERIOD

PASSING THE RIVER (*Buckland*)

A	B	C	D	E	F	G	H
I/J	K	L	M	N	O/Q	P	
R	S	T	U/V		W	X	Y	Z

GREEK

Greek letter	Greek name	English letter(s)[1]	Pronunciation	Magical pronunciation[2]
A α	alpha	A	All	"with an open mouth, undulating like a wave"
B β	beta	B	Bard	
Γ γ	gamma	G	Gift	
Δ δ	delta	D	Door	
E ε	epsilon	E	mElt	"like a baboon"
Z ζ	zeta	Z	aDZe	
H η	eta	E'	fEY	"with enjoyment, aspirating it"
Θ θ	theta	TH	THorn	
I ι	iota	I	ravIne	"[pronounce] IAO' to earth, to air, and to heaven"
K κ	kappa	K	Kiss	
Λ λ	lambda	L	Lore	
M μ	mu	M	Moon	
N ν	nu	N	Nick	
Ξ ξ	xi	X	flaX	
O o	omicron	O	nOr	"succinctly, as a breathed threat"
Π π	pi	P	Pyre	
P ρ	rho	R	Ride	
Σ σ,s	sigma	S	Song	
T τ	tau	T	Tell	
Y υ	upsilon	Y or U	nUde	"like a shepherd, drawing out the pronunciation"
Φ φ	phi	PH	Fish	
X χ	chi	CH	elK Hide	
Ψ ψ	psi	PS	tiPS	
Ω ω	omega	O'	Olde	"[pronounce] IAO' to earth, to air, and to heaven"

[1]An apostrophe after an E or O represents the long form of the vowel, which the Greek alphabet distinguishes from the short form but the English alphabet does not.
[2]The "Oracle of Sarapis," a spell in the *Greek Magical Papyri (PGM V.1-53)*, gives these instructions for pronouncing the nine letters in the Barbarous Words AOIAO' EOE'Y.

RUNIC

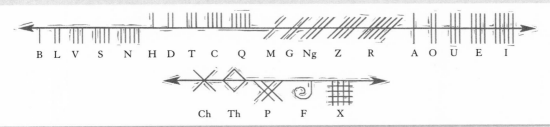

| F | U | Th | A | R | K | G | W | H | N | I |
| J | E | P | Z | S | T | B | E | M | L | Ng | O | D |

OGHAM

| B | L | V | S | N | H | D | T | C | Q | M | G | Ng | Z | R | A | O | U | E | I |

| Ch | Th | P | F | X |

Herbs, pg. 449). The latter is highly toxic and odiferous, so label it as a poison-ous bane, add a few drops of any essential oil to minimize its repellence, and shake it thoroughly for optimum consistency before each use.

Experiment with your own ideas regarding kitchen ingredients or garden plants that you think could produce goodly magical inks. Label and date con-tainers, and stow several varieties for future use.

When working with magical alphabets, don't confine yourself to conven-tional left-to-right writing:

- Write from right to left and upside-down. Such a message, called a *wendrune,* is best read reflected in a mirror.
- Use your sentences like brush strokes—write them in spirals, or word labyrinths that meander around a page.
- Paint a picture by filling in a faint line drawing with repeated phrases.
- Form "letter trees" by stacking one character atop another.
- Divide geometric shapes such as circles or triangles into sections, assign letters to each slice, then use only the curves or angles of the appropriate section to denote characters.

You can also convert numbers into a mystical script. This is particularly helpful whenever you're conjuring money or creating a spell or communiqué that involves a time, a date, coordinates, or other identifying numerals, such as an address or a telephone or social security number.

AGRIPPA'S SECRET NUMBER SIGNS

Agrippa describes these in his *Three Books of Occult Philosophy,* Book II, Chapter 19:

> *"I found in two most ancient books of Astrologers, and Magicians, certain most elegant marks of numbers, which I thought good to set down in this place; Now they were in both Volums [volumes] such."*

1. 2. 3. 4. 5. 6. 7. 8. 9.

"Now by these markes turned to the left hand are made tens, after this manner."

10. 20. 30. 40. 50. 60. 70. 80. 90.

"And by those markes which are turned downwards on the right hand, are made hundreds; on the left thousands, viz. thus."

100. 200. 300. 400. 500. 600. 700. 800. 900.

1000. 2000. 3000. 4000. 5000. 6000. 7000. 8000. 9000.

"And by the composition, and mixture of these markes other mixt and compounded numbers also are most elegantly made, as you may perceive by these few."

1510. 1511. 1471. 1486. 2421.

"According to the example of which we must proceed in other compound numbers."

When you've mastered traditional magical alphabets, create your own, using dots, dashes, or dingbats. Use any simple idea or image you can conceive of to stand for each alphabet letter. Experiment with letter position: For example, you can assign one *A* four different meanings depending on how you align it on a page—straight up, inverted, or pointing sideways left or right.

MAKING BINDRUNES

A bindrune is a symbol made from a combination of letters, similar to a monogram. Making a bindrune involves reducing one or more spell desires into a single glyph that you then use as a spell ingredient, or wear to achieve your wishes. First, translate your ideas into a few key words, and then translate them into a magical alphabet. Finally, morph the letters together or join them in places to produce an aesthetically pleasing, magically powerful pictogram.

Before making a bindrune, select the magical alphabet to work with that seems most appropriate for your needs. Sometimes your primary consideration may be the alphabet's ease of execution; at other times, you may want a complex alphabet to help prevent anyone from deciphering your work.

Making bindrunes takes practice, so for your initial efforts, minimize the learning curve by using a linear alphabet such as Runic or Ogham. Runic is quickly executed compared to other alphabets, and can be surreptitiously scratched in the dirt with your foot, or readily carved, painted, or wood-burned onto spell ingredients or magical crafts. Such primitive alphabets are especially suitable whenever you're working primal magic.

More embellished alphabets, such as Theban, Celestial, Enochian, or Passing the River, lend a calligraphic style of adornment for needlework, decorative borders on mystical messages, announcements, invitations, gift tags, and so forth. Such stylized alphabets are excellent to use when you crave flourish in your magical workings.

When composing bindrunes, eliminate any recurring letters or letter portions in your key word(s) or focus phrase. For instance, suppose you want to create an identifying bindrune in the Runic alphabet for your Craft name—say, Rainbowmare. Write down your name; then delete any repeated letters. In this example, getting rid of one *a* and one *r* should result in the core word *Rainbowme*.

RAINBOWMARE

RAINBOWM~~AR~~E

RAINBOWME

After you've removed all extraneous letters, convert the letters that remain to their corresponding matches in your chosen magical alphabet. Then connect the letters in various places until you achieve one symmetrical glyph. Polish your drawing until you're aesthetically satisfied with your results and it seems to practically buzz with power of its own accord.

Another way to create a bindrune is to use the Magic Grid Cipher[38] (also called the Rose Cross Cipher). Draw a tic-tac-toe template. Beginning in its upper left, write three letters of the alphabet at a time in each compartment.

ABC	DEF	GHI
JKL	MNO	PQR
STU	VWX	YZ&

For each letter of your key word(s), draw the grid compartment in which it appears; and zero, one, or two dots in its compartment depending on whether it is the first, second, or third letter, respectively. For example, here is the Magic Grid Cipher for the word *love*:

L   O   V   E

To convert these letters into a bindrune, superimpose them and eliminate all overlapping lines and dots.

LOVE

The charm is most potent if it resembles your magical goal. In the bindrune above, the word *love* has been reduced to two dots inside a square, suggesting two mates sharing a home.

---

[38] *Bill Whitcomb,* The Magician's Companion: A Practical and Encyclopedic Guide to Magical and Religious Symbolism *(Los Angeles: Llewellyn Publications, 1983). Whitcomb accords it Masonic/Rosicrucian derivation.*

Although transposing an ordinary alphabet into a more magical form and transforming letters into bindrunes requires practice and precision, sanctifying your desire in such fashion sharpens your spellwork concentration, thereby increasing the likelihood that your spell will succeed. Wear bindrunes you create until your wish is granted.

Making Sigils and Seals

A sigil is a mystic sign that conveys a central idea. Sigils are artistic depictions or shorthand summations of a status, an issue, or a directive. For example, a smiley face signifies happiness, whereas a frowning face with knit brows signifies worry, sadness, or anger.

Sigils pervade the planet, ranging from the recycling symbol on plastic bottles, to the skull and crossbones warning of piracy or poison. When a sigil is perpetuated long enough, it can become universally recognizable, such as the "no" sign, a red circle with a diagonal slash.

The peace sign is a goodly example of a sigil derived from a secret source—the maritime semaphore alphabet that employs waving flags to communicate messages from ship to ship. According to its inventor, a 1950s British peace activist who was a professional graphic designer, the peace sign takes its vertical line from the semaphore for *D*, and its inverted V shape from *N*—together, ND for nuclear disarmament. The designer also intended its shape to suggest a human figure holding its arms downward in a gesture deploring violence. The whole is surrounded with an encompassing circle connoting unity, similar to the way in which magical seals are encapsulated (as with the love bindrune above). People protesting the Vietnam War in the 1960s adopted it as a more general symbol of peace.

For every idea that you'd like to portray symbolically, a powerful mystical sigil for it probably already exists to help you convey it. Below is a smattering of sigils[39] you can refer to when beginning to compose your own:

N

D

[39] *Adapted from* Magic Symbols, *Frederick Goodman (London: Brian Todd Publishing House, 1989).*

ankh—*an Egyptian hieroglyph meaning life and reincarnation*

arch or rainbow—*equates with spirit*

asterisk—*denotes a dead language, such as Oscan, or a secret message*

circle—*unity; encompassment; zodiacal applications*

clover—*goodly luck; serendipity*

crescent—*magic; mysticism; secrets; nighttime; (horns of) power*

cross—*the Four Elements; the Four Directions; the Four Lesser Sabbats (the equinoxes and solstices)*

egg—*fertility; potential; birth; progeny*

eight-fold Wheel of the Year—*time; the seasons*

eye—*a Strega sigil for protection against the Evil Eye; perception; vigilance*

flower—*attraction; beauty; ambiance*

foot—*travel; journey*

heart—*love; desire; altruism*

hexagram, or Star of David *(overlapping, opposing triangles)—As above, So below; spiritual and material realms combined; totality; often used to symbolize the Sun*

infinity symbol *(a horizontal figure 8)—eternity; an ongoing event or circumstance*

intertwined rings—*a couple; twins; siblings; relatives; a bond*

inverted pentagram *(five-pointed star pointing down)—the Horned God, such as Pan; the Second-Degree symbol in Gardnerian Witchcraft*

keys—*wisdom; the power to decipher occult secrets or find lost objects*

ouraboros *(a circular serpent that bites its own tail)—cyclicity; perpetuity; encompassment*

outward palm—*stop; "none shall pass"*

Piscean fish *(two fishes portrayed yin-yang style)—harmony of soul and spirit*

slash or cross-hatching—*forbiddance; prohibition; strife; suffering*

spiral—*way; route. An inward spiral symbolizes a quest for, or the attainment of, wisdom; an outward spiral represents a physical journey.*

square—*an ancient symbol for planet Earth; matter; foundation; containment; constriction*

star—*an Egyptian hieroglyph meaning "night"; aspiration; hope; goal*

sun—*health; growth; daytime; summer*

sword—*force; physical strength; will*

triangle—*Spirit; the shape that constrains a conjured spirit; harmony; a group effort*

turtle—*longevity; a Native American symbol for land and planet Earth* udjat *(a stylized, Egyptian eye)—the all-seeing eye of Horus, a Sun God; protection against the Evil Eye*

upright pentagram *(five-pointed star pointing upward)—protection against ill luck; the Four Elements plus Spirit; the generative template for organic life; a hand; the human body*

vesica piscis *(the intersection of two overlapping circles)—female genitalia; the generative universe*

vines *(flowing from an urn)—an ancient sigil for prosperity; growth; plenitude*

wheel—*movement; steerage; command*

X—*no; here; yourself; the Four Greater Sabbats of Imbolc, Beltane, Lammas, and Samhain*

yin-yang symbol—*balance of light and dark; polarity; sexual parity*

SIMPLE SIGILS

To Thwart Theft

To Prevent Jealousy

To Dispel Depression

For Luck & Longevity

Many books detailing magical symbolism exist to help you learn the meanings of basic sigils. Once you realize how simple and targeted such signs are, you'll feel more capable of devising your own when the need arises. For instance, say you desire to protect your premises from the Evil Eye. Crafters' most common protective sign against the phenomenon is one open staring eye, occasionally depicted with lids, but rarely lashes.

Generally, the more primitively you draw your sigils, the more powerfully they serve your magical purposes. When you're beginning, every flourish and curlicue could correspond to a pre-set meaning of which you're unaware, so avoid making unexpected and unintended magical mistakes caused by excess embellishment until you're well on your way to mastering this skill.

When beginning to devise a sigil, consider what your main idea or magical wish is, or what changes must occur for your wish to be fulfilled. Conceive of a glyph that summarizes your desire, and then draw it on parchment or virgin (unused) paper. Ensure that your basic design is symmetrical and aesthetic, then add any necessary symbolic details, such as the manner in which your wish should manifest—add an elemental glyph, for instance. To depict its material or spiritual nature, draw it slanting, pointing, or facing right or left, respectively.

You can also construct time-specific sigils. Use a cross or an X template that indicates the applicable season or Sabbat; then add simple, appropriate signs that symbolize your magical need or goal.

Don't attract ill luck by drawing something negative—create only positive

---

EXAMPLES OF TIME-SPECIFIC SIGILS

BELTANE   LAMMAS

IMBOLC   SAMHAIN

1. Make an X representing the 4 annual Greater Sabbats.

For food through winter   For Divine aid traveling to a Beltane Gathering   For Divine aid in making Yule gifts

2. Add a specific symbol at the appropriate Sabbat point to create different spell sigils.

---

sigils that depict your desired outcome. For instance, if your car is kaput and you need reliable transportation, don't draw the old wreck that's the source of your quandary—instead, draw your dream machine.

MAKING MAGICAL SEALS

Magical seals are everywhere—mounted above a judge's bench, embroidered on a state flag, etched on coins and currency. The seal is an object imbued with numinous power, with energy. Without the bit of gold foil or red wax that certifies your diploma as authentic, it's nothing but worthless wallpaper.

Such seals follow the same principle of design that spellcrafters have used for millennia: Meaningful sigils are surrounded by a sacred enclosure. Ancient Egyptian cartouches were seals that depicted the Pharaoh's name in hieroglyphs encircled with a cord tied by a knot. In Greco-Roman times, Crafters carved gemstone talismans with seals that enclosed sigils such as the figure of a God/dess or Barbarous Words of Power within an ouraboros, a snake that bites its own tail—an image likely descended from the cartouche cord. (See the Abraxas seal on page 278.) Today, official seals still include God/dess figures and such traditional symbols as sheaves of wheat or a cornucopia (for plenty), an eagle (for power), or a scepter or crown (for rulership), typically encompassed by a circular band inscribed with a motto or stars.

The following traditional technique for making a magical seal summons the power of a particular planet to your cause. You convert the letters that make up your target's name or a key spell word(s) into their numerological equivalents, then draw them on the magic square of the corresponding planet. In a magic square, all the numbers in any given vertical, horizontal, or diagonal row add up to the same total. For example, in the square of Saturn, every row of numbers totals 15.[40]

First, decide which planet best corresponds to your magical purpose. For example, use Saturn to bind or constrain someone from doing harm; Jupiter, to draw wealth and prosperity; Mars, to evoke strength and courage to face an intimidating situation; the Sun, to improve health; Venus, to attract a lover; Mercury, to instill mental clarity and eloquence; and the Moon, to increase psychism and hone your instincts.

Your seal will be all the more powerful if you draw it during the day and hour of the planet you're working with. (See Timing Spells for Maximum Efficacy, page 102.) You will need a couple of pieces of parchment or virgin paper, scissors, ruler, a drawing compass, and a pen and ink of the appropriate planetary color.

SATURN = black

JUPITER = purple or blue

MARS = red

SUN = gold

VENUS = green

MERCURY = gray (pencil color)

MOON = silver

You will also need the appropriate planetary incense with which to consecrate the seal after you are finished making it. (See The Seven Planets and Their

[40] Tyson, "Appendix V—Magic Squares," in Agrippa, *Three Books of Occult Philosophy, 1531/1993. This is the best exploration anywhere of the planetary magic-number squares and the sigils derived from them.*

Properties, page 88.) You may want to use a light table or a piece of white cardboard to help you see and trace the designs.

Next, write either the name of the person you wish to affect (your name or another's) or one or two words that concisely express your magical desire. For example, if you want to heal a particular person, you might write his or her full name. If you want to make an all-purpose talisman for health, you might use the words *health* or *get well*.

Convert the letters of the name or word(s) into their numerical equivalents, using the following diagram.

THE LETTER-TO-NUMBER SYSTEM we show here is the very same one the olde magicians used, but adapted to the English alphabet, which we've rounded out with the ampersand (&) rather than the Greek or Hebrew alphabets they used. This method works better than the conventional modern numerological system that reduces all the letters to 1 through 9 without any 10s or 100s, which makes for some dreadful-looking sigils on the larger number squares as you scribble lines back and forth over the same handful of nine cells.

1	2	3	4	5	6	7	8	9
A	B	C	D	E	F	G	H	I
10	20	30	40	50	60	70	80	90
J	K	L	M	N	O	P	Q	R
100	200	300	400	500	600	700	800	900
S	T	U	V	W	X	Y	Z	&

In this case, *health* would convert to:

H=8, E=5, A=1, L=30, T=200, H=8

Get well translates into:

G=7, E=5, T=200
W=500, E=5, L=30, L=30

Now you're ready to make your sigil by tracing the sequence of numbers you obtained atop the appropriate planetary magic square (see below). But there's a wrinkle—each magic square contains only *some* of the numbers you are likely to need. For instance, the square of the Sun contains only the numbers *1* through *36*, but the numbers of *get well* include *T=200* and *W=500*.

If the number for a particular letter is too high to fit in the square you are using, divide it by *10* or *100* (that is, drop the zeros) until it does fit. For *get well,* you would reduce *200* to *20,* and *500* to *5.* For quick reference, the highest number in each magic square is next to the name of its corresponding planet.

Copy the number square you are going to use onto one sheet of paper; then place your other sheet of paper atop it. Here is where the light table or white cardboard will come in handy, because you need to be able to see the numbers through the top sheet of paper.

The following table shows the seven planetary sigils and their corresponding magic squares. The symbol at the left of each is a sigil (from Agrippa) that is based on the numerical structure of that square. It is the special, secret sign of that planet, and can be used in the same kinds of ways you use the sigil you are going to create. The planetary sigil also plays a role in the *lamen* seal to follow.

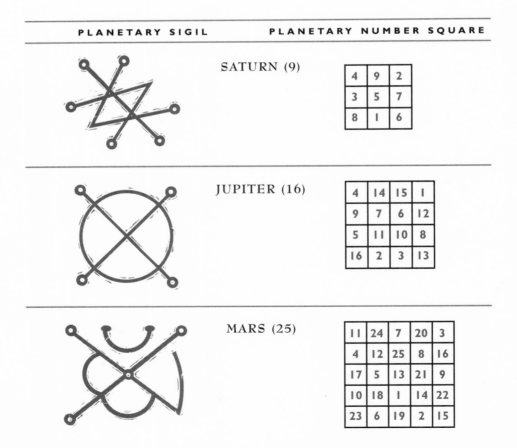

PLANETARY SIGIL	PLANETARY NUMBER SQUARE

SATURN (9)

4	9	2
3	5	7
8	1	6

JUPITER (16)

4	14	15	1
9	7	6	12
5	11	10	8
16	2	3	13

MARS (25)

11	24	7	20	3
4	12	25	8	16
17	5	13	21	9
10	18	1	14	22
23	6	19	2	15

SUN (36)

6	32	3	34	35	1
7	11	27	28	8	30
19	14	16	15	23	24
18	20	22	21	17	13
25	29	10	9	26	12
36	5	33	4	2	31

VENUS (49)

22	47	16	41	10	35	4
5	23	48	17	42	11	29
30	6	24	49	18	36	12
13	31	7	25	43	19	37
38	14	32	1	26	44	20
21	39	8	33	2	27	45
46	15	40	9	34	3	28

MERCURY (64)

8	58	59	5	4	62	63	1
49	15	14	52	53	11	10	56
41	23	22	44	48	19	18	45
32	34	38	29	25	35	39	28
40	26	27	37	36	30	31	33
17	47	46	20	21	43	42	24
9	55	54	12	13	51	50	16
64	2	3	61	60	6	7	57

MOON (81)

37	78	29	70	21	62	13	54	5
6	38	79	30	71	22	63	14	46
47	7	39	80	31	72	23	55	15
16	48	8	40	81	32	64	24	56
57	17	49	9	41	73	33	65	25
26	58	18	50	1	42	74	34	66
67	27	59	10	51	2	43	75	35
36	68	19	60	11	52	3	44	76
77	28	69	20	61	12	53	4	45

To draw your sigil, denote your first letter by making a tiny circle on the top sheet of paper over the first letter's number equivalent.

Use straight lines to connect each successive letter/number until you've spelled out the entire word.

If you wish, you can draw a loop instead of an angle when you change direction during the process. Signify repeated letters or numbers with a hump or a half circle.

End the sigil with a small, anchoring square or transverse line on the last letter/number.

6	32	3	34	35	1
7	11	27	28	8	30
19	14	16	15	23	24
18	20	22	21	17	13
25	29	10	9	26	12
36	5	33	4	2	31

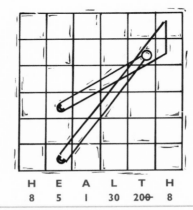 

H	E	A	L	T	H
8	5	1	30	200	8

You may have noticed that this letter-to-number system, applied strictly, gives you only numbers from *1* to *9* and their multiples by *10* and *100*. Tradition allows a way out of this: You can add two sequential letters' numbers together to obtain a third number. In *health*, for example, if you add *A=1* plus *L=30*, you get *31*. You can add reduced numbers, too—for instance, *T=200=20* plus *H=8* yields *28*. You can use these combined letter/numbers to improve your sigil's symmetry.

H	E	A	L	TH
8	5	1	30	28

The best sigils produce an evocative shape. This second health sigil, for example, looks like a doctor holding up an instrument to examine a patient.

Once you have the sigil, you can experi-

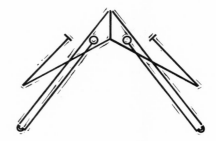

ment with its shape and position to emphasize its symbolism or enhance its mystery. As Donald Tyson observes of Agrippa's planetary sigils: "Sigils may be disguised through the simple but effective tricks of rotating or reflecting them once they have been extracted from the squares. Without some grasp of how the sigils were created, it is then impossible to relate them to the squares directly."[41]

To turn any sigil into a magical seal, simply enclose it in two concentric circles. Just like the ritual circle Wiccan Priest/esses cast to delineate sacred space, this double enclosure contains and concentrates the sigil's power and prevents magical leakage. You can also add cryptic writing in the space between the circles.

Seals are often inscribed on a double roundel of parchment or virgin paper, called a lamen. This form resembles a cosmetic compact or an old-fashioned covered pocket watch.

To construct a lamen seal, fold the paper and cut two small parallel incisions about a quarter-inch apart; then, starting at the end of one incision, cut a circle until you reach the end of the other incision. When unfolded, the paper-doll–style cutout should resemble a dumbbell.

Draw enclosing circles on each side of your seal. (See the illustration next page.)

On the inside of roundel B, inscribe the magic square of the planet you've chosen to work with. (The following example once again relies on the square of the Sun to create a talisman for health.) Fold roundel A over roundel B, and align the two roundels so that you can see the magic square through roundel A.

Draw your sigil on the outside of roundel A in the same way as described

---

[41] Tyson, "Appendix V," ibid. 747.

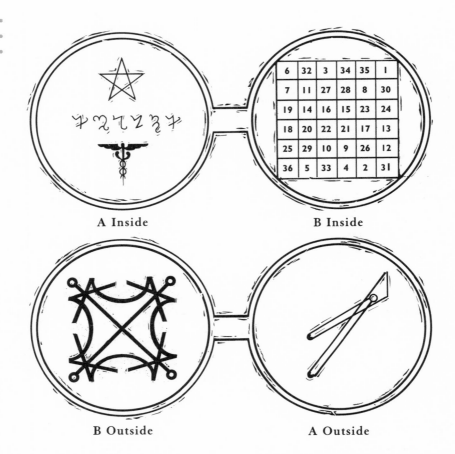

A Inside   **B Inside**

B Outside   **A Outside**

earlier. When the ink is dry, turn the seal over and inscribe the planetary sigil on the outside of roundel B, aligning it with the numbers of the magic square. Finally, on the inside of roundel A, inscribe symbols and writing that reinforce the purpose of your talisman.

When your seal is complete, consecrate it by fumigating it in the appropriate planetary incense.[42] Then put it to use. Place it on an altar, slip it under a pillow or doormat, or secrete it in a crack in a wall—whatever suits your magical purpose.

Finally, remember the power of North and be silent. Be very selective about whom you share your encryption techniques with—anyone who cracks your code could expose your spellwork, or even work magic against you. Teach others basic methods if you like, but always retain a trick or two that are uniquely yours.

[42] *This technique for making a lamen is a variation of the one illustrated in Francis Barrett's* The Magus, *1801; (reprint York Beach, Maine: Red Wheel/Weiser, Weiser Books, 2000).*

MUSICAL SPELLS

SINGING, HUMMING, AND DRUMMING MAGIC

*"See deep enough, and you see musically; the heart of Nature
being everywhere music, if you can only reach it."*
— THOMAS CARLYLE
SCOTTISH ESSAYIST

Folks have always known the power of music to affect the spirit and emotions. The word *chant* comes from the Latin *cantare,* to sing, and *charm* from *carmen,* a hymn, or sung spell. Like all forms of magic, music can be used to heal or harm; religious chants and sacred songs can entice worshippers into spiritual ecstasy, whereas martial beats and battle hymns can spur warriors into blood frenzy.

But the effects of music aren't merely psychological. Just as with spoken or written spells, you can affect time and space by converting your magical energy and intention into sung, hummed, whistled, played, or drummed patterns of vibrations. Throughout history and around the world, spellcrafters have applied the Art of Correspondences to their culture's traditional melodic scales or drum rhythms, and used them to fashion potent chants and charms.

Explore the magic hidden in scales and rhythms; then learn to encode a magical name or spell word into powerful tones and rhythms by using an encryption technique called the Musical Cipher.

The Magic in Musical Modes and Rhythms

"What passion cannot Music raise and quell?"
—John Dryden
English poet

From earliest times, musicians, philosophers, Priest/esses, and magicians have believed that modes—those strangely named scales, such as Aeolian, Mixolydian, and so on—are the principal key to the power of music. The modes are different moods of the musical scale—they all use the same collection of seven diatonic notes (the white keys of a piano), but each begins the scale on a different note. Modes are the patterns from which the cloth of melody is cut—rarely recognized, but always influencing the particular notes a chanter, singer, or player uses to express what he or she wishes to communicate, whether to human or divine ears.

Most people are familiar with the differences between major and minor scales and keys and the emotional polarity they express: the yang of bright and joyful major versus the yin of dark and mournful minor. The subtler spectrum of the modes, however, refracts this basic contrast into a range of shades of major and minor, each tinted by its own emotional character.

Their traditional names, which come from those of archaic Greek tribes, hint at the fact that individual modes are commonly associated with the distinctive musical styles favored by cultural or ethnic groups. For example, Wiccan chants are often in the antique, majestic minor mode called Dorian, such as "Darksome Night and Shining Moon," as are many olde European folksongs, such as "Scarborough Fair." In contrast, most Protestant hymns are in the plain, straightforward major mode called Ionian, such as "Amazing Grace," as are most country-and-western songs, such as "Okie from Muskogee." The blues have been wailed in the soul-of-the-night Aeolian minor mode since black Americans first sang them to lament their sorrows.

Many are the tales told of the modes' magical effects. According to one famous legend, Pythagoras was watching the stars one peaceful evening with his students, listening to a musician perform on an aulos, a kind of double oboe often played at the ecstatic rites of Dionysus. Suddenly, one of the students leaped up in a rage and shouted that he was going to go into town and kill a rival who had been sleeping with his lover. While the other students struggled to restrain the youth, Pythagoras calmly walked over to the aulos player and requested that he change the mode of his music from dramatic Phrygian (now called Mixolydian), to a slow, dirge-like rhythm. The irate student immediately calmed down and returned quietly to his seat.

Another tale also reveals the potent effect that rhythm has on the human psyche. In *Witchcraft Today*, Gerald Gardner wrote about a drumbeat the New Forest Coven had preserved that was traditionally used to drive men into a battle frenzy:

> *"They told me they could make me fighting mad; I did not believe it, so they got me to sit, fixed in a chair so that I could not get out. Then one sat in front of me playing a little drum; not a tune, just a steady tom-tom-tom. We were laughing and talking at first . . . it seemed a long time, although I could see the clock and knew it was not.*
>
> *The tom-tom-tom went on and I felt silly; they were watching me and grinning and those grins made me angry. I did realise that the tom-tomming seemed to be a little quicker and my heart seemed to be beating very hard. I felt flushes of heat, I was angry at their silly grins. Suddenly I felt furiously angry and wanted to pull loose out of the chair; I tugged out and would have gone for them, but as soon as I started moving they changed their beat and I was not angry any longer."*[43]

In African-based religions such as Voudon and Yoruba, which have always embraced the power of the drum, certain rhythms are associated with certain God/desses. Musicians at a ritual will use those rhythms to draw a Deity down to ride (temporarily possess) a worshipper. Some Middle Eastern tribes use rhythms to literally dance their demons out. They correlate drum patterns with negative Entities they believe are responsible for certain illnesses, and play the rhythm that corresponds to a sufferer's illness to call forth the offending demon and drive it out.

It's no coincidence that the history of the modal scales parallels the history of

[43] Gerald Gardner, Witchcraft Today, *chap. 13 (England, 1954).*

magic. The modal scales were widely used by musicians from the most ancient times up through the Renaissance—then discarded in the eighteenth century during the Age of Reason, which replaced them with the simple major scale that dominates classical music. Minor scales were dismissed as mere aberrations of major scales, useful only for expressing a few stock emotions, such as melodrama, sadness, or terror. Then, starting in the 1960s, the olde modes were revived in psychedelic rock music, inspired by the Aeolian pentatonic mode of the blues scale, and have become increasingly common in popular music ever since.

Using modal magic in your music affects more than mere emotions. Music resonates on many planes of being. As you listen to a melody and move to a beat, it's not only the air that's being stirred into harmonious vibrations. Your blood, your breath, and your brainwaves also pulse in time with the music. As you stir your passions and project your intent, the ether vibrates in tune with you, too, bringing your sweet or sultry, sorrowing or soaring strains to the very ears of the God/desses.

When you are in the middle of a spell, moved by the passion of your magical will, your inspiration and intuition will often bring you a melody and rhythm for your chant. You won't need to question whether it's the "right" one for your spell—it will be. But just as an Eastern martial-arts expert meditates between fighting matches, so should you hone your intuition between spellcastings by contemplating the magical wisdom inherent in the modes, rhythms, and other archetypal forms of music.

SEVEN MODES FOR SEVEN PLANETS

Music is an art of time. It measures its rhythms in time signatures and its tones in cycles per second. It's only natural that spellcrafters recognize correspondences between the forms of time, such as the astrological planets, and the forms of music, such as the modes.

Throughout recorded history, there have been many systems of correspondences applied to the modes. For more than two decades, *Diuvei, whose academic background is in musicology and music theory, has collected and experimented with countless systems of modal correspondences, both ancient and modern. He has found that these vary widely and are all too often based on abstract, self-contradictory theories that don't work well in practice. The system

THE SEVEN MODES

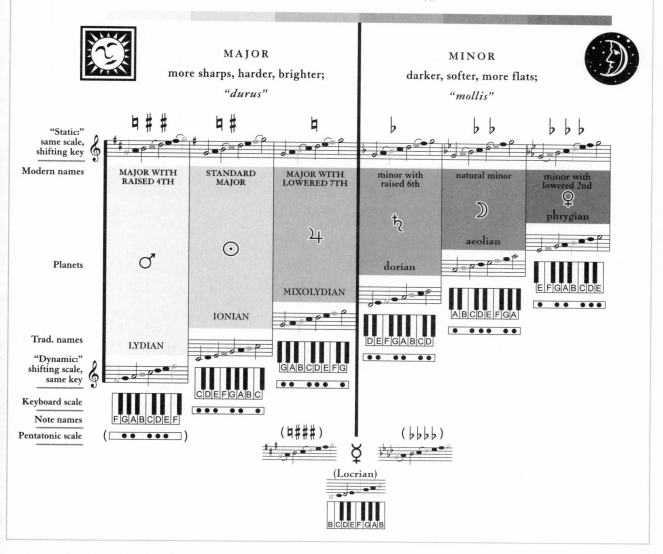

	MAJOR more sharps, harder, brighter; *"durus"*	MINOR darker, softer, more flats; *"mollis"*

"Static:" same scale, shifting key

Modern names

MAJOR WITH RAISED 4TH	STANDARD MAJOR	MAJOR WITH LOWERED 7TH	minor with raised 6th	natural minor	minor with lowered 2nd

phrygian

Planets

dorian

aeolian

MIXOLYDIAN

IONIAN

					E F G A B C D E

			A B C D E F G A

Trad. names

LYDIAN

			D E F G A B C D

"Dynamic:" shifting scale, same key

		G A B C D E F G

Keyboard scale

Note names

Pentatonic scale

F G A B C D E F	C D E F G A B C

(♮###)

(♭♭♭♭)

☿

(Locrian)

B C D E F G A B

- Six of the modes are arranged in order from the most major (Lydian, on the far left) to the most minor (Phrygian, on the far right). The seventh mode (Locrian), which is neither major nor minor, is paradoxically both in the center and at the peripheries of the modal spectrum.
- Running along the bottom of the diagram is a series of small flute-like bars, each marked with five or six dots that indicate which notes on the keyboard above compose that mode's pentatonic (five-note) scale. These five notes are the mode's framework, the armature on which its melodies are molded; in folk music, they are often the only notes used. (The Lydian pentatonic appears in parentheses because it is hypothetical and never actually used.)
- Exemplifying the law of polarity, each of the modes and planets has its complementary opposite. The Mars mode is the inversion of the Venus mode, the Sun mode of the Moon mode, and the Jupiter mode of the Saturn mode.

In the following descriptions of the modes' magical and psychological affects, we give the seven modal scales in the key with no sharps or flats—that is, played on only the white keys of a keyboard. The most important and powerful notes in each scale—the tonic, or final note, and the dominant, or co-final note—are distinguished by bold letters in the sequence labeled Scale. The tonic is the first and last note, and the dominant is in the middle.

We also provide the harmonies (labeled Chords) most closely associated with each mode. These are pairs of chords that you can alternate repeatedly, in a goodly rhythm, as the basis for a magical chant that you spontaneously improvise or, if you prefer, compose ahead of time. The first chord of the pair is the main one in each case, with which you should begin and, usually, end your chant. For example, in the Lydian mode, you would play F-A-C, then G-B-D, then F-A-C, and so on. To make them easy to play on a guitar, we also show these same chord pairs transposed to the key of A or A minor.

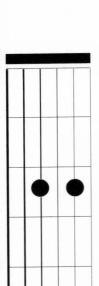

Guitar neck.

- <u>**Lydian Mode**</u> = Mars
  Scale: **F**-G-A-B-**C**-D-E-**F**
  Chords: F-A-C, then G-B-D **or** F-A-C, then E-G-B
  Guitar Chords: A-C#-E, then B-D#-F# **or** A-C#-E, then G#-B-D#

Use this mode to raise fast, frenetic energy or to express anticipation and anger. Chanting loudly in this mode while you're driving during morning rush hour is a great way to both wake yourself up and vent your frustration with traffic.

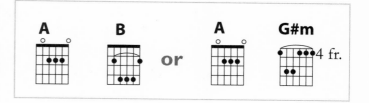

- **IONIAN MODE** = Sun
  Scale: **C**-D-E-F-**G**-A-B-**C**
  Chords: C-E-G, then G-B-D
  Guitar Chords: A-C#-E, then E-G#-B

This is the basic major mode. Use its sunny feeling for dispelling clouds of gloom and for spells involving health or friendship. We especially like to use the pentatonic version of this mode (**C**-D-E-**G**-A-**C**).

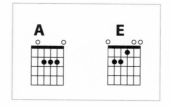

- **MIXOLYDIAN MODE** = Jupiter
  Scale: **G**-A-B-C-**D**-E-F-**G**
  Chords: G-B-D, then F-A-C **or** G-B-D, then D-F-A
  Guitar Chords: A-C#-E, then G-B-D **or** A-C#-E, then E-G-B

Often heard in rock music, especially songs with a psychedelic flair (it was Jerry Garcia's signature mode, for example), Mixolydian is also very common in folk music. This mode, which the Greeks played in the rites of

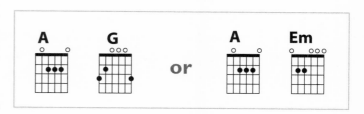

Dionysus, can induce ecstasy in listeners. Use it for spells of expansion, increase, prosperity, hope, and optimism. It's also excellent for travel magic—hum it for good luck when your plane is taking off or landing, or while you're dodging trucks on a freeway.

- **DORIAN MODE** = Saturn
  Scale: **D**-E-F-G-**A**-B-C-**D**
  Chords: D-F-A, then C-E-G
  Guitar Chords: A-C-E, then G-B-D

Dorian is a haunting, olde-timey mode often associated with folk ballads ("Scarborough Fair"), sailor's chanteys ("What Do You Do With a Drunken Sailor"), and Gregorian chants. It's also one of the favorite modes of Witches.

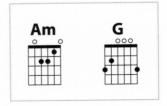

Use it to invoke antiquity, dignity, continuity, stability, solidity, and a sense of transcendence beyond time. Appropriately, Dorian's nickname among folk musicians is "mountain minor."

- **AEOLIAN MODE** = Moon
  Scale: **A**-B-**C**-D-**E**-F-**G**-**A**
  Chords: A-C-E, then E-G-B
  Guitar Chords: A-C-E, then E-G-B

This is the basic minor mode and perhaps the most expressive and soulful of all the modes. Use it for pouring out your heart to the God/desses in times of trouble, for meditation and reverie, and for calming, soothing, and healing.

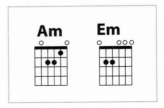

Aeolian is the mode most spellcrafters instinctively use for chants, especially in its hexatonic (six-note—the F omitted) version: **G**-**A**-B-**C**-D-**E**-**G**-**A**. In the hexatonic version, the notes shown in bold type alternate with the ones in regular type; for example, notes from the A minor triad, A-C-E, alternate with notes from the G major triad, G-B-D. This A minor–G major harmony is common the world over—in Celtic, reggae, medieval European, and many other styles of music. It expresses the fundamental cosmic polarity of Goddess and God, female and male, dark and light, with the Goddess (the minor triad) accorded precedence.

• **PHRYGIAN MODE** = Venus
Scale: **E**-F-G-A-**B**-C-D-**E**
Chords: E-G-B, then F-A-C **or** E-G-B, then D-F-A
Guitar Chords: A-C-E, then B♭-D-F **or,** A-C-E, then G-B♭-D

This mode can be as sensuous and sultry as a Gypsy flamenco, or as sorrow-
ful and sad as a lament for lost love. It's
very common in Arabic and Hindu
music, but its mystical quality sounds
exotic to Western ears, as in the 60s ode

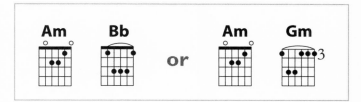

to psychedelia "White Rabbit." Phrygian's most distinctive feature is the close
interval between its tonic E and the next note, F. This interval, called a minor
second, is what you should emphasize when you use this mode. Played or sung
softly, this mode is made for lullabies, calms frenetic energy, and induces a deep
trance state. Performed passionately, however, it's very effective in raising sexual energy.

• **LOCRIAN MODE** = Mercury
Scale: **B**-C-D-E-**F**-G-A-**B**
Chords: B-D-F, then C-E-G **or** B-D-F, then A-C-E
Guitar Chords: A-C-E♭, then B♭-D-F **or** A-C-E♭, then G-B♭-D

Because of the dissonant tritone
(diminished fifth) interval between its
main notes, B and F, this mode rarely
stands on its own, but is usually part of
other modes. Medieval Church musicians considered it the mode of the

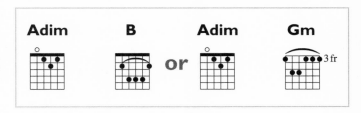

devil—which hints, of course, that it has great magical power, as indeed it does.
Use it for working between worlds, for opening portals and gateways, for being
neither here nor there—for example, when practicing invisibility, telepathy, or
astral travel.

The modes also correspond to times of day.

Lydian = morning
Ionian = midday
Mixolydian = afternoon
Dorian = evening
Aeolian = midnight
Phrygian = pre-dawn
Locrian = twilight, between day and night

DRUMMING WITH THE ELEMENTS

In the music of Western culture, there are four fundamental types of rhythm: three, four, six, and nine beats to a measure. These are represented by the time signatures 3/4, 4/4, 6/8, and 9/8. The most common beats are three, four, and six; nine is rarely used. Of course, there are countless variations and combinations of these rhythms, not to mention irregular beats, such as five or seven to a measure, or the syncopations that add spice to a regular rhythm.

You can apply several magical correspondences to these rhythms. Three-beat (3/4), sometimes called waltz time, traditionally corresponds to Spirit. Four-beat (4/4), march time, corresponds to Matter. Witches also use the three-beat to signify the Threefold Goddess (who is Maiden, Mother, Crone), and the four-beat—twice two—to signify the God, whose two horns symbolize his dual nature. Six-beat (6/8), swing time, signifies their union because six can be played as either two groups of three beats, or as three groups of two beats.

The association of three-beat with Spirit and four-beat with Matter is very ancient—in fact, it's the origin of the common-meter sign, C, which music printers still often use to denote 4/4 time. In medieval music, a whole circle, representing the perfection of Spirit, was used to signify triple time, and a broken circle, representing the imperfection of Matter, signified double or quadruple time.

Including the nine-beat, the four basic rhythms correspond to the Four Elements. The correlation shown here derives from medieval music theory, in which these four rhythms were called the Four Prolations. Their symbols were based on the whole and broken circle, as shown below. The square beat of 4/4 fits with Earth. Water's fluid 6/8 beat readily converts to Air's swirling 3/4, just as water readily evaporates into steam. Alternating measures of 6/8 and 3/4 is the energizing beat called *hemiola*, popular in Latin music. The purely triangular rhythm of 9/8 illustrates the flames of Fire; but if you find this too hard to play, use an African-derived rhythm, 3+3+2 beats per measure, often heard drummed around a balefire.

THE FOUR PROLATIONS

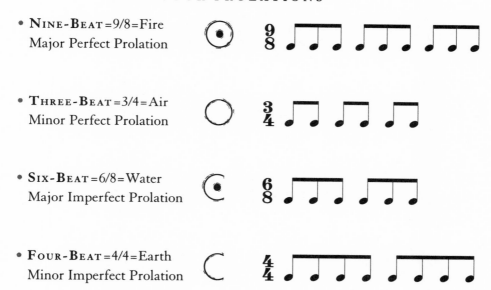

* **NINE-BEAT**=9/8=Fire
  Major Perfect Prolation

* **THREE-BEAT**=3/4=Air
  Minor Perfect Prolation

* **SIX-BEAT**=6/8=Water
  Major Imperfect Prolation

* **FOUR-BEAT**=4/4=Earth
  Minor Imperfect Prolation

Applying the correspondences of the Four Elements to the four basic beats is just one way to use rhythm in spellwork. Spellcrafters also draw on principles of magic such as polarity and sympathy/antipathy, as illustrated by the drum rhythms of a pair of African Yoruba invocations to Ogun, the God of iron and war.[44] The first invocation is drummed and chanted before a tribe goes to war. Its rhythm is an exciting, energy-pumping hemiola that repeatedly steps up from its two longer notes in 6/8 to three shorter notes in 3/4:

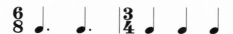

[44] *These invocations are recorded on Babatunde Olatunji's album* Drums of Passion: The Invocation. *1990.*

The second invocation is drummed and chanted after the tribe returns from war, to integrate the warriors back into peaceful society. It starts with an even, steadying 4/4 beat, then breaks into another hemiola. This time, however, the hemiola rhythm steps down from 3/4 to 6/8—the reverse of the going-to-war rhythm, as if to taper down the martial energy that the first rhythm raised. Even the shorter eighth notes in the 6/8 part give way to longer quarter notes:

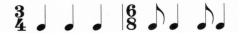

Making Musical Ciphers

You can turn any word or name into a musical melody and rhythm, which you can then sing, play, or write for spellwork in much the same way you would use a sigil. The cipher, or secret code, by which you do this is very simple—each letter of the alphabet corresponds to a note of the scale, according to the diagram shown here. Half the notes are long ones, which count for two beats; half are short notes, which count for one beat. Even if you can't read music, you can still make musical ciphers by using just the rhythms corresponding to the letters.

We adapted this cipher from a system described by Giovanni della Porta in *De furtivis literarum notis* (On secret notations for letters), which was widely used for secret communications by spies, diplomats, and generals throughout the seventeenth and eighteenth centuries. [45]

A TO Z MUSICAL CIPHER

A B C D E F G H IJ K L M N O P Q R S T U,V W X Y Z

[45] *Della Porta used a C-major scale, omitted the letters* k *and* w, *and only went up to the note* f# *and back. Our version employs a more natural correlation between letters and pitch names—essentially the same system composers (such as Bach and Schumann) used for centuries.*

Some tips for using the cipher:

- To create a simple chant or ritual drumbeat, use just the rhythms of the notes, minus the pitches.
- Transpose any pitch up or down an octave as needed to improve your melody.
- Any pitch can be natural, sharp, or flat—for example, the letter *T* can be pitch F or F#, as in *wealth*, below. Altering a pitch will change your melody's mode, which you may wish to do to add an appropriate modal correspondence to your spell, or you may simply find that your melody sounds better in a minor mode than in a major one.

QUICK REFERENCE TABLE

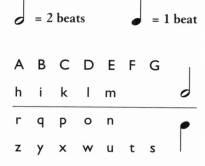

CIPHER EXAMPLES

HECATE   HERNE   WEALTH   _ _ _ _

MAGICAL MOVEMENT
AND GESTURES

*"Movement never lies. It is the barometer telling
the state of the soul's weather."*
— MARTHA GRAHAM
AMERICAN CHOREOGRAPHER

Actions reinforce magical measures by converting your spiritual intention into physical form. Magical movement and gesture actively bridge the gap between your inner world, and the world without. When you work magic alone, dancing and employing magical gestures help you feel as one with nature and other Witches.

Movement is also a vital part of any group ritual, though far too underutilized. Dance and gesture unite, raise, and direct a group's energy and are much more empowering for participants than standing stock-still in the cold, straining to hear lengthy recitations of words.

Magical movement shouldn't be confined solely to ritual, but should be a part of your everyday life. Witches know that true grace and beauty come not from a surgeon's knife or a cosmetic bottle but from enhancing the natural charm each person is born with. The arts of fascination and glamoury involve embracing the spiritual aspects of your unique physique, liberating your attire and movements, increasing your charisma, and developing a magical persona— all of which aid in mesmerizing and attracting others.

Mystical Dance

*"To dance is to be out of yourself, larger, more powerful, more beautiful.
This is power, it is glory on earth and it is yours for the taking."*
— AGNES DE MILLE
AMERICAN CHOREOGRAPHER

ife is one long dance through air—indeed, even the stars above are but heavenly bodies dancing on a cosmic stage. Humans have danced since the dawn of time. We sought to define the boundaries of our bodies' range of motion—to press the limits of our capabilities. Our steps propitiated predator and prey alike. We coaxed our crops to grow high as we leapt astride our besoms. We used dance to connect with nature and our pasts—to tell stories, celebrate, beguile mates, and even mourn. Dance afforded everyone a common context of communication that transcended language barriers, and the cathartic joy it engendered made hardships easier to bear.

Centuries before rock and roll and rave dancing became synonymous with the San Francisco hippies, dance pervaded the culture of their indigenous predecessors, the Ohlone Indians of northern California.

"Dancing was almost as natural a form of expression as talking. Shamans danced to achieve clairvoyance, to influence the weather, to thwart death, or to make contact with their ancestors. . . . There were wild dances to prepare for war, and even wilder dances to celebrate a victory. There were strictly social dances where enjoyment was the only object, and a multitude of religious dances such as the First Grass dance, the Coming-of-Age dance for girls, the Mourning Ceremony dances, or the Acorn dances. . . . Dancing was a natural part of living, like eating or sleeping; it would have been unthinkable to live a life without dance."[46]

Monotheistic regimes have repeatedly prohibited group dancing. Their hatred of the body has caused them to force worshippers into rigid standing,

[46] *Malcolm Margolin, "Dancing,"* The Ohlone Way: Indian Life in the San Francisco–Monterey Bay Area *(Berkeley: Heyday Books, 1978).*

Puritan police glower at Pagan dancers, as the Merrymount colonists celebrate May Day (Beltane) around a Maypole with the native people of Massachusetts in 1627.

sitting, or kneeling postures that are intended to induce feelings of humility and penance, and to repress the feelings of ecstasy that dance produces. The Plymouth Puritans' ban on dance shaped the United States' destiny in a pivotal way: William Bradford and Miles Standish used the ban as a means to destroy the Pagan Thomas Morton's more successful nearby settlement of Merrymount. Morton invited local Native Americans to join Merrymount colonists in celebrating a traditional Maypole dance. The outraged Puritan leaders arrested and deported Morton. His tolerant Pagan way of respecting the land and its native inhabitants was thereafter suppressed, and the Puritans' way of subjugation and slaughter predominated.[47]

Modern Witches continue to dance for myriad reasons—to express ourselves (ecstatic dancing), to celebrate a Sabbat (a Maypole dance on Beltane), to conjure fertility (fire-leaping), and to raise energy in spells (a Cone of Power). Pagans love to dance. We dance to please God/desses we cherish and to inspire others to reclaim their dormant grace and shake their tail feathers for a change! Witches knew long ago what remains true today—human contentment is gained not in a plodding, pedantic approach to life, but in *how* people live it, and with what *style*. Losing yourself in a nightlong trance dance can liberate your soul, as the Ohlone knew:

> *"The dance went on for hours, sometimes for a whole day or even longer. The dancers stamped and stamped. They stamped out all sense of time and space, stamped out all thoughts of village life, even stamped out their own inner voices. Dancing for hour after hour they stamped out the ordinary world, danced themselves past the gates of common perception into the realm of the spirit world, danced themselves toward the profound understanding of the universe that only a people can feel who have transcended the ordinary human condition and who find themselves moving in total synchronization with everything around them. In such a state the dancers were totally transformed and filled with supernatural powers."*[48]

[47] Thomas Morton, New English Canaan *1637; (reprint, ed. Jack Dempsey, Digital Scanning, 1999) and* Glory Here: Thomas Morton and the Maypole of Merrymount *(N.p.: Pagansword Press, Thomas Morton Alliance Publications, 1992).*
[48] Margolin, The Ohlone Way.

It pays to learn about different kinds of traditional Pagan dances and the effect each has on both participants and observers. Some dances can cure: When southern Italian women could no longer bear the maddening confinement of their rigidly patriarchal society, they would begin dancing in a frenzy—symptoms observers ascribed to a bite from a tarantula. The women would dance the *tarantella* for days, until they were exhausted—and cured. Rejuvenated, they would resume their mundane tasks with aplomb as if they'd never taken ill.

Traditional Wiccan dances are passed down from generation to generation—examples include the Circle, Meeting, Spiral, Labyrinthine, Snake, Cord, Mill, free-form, ecstatic, and trance dances. The Pagan presumption is that the God/desses will look down from on high and delight in the arabesques the dancers trace with their moving bodies. Specific Witch tunes and evocative drumbeats often accompany such dances. Once memorized, the form of traditional Wiccan dances should remain unaltered so that no matter where you may circle, you will know exactly what to do and, hence, flow like a pro.

Wiccan dances convey key Craft principles without proselytization. For example, the Spiral dance, while enacting the form and movement of a galaxy, conveys both our understanding of how cyclicity confers life, and our acknowledgement that we have our own part to play within the universe's vast expanse. The dance symbolizes birth, death, reincarnation, infinity, perpetual motion, and many other profound cosmological concepts. For transmitting spiritual bliss, prancing is far preferable to preaching:

> *"Throughout the entire dance the expressions on their faces never altered, but an unrestrained joy made itself felt within them, an unspoken joy that spread invisibly among the dancers, the singers, and spectators, joining them to one another and indeed joining them to the world around them: a joy, an order, a balance, and a sense of the oneness of all things . . .—not through dogmas and religious tenets—but through the all-embracing religious experience of the dance."*[49]

TRADITIONAL PAGAN DANCES

The most basic form of Pagan group dance is an inward, hand-to-hand Carole or Circle dance. Ritual ring dances are the oldest form of dance

[49] *Ibid.*

known—some of the earliest human footprints were discovered circling around an altar in a mud-floored cave. The Circle dance was depicted on Bronze Age rock carvings of proto-Egyptians who lived prior to 3400 B.C.E. The ring dance's later Greek name, *choros,* described the practice of worshippers of Dionysus, who sang and danced at their festivals on circular threshing floors. Their rite begat the chorus in Greek drama.

In the Middle Ages, the popularity of the Carole flourished in spite of efforts by the Church to censure and punish the dancers. Bulgarians, Russians, and Jews danced the similarly named *hora*; the Yugoslavians, the *kolo,* or Wheel dance. The Basque country has the *dantza khorda,* or String dance—a rather wild, hand-to-hand circle dance that becomes a line or chain dance. In Switzerland, the Carole is known as the *coraule;* in Belgium, as the *coro'des.* However, due to the hostile pressure of the Church, seasonal Carole dancing eventually devolved into staid "Christmas caroling." Circle dances are popular children's dances, often accompanied by such common tunes as "All Around the Mulberry Bush" and "Ring Around the Rosie." Circle dances are also the basis of modern contra dancing and, paradoxically, "square" dancing.[50]

Circle dances are done either sunwise or ayenward. They typically start slowly and naturally gain speed, thereby increasing their centrifugal force. Circle dances help Witches raise energy toward creating a Cone of Power, an occasionally visible, whirling vortex of energy. This type of dance often ceases by unspoken mutual consent when everyone becomes happily breathless.

A Meeting dance is often done at the beginning of a rite or gathering to help folks eliminate emotional and physical barriers before doing magic together. It accomplishes this lofty goal by getting them to kiss one another in the spirit of occult fellowship.

The High Priestess or other dance leader gathers all participants into an outward-facing, hand-to-hand circle, and guides them to move ayenward. In anticipation, the dancers pick up speed. At some point, the High Priestess lets go of one person's hand and reverses direction without warning. Still holding hands, everyone mimics the High Priestess's movement. The participants kiss as they dance by in front of one another. When all are laughing and the mood is

---

[50] *"Carole,"* Man, Myth & Magic: The Illustrated Encyclopedia of Mythology, Religion and the Unknown, *vol. 15 (London: Purnell, Inc./BPC Publishing, 1970), 413–414.*

STEPS KEY

- 🦶 Silhouetted foot leads
- 👣 Outlined foot follows
- ◀ Directional arrows

SUNWISE CIRCLE DANCE

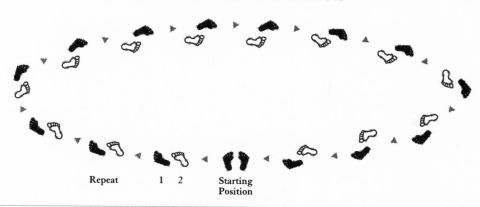

Repeat   1   2   Starting
Position

MEETING DANCE

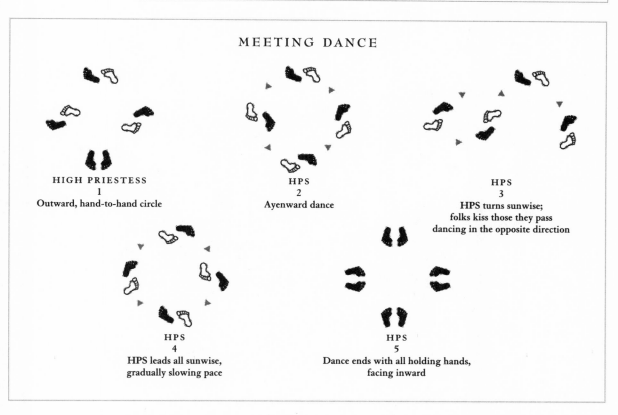

HIGH PRIESTESS
1
Outward, hand-to-hand circle

HPS
2
Ayenward dance

HPS
3
HPS turns sunwise;
folks kiss those they pass
dancing in the opposite direction

HPS
4
HPS leads all sunwise,
gradually slowing pace

HPS
5
Dance ends with all holding hands,
facing inward

jolly, the High Priestess draws everyone into an inward-facing circle going sun-wise, and slowly brings the dance to conclusion.

Without a word, the Meeting dance reiterates the importance of having perfect love for and perfect trust in everyone with whom you practice the Art Magical.

Spiral dances resemble meeting dances minus the cheek-pecks. They may

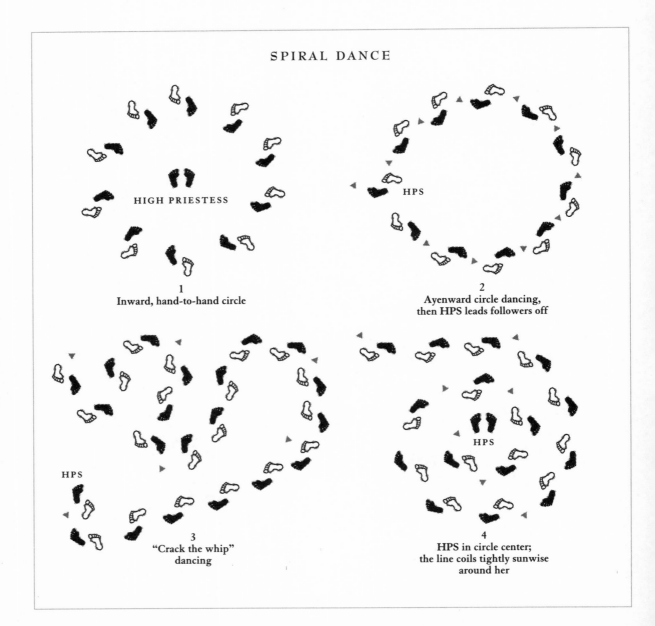

SPIRAL DANCE

HIGH PRIESTESS

1
Inward, hand-to-hand circle

HPS

2
Ayenward circle dancing,
then HPS leads followers off

HPS

3
"Crack the whip"
dancing

HPS

4
HPS in circle center;
the line coils tightly sunwise
around her

involve hundreds, or even thousands, of participants, and are often executed over a long period to induce an altered state of consciousness. A true Spiral dance begins in the center of sacred space. The High Priestess grabs a hand and leisurely waltzes away in an outward spiral pattern. Everyone follows suit until all are part of a hand-to-hand chain dance. The High Priestess guides everyone hither and thither in complicated variations of spiral patterns and, eventually, back to the center of the circle in an inward-curving spiral with everyone pressed up close together.

Fast Spiral dances are exhilarating, but can be a bit dangerous for folks with weak joints or bones. Participants on the end bear the accumulated force of the speed of everyone in front of them, and can sometimes feel whip-cracked back and forth. Fortunately, when this happens, one person typically lets go of another, and the line behind them continues the dance as a separate subset of the larger dance line.

Labyrinthine dances are hand-to-hand and linear, with frequent angular turns. Sometimes the High Priestess leading the dance dives under random sections of the line, intricately weaving the dancers in, through, and around themselves.

Snake dances are also hand-to-hand and linear, but involve making graceful, undulating waves with long, sinuous chains of participants. Snake dances

SNAKE DANCE

HIGH PRIESTESS

can be lurid or innocently provocative, depending on the mood and ritual purpose. Both Labyrinthine and Snake dances cease to be linear the moment folks come back together in a concluding Circle dance.

The Mill dance is another hand-to-hand dance, but it is circular rather than linear. Standing in a circle, participants hold their right arms horizontally straight out, away from their bodies and parallel with their shoulders; pile their right hands atop one another in the middle to resemble the hub of a wheel or a millstone; then move sunwise as one, usually while intoning the Mill Chant. (See below.) As their magical energy builds, they dance faster and faster until they raise a Cone of Power, then lift their hands to send forth their spell at precisely the right moment.

THE MILL CHANT

Air breathe, and air blow—
Make the mill of magic go!
Work the Will for which we pray!
Io, dia, ha, he-yay!

Fire flame, and fire burn—
Make the mill of magic turn!
Work the Will for which we pray!
Io, dia, ha, he-yay!

Water heat, and water boil—
Make the mill of magic toil!
Work the Will for which we pray!
Io, dia, ha, he-yay!

Earth without, and Earth within—
Make the mill of magic spin!
Work the Will for which we pray!
Io, dia, ha, he-yay!

The last line is passionately pronounced **EE-oh, DEE-ah, HA, HE-YAY!**

A variation of the Mill dance is the Cord dance, which involves looping, knotting, or braiding together nine-foot cords to form occult symbols. Participants then grasp the tangible glyph produced and dance around, typically, in a circle, so the God/desses can see it from above. One such symbol is the Wheel of the Year, representing seasonal progression, the eight annual Sabbats, or the 12 months in a year (or 12 signs of the zodiac). Three or more cords are tied together to form an outer circle that others then tie their ropes onto to fashion the appropriate number of spokes. Cord symbols serve as a great ritual focus to look at while intoning the Mill Chant or Barbarous Words of Power.

A Cord dance can be either simple or elaborate—participants may alternate sunwise or ayenward steps, or females and males can take turns elevating and lowering their ropes, as they would while weaving ribbons onto a Maypole. Cord dances are goodly for bonding a group together or increasing magical energy preparatory to raising a Cone of Power.

Free-form, ecstatic, and trance dances are performed by both solitaries and groups. The free-form style involves dancing as you feel inclined. An ecstatic dance often results from circle bliss (euphoria induced by a powerful ritual), and is characterized by rapid movement. Trance dances are usually slower and recognizable because of the expressions on the dancers' faces as much as by any particular movements. Folks in trance can walk through balefires without

CORD DANCE

PENTAGRAM CORD GLYPH

WHEEL OF THE ZODIAC CORD GLYPH

EIGHT SABBATS CORD GLYPH

injury, play with hot coals, walk on glass without bleeding, and often only dimly recall their exploits the morning after.

Ecstatic dances often erupt during Sabbats, particularly Beltane, Lammas, Mabon, and Samhain. We've witnessed many instances of spontaneous levitation and supernatural abilities while dancing entranced or watching others obviously "in the zone."

Trance dances are fluid and introspective, and reflect dancers' reaction to a mystical experience—often, a heightened attunement with nature, or a sharpened awareness that magic pervades everything. A trance dance may induce past-life recall; a shape-shifting sensation; a feeling of oneness with all Witches, be they ancestral, unknown in the present, or yet unborn; and an infinite variety of other exotic phenomena.

Music type and speed—energetic, languid, and so on—easily influence trance dancers. Because folks in the throes of any free-form, ecstatic, or trance dance often get too close to balefires while in an altered state of consciousness, savvy observers should inconspicuously monitor the dancers for signs of dehydration—profuse sweating followed by chills, muscle cramps, profound fatigue, and even fainting. Approach the dancers respectfully, careful not to impede their movements. Restrict your comments to brief declarations of appreciation of their efforts, then kindly offer them replenishing fluids. Many dancers will not want to stop moving, so consider squirting water into their mouths from a *bota,* a bladderlike reservoir that holds liquids and is often carried over the shoulder like a satchel or purse.

A High Priestess often employs a combination of dances in rites. For instance, she may start a ritual with a Meeting dance, keep everyone in a hand-to-hand circle while she relates the purpose of the night's working, follow with a sunwise Circle dance that transforms into a Cone of Power, then end the spellwork with an uplifting Spiral dance. Innumerable ways exist to incorporate several dance forms within one ritual.

The content of certain spells, however, practically dictates the type of dance that should accompany them. For instance, because a feminine Moontime ceremony involves recognizing a young woman's ability to conceive like other women, it traditionally includes a Circle dance that symbolizes the womb, or a hand-to-hand Spiral dance that symbolizes unity with generations of mothers. When a woman is amorously active, she may attract a mate by performing a provocative fascination dance. Primal, tribal, or masculine-style dances feature angular, linear movement, as in the hand-to-hand Line and Labyrinthine dances.

A conducive dance can polish a ritual and embolden a crowd. It is hard to describe the endless list of unforgettable memories that group Pagan dancing engenders. Our own Coven memories are considerable and include a time when we danced for hours with hundreds in an infinity pattern, and one when Lady Passion led hundreds in an eight-minute-long Snake dance that spanned a football field.

The liberating, life-changing, mystical effect that magical dancing has on individuals, crowds, and Craft communities is profound. A transitory and haunting experience, intentional dance fosters group cohesion, accords attendees protection while circling publicly, and inspires future creative projects.

Magical dances often take on a life of their own. You may plan a particular dance for a rite, only to have it end in a completely different dance than you assumed. For instance, it's fairly common that folks start with a Circle dance, break out into a Snake dance, speed up into a fast Spiral dance, then reconnect and end in a slow Circle dance. You never really know how such dances will evolve. If a dance is working and everyone is high-spirited and happy, simply enjoy and participate until the dancers naturally grow breathless—then resume the reins if need be, and steadily wind the dance down to a halt.

Before leading a large group of dancers in a public ritual, note their mood and probable physical stamina. Depending on what you deduce, you may elect to substitute a different kind of dance for the evening. You can try to break the ice with rapid steps, but if that doesn't work quickly, gradually slow the dance down to a more contemplative shuffle with swaying, humming, and similar soothing elements.

Maintain experienced control to keep participants from being accidentally injured by other dancers' exuberance. If a dance is held adoors at night, post guardians by torches to prevent people from inadvertently crashing into them.

Temperature permitting, dancers should be barefoot—mostly so they can freely absorb and radiate the Earth's energy, but also to minimize harm should someone accidentally step on another's toes.

Even the young, infirm, or paralytic can participate in large dances. For instance, guardians can accompany them into the center of the dance space. When the dance begins, they can absorb the magical or healing energy the dance produces. If they can or wish to, they may be allowed to direct the release of the Cone of Power when the spell peaks.

If you're a solitary practitioner, consider spinning for an extended period of time, dancing free-form, or mimicking a bird or an animal's movements. You may elect to wear a costume or use props, such as a wand, a musical instrument, glow sticks, torches, or *sai*.[51]

Fine-tuning your unique dancing style necessitates experiment, practice, occasional failure, and unintentional success. One of Lady Passion's signature dance styles developed as a result of her forgetting to remove three heavily laden charm bracelets prior to the main rite at a gathering. Caught without a musical instrument on hand, she simply twisted her wrists in time with the music—the charms clinked together like fairy bells, and she quickly incorporated the new dance form into her repertoire.

Ultimately, dancing is not merely fun—it's an act of defiance—of grace and freedom asserting themselves against madness and repression.

> " . . . *everything was falling into chaos. By dancing, though, the people could repair the world. With dance and song they could restore order and balance. They could unite people and power once more into a deeply felt, rhythmic whole, summoning the powers of the spirit world close and returning . . . to the purity of Sacred Time. By dancing and singing they could fend off . . . the inevitable disintegration of their world.*"[52]

Spellbinding—The Art of Fascination and Glamoury

For both men and women, fascination and glamoury involve embracing the spiritual aspects of your unique physique; liberating your attire, movements, and mannerisms; creating charisma and sex appeal; and developing a magical persona—all of which aid in mesmerizing and attracting others.

---

[51] *Chinese martial-arts practice swords, short and blunt on the ends with three-pronged, trident-like projections. Coincidentally, they look like the Greek letter* psi.
[52] *Margolin,* The Ohlone Way.

Witches have innate mystique. Our eyes sparkle with secrets. Our hair is long and loose. We dress Gypsyesque and saunter with feline grace. We are sacredly sexy, beautifully wild and free. We have magical powers, work with elemental forces, and are adept in the occult arts—all classic aphrodisiacs on the human psyche. Crafters intensify our automatic ability to attract by practicing glamoury.

Glamoury is like a magical makeover wherein you make yourself irresistible to others:

- Dress in an alluring style.
- Adorn yourself with intriguing jewelry and accessories.
- Line your eyes with kohl.
- Dust yourself with micro-fine glitter.
- Wear a haunting, seductive scent—an evocative essential oil is a potent potion, indeed.
- Lower the timbre of your voice, or whisper.
- Move with an air of mystery, a smile of secrets about your lips.
- If you're a woman, entice by acting extremely feminine; if you're a man, lure by epitomizing masculinity. Either way, retain or adopt a characteristic or two of the opposite sex, to toy teasingly with conventional sexual stereotypes.
- Visualize others as being captivated by your charm, hypnotized by the sound of your voice, or impressed with your wisdom.

To magically incline (attract) someone, closely observe their behavior and memorize his or her idiosyncrasies. Mentally classify the person's basic nature; for example, are they jovial, melancholic, or sensitive? Ruminate often about their unique characteristics. Feel within yourself what you hope to inspire in their mind and heart. Fantasize in a detached manner—let your yearning build without physically relieving the strain (abstain from masturbating to orgasm).[53]

Conduct a private ritual and express your desire through song or dance.

---

[53] *Ioan P. Couliano,* Eros and Magic in the Renaissance *(Chicago: University of Chicago Press, 1987). Summary of Giordano Bruno's attraction technique. According to Bruno, the person will soon share your hunger and try to assuage their desire by feeding on your victuals, so to speak, leading to mutual satisfaction.*

Woo your target from afar by describing why you love them, how deep your love is, or what you hope to accomplish as a couple. Abandon your inhibitions and move in ways you normally wouldn't—wiggle your hips, bend, shimmy, crouch, or gyrate in a tantalizing manner. Raise energy equivalent to the amount of your desire. For instance, if your goal includes sex, you must break a sweat in circle. If your intended is currently uninterested, dance especially provocatively to magically attract their attention.

Convert your desperation into such a powerful beacon of attraction that it overwhelms the seeming impossibility of your desire. Banish your doubts and trust in magic's efficacy—it works well in rectifying lost causes and fulfilling the most unlikely of dreams.

Languid movements, sultry song, lithe dancing, billowing incense, primal music, candlelight, and scented oils rarely miss their mark. Add targeted spell components, such as a person's birthstone or carnelians, and you'll melt their reluctance into an ethereal embrace.

Often, such spells bring results shortly after you release them from your conscious will. After intently wishing, you inadvertently release the wish—perhaps something unexpectedly humorous diverts your attention for a moment, perhaps you reach a moment of peaceful resignation. Paradoxically, the instant you stop desiring is often just when the object of your desire appears—as if it had to wait until you stepped away from the space you'd created for it before it could manifest.

The Two Perfect Pentacles—The Power of Human Hands

"Gestures of the arms and hands ... express universal moods and thoughts, and also regional and individual variations. ... Everywhere gestures can be imitative or symbolic, involving the whole arm or just the fingers, executed with or without props."

"Speaking with Their Hands"
Man, Myth & Magic

itches have deft, healing hands and a powerful touch; therefore, we can always work magic even without other magical tools because our hands themselves are potent magical tools. With five fingers each (one point for each of the Four Element plus Spirit), hands are often referred to as the "two perfect pentacles" in the Craft.

Using ancient, sacred, magical hand gestures is a graceful way to maintain spell secrecy. After all, with silent rites, there's no proof regarding what was, or wasn't, done. Magical gestures are a goodly option if you're in restrictive or repressive circumstances, such as in court, in prison, when biding with intolerant relatives, and so on.

Spellcasters employ many magical hand gestures to aim their power and convey deep, occult meaning. Some are beneficent (averting, protecting, blessing, or healing signs), and some are malefic (banishing, hexing, or cursing signs). Magical gestures can be realistic, emotive, graphic, descriptive, or decorative. They may serve as a silent narrative adding details to a sacred myth reenactment.

Wiccans use myriad secret signals and multiple methods to derive yet more signs for magical purposes. We draw targeted pentagrams in the air with our athamés to invoke or banish each Element. We can convert any written sign into an "air glyph" and mark it in the ethers with our hands, fingers, wands, or athamés.

Whenever you need to silently summon elemental forces, face the appropriate Quarter, concentrate, and use one or both hands to form the following signs:

AIR (EAST)—palm(s) forward, fingers splayed and wiggling, like wind rustling tree leaves;

FIRE (SOUTH)—hand(s) fisted, knuckles forward, in the universal sign of power and resistance;

WATER (WEST)—hand(s) curved upward, resembling a cup;

EARTH (NORTH)—hand(s) flat, parallel to the floor, as if to pat the ground.

Include in your repertoire the gestures of other polytheistic religions. For instance, Hindu and Tibetan/Nepalese Buddhist statuary and iconography is replete with God/desses in stylized postures, making *mudras* (gestures) that indicate their powers and attributes. A comparison between mudras[54] and conventional Western gestures reveals their close similarities:

Mudras		**Western Gestures**
Abhaya—A gesture of protection. Arm elevated, bent slightly, with hand at shoulder height, palm facing outward with fingers extended upward.		**"Stop!" sign**—Self-protection and forbiddance. Arm elevated, rigid, with hand at shoulder height, palm facing outward, with fingers extended upward.
Tarjani—Warning, threatening. Fist with raised index finger.		**Heed sign**—Warning, threatening. Fist with raised index finger.
Vitarka—Sign of argument. Thumb and index finger touching at their tips, all other fingers pointing upward.		**Making a point**—Used in debate. Thumb and index finger touching at their tips, all other fingers pointing upward.

[54] *Jnan Bahadur Sakya, comp.,* Short Description of Gods, Goddesses and Ritual Objects of Buddhism and Hinduism in Nepal *(Kathmandu, Nepal: Handicraft Association of Nepal, 1989). Illustration.*

The implication is that many common cultural gestures derive from age-old sources and convey secret magical significance.

Strega (Italian Witches) employ magical gestures called *gettatura*. The ancient Roman sign of beneficence (blessing), which they now use as protection against the Evil Eye, is the *mano pantea*. Form this by extending your thumb, index, and middle finger, keeping them stiffly pressed together, and folding your ring and pinky finger downward over your palm.

Strega use other, more graphic hand signs as well. Their feminine hex sign is called the *fare la fica,* or fig sign, and resembles female genitalia. Form the fig by making a fist and inserting your thumb between your index and middle fingers.

Their masculine hex sign is called the *mano cornuta,* or horns sign, and resembles an animal head with horns. Form the horns by tucking your thumb beneath your curled middle and ring fingers and keeping your index and pinky fingers rigidly extended.

In chiromancy (palmistry), the planets rule fingers and parts of the hand.

Mano pantea: A blessing gesture.

Fare la fica: "Make the fig," a feminine hexing sign.

Planets ruling the parts of the hand.

SATURN = middle finger
JUPITER = index finger
MARS = center of palm
SUN = ring finger
VENUS = thumb
MERCURY = pinky finger
MOON = outer side of palm

Mano cornuta: Sign of the "horns," a masculine hexing sign.

These can be useful correspondences in spellwork. For example, you can stir a spell ingredient, such as a powdered herb for incense, with the finger corresponding to its planetary ruler.

Consider converting spell incantations or ritual texts into finger spelling; or accompanying a timeless Craft chant with the silent song of sign language.

To physically reflect our verbal assertion that our spell will manifest itself,

Finger-spelling alphabet. *Source: Funk & Wagnalls Dictionary,* 1966.

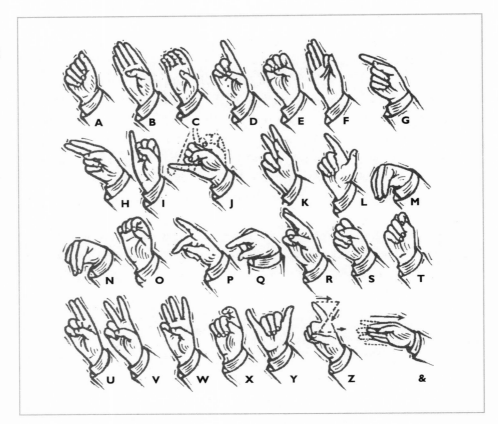

Coven Oldenwilde uses an American Sign Language (Ameslan) gesture when saying "So mote it be!"—one raised hand with fingers together, forcefully moving downward like a karate chop.

Magical gestures can be both beautiful and sinister, so always aim them away from yourself, and either toward your target or in the direction you want to discharge your spell energy. Like smoke let out of a container, energy dissipates if it isn't consciously directed, aimed with intention. Gestures help you point your spell toward a specific goal, to show in motions as well as words how you would manifest your magical will.

HANDS-ON SPELLCRAFTING

> "Then Éowyn gave to Merry an ancient horn, small but cunningly wrought all of fair silver with a baldric of green; and wrights had engraven upon it swift horsemen riding in a line that wound about it from the tip to the mouth; and there were set runes of great virtue.
>
> 'This is an heirloom of our house,' said Éowyn. 'It was made by the Dwarves. . . . He that blows it at need shall set fear in the hearts of his enemies and joy in the hearts of his friends, and they shall hear him and come to him.'"
>
> —J.R.R. Tolkien
> *Return of the King*

Your two perfect pentacles are good for more than making gestures in the air. Handicrafts are the most tangible, physical way to project your spiritual intention into the material world. Unlike spells that are spoken, written, sung, or danced, hand-worked spell objects, such as knotted strings, bottled potions, molded poppets, or engraved talismans, can be traded or given to people who need magical aid, but lack the skills to perform a spell themselves.

The hands-on spells presented here have for centuries been some of the best-known and most widely used magical crafts, as proven by the Witch's Ladders and waxen poppets that are frequently discovered in old attics and chimney cracks.

Knot Magic

itches use knots to bind things magically—after all, there's always a bit of string handy. For example, in the days of sailing ships, Witches sold mariners three-knot string poppets, which, if all were untied when needed, granted them gale-force winds.

You can employ knot magic to attract a mate, to bond with someone formally (such as during a Handfasting, a Pagan marriage commitment that lasts a year and a day), or to prevent someone from doing harm—among many other practical applications.

The following is a powerful spell to use for almost any purpose. The olde chant helps keep your concentration focused on your goal, and the nine knots cement your wish three times threefold.

KNOT SPELL CHANT

By knot of one, my spell's begun.
By knot of two, it cometh true.
By knot of three, so mote it be!
By knot of four, this pow'r I store.
By knot of five, this spell's alive.
By knot of six, this spell I fix.
By knot of seven, events I'll leaven.
By knot of eight, it will be fate!
By knot of nine, what's done, is mine!

You can use any kind of cord for this, but a length of strong hemp or silk is best. Holding the cord with both hands, intone the first line exactly nine times in succession; on the ninth repetition, make your wish and tie a knot with all your might. Repeat the procedure for each line. To help establish a goodly magical flow, rock back and forth as you recite the charm.

To attract a mate, go adoors and select two equal lengths of pliant vine, twig, wheat, or grass. (Because of its green, Venusian color, many folks prefer ivy.) Grip like handlebars the length that stands for you. Impress upon it the skills or experience you intend to bring to the equation. Then lay it down and similarly grasp the other, which represents the type of lover you desire. Visualize attributes or characteristics you'd like your lover to possess, and see such a person fulfilling your needs. Then hold both, one in each hand. See yourself locked in a passionate embrace with a new and wondrous love. Tie one in a circle, insert the other one into the center of the circle, and secure the end of the second vine so that you end up with an interlacing ring fetish. Carry the charm in a green bag above your heart every Friday until your dream lover appears in the flesh.

To determine whether you're destined to marry an existing love, repeat the above, but use a single living vine that's still attached to a tree. Tie one knot in it that represents you and your beloved as a couple; then walk away without looking back. Check on its status three days later or whenever you're in doubt about the relationship. If the vine undoes the knot—or worse, if the vine withers—it is a sad, but sure sign that you are star-crossed lovers not meant to be together.

When you're ready to make a commitment, "tie the knot" in a Pagan Handfasting, complete with a feast. During the ceremony, have the High Priest/ess marrying you bind one of your and one of your partner's hands (one atop the other) with a ribbon-bedecked vine you pre-decorated for the occasion. Some couples opt to remain so bound for an hour and a minute, or even for a day and an hour, as a microcosm of their year-and-a-day union to come. Store your binding knot well—should your love ever wane, use it in ritual to officially Handpart as friends.

To bind someone from doing harm, make a string-knot poppet called a Witch's Ladder. Use anywhere from 9 to 13 inches of string or, preferably, black hemp. Assemble tiny spell components, such as pieces of the person's hair, fingernail parings, clothing swatches, or bits of jewelry, or use natural items that remind you of their behavior. If the person is angry, you might use fangs, claws, or sharks' teeth to represent their ire. If the person is acting sinister, you might substitute a rattlesnake's rattle or a piece of shed, dried snakeskin. Hold the string and focus on what the person has done, how they are acting, and the negative future outcomes you anticipate if their behavior should continue to deteriorate. Then rock back and forth, occasionally tying up a bit of the ingredients in a knot, and verbally exhorting them to cease and desist immediately. Tie as many knots as you need so long as you don't exceed 12. Traditionally, tying 13 knots in succession—as in a hangman's noose—causes a target's death.

Hide the poppet from all prying eyes—a mirrored black box is goodly. This spell works so well and swiftly, the problem person's ensuing timidity or silence will amaze you.

Stir Up Something Goodly—Kitchen Witchery

itchen Witchery is a goodly way to heal family and friends. They'll appreciate that you made a time-tested potion or magical meal with your own, caring hands—a far more effective response to illness than merely giving them get well cards.

Anyone who can read and follow simple recipes can use what they have on hand to make powerful potions, potent herbal medicines, magical salts, brews, oils, powders, and impressive ritual pyrotechnics.

When you're ready to begin practicing the simmery arts, first familiarize yourself with the basic magical, chemical, and allergic effects of common food-stuffs. For example, in most folks chocolate's renowned endorphin-like effect evokes a sense of pleasure. However, its high glucose composition poses peril for diabetics, its vaso-constrictive quality can trigger migraines, and because it stimulates the release of prostaglandins, chocolate can worsen menstrual cramps.

Before mixing anything people will ingest, consider their food allergies and avoid using a known allergen, even if you're following a recipe that stresses its necessity. For instance, if a family member who is allergic to almonds asks you to prepare a salve to relieve dry skin, but the recipe you have for making it calls for you to use almond milk as a base, substitute a similar soft ingredient, such as rose oil. In addition, separate myth (Spanish fly is a great aphrodisiac) from fact (the herb damiana works far better in this capacity).

Arrange your counters, ingredients, and kitchen surfaces for maximum ergonomic ease of use, utensil availability, emotional comfort, and feng shui energy flow. A messy kitchen invites needless breakage and attracts mischievous brownies.

Model your practices on the simplicity of the ancients. Don't feel compelled to rush out and buy obscure spices—start spelling with whatever your cabinets currently contain. A Witch can work much magic with only a few rudimentary makings. Sugar, honey, basil, anise, and fennel possess wondrous powers of attraction. Table salt provides money, abundance, and protection. Paprika and cayenne pepper banish nefarious folk. Raw egg makes a goodly binding agent to blend diverse ingredients. To magically dilute negativity, add water to any spell; to instill positivity, add milk. Recycle empty tincture bottles, Mason jars, wine bottles, and so on. Refill them with your own concoctions and brews.

To prevent fires, cuts, scalds, and accidental food poisoning, make a protective Kitchen Witch. Acquire or save a bottle no taller than 4 or 5 inches—dark glass is preferable to clear glass. Fill it with table salt; sharp objects, such as nails, glass, mirror or pottery shards, tacks, or pins; and some of your personal bodily fluid (any type). Cork or cap the bottle, label and date the contents (for instance, Kitchen Witch 5/15/05), then drip wax from a lit black candle all the way around the top to seal the bottle thoroughly. Store it in the back of a cupboard behind the rest of your spices. Should you ever start to experience a spate of close calls, such as knife nicks, check the primitive figurine to ensure that its seal remains intact; if the wax has flaked off, reseal the bottle, or discard it and make another from scratch.

To crush herbs, use two mortars and two pestles. Reserve one set solely for making toxic compounds, such as inks, dyes, or incense, and use the other for crushing culinary herbs that may be ingested. Grind sunwise when you're preparing a healing potion or to evoke goodly feelings in others, and ayenward whenever you make a magical repellent or banishing incense.

Consider the phase of the Moon before cooking. Dough rises higher and faster during a waxing or full Moon, and ingredients blend more easily when la Luna is waning or new. Label and date mixtures you make that require time to ferment or magically charge beneath the Sun or the Moon.

If you prepare something during the day but want the Moon to infuse it with lunar energy, transfer it to a silver platter and keep it in a shadowy corner until nightfall, when you can magically charge it adoors for seven, nine, or 28 minutes. To evoke solar energy in a healing soup, spoon it into a clear glass or golden bowl, set it on a windowsill, and let it soak up the Sun's rays for four, eight, or 12 minutes. If you're trying to win your way to a mate's heart by pleasing their belly, add extra Venusian energy to the enchanting edibles you prepare by serving them on a copper platter.

Make directional stirring second nature. For instance, whenever you crush herbs with a mortar and pestle, or mix, cook, or decorate a dish to conjure a positive effect, stir each ingredient you add and the resultant mixture sunwise a magical number of times. (See The Qualities of Quantities, page 136.) Intone a rhymed incantation to help you stir intentionally. Gaze intently into the mixture and become mesmerized by its swirling. Mentally infuse each ingredient with the specific attribute you expect it to contribute to the spell and the completed dish with your aspirations for the outcome you wish it to produce. Conversely, if you want to banish a problem, mix the ingredients in backward order if possible, and stir everything ayenward. Throughout, concentrate on the ways in which you'd like the problem to disappear; then see your loved ones acting relieved and happy again.

Mutter, whistle, or sing while cooking to alert the God/desses to your efforts. Set the heat to a magical number (three, five, seven, or nine on a burner) or, when possible, to a number that corresponds to your working. For instance, bake a round Sun cake at 365 degrees. Refrigerate, steep, ferment, or age your concoctions for a magical amount of time; for example, steep herbal tea for three to five minutes, and wait 21 days before sampling a medicinal tincture you made.

Tell your family or guests whenever you're brewing something magical so they won't inadvertently throw it out or sample it. Teach your friends or family the rudiments of basic amounts of herbals and magical concoctions that are normally safe to ingest—typically one to three droppersful of an herbal tincture, and one to three herbal capsules at a time. Further, scrupulously label and date everything you dry, save, or prepare for use. Cover the entire paper label with clear tape to prevent future spills from smudging the ink detailing the name of the preparation, its contents, and the date you made it.

Note the different results you elicit when you concoct by candlelight or enveloped in incense or soothing music—and when you cook beneath artificial lighting or while embroiled in familial supper-crunch tumult. The former conditions help produce precise, potent results; the latter are often responsible for unappealing or erratic results.

Candlelight is not the only way to create ambiance for magical meals you prepare. Accompany feasts with a Witchy centerpiece, such as a *Strega* spirit flame. Half fill a clear, heatproof glass bowl with some goodly cologne or alcoholic spirits. Ignite the liquid, dim the lights, and savor the haunting, sapphire-blue flames. Legend has it that camaraderie prevails as long as the fire dances.

Whenever you prepare something especially elaborate or traditionally magical, offer the first, best portion to the God/desses, garden devas (plant spirits), elementals, or animals. Save a few pinches of the dried, raw ingredients with which you made the masterpiece, and toss them adoors when you're done or put a small portion into a bowl atop your outdoor altar. The appeased spirits will in turn help ensure that your soufflés don't fall, your toast doesn't burn, and your kitchen Witchery skills deepen over time.

During the Victorian era, folks associated a meaning with each flower. Foods also have specific meanings that you can use in magical ways. For example, to entice a prospective mate, prepare a platter of fruit. Peaches mean "you're wondrous," grapes mean "you please all," and pears convey affection. To reestablish peace following a quarrel, offer olives, or show your remorse by serving raspberries. Delve into the fascinating realm of food correspondences and incorporate them into your magical repertoire.

Replenish your strength following lively spells or coven rites by eating ancient Witch cakes, traditionally consumed during the Cakes and Wine ceremony after raising a Cone of Power in circle. Mix several handfuls of wheat meal and 1 to 2 tablespoonfuls of honey into a paste. Add enough water to make the mixture malleable and a dash of table salt to taste. Finger-form the dough into numerous crescents (or horned Moons), and place them on a lightly greased baking sheet. Preheat the oven on a low setting; then bake slowly until the batch is done.

Make cookie stamps that promote healing or produce occult symbols on your culinary creations. Using self-hardening clay, finger-form several three-dimensional toadstool (mushroom) shapes. On each, indent two opposite sides of the stem portion to serve as a non-slip grip for your thumb and forefinger. Flatten each cap part, and sculpt on it a bas-relief of your chosen design. Perennial favorites include an interlaced pentagram, a lunar crescent, a solar disk with perimeter rays, or a symbol that signifies your coven. Poke a hole through each stem. Air dry the stamps, and then thread them onto a string and hang them to prevent breakage. When need be, wash them quickly with warm water. Use them to decorate cake tops, sugar cookies, Sabbat pies, and so on.

Making Healing Poppets

*M*ost ill folk simply don't feel well enough to work healing magic on themselves, so caretakers must often assume the task on their behalf. Although myriad healing spells exist (see Healing Spells, page 267), making a poppet of someone sick is one of the oldest and most effective ways to target and ameliorate a medical and mental condition—and the wax or string employed are very forgiving mediums for beginning spellcrafters.

A poppet is a simulacrum, or microcosmic representation, of a human body, animated by the energy you instill in it when you create it. Because it incorporates a bit of the ill person's DNA, their picture or signature, and so forth, it is connected to them by the magical principle of contagion.

To make a traditional healing poppet, assemble the following:

- a double boiler or two non-aluminum pots, one large enough to hold the other
- enough water to half fill the large pot
- several handfuls of beeswax or clear paraffin, or a virgin white candle or an appropriately colored used candle
- herbs that relieve or heal the infirm person's condition
- one or more intimate parts or representations of the ill person, such as a sample of hair, fingernail parings, any bodily fluid (cough sputum, urine, exudate, and so forth), a swatch of sweat-soaked garment, their photograph, and so on
- a heat source, such as a stove or hot plate

Half fill the bottom of your double boiler or the larger pot with distilled water (preferred) or tap water (will suffice in a pinch). Set the smaller container inside the other, and bring the water to a boil. If necessary, keep the smaller container from tipping over by holding its rim with a potholder. Place beeswax, paraffin, or candle wax in the top container, and melt it thoroughly. If you elect to recycle used candles, take care regarding their color—green can inadvertently induce infection, red can exacerbate fever, yellow can cause jaundice, black can cause tissue necrosis, and so on. Remember to remove wicks from the melted wax before sculpting.

Remove the top container, and pour the wax onto either a cool stone or concrete floor or waxed paper. Let the wax cool until you're able to finger-sculpt its gelatinous mass into a palm-sized, pentagram-shaped figure with a primitively fashioned head, arms, and legs. Put the representations of the person wherever they'd normally go—hair atop head, fingernail on hand, and so on. Poke holes in the figurine where their disorder is manifesting itself, and put in pinches of the herbs and seal the indentations with more wax.

When the poppet is air dried, cup your hands and comfortingly cocoon it in them. Coo to it, soothe it, sing, hum, or gently rock it awhile as you would a newborn infant or kitten. Hold a crystal or other healing stone in one hand, and make passes with it over the poppet, giving special attention to any weak area whence the symptoms or infirmity originates, or where their pain seems localized.

Lay the doll down on a soft bed of cotton balls or cool grasses in the curative and secretive Earth direction (North). Conceal the poppet carefully. You don't want it found by someone prejudiced or ignorant who has seen too many B horror movies about voodoo dolls and would leap to the worst conclusion, or clumsily or unethically misuse it.

When the infirm person fully recovers, pulverize the poppet and return it to Mother Earth through burial.

To make a healing poppet that is decorative and can be openly displayed, refer back to the Witch's Ladder on page 245. While praying for the person to recover, insert healing herbs, tiny quartz crystals, and fever-cooling feathers inside the knots you tie. If the patient is willing, place the healing string poppet above their sickbed and within the person's line of sight to serve as a focus for their recuperation.

Ever remember that all medicines can be used to harm as well as heal. Take as much care crafting a poppet as you'd lavish on a sick child.

Making Amulets and Talismans

*P*agans' belief in the merit of amuletic and talismanic magic is borne out by our penchant for wearing a pentagram to protect us with the power of the Four Elements plus Spirit. We consider it the best default sacred object because it incorporates so many powerful virtues. For example, because the pentagram represents the geometric template of a complete human body, it is a natural symbol of holistic health. The head and four limbs form the pentagram, and the proportions of human parts harmonize with the pentagram's Golden Mean proportions. A Pagan usually wears one around their neck as a periapt, (from the Greek *periaptós,* "hung around").

There is much debate in the Craft regarding the difference between an amulet and a talisman. Some say an amulet is any natural item that attracts, protects, or averts something in a broad way, such as a buckeye nut that conjures general abundance. Others insist that an amulet is anything worn in necklace form above the heart. Along the same vein, some say there is little distinction between an amulet and a talisman. Still others maintain that a talisman is any natural item bigraved with occult symbols or otherwise embellished, then magically charged by a Witch to accomplish a targeted magical goal. Originally, *amulet* was the Latin word and *talisman* was the Greek word for essentially the same thing—a magical object—but the two had slightly different connotations: a rough-and-ready Roman attitude as opposed to a Priest/essly Greek perspective.

In his *Natural History,* the Roman naturalist Pliny described an amulet—*amuletum*—as "an object that protects a person from trouble." An amulet in its most basic form is a natural item that is innately magical, and therefore requires no human alteration or influence in order to act on your behalf. Although you can always hold such items and work wish magic over them, or use them in basic spells as a focus that represents your desire, their powers are so intrinsically mighty that they're quite capable of working without such ritual accompaniment.

Millions of natural amulets exist, including precious and semiprecious gems, feathers, bones, resins, blossoms, nuts, herbs, metals, shells, and so on. Each one possesses one or more particular virtues, powers, or correspondences that can exert a specific influence regarding issues or circumstances that occur in your life.

Wearing an amulet is a goodly way to take your spellwork on the road with you. For instance, if you know in advance that you will be dealing with angry sorts of people and, hence, desire protection from their cursing, you can take steps ahead of time to repulse their ire by donning a reflective hematite necklace.

Talismans—derived from the Greek root *teleo,* "to consecrate to a purpose, accomplish"—are typically objects that humans alter or adorn in some way, then magically charge to achieve a specific spell purpose. Talismans are similar to amulets because they are composed of one or more natural ingredients, but they differ from amulets in that their structures are intentionally augmented to increase and refine their innate magical efficacy.

Talismans are usually crafted in exact ways. A spellcrafter often employs ancient methods and existing templates; for example, designs that invoke planetary powers to grant desirable qualities, such as eloquent speech or profound wisdom.

Witches often make a talisman by bigraving or casting occult symbols into a flat disk made of the metal sacred to the planet that corresponds to their magical cause. For a basic list of symbols, see Making Sigils and Seals, page 200. For metal/planetary correspondences, see The Seven Planets and Their Properties (page 88), or peruse the books we list as sources.

In the same manner, wooden or clay disks, a parchment roundel, a mirror, or any other appropriate (and corresponding) surface may be inscribed, decorated, or otherwise augmented to elicit a precise magical effect. Talismans can be hung above a bed or doorway, concealed, left to work continuously atop an indoor altar, or carried until their aim is achieved.

You can also construct a talisman by combining several amuletic components together synergistically—after all, if one spell element is goodly, three of a kind should work with triple intensity. For instance, to make someone impervious to withering looks and stinging stares, a Witch might fashion a fetish of fringe and peacock feathers wrapped around with blue lapis lazuli beads—all ancient ingredients renowned for bestowing that particular invulnerability. For the magical theory supporting the ingredients' efficacy, see To Avert the Evil Eye, page 425.

The line between amulets and talismans can be rather fine. For instance, if you yearn for the good will of others, you could simply carry an amulet in the form of a lump of raw copper, the metal sacred to the Goddess Venus. Should you pine for love from a particular belle or beau, however, you could fashion two interlacing rings from copper wire, then use them in a spell to win their love immediately. In this case, carrying the raw copper would be using an unaltered *amulet* to evoke a goodly response from people in general. Manipulating the metal into human symbols of commitment would be making a *talisman* to elicit requited love from a specific person.

By the same token, a silver ingot is innately magical without necessitating human intervention to make it more so. Because the metal resembles and corresponds to the Moon, you might elect to carry a raw lump of it to automatically attract mystical, lunar powers. You could also melt the reflective ore, design a charm or ring, cast it, bigrave it, and embed it with gems or otherwise embellish it to form a talisman to strengthen a magical bond.

Before working with amulets or designing talismans, read grimoires that document the age-old powers of objects. Delve into the subject at large in such tomes as *The Complete Book of Amulets & Talismans* or *Three Books of Occult Philosophy*. Particularly note illustrations of magic seals, occult symbols, or charms, such as the protective Hand of Fatima that you can then draw or otherwise duplicate.

Peruse ancient Books of Shadows, such as the *Greek Magical Papyri,* the *Picatrix,* and the *Greater and Lesser Key of Solomon*—just three of many sources replete with diagrams and step-by-step instructions for constructing, activating, and using amulets and talismans in spellwork.

Practice looking around and classifying objects in terms of their innate amuletic virtues versus their potential talismanic uses. For instance, a single rose thorn inherently repels ill will, but a thorn bigraved, say, with a violent ex-spouse's initials could serve as a potent, targeted talisman to prevent them from physically harming you.

Rather than buying expensive, prefabricated fetishes or lucky charms, go adoors, collect components, and make your own. For instance, if a thing seems strong or fire-resistant, carrying or wearing it could inspire courage within you.

Identify any quality you'd like, such as wisdom, eloquence, occult prowess, and so on; then make a talisman to accord you the power. Find the sigil or seal that's already proven its efficacy in endowing the ability you want. Then determine the metal the talisman is supposed to be cast in, and any gems that are traditionally inset in it. Cast the talisman yourself, or have it made by a trustworthy jeweler. Consecrate the talisman before use by immersing it in the Element it's associated with. For instance, wisdom and eloquence equate with the element Air, so you'd pass a talisman for that through incense smoke. Occult prowess equals Earth, so you should bury that type of talisman during Moondark. When you dig it up, it will transfer Earth's mystical secrets to you.

Make a mojo bag to hold tiny, but potent, amulets or talismans—you can change the contents at will depending on your need. Cut out a cloth or leather circle about 3 inches in diameter. Use an awl or a nail to punch holes every half-inch or so around its perimeter. Weave a leather thong or hemp cord through the holes, pull it tight to form the fabric or leather into a bag that will contain your ingredients, then tie the cord closed to complete your necklace.

A goodly way to dive into amuletic magic is to make a portable spell kit that you can use anywhere at a moment's notice. Such sets are indispensable additions to backpacks, tote bags, purses, or vehicle glove compartments. They afford Crafters the security of knowing that regardless of where they end up or what they become embroiled in, they can always retreat to a quiet corner and work magic to help themselves or others.

In choosing what to include in your kit, consider archetypal similitude and opposition—which things correspond with other things—as well as what constitutes a small version of its larger counterpart. For example, Lady Passion's portable spell kit, housed in a zippered, black leather bag, includes:

- a black and white tiger-striped scarf to use as a layout cloth
- a tiny spiral seashell, which represents the Goddess
- a black shark's tooth, which represents the God
- colored birthday candles, with holders for standing them up in dirt or sand
- matches and a striker
- a packet of black Witch's salt and a packet of white table salt
- a vial of amber and a vial of patchouli essential oil, representing women and men, respectively
- a compass to determine the Four Quarters
- a piece of black and a piece of red hemp string for knot magic

- a micro-sized Ouija board complete with a tiny planchette
- a scallop shell and a packet of sand, to combine and use as an incense burner
- cone incense
- several small lids or cups to serve as libation bowls or chalices
- a vial of water and a vial of wine
- a tiny pocketknife to serve as an athamé
- two toothpicks and two drilled gemstone star beads, one black and one white. When a toothpick is inserted into a bead's hole, it makes a diminutive magic wand—the dark star becomes a blasting rod, and the light star, a blessing baton.

$\mathscr{H}$OW TO KNOW YOU'RE
DOING SPELLS PROPERLY

"Call to mind, I pray you, how often ceremonies are repeated, because through negligence or accident some detail of the ancestral ritual has been omitted."

—LIVY
History of Rome

Spells succeed when you follow their formulas and earn the favor of the God/desses through your goodly and ethical intent. Spells don't work or can backfire if you perform them haphazardly or irreverently, or use them to serve an unethical agenda. Sometimes, even though your technique is perfect and your conscience pure, a spell fails because the God/desses know more about the situation than you do. If they allowed the spell to succeed, it could go against your true intention or inadvertently harm you or others. At other times, the problem you are dealing with is just so complex or entrenched that one casting isn't sufficient to resolve it. Following the magical principle of repetition, you may need to cast the same spell more than once.

At all times before, during, and after you undertake a spell, it's wise to observe omens and portents that bear on the problem your spell is intended to address. You can also troubleshoot during a spell for omens that indicate how it is progressing. For example, an easy ritual setup bodes well, but breakage suggests that you should postpone the working.

Stop your spell when you get a feeling of certainty that it has "taken hold."

This feeling is often an inner tingling, but may resemble hyper-alertness, or even a slight shock. One moment the spell is moving apace; the next, you suddenly realize that what was a work in progress has become perfect, powerful, and complete. Your ears may ring, your body buzz, and a sense of accomplishment seem to resonate in the air for some time. There is simply nothing more to do—your passion is spent, the God/desses have heard, and the spell has hit its target. Afterward, you will see the results for yourself in the changes that occur in the situation.

Spellwork Rules of Thumb

WRAP YOURSELF IN THE BEWITCHING BEAUTY OF THE OLDE RELIGION. While modern mundane life saps the soul, Craft rites make you bloom. Personal experience practicing magic teaches you to think for yourself— to reject repressive dogma, political propaganda, and militaristic tyranny in favor of achieving your highest ideals, developing Crafty talents, and helping the world in truly life-affirming ways.

DON'T RESERVE SPELLS AS A MEANS OF LAST RESORT—INTEGRATE MAGIC INTO YOUR DAILY LIFE. Revel in your mystic might and enjoy being able to pad life's corners for your loved ones.

CONSECRATE A PRIVATE PLACE TO USE SOLELY FOR SORCERY. If you practice indoors but can't spare an entire room, designate a shelf or table as an altar to be used for magical purposes only.

IF POSSIBLE, ERECT AN ALTAR IN EACH OF THE FOUR DIRECTIONS TO HELP YOU WORK WITH THE FUNDAMENTAL ELEMENTS OF MATTER. To know a thing is to master it, so decorate each altar with its appropriately corresponding things that you can find around you in nature:

EAST—Airy things, such as incenses; crystalline, birch-wood, and golden fetishes; feathers, butterfly wings, pictures of fairies, and so forth; transparent, white, or yellow décor

SOUTH—Fiery things, such as candles; phosphorescent, redwood, and iron fetishes; horns, claws, fangs, thorns, and so forth; red, orange, or pink décor [55]

WEST—Watery things, such as potions and oils; shell, driftwood, and silver fetishes; a chalice, fountain, mirror, and so forth; blue, iridescent, or silver décor

NORTH—Earthy things, such as herbs; clay, ebony, and copper fetishes; stones, bones, coins, rice or wheat, and so forth; green, brown, or black décor

EMBELLISH YOUR DEVOTIONAL SURFACES WITH A PLETHORA OF NATURAL SYMBOLS AND COLOR-COORDINATED CANDLES—LET THE WIND OF YOUR WHISPERED WISHES MELT THEIR WAX INTO DRIPPY DECORATIONS. Coven Oldenwilde's Quarter altars are filled with manifestations that have occurred during spells, components donated by grateful students and clients, and precious trinkets acquired during backpacking adventures. Selenite and citrine wands and quartz crystals glitter on our eastern altar; carnelians, garnets, rose quartz, knives, and red peppers vie for attention on our southern altar; conch and scallop shells, sea salt, and a bowl of Nile water overflow our western altar; and lodestones, etched slate, and ceramic skulls rest upon our northern altar.

RECYCLE MUNDANE OR ODIOUS OBJECTS FOR THE POWER OF GOOD. Sheaves of wheat put in a female-shaped syrup bottle can be a simple and lovely Demeter statuette; a silver thrift store platter, a dazzling ritual Cakes plate.

BEGIN PRACTICING MAGIC WITH BASIC TOOLS AND ACQUIRE MIGHTIER MAGICAL TOOLS AND CIRCLE PARAPHERNALIA OVER TIME. Fill a clear cup with salt and another with water. Use string for working knot magic. Obtain a round piece of wood, a tile, or a metal trivet to act as a pentacle on which to magically charge (energize) and bless things.

PURCHASE OR MAKE CANDLES. If you lack the traditional colors associated with the Four Directions, substitute white, which symbolizes purity of spirit, or red, which stands for the blood of life.

ACQUIRE A BELL TO RING TO BEGIN A SPELL, TO TRANSITION BETWEEN DIFFERENT PARTS OF A SPELL, AND TO SIGNAL ITS END. Make pouches from leather and fabric scraps. Find an appealing wooden stick, and whittle it into a personal

---

[55] *If you are south of the equator, Fire is the North Quarter altar, and Earth is the South Quarter altar.*

staff, either walking stick–size, or no taller than a head above your height. Make a wand—the traditional size is no longer than a cubit, the distance from your inner elbow to the tip of your middle finger. Prepare potions from a variety of herbs, oils, and waters, and saved storage bottles and jars.

ACQUIRE A BLACK-HILTED, DULL, DOUBLE-EDGED KNIFE TO USE AS AN ATHAMÉ FOR CONDUCTING ETHEREAL OPERATIONS, SUCH AS DRAWING MAGIC SIGNS IN THE AIR, CASTING OR EXITING A CIRCLE, SUMMONING THE ELEMENTS, AND DIRECTING AND DIS-CHARGING RAISED POWER. Cut nothing but air with this knife. (You can cut wicks, bigrave candles, or scrape up wax and so forth with a white-hilted utility knife, or boleen.)

USE BEAUTIFUL, VALUABLE, OR RUGGEDLY RAW MAGICAL INGREDIENTS. Determine what evokes your most magical response—silver candelabra, or candles set in dirt. Both approaches have equal validity, and your preferences will naturally change over time as you spiritually deepen.

CONDUCT YOUR RITES BAREFOOT, TO ENHANCE YOUR SENSITIVITY TO MAGICAL ENERGIES. Don't wear a watch and don't allow an electrical device in circle—they break when you tweak space-time. Spurn plastic in sacred space.

PURIFY, THEN CONSECRATE YOUR MAGICAL TOOLS TO RECOGNIZE THEIR SACRED-NESS AND TARGET THEIR POWER TOWARD YOUR DESIRE. No matter the tool, first consecrate it to the East. Verbally introduce it to that direction—hold it in your left hand, then call on Air and pass the tool through incense or smoke. Next, consecrate it in the South (or Fire) Quarter—pass it through a candle flame or cauldron fire. Consecrate it in the West—dowse it with Water, scented oils, or viscous liquids. Finally, cast dirt on it, place moss on it, set it on the ground, sprinkle it with salt, or keep it for a time in close proximity with Earth in the North Quarter. In this way, you immerse the tool in each of the Four Elements necessary for powerful magic. You may want to do this during the day or hour of the planet that corresponds to the tool. Mercury is good for most tools, but it is traditional to consecrate an athamé during the day or hour of Saturn.

PERFORM SPELLS WHEN SPECIFIED OR AT THE MOST ASTROLOGICALLY OPPOR-TUNE TIME. If no particular time is mandatory, do spells on the weekday that has traditional influence regarding your problem or desire, or consult a lunar or an astrological calendar to determine the most powerful time to augment your intent.

ANCIENT FORMULAS HAVE A LONG HISTORY OF PRODUCING RELIABLE RESULTS, SO

ALWAYS OPT TO WORK THE OLDEST RITE OR CONCOCT THE RAREST RECIPE YOU CAN FIND. Do modern workings only when they clearly derive from traditional Craft practices.

MAGIC WILL NOT MANIFEST ITSELF AMIDST THE IRREVERENT OR OBNOXIOUS, SO AVOID FEAR-BASED FEIGNERS AND PAGAN POSERS. Circle with competent folk in an evocative setting permeated with alluring ambiance. Work beneath moonlight or by candlelight, enveloped in copious clouds of incense and encircled by enchanting accoutrements.

GENERALLY, USE ODD NUMBERS IN SPELLWORK, ESPECIALLY *3, 7, 9, 13,* AND *21.* When necessary, however, use appropriately corresponding numbers of ingredients, knots, or gestures during workings. For instance, use the powers of *3* whenever you want to represent feminine force, and the powers of *2* to represent masculine energy.

A SUBSTITUTED SPELL INGREDIENT WILL CREATE THE SAME MAGICAL EFFECT AS AN UNAVAILABLE INGREDIENT IF THEY MAGICALLY CORRESPOND TO EACH OTHER. If you must simulate specified components, use your Wiccan common sense to deduce natural alternatives. For instance, should you lack winter snow to break a summer drought, you could shave an ice block into passable snow; however, your spell will likely fail if you use Christmas-tree flocking instead because it's plastic and its ozone-depleting propellant contributes to global warming.

NATURE ABHORS A VACUUM. WHEN ALTERING THE PRESENT COURSE OF EVENTS WITH SPELLWORK, PREVENT THE UNIVERSE FROM RUSHING IN TO FILL THE VOID YOU CREATE. Recompense the cosmos with an offering, or vow to reciprocate in some way should your request be granted. Every goodly gain is paired with a potential backspin, or afterclap, to use the Witch word for it. Proceed only when you're sure that your magical might will be sufficient to overcome all possible side effects that could result from impressing your human will to alter time, space, and the orthodox laws of physics.

SUMMON, STIR, AND CALL UP SPIRITS AT WILL. Resist conditioned fear of the unknown. Many beneficent ancestral spirits yearn for your contact, heed, and reciprocal relationship. Conjure, invoke, evoke, chant, cavort, dance, sing, laugh, love, and appeal to deeply powerful God/desses at any time during spellwork. The more often you pray to God/desses and spirits, the more they will know you, remember your previous efforts on their behalf, and thus be inclined to grant boons you humbly request.

PAY PARTICULAR HEED TO EVENTS THAT OCCUR DURING SPELLWORK OR IN SACRED CIRCLE. An eerie calm foretells as much as a sudden storm. Every unusual bird chirp, dog bark, frog croak, floorboard squeak, wind-chime ring, siren wail, blaring car horn, or power outage can betoken a meaning relevant to your rite. As a magical practitioner, your task is to give due weight and credence to such divine messages, and to interpret their purpose for the benefit of all.

FAMILIARS' MOVEMENTS DURING SPELLWORK OFTEN CONVEY HOW THE GOD/DESSES PERCEIVE YOUR MAGICAL EFFORTS. Witches value practically every species for its ability to produce accurate omens—parrots, ravens, doves, frogs, cats, and dogs, to name a few. You can interpret their omens according to the number of animals that appear, the direction they come from or move toward, the sequence of their vocalizations, their color, and so on.

MAGIC TAKES AS LONG AS IT TAKES. Invocations or supplications to Deities may last only minutes, but most rituals necessitate an hour or more. Not to worry—if you're properly focused on your task, time will be the last thing on your mind. Further, if your need is dire, you won't care how long a spell takes as long as it rectifies the problem.

LEARN TO LET GO AND ENJOY OCCULT MYSTERIES AS THEY OCCUR. Although you may prepare for an elaborate rite for days, weeks, or even months, there comes a time when your preparation should be complete. When you've prepared well, simply relax, begin, and revel in the spirit of your spell. When awe-inspiring things happen, don't analyze away the miracle—appreciate that you saw them.

DON'T RUSH THROUGH RITES—ENJOY YOUR MYSTIC TIME. Say everything that needs to be said. Do everything that needs to be done, and often more, but never less. Better yet, attack your problems with passion, relish your rites, and indulge your creative whims within the embrace of safe magical space. With practice, you'll find your flow, get into a rhythm, determine your best way of working and, most important, experience satisfaction when your spell takes hold.

A SPELL'S SUCCESS IS OFTEN PROPORTIONATE TO THE AMOUNT OF RISK THE WITCH HAS TAKEN TO WORK IT. The wild unbridled thrill you get from procuring grimoire ingredients or conducting a secret grove or graveyard rite innately boosts your magical power.

ALTHOUGH MOST SPELLS PRODUCE CONSISTENTLY PRECISE RESULTS, REMAIN OPEN FOR YOUR WORKINGS TO MANIFEST YOUR DESIRES IN A VARIETY OF FORTUITOUS

FORMS. If you do a rite for a new roof, for instance, don't assume you'll win a lottery to help you pay for it—you may be blessed instead with meeting a talented, honest, and affordable contractor.

THE PROPER DISPOSAL OF RITUAL REMAINS IS THE CRUCIAL FINAL STEP IN MOST CRAFT SPELLS. Therefore, Witches often target their choice of methods to reinforce their magical intention. For example, because things that foster communication are akin to Air, we cast eastern ingredients to the winds. Southern anger eradicators we consign to candle flame, a cauldron fire, or a fireplace. We throw western ingredients that resolve emotions into a soothing stream, and bury wealth-bringing northern materials. Spell remains (*katharmata*) are sacred to Hecate, to whom you may offer them. A note of caution, however: Don't be too hasty in disposing of your spell ingredients—spells need time to work, and if you break up their components too quickly, you risk negating the magical good you've done. Wait about three times longer than you think you should before disposing of your spell ingredients.

DON'T WORRY DONE SPELLS TO DEATH. To obsess over a spell is to doubt the powers that enable your rites, which could nullify the working. Once done, simply leave your circle without looking back. Banish the deed from your mind to give the God/desses time to effect the change; and to prevent your work from being jinxed or negated by another, avoid bragging about your magical expectations.

THE UNIVERSE WILL PROVIDE YOU WITH PROMPT FEEDBACK ABOUT HOW YOUR SPELL IS PROGRESSING. If you haven't received any validation after three nights or, at most, a week, anoint a virgin black candle with your Witchiest essential oil, then light it and scry its smoke for omens about the matter. Should you see a negative omen, you'd be in a welcome minority if you abandon the enterprise as being obviously at odds with the God/desses' will or foreknowledge. If after careful thought, however, you still feel that the situation necessitates mystical measures, breach the impasse by either doing a similar spell, or repeating your original rite during a more astrologically auspicious time.

RECORD ALL PERTINENT PORTENTS AND SPOOKY SYNCHRONICITIES THAT OCCUR DURING AND AFTER SPELLWORK. Let the feelings they evoke guide your actions. Refer to your records upon occasion to track your magical progress.

> KATHARMATA ARE RITUAL REMNANTS, such as candle stubs, leftovers from the Cakes and Wine ceremony, or half-burnt incense, and so forth, sacred to the Goddess Hecate in her aspect of wizened crone. To give such an offering to the Goddess of Witches, leave it at a triple crossroads and depart without a backward glance.

The Rule of Two

*Y*OU MAY NEED TO REPEAT A SPELL SEVERAL TIMES BEFORE YOU'RE ABLE TO MASTER IT. The first time you work an unfamiliar spell, beginner's luck will help you succeed.

THE SECOND TIME YOU TRY IT, HOWEVER, YOU'RE LIKELY TO ENCOUNTER A PHENOMENON THAT WE CALL "THE RULE OF TWO." Opposition enters in, and you will likely run into difficulties that test your magical resolve. Often, on your second attempt, whatever can go wrong does.

NO MATTER WHAT HAPPENS, REMAIN PRECISE AND PERSISTENT THROUGHOUT. Stay your course, and by the third time around, the spell typically works flawlessly. Ever remember that three times is the charm!

The 24-Hour Rule

*R*IGHT AFTER YOU CAST A SPELL, YOU MAY BE TEMPTED TO SPECULATE ALOUD ABOUT WHETHER YOU DID IT CORRECTLY. You may attend a rite that you find boring, confusing, hard to hear, or clumsily performed, and feel compelled to critique it as soon as you're out of the Priest/ess's earshot. Even after experiencing an undeniably powerful working, you may erect a mental wall of disbelief in reaction to the mind-blowing phenomena you witnessed.

THE GREEKS DEPICTED THE DESTRUCTIVE EFFECT OF DOUBT OR MISTRUST ON MAGIC IN THE STORY OF ORPHEUS AND EURYDICE. The magical musician Orpheus charmed his way past the gates of the Underworld and succeeded in winning his beloved Eurydice back from the Deities of Death—on the single condition that he not look backward on the return journey to the world of the living. Orpheus couldn't resist giving in to his skepticism, however. He turned around to prove to himself that Eurydice really was following behind—and caught just a glimpse of her before she disappeared forever.

HEED THIS TALE, AND EMBODY THE WITCHES' POWER TO BE SILENT. Invoke the 24-Hour Rule and wait at least a day before you make any negative comments or pass any judgments about any spell or rite. Ever remember: A spell you can't fathom may gladden the Gods.

PART III

SPELLS

*"O come
magical one
and feel the mystic thrill
Practice
practice magic
to master the Witches' skill."*

— LADY PASSION

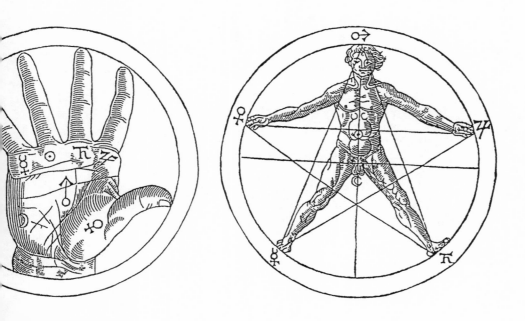

Spell Recipes for Common Needs and Problems

Here are hundreds of powerful spells and spell variations drawn from many cultures throughout history, as well as some we've created and used successfully ourselves. Beneath each spell is information about its culture of origin; the best time to perform it; its necessary ingredients; the best ambiance, or physical and psychic milieu, in which to perform it; the magical principle(s) on which it's based; and any Deities to invoke during the working. Should a spell not require the aid of a specific God/dess, feel free to supplicate your favorite Deity.

· Healing Spells ·

"Therefore among all people who use charms and spells those which are devoted to cure occupy the principal position."
—Charles Godfrey Leland
Gypsy Sorcery and Fortune Telling

Modern medicine can be great—when you can get it. However, between unaffordable insurance, expensive synthetic drugs, indifferent doctors, infection-ridden hospitals, and many medical industries' priority of profits over patients, you're lucky to get an illness even treated, much less cured. It's only prudent, then, to rely as much as possible on nature's effective remedies—including the traditional magical medicine of spellcraft.

TO BREAK A FEVER

FEVERISH FOLKS RISK DEVELOPING CONVULSIONS, BRAIN DAMAGE, coma, and even death. So, when the chill-sweat cycle grips your loved ones, take immediate curative action.

Comfortably situate your ill one above the waterline on a sandy beach during high tide. Let the retreating waves carry the disorder out to sea. Alternatively, brew an infusion of one teaspoon of feverweed in one cup of hot water and have the ill person drink it. (Don't exceed one dose per day.) While the sick person sips the drink, recite the olde Abracadabra Charm:

Abracadabra
Abracadabr
Abracadab
Abracada
Abracad
Abraca
Abrac
Abra
Abr
Ab
A

Say the words and word parts as if you were reading from left to right. Note that the glyph has a left line of *A*'s, and spells out *abracadabra* on its top and (from below, upward) its right side. Further, the inverted triangle is the same shape as the symbol for the element water. Conjuring water helps the sickly sweat a fever off. The rune's diminishing appearance visually depicts your desire to lessen something—in this case, a fever.

Gently rock or stroke the feverish as you recite this charm. We advise rocking forward during the initial **Ab** sound, then backward during the following **brah**. Skip a beat to breathe, then rock forward again to punctuate **kah-dah** and back again to finish the second **brah** in a mere whisper.

Begin by intoning *abracadabra* nine times in a row. When you've completed that first series, repeat the process, but drop the last letter: Say *abracabr* nine times in a row, without the final *a*. Keep repeating this pattern, always remembering to drop a letter after you've intoned a series nine times consecutively. Eventually, you'll have to say only the first letter (*a*) nine times in succession (pronounce it as *ah*). To prevent the patient from relapsing, be sure to complete the entire charm. You'll chant *abracadabra* either completely or in part a total of 99 times.

To prevent or cure fevers, make the following talisman from the *Papyri Graecae Magicae* for folks to carry or wear. Inscribe it on parchment on a Sunday just before midnight.[56]

ΑΒΛΑΝΑΘΑΝΑΒΛΑΝΑΜΑΧΑΡΑΜΑΡΑΧΑΡΑΜΑΡΑΧ
ΒΛΑΝΑΘΑΝΑΒΛΑΝΑΜΑΧΑΡΑΜΑΡΑΧΑΡΑΜΑΡΑ
ΛΑΝΑΘΑΝΑΒΛΑΝΑΜΑΧΑΡΑΜΑΡΑΧΑΡΑΜΑΡ
ΑΝΑΘΑΝΑΒΛΑΝΑΜΑΧΑΡΑΜΑΡΑΧΑΡΑΜΑ
ΝΑΘΑΝΑΒΛΑΝΑΜΑΧΑΡΑΜΑΡΑΧΑΡΑΜ
ΑΘΑΝΑΒΛΑΝΑΜΑΧΑΡΑΜΑΡΑΧΑΡΑ
ΘΑΝΑΒΛΑΝΑΜΑΧΑΡΑΜΑΡΑΧΑΡ
ΑΝΑΒΛΑΝΑΜΑΧΑΡΑΜΑΡΑΧΑ
ΝΑΒΛΑΝΑΜΑΧΑΡΑΜΑΡΑΧ
ΑΒΛΑΝΑΜΑΧΑΡΑΜΑΡΑ
ΒΛΑΝΑΜΑΧΑΡΑΜΑΡ
ΛΑΝΑΜΑΧΑΡΑΜΑ
ΑΝΑΜΑΧΑΡΑΜ
ΝΑΜΑΧΑΡΑ
ΑΜΑΧΑΡ
ΜΑΧΑ
ΑΧ
Α

Were you to pronounce it, the topmost word of this talisman would be rendered *ah-BLAH-nah-THAH-nah-BLAH-nah-MAH-khah-RAH-mah-RAH-khah-RAH-mah-RAKH*. It derives from a mystical appellation of the Sun God, ABLANATHANALBA AKRAMMAKHAMARI, which appears in a

---

[56] PGM, *XXXIII, 1–25.*

number of invocations in the *Papyri Graecae Magicae,* usually in association with the Deity Abraxas. (See To Summon Strength, page 278.) The name *ABLANATHANALBA* is a palindrome—it reads the same way backward as it does forward. This is even more obvious when it's written in its original Greek, in which the central *th* sound appears as the round, sunlike letter *theta* (Θ) from which the other letters symmetrically radiate:

ΑΒΛΑΝΑΘΑΝΑΛΒΑ

In the talisman, a variation of this Solar name on the left side is paired with an Earthy palindrome on the right,

ΧΑΡΑΜΑΡΑΧΑΡΑΜΑΡΑΧ

which is centered on, and flanked by, the four-quartered letter *chi,*

Χ

pronounced *kh.*

As you whittle away the topmost word's letters one by one from both ends, the other two sides of the triangle repeat each half of it—the first half (ΑΒΛΑΝΑΘΑΝΑΒΛΑΝΑΜΑ) running down the triangle's left side and the second half (ΧΑΡΑΜΑΡΑΧΑΡΑΜΑΡΑΧ) running down its right.

SPELL VARIATIONS

- Transfer the sufferer's illness to another life form. Tie a small lock of the person's hair to an aspen tree (or any shrub the wind frequently stirs) while intoning this spell:

> *Aspen tree, aspen tree.*
> *I prithee to shake*
> *and shiver 'stead of me!*

- Put some of the ill person's nail parings in a cleft of a tree, and seal the opening closed with a cork or wax.
- Keep a cut onion under the ill person's bed.

- An olde home remedy calls for feeding the patient a dead, non-poisonous spider in fruit or something sweet, such as jam.
- If the ill one is able, have him or her pull up some dwarf nettle roots.
- Caretakers can poke elder tree twigs into the ground, or give the ill a moonstone, agate, or garnet talisman to wear.

SPELL ORIGIN: Irish and European magic

SPELL TIMING: During high tide; chant the Abracadabra Charm as needed; make the talisman just before midnight on a Sunday.

INGREDIENTS: a beach at high tide; one teaspoon of feverweed, a teakettle, and one cup of water

> FOR THE VARIATIONS: a lock of hair and an aspen tree; a cut onion; a non-poisonous, dead spider; dwarf nettle roots; elder tree twigs; a moonstone, agate, or garnet talisman

AMBIANCE: a cooling river or ocean; in your kitchen, then near the ill person; alone in your ritual space

MAGICAL THEORY: Abracadabra likely derives from the ancient Chaldean phrase *abbâdâ ke dâbrâ,* meaning "perish like the word."

> SYMPATHETIC MAGIC: As you discard more of *abracadabra*'s letters, so the fever diminishes by degrees. Moonstone cools the fevered brow, the swirling colors of agate confuse fever spirits, and garnet challenges high temperatures with its own russet glow.

> INVERSION: The ABLANATHANALBA talisman is an intricate acrostic that channels magical energy in much the same way as a rhymed spell. Although the Sun is primarily associated with health, it's also hot, like fever. When you make the ABLANATHANALBA talisman, you should appeal for the Sun's favor (health) on Sunday, but when his power is weakest—before midnight leading to Monday. You can use a thing's qualities to relieve a condition it resembles—an onion is hot like fever, garnet stones are red like fire, and the leaves of the aspen tree shiver like someone sick with chills.

> ANTIPATHETIC MAGIC: As water quenches fire, so ocean waves can eliminate bodily fire (fever).

TO PROMOTE WELLNESS

FOR LONG-TERM HEALING AND TO PREVENT ILLNESS, PRECIOUS AND semiprecious stones are effective magical partners of the physical medicine of herbs. Gems are most effective when worn continuously—especially when set in a ring to wear on a finger or as a pendant to rest atop the heart.

Rings have a long history of magically binding certain powers to the wearer. The ancients often bigraved Deities' images onto precious stones and set them into signet rings used to seal important documents. To this day, people accord wedding rings such power that they consider it a terrible omen for a marriage if they lose theirs—or, conversely, they will throw the ring away on purpose as a magical act to break the marriage bond. As Agrippa wrote,

> *"Rings . . . do fortify us against sickness, poisons, enemies, evil spirits, and all manner of hurtful things, or at least will not suffer us to be kept under them."* [57]

Constructing and wearing a ring with a specific stone to target, treat, and banish an infirmity works by either sympathetic or oppositional magic. A stone has magical virtues and qualities based on its density, shape, color, clarity, reflectivity, and other geological properties. These correspondences can be used sympathetically, to conjure health, or antipathetically, to repel illness.

For example, when Lady Passion developed life-threatening *grand mal* seizures because of a vascular disorder, her symptoms were alleviated when our Third Degree Rowan Greenleaf cast a silver ring for her with an inset bloodstone cabochon. Lady Passion wears many magical rings—lapis lazuli to suppress the disorder; rainbow moonstones to augment her magic; alexandrite to attract luck, love, and good fortune; hematite to repel the Evil Eye; and aquamarine for calm amidst chaos.

The best way for a healing stone to be set in a ring is as a cabochon, or dome-shaped gem, with the flat underside of the stone touching or very close to the skin. To speed healing, wear the ring on your index, or pointing, finger. Avoid synthetic stones.

---

[57] Agrippa, *"Of Rings, and their Compositions,"* in Three Books of Occult Philosophy.

If you can't afford to contract with a jeweler to set the stone you need, do the next best thing: Purchase a thick, bendable gauge of silver or copper craft wire, consult a book on wire-wrapping techniques, and duplicate your favorite style. String on a central gem that alters your mood for the better, or a stone known to heal your specific ailment.

Here is a list of readily available gemstones and their tried-and-true healing virtues:

agate—*makes the wearer amiable; eliminates jealousy and spiteful behavior*

alexandrite—*attracts luck, true love, and good fortune*

amber—*dispels gloom; instills positive energy; when rubbed against wool or silk, produces static electricity (its ancient Greek name was* elektron, *whence the word* electricity *derives); imbues the wearer with wisdom, balance, and patience; promotes altruism; provides protection, luck, solar strength, and healing*

amethyst—*cures alcoholism; increases psychism and spirituality; instills calm and contentment; heals illnesses; manifests peace, love, and happiness*

aquamarine—*soothes sadness; promotes tranquility; protects travelers across waterways*

beryl—*prevents seasickness; stops hurtful gossip against the wearer; protects the wearer from being easily manipulated by others*

bloodstone—*treats vascular disorders; stanches hemorrhage and heals wounds; helps the wearer win physical competitions*

blue lace agate—*imbues the wearer with peace and happiness; sacred to girls*

blue quartz—*promotes serenity and psychism*

carnelian—*lures lovers; increases sexuality, strength, and fertility*

chalcedony—*increases lactation; banishes fear; stops hysteria; treats mental illness*

chrysolite (olivine/peridot)—*banishes night phantoms, thereby promoting sleep; imbues the wearer with a positive attitude; attracts love and money*

chrysoprase—*minimizes selfishness; aids eloquence*

clear quartz—*purifies; imbues folks with added energy*

coral—*protects children; regulates women's menstrual cycles; dispels panic and murderous ideation*

diamond set in onyx—*imbues the wearer with control over sexual appetites*

emerald—*improves the wearer's memory and eyesight*

garnet—*makes dreams reality; reinvigorates; increases endurance; inspires love; enhances sexuality*

green aventurine—*improves intelligence and eyesight; calms emotions; speeds healing*

green jasper—*protects the wearer against illness*

heliotrope—*makes the wearer invisible*

hematite—*protects by deflecting negativity away from the wearer and reflecting it back to its origin*

iolite—*calms the wearer; improves emotional clarity; dispels discord*

jade—*heals the body; protects the wearer from mishaps and inclement weather; grants long life and wisdom; lures love and prosperity*

jasper—*minimizes dangerous impulses and protects the wearer from hazardous situations*

jet—*prevents illness, nightmares, violence, and psychic attack; stabilizes mood swings; absorbs negativity*

labradorite—*stimulates the imagination, producing contemplation and introspection; relieves stress and induces calm*

lapis lazuli—*reduces fever; alleviates blood diseases*

malachite—*breaks into pieces to warn the wearer of impending peril; attracts money; calms the nervous system; promotes tranquility; induces therapeutic sleep*

milky quartz—*aids lactation*

moonstone—*aids dieting; imbues the wearer with joy and youthfulness; grants magic powers; stimulates intuition; reduces tension; lures good luck; protects travelers*

onyx—*helps the wearer face adversaries and conflicts; reduces sexual desire*

opal—*when wrapped in a bay leaf, imbues the wearer with inner beauty and invisibility; helps the wearer remember past incarnations and travel astrally*

red jasper—*cures fevers*

rhodocrosite—*draws love; imbues the wearer with extra physical energy during exertion or peace during a bath*

rhodonite—*minimizes confusion; makes the wearer coherent; banishes self doubt and others' paranoia*

rose quartz—*attracts innocent love*

ruby—*darkens to warn the wearer of peril; imbues the wearer with invulnerability; encourages folks to "follow your bliss"; aids in retaining wealth and passion; increases body temperature; shields from psychic attack. Olde spells that require a carbuncle mean a ruby cabochon.*

sapphire—*strengthens vision and heals disorders of the eye; reduces fever and stops nosebleeds; reduces anger and reconciles foes; protects the wearer from being captured or imprisoned; promotes chastity or fidelity; imparts wisdom; enhances meditation*

sard—*promotes easy childbirth*

sardonyx—*imbues the wearer with fearless eloquence (especially helpful regarding legal testimony); stops domestic strife*

serpentine—*prevents snakebite and guards against stinging or poisonous insects and animals; imbues the wearer with double blessings from the God/desses; increases lactation*

sodalite—*eliminates nervousness and heals stress-related illnesses; dispels guilt; reduces inner turmoil*

sugilite—*aids healing and meditation; grants wisdom; increases the wearer's awareness of the spiritual world (versus the material world)*

sunstone—*imbues the wearer with the strength of the Sun; increases physical power and will; stimulates sexual arousal*

tiger's-eye—*protects the wearer; averts the Evil Eye; conveys the awareness and strength of a tiger to the weak or infirm*

topaz—*regulates digestion (aids weight loss); relieves joint pain; stops sleepwalking; protects the wearer against jealousy, disease, accidents, injury, and lunacy; confers invisibility*

tourmaline—*when rubbed or heated, becomes polarized (positively charged on one end and negatively charged on the opposite end). Magical attributes depend on its color. Pink attracts help and sympathy; red promotes courage and strengthens will; green draws money for medical bills and increases creativity; blue reduces anxiety and fosters sleep; black grounds scattered energy and free-floating anxiety; watermelon-colored*

balances feminine and masculine energies (particularly helpful for
transgendered folks).

turquoise—*protects the wearer from diseases, falls, violence, accidents,
injury, poison, snakebite, and all danger; when given to a mate, will fade
to warn if their love wanes; heals eyes; reduces fevers; minimizes
headaches or migraines; imbues the wearer with joy and makes him or her
amiable; attracts friends*

SPELL VARIATIONS

- An ancient way to remain disease-free for a solid year is to walk thrice around a balefire during Litha, on June 21 or 22. Pagans often repeatedly jump over a balefire during this summer solstice Sabbat.
- Time healing actions for when the Moon is passing through the sign associated with the part of the body with which you're concerned. To strengthen a particular body part, work magic when the Moon is waxing in the sign associated with it; to banish pain or minimize a malady, act when the Moon is waning in the appropriate sign.

ASTROLOGY AND ANATOMY

Aries—*head, face, upper jaw, brain*
Taurus—*neck, throat, mouth, vocal chords, lower jaw, ears*
Gemini—*arms, hands, shoulders, lungs, bronchial tubes*
Cancer—*chest, breasts, abdomen, stomach, womb*
Leo—*heart, eyes, upper back, head and facial hair*
Virgo—*intestines*
Libra—*kidneys, ovaries, lower back*
Scorpio—*genitalia; urinary and excretory organs*
Sagittarius—*thighs, liver*
Capricorn—*knees, bones, skin, nails*
Aquarius—*lower legs, circulatory system*
Pisces—*feet, lymphatic system*

- Schedule basic medical procedures for these times, with one important exception: Avoid surgery on a particular body part when the Moon is in that sign, or you risk hemorrhaging or developing an infection. Instead, schedule surgery for when the Moon is in a sign that rules a body part that's as far away as possible from the one that ails you. For instance, if you need foot surgery, don't schedule it for when the Moon is in Pisces, which rules the feet—wait until the Moon is in Aries, which rules the head, or Taurus, which rules the neck.

SPELL ORIGIN: traditional European magic and gemology

SPELL TIMING: Make healing talismans on the weekday and hour when the planet ruling the sign associated with a problem body part is most powerful. (See The Seven Planets and Their Properties, page 88.)

    For annual immunity from illness, celebrate the Litha Sabbat each June 21 or 22.

    Strengthen weak body parts during a waxing or full Moon; banish illness during a waning or new Moon. Schedule basic medical procedures for when the Moon is in the planetary sign that rules the pained body part, but avoid surgery during such times.

INGREDIENTS: selected gemstone(s) and, if necessary, bendable silver or copper craft wire

    FOR THE VARIATIONS: a balefire on June 21 or 22; an astrological calendar showing Moon signs

AMBIANCE: surrounded by aesthetic pleasures—incense, candlelight, and so on

MAGICAL THEORY: Wellness is a subjective state—optimal health involves self-respect, a clear conscience, a goodly outlook, helping others, and expressing bliss. Stones convey their magical virtues to a wearer through their correspondences, which are based on their geological properties.

    SYMPATHETIC MAGIC: Walking around or jumping over a balefire at the height of summer purifies you, immunizes you against illness, and infuses you with the Sun God's own vigor. In astrology, the Sun is associated with good health.

DEITIES TO INVOKE: a Sun God, such as the Egyptian Ra or Horus, or the Greek Helios or Apollo

TO SUMMON STRENGTH

Adoors at noon on a Sunday, preferably during a waxing or full Moon, intone the following invocation seven times while holding your two thumbs:

"PHNOUNEBEE'
PHNOUNEBEE'
Give me Your Strength,
IO' ABRASAX,
Give me Your Strength,
for I am ABRASAX!"[58]

SPELL VARIATION

ABRASAX: This Solar Deity, invoked for strength and power, is depicted on this Roman-era seal.

- Make a power amulet to grant stamina on demand. Acquire a yellow flannel bag and put a pinch[59] of ironweed,[60] snakeroot, or saffron in it. Add a golden daisy or chrysanthemum bloom and a warming sunstone, an energizing clear quartz, and/or a health-inducing bloodstone. Using a fingertip, anoint the pouch with safflower oil. Hold the pouch in both hands and invoke the aid of Olwen, a Welsh summer Goddess with streaming blond hair, willowy limbs, and rosy cheeks.

    Wear the mojo bag like a necklace, or carry it in your pocket whenever you need energy and endurance.

SPELL ORIGIN: Egypto-Greco and Roman magic; Voudon, Welsh, and Chinese magic; gemology

SPELL TIMING: at noon on a Sunday during the waxing or full Moon; as needed

INGREDIENTS:

FOR THE VARIATION: a yellow flannel bag; ironweed, snakeroot, or saf-

---

[58] PGM, *LXIX, 1–3.*

[59] *For explanations of* pinch, handful, *and* equal parts of *plant measurements, see Magical and Medicinal Herbs, pages 449.*

[60] *To determine the specific species or variety of herbs listed throughout* The Goodly Spellbook, *see Magical and Medicinal Herbs, pages 449.*

fron; a golden daisy or chrysanthemum blossom; a sunstone, clear quartz, and/or bloodstone; safflower oil; hemp or yellow cording

AMBIANCE: adoors, adoring the Sun at his zenith

MAGICAL THEORY:

SYMPATHETIC MAGIC: The Barbarous Word of Power *phnounebee'* (f'noo-NEH-beh-eh) may derive from Phanes, a solar creator Deity often depicted as a serpent coiled around the cosmic egg—another possible significance of the thumb-holding gesture. Sunday is named for the Sun, the strongest astrological planet. The spellcaster harnesses the power of the Sun and the Moon by saying the charm at noon during Luna's waxing phase. The thumb is the strongest finger; holding it in the fist (or each thumb in the opposite fist—the spell doesn't specify) is a strength-inducing gesture. It is similar to the sexual act and, if you're familiar with electromagnetic theory, to the great strengthening of power that occurs when an iron rod is introduced into a copper transformer coil.

The spellcaster assumes the God inside—"I *am* Abrasax!" Abrasax (or Abraxas) is a Sun God worshipped as the creator by the Gnostics of the late Roman Empire. He is traditionally depicted as a man with a rooster's head (whose crowing heralds the rising Sun) and two serpents for legs. He often bears a shield for wisdom and protection, and a whip for mastery. In Grecian numerology, the numerical equivalents of the letters of his name add up to 365—the number of days in a solar year. The seven letters of his name represent the Seven Planets; therefore, to summon the power of all the cosmos, intone his incantation seven times.

DEITIES TO INVOKE: Abrasax, a Gnostic solar God, and Olwen, a Welsh Goddess so pure, she leaves white footprints

TO MAKE PEACE

CAST A SUNWISE CIRCLE. SET A GLASS CONTAINER OF WATER IN THE South, West, and North Quarters, and then stand in the center of the triangle produced. (Temporarily ignore the East.)

Summon the Goddesses Pax and Concordia. Verbally extol their virtues (peace and concord) in lengthy, descriptive form, such as "She who becalms the savage beast," "They who instill mildness in the mad," and so forth. Entreat the

Deities to negate the contentious circumstance and imbue all involved with serenity concerning the subject. Thank them in advance by sprinkling a pinch of sugar in the southern, western, and northern water vessels.

Dispel discord by donning an iolite, promote peace by putting on green jade, or encourage clear communication by carrying a blue quartz or azure topaz until the matter is resolved to your satisfaction.

SPELL ORIGIN: European magic and gemology

SPELL TIMING: as needed—attract accord during the waxing or full Moon; dispel discord during the waning or new Moon phase

INGREDIENTS: three glass containers filled with water; sugar; an iolite, a green jade, a blue quartz, or a cobalt-colored topaz gem, inset ring, or pendant

AMBIANCE: a serene circle environment

MAGICAL THEORY:

SYMPATHETIC MAGIC: North equates with Earth's calm stability, South creates conflict, and feelings originate in the West Quarter. To make peace, spellcrafters must deal with both the problem (South and West) and its solution (North). To break a deadlock, spurn the oppositional number *2* in favor of working with *3,* the first number that involves accord. Sprinkling sugar in water (feelings) sweetens everyone's outlook regarding the subject. The color blue softens stances, and pale green promotes peace.

DEITIES TO INVOKE: the peaceful Roman Goddesses Pax and Concordia

TO SOOTHE FRAYED NERVES

CUT A HANDKERCHIEF OR THIN PIECE OF MUSLIN INTO THREE sachet-sized squares approximately two to three inches in diameter. In the center of each, put one teaspoon each of dried lavender buds, chamomile flowers, and basil. Tie the potpourri bags closed with twine.

Place the herbal bundles in your bathtub, then fill it and let the herbs' healing essence and fragrance diffuse in the warm water as if you were making a soothing cup of hot tea. Melt into the water. Let your mind wander at will. After appropriate acclimation time, mentally appeal for tranquility from the Goddess Eirene. Afterward, trustingly relax.

When you're restored and ready to exit your ritual bath, visualize your stresses and worries dripping off you and bonding with the liquid's molecules—banished away from you as the water funnels down the drain.

SPELL VARIATION

- Wear a cat's-eye amulet pendant or a ring or earrings inset with the gem.

SPELL ORIGIN: European herbalism and gemology

SPELL TIMING: as needed—the spell works best during the waning or new Moon

INGREDIENTS: scissors, a threadbare handkerchief or thin piece of muslin (three sachet-sized squares of either fabric two to three inches in diameter), twine, 1 teaspoon each of dried lavender buds, chamomile flowers, and basil, warm water

FOR THE VARIATION: a pendant, rings, or earrings inset with a cat's-eye gem

AMBIANCE: meditative, surrounded by pleasing incense, lit candles, and conducive taped or CD music

MAGICAL THEORY:

SYMPATHETIC MAGIC: Lavender and chamomile have relaxing properties, and basil magically banishes negativity or a jinx. Three is an odd (that is, an especially magical) number that can symbolize a balanced mind, body, and soul. The force of gravity is employed to prevent purged worries from reattaching to you. A cat's-eye gem can assume the burden of your concerns and acts magically to protect your interests vigilantly.

DEITY TO INVOKE: Eirene (or Irene), a serene Greek Goddess and one of the three Horae, female Deities who ruled the hours, seasons, and natural order as Goddesses of law, justice, and peace

TO INDUCE THERAPEUTIC SLEEP

CONCOCT A SLEEP CONCENTRATE IN ANTICIPATION OF INSOMNIA. Half fill a Mason jar with equal parts of dried skullcap and dried valerian root. Pour moonshine or vodka over the herbs to the container's rim. Cap the container, label and date its contents, shake vigorously, and store in a dark place for

21 days. Jostle the jar every three nights or so. When three-fourths of a month has passed, transfer the liquid to tincture bottles and label and date their contents. Whenever you experience insomnia, squirt one to three droppersful beneath your tongue, or add some to a relaxing cup of chamomile tea you brew before retiring.

If you've neglected to prophylactically prepare the potion and insomnia imposes itself, fill a muslin bag or thin cotton handkerchief with equal pinches of powdered rose petals, dried lavender, bay leaves, and catnip. (If your muscles ache, use equal amounts of sage and rosemary instead.) If you're using a hanky as a sachet pouch, tie together two ends at a time in cross-quarter fashion. Place the potpourri in the tub, draw warm bath water, and enjoy a long, languid soak.

Afterward, brew a Somnus simple, a sleep-inducer named for the Roman God of sleep and composed of one herbal ingredient: either one teaspoon of dried skullcap or one teaspoon of dried valerian root. Steep the therapeutic tea in a cup of hot water for three to five minutes before ingestion. Drink in the evening or at a time you won't need to drive or operate machinery.

Retire clutching a restful gem in your left hand. Chrysolite (olivine/peridot) banishes phantoms, topaz treats insomnia, crystal creates serene sleep, and amber, amethyst, coral, and ruby prevent nightmares.

Invoke the Gods Hypnos and Somnus for sound sleep. If you desire goodly dreams in addition, also appeal to Morpheus.

SPELL VARIATIONS

- Arrange your bed to promote sound sleep—ensure that your head points toward the restful North.
- Decorate your bedroom in colors and textures that promote repose.

    Blue tones, deep greens, dark beige, and black support sleep, while red, orange, yellow, and white stimulate insomnia.

    Prefer plain paint to striped, diagonal, or intricate wallpaper patterns. Soft upholstery, plush pillows, and velvety fabrics promote rest better than metallic surfaces and abstract ambiance.

    Drape scarves hither and thither. Make natural curtain rods by attaching deadfall branches above your windows with scrap leather strips.

- Troubled by night terrors? Mollify Morpheus, the Roman God of dreams.

  Before retiring, cut out pictures from magazines that convey a happy dream state and offer them in his honor. When you have a goodly dream, throw the pieces away. If necessary, you may add to the pile each evening until you cease having nightmares.

  Or, make a dreamcatcher.

  Purchase from a crafts store a metal ring or wooden embroidery hoop three to five inches in diameter and an instruction booklet with diagrams showing several simple dream catcher designs. (You can find this information free at a library or online if you have Internet access.) Wrap the hoop with soft strips of undyed leather. Tie them on or affix ends with hot glue if necessary. Using sinew, weave the inner design of the dreamcatcher. As necessary, loop the sinew around the leathered hoop to ensure the design's integrity. Occasionally intersperse restful charms, gems, shells, or feathers. Hang the dream catcher over your bed above your head to mute nighttime worries, trap phantasms, and allow only goodly thoughts and dream imagery to enter your mind.

- If you're adoors, sleep beneath a bay tree—inhaling the leaves' vapors induces a trance-like sleep state.

Spell Origin: Greek and Native American magic; herbalism; gemology

Spell Timing: as needed—insomnia is worst when the Moon is waxing or full

Ingredients: a Mason jar; moonshine or vodka; several equal handfuls of dried skullcap and valerian root (a cup of chamomile tea optional); muslin sachet bag or cotton handkerchief; equal pinches of powdered rose petals, lavender, bay leaves, and catnip (or sage and rosemary); one teaspoon of either skullcap or valerian root; a teakettle; one cup of hot water; a relaxing gem

  For the variations: restful bedroom décor; restful pictures; dream catcher supplies: a three- to five-inch diameter metal ring or wooden embroidery hoop; pliant leather lashes, sinew, restful charms, gems, shells, or feathers; a bay tree

Ambiance: at home, in a soothing, restful setting; adoors

Magical Theory:

  Sympathetic magic: Stones that possess sleep-inducing properties transfer those properties to the holder by proximity. The soothing waterfall effect of draped scarves serves as a visual cue for you to relax, helps reduce your blood pressure, and promotes pre-sleep serenity. Because curtain rods made from fallen tree limbs or bamboo have natural curves and asymmetries, they are more visually restful than rigid, linear, metallic rods. If the head of your bed points toward the South, you'll be prone to headaches and nightmares.

DEITIES TO INVOKE: Hypnos, the Greek God of sleep, or Somnus, his Roman equivalent, and Morpheus, the Greek God of dreams

TO RECEIVE A DIAGNOSIS OR CURE IN A DREAM

EVERYONE KNOWS THAT THE SERPENT-TWINED STAFF IS THE conventional symbol for medicine. Some know that it is called the "staff of Asclepius" after the ancient Greek physician and healing God. Very few are aware however, that in pre-Christian times, people with serious illnesses were diagnosed or healed during dreams in *Asclepiums,* or temples to Asclepius, throughout the Mediterranean region. According to countless inscriptions of gratitude carved on temple walls, we know that Asclepius was successful in curing illnesses that would confound even modern medical experts. Although early

ASCLEPIUS: The Greek God of healing was exalted in the sky as the constellation Ophiuchus, the Serpent-bearer.

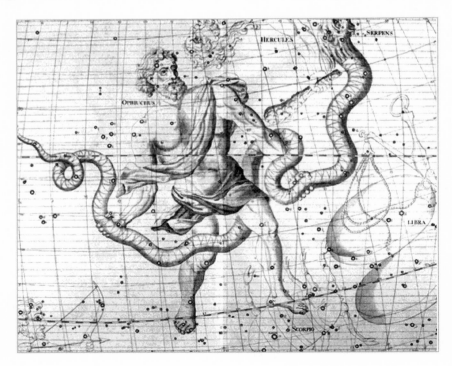

Christian zealots destroyed his sanctuaries, Asclepius still heals. He visits suffering sleepers from his abode in the stars, where the Greeks said Zeus placed Asclepius in the form of the constellation Ophiuchus, the Serpent Bearer.

If you're afflicted with a serious illness whose cause or treatment stumps your doctors, perform the ancient practice of incubation. Pray and request a consult from Asclepius in the form of a dream. He will attend you and accurately diagnose your disease. He may prescribe a treatment, or he may cure you on the spot.

When Lady Passion suddenly developed debilitating *grand mal* seizures that doctors could not explain, she was unsure whether they signaled a worsening of her congenital migraines or represented an entirely new disorder. She prayed that Asclepius would tell her which it was, then fell asleep. Asclepius appeared to her in his traditional guise as a long-bearded, kindly gent; touched her right arm; and confirmed that the seizures were associated with her migraines and did not represent a new condition. Relieved, Lady Passion approached her symptoms with less panic and treated them magically until they disappeared.

Before sleep, place a pen and paper close by so you can later document your dream. Begin by taking a therapeutic bath, as described in To Induce Therapeutic Sleep, page 281. Then settle yourself into a comfortable, conducive position. Pray to Asclepius to come to you, either in your own words or using this ancient invocation:

> *"Awake, Paieon Asclepius,*
> *commander of peoples,*
> *Gentle-minded offspring of Apollo and noble Coronis*
> *Wipe the sleep from thine eyes*
> *and hear the prayer Of thy worshippers,*
> *who often and never in vain*
> *Try to incline thy power favorably, first through Hygieia,*
> *O gentle-minded Asclepius,*
> *Awake and hear thy hymn;*
> *greetings, thou bringer of weal!"*[61]

---

[61] G. Kaibel, *Epigramma Graeca, Epigram no. 1027, p. 433, originally printed in Berlin, 1878;* C. A. Meier, Healing Dream and Ritual: Ancient Incubation and Modern Psychotherapy *(Einsiedeln, Switzerland: Daimon Verlag, 1989), 51.*

You can also place a representation of Asclepius or his serpentine staff near your bed. (In an ancient Asclepium, the incubation couch—*kline* in Greek, the origin of the word clinic—was usually placed near a statue of the God.) Consider your symptoms in detail, and try to ensure that they are your last thought before falling asleep.

Asclepius typically manifests himself as an intelligent animal, two boys, or a bearded old man. He may silently gaze in your direction to discern the cause and extent of your medical crisis, or engage you in conversation. (If you doubt his identity, he'll gladly prove his psychic prowess by revealing a secret you've never shared with anyone.) The God may touch a particular part of your body and heal your disease or disorder, or he may advise you to change your routine, take a therapeutic bath with specific minerals added, or offer similar solutions.

Upon waking, immediately record everything you can remember about the visitation. Strange imagery that initially seems nonsensical may be a symbolic communication of the perfect treatment for which you've been pining. For instance, if you recall that a snake sniffed you with its forked tongue, it could simply mean that you'd achieve relief by ingesting the herb adder's tongue.

Follow Asclepius's prescriptions to the letter as much as possible. When you receive a complete cure, thank him in the traditional manner by fashioning a clay or metal tablet with the details of how he saved your health. Place it in his preferred shrine site, a quiet grove.

SPELL ORIGIN: Greek magic

SPELL TIMING: as needed, prior to sleeping; while the Moon is passing the constellation Ophiuchus (7°–26° Sagittarius)

INGREDIENTS: pen and paper (optionally, a picture of Asclepius or his serpentine staff)

AMBIANCE: a place that encourages deep sleep

MAGICAL THEORY:

SYMPATHETIC MAGIC: When effecting self-cures, fondly invoke God/desses proven skillful in the healing arts.

DEITY TO INVOKE: Asclepius, a Greek healing God

TO RELIEVE BURN, STING, SCALD, AND RASH

EVERYONE INEVITABLY SUFFERS A BURN, STING, SCALD, HEAT RASH, OR hot flash. Witches know how to "bless the fire out."

When such an accident or a situation presents itself, delicately touch the area with your non-dominant hand. Close your eyes and concentrate, willing your heart, mind, hand, and fingers to work in tandem to magically pull the pain out of the body. When you're ready, repeatedly chant the Three Ladies Charm:

"Three ladies came from the East.
One with fire, and two with frost.
OUT with the fire!
IN with the FROST!!"

The sufferer may chant with you if he or she desires. Either way, intone the first two lines in a matter-of-fact manner. Pause for breath after the second line, then emphatically shout the last two lines. Emphasize the three most important words—*out, in,* and the final word, *frost.*

As you feel inclined, use your hands to fling the invisible pain away from the patient hither and thither around the room. Repeat until you feel the spell has taken hold or the person expresses relief.

SPELL ORIGIN: traditional European magic
SPELL TIMING: preferably during Moondark—blistering, swelling, and pain are minimal and more easily treated when the Moon is waning or new; as needed
AMBIANCE: a soothing setting
MAGICAL THEORY:
 ANTIPATHETIC MAGIC: Water puts fire out, so to banish hot pain, conjure cool frost

TO CURE AILING PLANTS

ENSURE THAT YOUR SEEDS GET A GOODLY START—SOW SPECIES THAT flourish above the soil during the waxing Moon and ground-dwelling plants when la Luna is waning.

If your soil lacks nutrients, invoke the Goddess Seia, who roots seeds. Should your shoots succumb, appeal to Segetia, who makes seeds sprout. If your worts wither, petition Tutilina for aid, for she invigorates vegetation.

Many Witches report achieving goodly results by putting clear quartz gem chips in a paper bag, pulverizing them with a rubber-coated mallet, then dusting the top of their plants' soil with the crushed mineral.

SPELL VARIATION

- Avert bad gardening luck—don't force-grow a plant out of season or its normal clime (such as a poinsettia), never bring flowers indoors that have bloomed out of season, avoid picking flowers that bloom in May, and don't pluck dead flowers or retrieve dropped ones.

SPELL ORIGIN: astrology, Roman magic, Irish herb lore

SPELL TIMING: Sow the seeds of plants that bear their fruits above the ground (such as corn) during the waxing Moon, and those that mature underground (such as potatoes) during the waning Moon.

INGREDIENTS: quartz gem chips or other mineral stones, a paper bag, and a rubber-coated mallet

AMBIANCE: adoors or in your greenhouse or solarium

MAGICAL THEORY: Because lunar phases influence tides, and plants are composed primarily of water, gardeners can use the Moon's monthly rhythms to encourage species to root and thrive.

SYMPATHETIC MAGIC: Forcing plants to grow out of season, in atypical climes, or in bizarre ways offends the plants' devas (protective Entities). To secure the devas' favor, abide by their rules. Flowers that bloom out of season are considered unnatural and can transfer their bad luck to your home's occupants if you bring them indoors.

Certain God/desses rule specific stages of a plant's growth cycle, so appeal for aid from those who can alleviate your particular plant problem.

DEITIES TO INVOKE: Seia, Segetia, or Tutilina, Roman Goddesses who rule planted seeds, sprouts, and seedlings, respectively

TO BREAK A DROUGHT

POUR WATER THROUGH A SIEVE ONTO THE GROUND AND APPEAL FOR relief from the Korean rain Goddess, Aryong-Jong.

Another traditional means to conjure cloudbursts is to perform a rain dance. Myriad methods exist, but each typically involves:

- a blazing fire and bubbling cauldron that produce steam
- a musical instrument famous for evoking rain and thunder, such as a drum, bell, or rain stick
- either ayenward or sunwise dance steps (ayenward to dispel drought, or sunwise to attract rain)

SPELL VARIATIONS

- Stop a drought in deliciously Witchy fashion—strip skyclad, go adoors, and dance in the light of the full Moon amidst droplets from a water sprinkler.

  Coven Oldenwilde did its own variation of this, with goodly results. After patiently enduring two years of a relentless lack of rain, we decided to take advantage of several pints of snow we'd collected and stored in our freezer. We built a balefire, stripped skyclad, and rubbed ourselves head to toe with the ice. An unpredicted, much-publicized freak snowstorm immediately buried the Atlantic Coast, preventing some participants from being able to return home following the rite.

- A different anti-drought spell involves holding jasper in your right hand and jade and an altar bell in your left. Ring the bell for several minutes without dropping either stone.

- Medieval Witches conjured rain by "stirring up a tempest in a teapot." The next time heat saps your strength and you're sure the sky will never weep again, stir a teakettle full of water ayenward with a silver spoon for several minutes. Rain will manifest itself out of nowhere.

- Construct your own rain stick. Acquire or harvest one complete segment of bamboo or river cane. Cut above one indentation, then below its opposite line—the indentations delineate the individual sections that compose an entire pole. Bore a hole through one end of the cane, and half fill it with uncooked rice, hard birdseed, or tumbled gem chips. Dip the end of a cork in melted wax, and then push it into the hole to seal the opening. Decorate the outer surface with silver ribbons, seed pearls, or tiny bells and shells.

Shake your rain stick whenever you want to conjure rain in your region.

Spell Origin: Korean, African, European, and Native American magic

Spell Timing: as needed, but preferably during a full Moon

Ingredients: a sieve and water; something that produces steam, such as a balefire and bubbling cauldron; musical instruments or loud noisemakers

> **For the variations:** a water hose or sprinkler; one jasper, one jade stone, and an altar bell; a teakettle full of water and a silver spoon; a segment of cane, a sharp boring tool, a cork, melted candle wax, dried rice, hard birdseed, or tumbled gem chips, and wateresque decorations, such as silver ribbon, seed pearls, or tiny bells and shells

Ambiance: facing West, either adoors, inside, or in your kitchen

Magical Theory:

> **Sympathetic magic:** A sieve strains water into droplet form, mimicking raindrops. Summon specific God/desses that rule rain. Drums mimic rumbling thunder, and tinkling instruments sound like rainfall. Jasper and jade lure rain because of their watery feel and appearance. A teakettle is a microcosmic representation of your realm and all water; by stirring a filled kettle ayenward, you dispel drought and conjure rain.

Deity to Invoke: Aryong-Jong, a Korean rain Goddess who opens up the clouds

TO HEAL A HEADACHE

PRESS YOUR THUMB AGAINST THE ROOF OF YOUR MOUTH.

Folks in antiquity relieved stabbing head pain by wrapping their heads with ivy harvested from atop a God/dess statue. Sadly, Christian zealots destroyed many idols. Undeterred, Pagans simply substituted a red cord for the ivy.

If you can't find ivy growing on the head of a statue, simply tie a vermilion ribbon around your head and repeatedly whisper this traditional incantation:

"Zeus sowed a grapeseed: it parts the soil; He does not sow it; it does not sprout."

You should be relieved within a short time. Should your pain return the following day, however, eradicate it once and for all. Go into a forest and transfer your headache to an inanimate object—tie the red ribbon around a dead tree.

SPELL VARIATIONS

- Prevent headaches by wearing a shed snakeskin inside your hat.
- Minimize migraines by wearing an agate ring or necklace, or a sapphire or turquoise talisman.

SPELL ORIGIN: European sorcery

SPELL TIMING: whenever a headache strikes, or during a new or waning Moon

INGREDIENTS: ivy from the head of a statue or a red ribbon

FOR THE VARIATIONS: a shed snakeskin; an agate, a sapphire, or a turquoise talisman

AMBIANCE: a tranquil indoor setting, or adoors in a grove

MAGICAL THEORY:

SYMPATHETIC MAGIC: A red cord resembles both the blood vessels responsible for causing most headaches and the binding pain the disorder produces. Tying your headache to a dead tree can't hurt the tree because it has already succumbed, but transfers it to the other life forms that subsist on it, for them to bear. Grapes are associated with fertilized eggs because their seed is visible, in the center, like a yolk, and the fruit is round like a pregnant belly.

INVERSION MAGIC: To prevent Zeus from devouring Athena at birth, Hera impregnated him by implanting Athena as a grapeseed in his head. The growing Goddess must have caused the divine scoundrel much head pain before Athena sprang, fully grown, from his head! Invoking Hera allows her to heal what she can deal.

DEITY TO INVOKE: Hera, the Greek Goddess who gave Zeus a royal headache

TO HEAL COMPUTER EYESTRAIN

ON A FRIDAY DURING A WAXING OR FULL MOON, MAKE AN HERBAL eyewash. Boil about a cup of water in a teakettle; then steep in the hot water for three to five minutes one teaspoon each of dried lavender, red eyebright, and daisy flower tops. Strain the liquid through muslin or cheesecloth. Pour the eyewash into a clean glass bottle. Cap when the liquid cools to room temperature. Flush your eyes with copious amounts as needed to achieve relief.

SPELL VARIATIONS

• Make an herbal-simple eyewash using the same recipe as nineteenth-century Gypsies—a pinch of saffron in spring or well water. As you flush your eyes with it, intone their incantation:[62]

> *"Oh, pain from my eyes, go into the water,
> Go out of the water into the saffron,
> Go out of the saffron into the earth.
> To the Earth-Spirit. There's thy home.
> There go and eat."*

• Wear an emerald to prevent eyestrain, or a lapis lazuli to relieve inflammation.
• Rubbing your eyes with the tail of a black cat is an olde cure for most ocular problems.

[62] *Charles G. Leland,* Gypsy Sorcery and Fortune-Telling: Illustrated by Incantations, Specimens of Medical Magic, Anecdotes, Tales *(Library of the Mystic Arts/Citadel Press, 1891), 27.*

- To improve bad eyesight, wear pierced earrings.

SPELL ORIGIN: European magic

SPELL TIMING: Concoct the eyewashes during Moonbright and charge them by letting the rays of the full Moon bathe the bottles. The best time to use the eyewashes is during a new or waning Moon.

INGREDIENTS: one cup of water, a teakettle, one teaspoon each of dried lavender, red eyebright, and daisy tops, a straining cloth, and a glass container

FOR THE VARIATIONS: saffron and spring or well water, and a glass container; an emerald or lapis lazuli gem; a black cat's tail (and a patient cat!); pierced earrings

AMBIANCE: comfortable in your kitchen or ritual room and as you go about your daily duties

MAGICAL THEORY:

INVERSION MAGIC: Red eyebright resembles the eye inflammation it reduces.

ANTIPATHETIC MAGIC: In the Gypsy spell, the sufferer benefits from washing the eyes while transferring the pain to the water and herb, then back into the Earth. The body (the source of the pain) is associated with the element Earth. Wearing pierced earrings repels bad eyesight because of their close proximity to the eyes; their sharp posts repel the stabbing pain.

SYMPATHETIC MAGIC: Cats' vision is renowned, and black cats are often considered unlucky. By rubbing ill eyes with a black cat's tail, the sufferer transfers his or her condition to an animal with superior visual acuity, which will run and take the problem away.

TO CURE A TOOTHACHE OR AN EARACHE

CONCOCT A TOOTHACHE-EARACHE TINCTURE: Half fill a Mason jar with equal amounts of dried echinacea and powdered goldenseal. Pour moonshine or vodka over the herbs to the jar's brim. Cap lightly—the plant matter will gradually ferment and off-gas, which could pop a too-tight top.

Label the contents and write the date you concocted the compound. Store the tincture in darkness for a month, shaking it three to nine times whenever you remember to. Fill a dark tincture bottle with the liquid—it will remain effective at room temperature for years if opened only when needed.

Whenever the stabbing pain strikes, soak a cotton ball—or, as the Irish advise, a piece of black wool—in the amber-colored medicinal liquid. Then insert it in your ear or atop your tooth, or drench the painful area with a dropperful or more. You'll feel noticeable relief within minutes.

A third-century magical cure for dental agony was to carry "a grain of salt, a crumb of bread, and a coal, in a red bag."[63]

Transylvanian Gypsies wound a barley-straw around a rock, then threw it into a coursing stream while chanting:

Oh, pain in my teeth,
Trouble me not so greatly!
Do not come to me,
My mouth is not thy house.

I love thee not all,
Stay thou away from me;
When this straw is in the brook
Go away into the water!

If you do their rite and intone the incantation, your toothache should abruptly abate.

Incrementally diminish dental pain by reciting a third-century spell similar in nature to the Abracadabra Charm—the "Song of the Acorn Sisters:"[64]

"Nine little,
Eight little,
Seven acorn sisters.

---

[63] Jacob Grimm, Über Marcellus Burdigalensis, *Gelesen in der Akademie der Wissenschaften* (Berlin: n.p., 1847). Cited in Leland, Gypsy Sorcery and Fortune Telling, *chap. III.*

[64] Leland, Gypsy Sorcery and Fortune-Telling, *221. Initially published by Marcellus Burdigalensis, this reduction spell is an ancestor of the familiar nursery rhyme "Ten Little Indians."*

Six little,
Five little,
Four acorn sisters.

Three little,
Two little,
One acorn sister—

No little acorn sisters!"

SPELL VARIATIONS

- Prevent toothache—don't shave on a Sunday, or eat while a funeral procession passes by, or when a bell tolls someone's death knell.
- To be immune to tooth pain, wear a mojo bag that contains a tooth from a loved one who has died.
- To cure acute dental despair, ingest a small amount of powdered jet stone, chew on lightning-struck wood, or rub your jaw with a horse's tooth.
- The tooth fairy isn't just for kids any more. Adults can actually prevent tooth loss by placating her—we call her Dentina. Put an offering of dried corn kernels or tiny quartz crystals and silvery coins into a small bag, and place it beneath your pillow. Sleep atop it until your toothache abates.

SPELL ORIGIN: European herb craft, Latin and Transylvanian spells
SPELL TIMING: Make and take the tincture during a waning Moon.
INGREDIENTS: equal amounts of dried echinacea root or tops and goldenseal powder, a Mason jar with a lid, an empty, dark tincture bottle with a dropper, moonshine, vodka, or another clear, high-proof spirit, cotton balls or black wool if desired; a grain of salt, a bread crumb, a cooled coal, and a vermilion-colored pouch; a barley stalk or piece of straw, a rock and a running river

FOR THE VARIATIONS: a tooth from a departed relative and a mojo bag; a pinch of powdered jet, lightning-struck wood, or a horse's tooth; dried corn kernels or tiny quartz crystals, coin offerings, and a small bag
AMBIANCE: a comfortable setting or conducive kitchen

MAGICAL THEORY:

HERB CRAFT: Medicinal liquid extracted from echinacea roots and tops will dull tooth and ear pain, and goldenseal powder extract heals tooth-aches and earaches.

SYMPATHETIC MAGIC: A grain of salt and a bread crumb represent food, which teeth chew; a coal symbolizes Earth, therefore, the body and the pain itself; and red equates with the blood of life, so carrying these encourages your tooth to remain functional and in place. Straw represents death—literally, of grass, and figuratively, when used for Samhain scarecrows. Therefore, the tooth is the stone and pain is the straw, and toothache is cured with healing water as the river carries the simulacrum away.

Jet is associated with death because it's black; therefore, jet can end pain just as death does. Lightning-struck wood has already had bad luck, so chewing it fools your mouth into believing you've had a toothache already. Rubbing your jaw with a horse's tooth transfers its notorious strength to your own teeth.

Traditionally, a person's magical strength is in the hair; folks who shave do so on skin above their teeth; shaving on a day associated with health (the Sun's day) risks fate's ire. Making all three magical faux pas pretty much guarantees you'll develop a toothache.

Tradition holds that the dead feel no pain, so carrying a tooth from a departed relative confers that person's immunity from toothache to you.

Offering Dentina objects that resemble teeth may fool her into believing that you've already lost your quota of teeth, so she'll spare them in your twilight years. Including silver coins shows that you value her work and promotes her favor.

DEITY TO INVOKE: the tooth fairy, known to Coven Oldenwilde as Dentina

TO ALLEVIATE AN INFECTION

To help prevent a localized infection from spreading systemically, suck on an amber gem.

Spell Origin: traditional European magic
Spell Timing: as needed—infections are minimized when the Moon is new or waning
Ingredients: a piece of amber
Ambiance: any soothing setting
Magical Theory:

Like can cure like: Amber is red, yellow, or green-colored, resembling the typical colors associated with infection, so sucking on such a gem tricks an infection into assuming it has already spread.

TO HEAL WOUNDS AND BROKEN BONES

*"Man is all symmetry,
Full of proportions, one limb to another,
And all to all the world besides.*

*Each part may call the farthest brother,
For head with foot hath private amity,
And both with moons and tides."*

—George Herbert
17th-century English poet

Spare your loved ones from developing permanent deformity, internal adhesions, or wicked scars following injuries. Psychically will their flesh, bone, sinew, and veins to cleave only to their own kind—to meet and mesh with the parts of themselves from which they've been so traumatically separated.

When you witness an accident or try to heal a victim, first bestill and calm yourself—consciously breathe slowly and deeply throughout all curative spells. Gingerly hold your dominant power hand slightly above the injured area until you achieve focused concentration and relaxed magical flow. Your hand will likely grow warm from your mental effort. Then rock rhythmically, caress the hurt person's cheek or forehead, and whisper the following healing charm, called the Boneset Spell:

> *This is the spell that I intone.*
> *Flesh, to flesh, and bone, to bone.*
> *Sinew, to sinew, and vein, to vein.*
> *And (injured's name) is made*
> *whole again!*

Pronounce the last word as a-GAIN to rhyme with *vein* two lines above it. Intone the charm numerous times during your initial healing session, then whenever you remember to throughout the patient's recovery time. Folks heal amazingly well and rapidly when this chant is employed.

Here is an olde German version of it, known as the Merseburg Incantation:[65]

> *"Bone-sprain like blood-sprain, Like limb-sprain.*
> *Bone to bone, blood to blood, Limb to limb—*
> *like they were glued."*

SPELL VARIATIONS

- Brew a tea of all-heal herb, and then sprinkle it around the injured person.
- Kill wound pain and prevent a wound from becoming infected by daily applying a poultice of powdered narcissus bulbs mixed with honey, preferably a local variety. Treat lacerations topically with antiseptic tea tree oil, readily available from health food stores and online sources.
- Rapidly cure contusions—heat a large stone in a fire until the rock becomes visibly red-hot; flash-cool the rock in water, then bathe the bruise with the resulting liquid. Twice daily treatments effect a cure within a day or two.
- Banish burns and prevent scarring—concoct Oldenwilde's skin balm.

---

[65] *D. L. Ashliman, comp., "Wodan Cures Balder's Injured Horse," Balder's Homepage, Germanic Myths, Legends, and Sagas, Folklore and Mythology Electronic Texts, 1999–2000.*

With a mortar and pestle, crush equal amounts of dried coltsfoot, jewel-weed blossoms and leaves, and comfrey. In a double-boiler setup, boil water and steep the herbs in it for three to five minutes. Stir the mixture ayenward throughout the process. Slowly melt in beeswax to serve as a base and binder; then add hemp oil or olive oil as needed to make the salve soft.

While the compound remains hot and liquefied, pour it into clean, shallow glass containers (sample gourmet jam jars are ideal). Cap when cooled to room temperature. Apply topically as needed to burns and skin disorders; the balm forms an organic, healing bandage.

- To prevent keloiding (developing puffy scars), buy sheep's suet from a feed store and boil it with some elder tree rind (the bark's inner pith). Cool, then topically apply the resulting unguent atop a burn or wound.

SPELL ORIGIN: traditional European magic, German variant, Voudon herbalism, Irish magic, and Coven Oldenwilde practice

SPELL TIMING: as needed, although wounds and broken bones heal faster during a waxing or full Moon

INGREDIENTS FOR THE VARIATIONS: a tea kettle, water, one teaspoon of dried all-heal herb, and an aspergillum (a small tree or plant limb with which to flick the liquid around); powdered narcissus bulbs, honey, and tea tree oil; one large stone and water; a mortar and pestle, a non-aluminum double-boiler setup, and water, equal parts dried coltsfoot, jewelweed blooms or leaves, comfrey, beeswax, hemp or olive oil, and glass jars; sheep's suet and elder tree pith

AMBIANCE: a calm, nurturing atmosphere

MAGICAL THEORY:

SYMPATHETIC MAGIC: The Boneset Spell directs confused, injured cells to cleave to their own kind of tissue and to avoid developing painful adhesions. The all-heal herb has such profound healing properties that you don't have to apply or ingest it in order for it to work. Water from a hot, then flash-cooled rock likewise cools fiery wound pain.

ANTIPATHETIC MAGIC: Because burned skin has been sapped of cellular moisture, heal it by drenching the area with a dewy salve.

DEITY TO INVOKE: Woden, a Norse God with healing powers

TO EASE CHILDBIRTH

- Don't incur a hard labor by making or knitting a cap for the baby's head before delivery.
- When your labor pains begin, remove your rings, necklaces, bracelets, anklets, and watch. If you have a piercing, remove the jewelry.
- Throughout delivery, wear your mate's slippers.
- To prevent excessive bleeding during delivery, hold a bloodstone in your left hand.
- Throughout delivery, always face or have your head pointing North (vice versa if you bide in the Southern Hemisphere).
- Don't allow any knots in your presence during delivery—unplait your hair and wear it loose. By the same token, never cross your legs or wring or cup your hands during labor, or allow any attendants to do so.
- If your labor goes long or grows difficult, have your attendants liberate as many things as they can around you—free pets, undo ties, laces, and knots, open doors and windows, and so on.
- Gain pain relief by quilling—have an attendant blow a tendril of tobacco smoke in your face through a hollowed turkey quill.

SPELL ORIGIN: Ozark Mountain, Hawaiian, Filipino, Roman, German, Sumatran, Chittagong, Punjabi, and Sumerian lore

SPELL TIMING: as needed before and during labor and delivery

INGREDIENTS: your mate's slippers; a bloodstone; a compass; tobacco; a turkey quill; and matches

AMBIANCE: a calm, nurturing atmosphere

MAGICAL THEORY:

MURPHY'S MAGIC: Knitting a cap for an infant not yet born tempts fate to thwart your desired outcome.

SYMPATHETIC MAGIC: Because rings bind their wearers, keeping them and similar jewelry on during labor can impede the baby from being able to detach from its mother.

Piercings are Martial, which could cause excess bleeding.

The baby's father's strength is transferred when you wear his slippers—instead of having feet of clay, you'll feel strong.

Bloodstone helps prevent internal hemorrhage or excessive blood loss during and after delivery.

Keeping your head toward the North (or South, if you are below the equator), the Earth Quarter (the direction of fertility and of caves, which resemble the vagina), keeps your mind focused on delivery and grants you the life-giving ability of the Great Mother.

Knots impede the baby's egress and could cause its umbilical cord to tangle around its neck. Therefore, freeing confined, constricted, or closed things eases the infant's progress.

INVERSION MAGIC: Olde midwives observed that women in childbirth were calmed by inhaling some smoke.

DEITY TO INVOKE: Mami, the Sumerian Goddess of childbirth

TO PREVENT HEMORRHAGE

WRAP STRANDS OF IVY AROUND YOUR BELLY OR INJURED BODY PART.

- Locate a goodly surgeon during the most auspicious time—when the Moon is waxing in Gemini, Aquarius, or Virgo.
- Avoid surgery when the Moon is in the sign that rules the pained body part. (See To Promote Wellness, page 272.)
- Prior to surgery, cook in iron pots.

SPELL VARIATION

- To promote the clotting of a wound or surgical incision, bind a bloodstone in your bandage.

SPELL ORIGIN: astrology and traditional European folk practices and gemology

SPELL TIMING: as needed—works best when performed during a new or waning Moon

INGREDIENTS: long strands of pliant ivy; an astrological calendar and a lunar calendar to determine auspicious times to locate a surgeon or schedule surgery; cast iron culinary equipment

FOR THE VARIATION: a bloodstone

AMBIANCE: surrounded by aesthetic pleasures, such as incense, candlelight, and so forth

MAGICAL THEORY: Success often depends on optimal timing. Being conscious of when your stars are working for or against you helps you ensure success or prevent problems.

SYMPATHETIC MAGIC: Ivy branches in multiple directions, resembling blood vessels, and binds other plants, so it can be used to magically prevent human bleeding.

Traces of ferrous sulfate in iron pots will leach into your food and reduce your risk of hemorrhaging by weighing down platelets inside your blood vessels, thereby slowing blood flow and encouraging quick clotting.

DEITY TO INVOKE: Asclepius, a plague-curing Greek doctor posthumously deified

TO STANCH BLOOD FLOW

IF POSSIBLE, WASH YOUR HANDS WITH SOAP AND HOT WATER. USING aseptic technique (working in ways that ensure you don't contaminate the wound), inspect the injury. Clean the wound by drenching the area with cold water. Pat the wound dry with a clean towel.

Reduce bleeding—apply hard pressure to the wound by firmly pressing down on it with both of your hands for three to five minutes. Bend your body toward or over the injury to help you maintain sustained pressure.

Aid clotting by covering the cut with copious amounts of the best ancient styptic around—spider webbing.

To prevent break-through bleeding and speed healing, bind a bloodstone, an agate, a jasper, or a carnelian in the bandage.

SPELL VARIATION

- Another goodly olde way to stop coursing blood is called "wristing." Loosely tie scarlet worsted or red woolen fabric around the wounded person's wrists and throat. Ensure proper circulation and respiration.

SPELL ORIGIN: traditional European folk remedies, gemology, and Irish magic

Spell Timing: as needed—blood clots easiest during a new or waning Moon

Ingredients: spider webbing and a bloodstone, agate, jasper, or carnelian

   For the variation: red worsted or woolen fabric

Ambiance: a calm area

Magical Theory:

   Sympathetic magic: The color and pattern of a bloodstone, an agate, a jasper, and a carnelian resemble blood; as stones, they represent solidity; together, their correspondences equate with clotted blood. Tied red fabric resembles a clotted gash and acts as a magical tourniquet.

TO CURE MENTAL PROBLEMS

- Make the mad meek. Obtain three magical ingredients made only by nature—honey, milk, and salt. Milk should make up the majority of your healing potion, to which you should add a tablespoon of honey and several sprinkles of salt. Serve the mixture to the delusional in a seashell before sunrise on a Wednesday during the waning Aries Moon.
- Bedeck a troubled person's neck with a bag of buttercups.

SPELL VARIATIONS

- To prevent yourself from developing psychosis, carry coral or a chrysolite.
- Make the sad smile—give the sufferer a blue chalcedony ring.
- Make a taciturn person talk—give him or her a blue chalcedony pendant.

Spell Origin: ancient Irish and modern European magic; gemology

Spell Timing: before sunrise on a Wednesday during the waning Aries Moon; as needed

Ingredients: a seashell, honey, milk, and salt; a bag of buttercups

   For the variations: a coral or chrysolite gem; a blue chalcedony ring; a blue chalcedony pendant

Ambiance: a calm, quiet, soothing setting

Magical Theory:

   Macrocosm = microcosm: Aries rules the head. Casting this spell on a Wednesday (Mercury day) increases the patient's cognitive clarity.

Buttercups resemble the Sun, the astrological ruler of health and wholeness. Coral and chrysolite's colors also resemble the Sun, therefore they are magically solar.

ANTIPATHETIC MAGIC: Because mental problems are human aberrations, they can be eliminated only with ingredients made by nature—honey, milk, salt, buttercups, and stones.

SYMPATHETIC MAGIC: Traditionally, chrysolite inset in gold not only promotes mental health, but can also prevent breakdown relapse. Blue chalcedony is the color of a clear sky, which elevates the mood and encourages the wearer to articulate his or her feelings.

· Protection Spells ·

"In the ecstasy of the Goddess, you be free from harm.
The more oft you attain, the easier it is."
—UNKNOWN AUTHOR,
TRADITIONAL SOURCE

Although Crafters are fearless, we also know that not everyone means well. These days it seems that many folks feel compelled to barricade themselves inside gated developments behind deadbolt door locks backed up by expensive security systems.

However, you can achieve a balance between naïveté and paranoia by learning how to magically protect what you value—be it privacy, safety, your home's sanctity, or the beleaguered Earth.

TO PREVENT OR QUELL RUMORS

RUMORS ARE NEBULOUS CREATURES BORNE ON THE WIND BY CLACKING TONGUES. To minimize others' ability to use you as phone fodder, resist the temptation to brag about your magical prowess. The more powerful your magic is, the less you should feel compelled to do so. Instead, practice being taciturn and noncommittal about your spell successes—embody the Witchy Power to Be Silent.

Discourage gossip by habitually closing all your doors, cabinets, chests, and drawers.

To negate a ruinous rumor, hold your thumbs and intone the following spell seven times:[66]

"ERMALLO'TH
ARCHIMALLO'TH

Stop the Mouths that speak against me,
Because I glorify Your Sacred and Honored Names!"

If circumstances dictate that you must occasionally interact with people who have lied about you, tie their tongues by wearing a spice-scented essential oil whenever they're around.

SPELL ORIGIN: European, Egyptian, and Voudon magic

SPELL TIMING: as needed—rumors abound during a full Moon and are more easily negated during Moondark

INGREDIENT: a spice-scented essential oil

AMBIANCE: alone indoors. You may elect to burn black candles and banishing incense during the rite.

MAGICAL THEORY:

SYMPATHETIC MAGIC: The most difficult spellcraft skill for many to master, Earthy secretiveness nonetheless innately protects those who don't divulge information regarding spells they've done.

Furniture that's ajar resembles a gaping, gossipy mouth and provides magical access for inquiring minds to enter your home and snoop around for foibles.

Holding your thumbs makes you focus your will more and highlights your restraint in the face of adversity. (See also To Summon Strength, page 278.)

Seven is an ancient magical number. Repeating a charm seven times protects you on both a microcosmic level (seven days a week) and a macrocosmic level (by invoking the power of the Seven Planets to your aid).

---

[66] *Abridged from* PGM, *XXXVI, 161–177.*

Spicy scents evoke feelings of comfort in humans, so wearing them around rumormongers reduces their insecurity and discourages their gossiping.

TO PREVENT YOUR PHONE FROM BEING TAPPED

MINIMIZE YOUR RISK BY REFUSING TO CONVERSE VIA CELLULAR telephone.

On a Wednesday during the waning or new Moon, assemble either ordinary playing cards or a tarot deck and cast a circle ayenward. Light black candles and burn several pinches of a banishing incense such as asafetida or mugwort. Face the North and remove from the deck either the queen and king of diamonds, or the queen and king of pentacles. These significator cards represent those with legal or financial means to eavesdrop. Place the queen atop the king, and lay the pair down on your left.

Next, match your sex with the corresponding highest spade or sword card. Women should select the queen, and men the king. This card signifies your adamant opposition to being entrapped or having your privacy violated. Hold it in your right hand, and concentrate on thwarting every attempt to infiltrate your sanctuary. Picture your powers unconsciously but continuously operating—creating constant interference for listening devices and severing mechanical methods.

When you feel the spell is sufficiently strong, loudly smack the card atop the cards on your left, then secrete the stack beneath the base of your telephone. You will negate sabotage as long as the cards are in direct contact with the device.

SPELL ORIGIN: Gypsy magic adapted by Coven Oldenwilde

SPELL TIMING: a Wednesday during Moondark

INGREDIENTS: ordinary playing cards or a Tarot deck, black candles, asafetida or mugwort, or a similar banishing incense, and a telephone

AMBIANCE: alone, indoors, amidst black candlelight, surrounded by clouds of banishing incense

MAGICAL THEORY:

SYMPATHETIC MAGIC: Moondark and black candles represent the obscuring cloak of darkness you want to cast over yourself, your actions, and your domicile. Significator cards work by both the principles of resemblance (to the problem and you) and proximity (in this case, contact with the device through which nefarious folk could entrap you).

ANTIPATHETIC MAGIC: Repellent odors drive off unwanted Beings—they work oppositely of enticing scents.

TO ENSURE A SAFE AND SPEEDY JOURNEY

ANIMATE YOUR AUTO TO WORK IN YOUR FAVOR BY GIVING IT A mighty moniker. Accord it with a name that befits its temperament and reflects your needs, such as:

Turtle (for protection from injuries)
Camel (if you typically drive on fumes)
Mojo (if you want radar invisibility).

Then, whenever you need to compel it over icy inclines and other perils, appeal to it by name.

For dependable transportation to and from work, use undyed hempen string to secure a horse charm to your rear-view mirror. Let it freely dangle or "gallop" beneath the glass.

Know that drivers unconsciously increase their speed during a waxing or full Moon, so proceed cautiously during those times to minimize your risk of being cited.

Prevent detours, delays, gridlock, and wrecks during your sojourns—harvest and put ten feathery yarrow leaves in your ride.

Another method to ensure a safe foray is to put several pinches of the herb bladderwrack into a red flannel bag and affix it to your steering wheel.

Decorate your dash and transform it into a protective altar. Attach fetishes such as God/dess statuettes and reflective, repelling hematites or Evil Eye–confusing agates.

For speedy travel, make a bird flight fetish:
- Thread tiny blue or iridescent seed beads.
- Wrap the string around a large feather just above its quill.
- Secure both ends of the spiraling band of beads to the feather with adhesive.

- When dry, attach the decorated plume to your car's rear-view mirror with sinew or hemp (use any color except red).

The fetish makes you practically fly to destinations, so monitor your speedometer to avoid speeding tickets.

SPELL VARIATIONS

- Morning glory protects travelers, so put a bloom on your dashboard, or tie a stem to the handlebars of your bicycle.
- On foot and need to cover ground quickly? Detach the bird flight fetish from your vehicle and wear it tied around your left leg.
- The fleet-footed God Mercury will ensure you safe and speedy travel if you pray to him before starting a journey—especially if you do so on his sacred weekday, Wednesday.

SPELL ORIGIN: Irish, Voudon, and European magic
SPELL TIMING: before commencing a journey
INGREDIENTS: hempen string and a horse charm; ten feathery yarrow leaves; bladderwrack and a red flannel bag; dashboard decorations; tiny pale blue or iridescent seed beads, one large feather, adhesive, and sinew or hemp
FOR THE VARIATIONS: a morning glory
AMBIANCE: comfortably calm in your car, garden, greenhouse, or craft-making room.
MAGICAL THEORY:
SYMPATHETIC MAGIC: Although machines are often considered inanimate, they nonetheless possess individual spirit. If you acknowledge this by giving them names and treating them accordingly, they will respond as friends. If you don't, they can capriciously thwart you.
Fetishes are a microcosm of the macrocosm that Crafters spell to produce. A horse charm in your transport compels it to act like a reliable workhorse. Yarrow is associated with fairies, so as a magical ingredient, it confers their famous flight abilities and invisibility. Affixing a bird flight fetish to your transport transfers birds' speed and agility to your car by means of proximity.

INVERSION MAGIC: The name of the herb bladderwrack and the red bag it's contained in conjure the image of mangled organs. Therefore, carrying them in your car is a form of Murphy's magic to fool harmful spirits into believing that you've already been injured, so they'll move on and leave you alone.

DEITY TO INVOKE: Mercury, the swift Messenger of the Gods and astrological ruler of travel

TO PREVENT CAR ACCIDENTS

CONSTRUCT COVEN OLDENWILDE'S PROTECTIVE CAR CHIME.

Acquire sinew, carved wooden or bone beads that resemble 2-inch-long fangs, and a horizontally sliced section of a walnut shell.

Attach each bone bead to the walnut-shell with a piece of sinew so that each bead dangles like a wind chime.

Ensure that your bead arrangement is balanced, then suspend the talisman from your car's rearview mirror.

We tap ours with our right fingers when we commence a trip, and the swinging charm rings delicately—instantly wafting our prayer for a peaceful journey straight to receptive, protective God/desses.

If peril looms—a tailing cop or an oncoming drunken driver, for example—we avert the crisis by tapping it again. We also tap it to secure help from Squat, Goddess of the needed parking space!

SPELL VARIATIONS

- Enchant an old car not to imperil you by breaking down in traffic. Obtain a silver spark-gap measuring coin from an auto parts store. Bury the metal medallion deep inside the car's glove compartment, where it will act as a magical pacemaker to coax more months or years out of your venerable vehicle.

- Protect a sluggish machine from accidents by applying a pentagram decal to the extreme right corner of both the front and rear windshields.

- Never refer to a wreck while driving.
- To avoid others' envy or being mysteriously prone to crashing, don't drive a green car.
- Avoid a "money pit" kind of car—never arbitrarily exchange a reliable car for a different model.
- Transfer a previous car owner's luck to yourself—buy a vehicle from a person of financial means.
- To promote your transportation's longevity, transfer items from your old car to your new one.
- If you wash your car by hand, add a handful or so of dried rosemary to water, and give your ride a ritual bath that promotes good will from other drivers. Rub in ayenward circles to repel road rage and collisions.

SPELL ORIGIN: Coven Oldenwilde and European practices and lore

SPELL TIMING: as needed; prior to long or hazardous trips

INGREDIENTS: sinew, carved bored wood or bone beads resembling fangs, and a horizontally sliced section of a walnut shell

FOR THE VARIATIONS: a spark-gap measurer that resembles a silver coin; two pentagram decals; rags, dried rosemary, water

AMBIANCE: calmly optimistic, but cautious and precise indoors; inside the vehicle; adoors, washing your car

MAGICAL THEORY:

MACROCOSM = MICROCOSM: A car's rear-view mirror not only symbolizes safety, but also acts as its psychic "third eye," just as its headlights correspond with humans' physical eyes.

Elementally, spark plugs correspond with Fire and the car's Spirit. In automotive terms, the medallion marked with all possible spark gaps is a cosmological talisman.

SYMPATHETIC MAGIC: Because it is associated magically with prosperity, the color green often evokes others' envy. Traditionally, green cars are prone to mysteriously crashing—perhaps because of incurring someone's Evil Eye. The smell of rosemary attracts the good will of others.

INVERSION MAGIC: Rosemary's needles act as sharp projectiles to deflect harm away from you.

Murphy's magic: If you avoid randomly getting a different vehicle, you minimize your chance of acquiring a "lemon" that makes you throw good money after bad, or repeatedly paying to fix a doomed car.

Deity to Invoke: Apollo, the Greek God who daily drives the Sun in the form of a chariot across the sky

TO ENSURE A BABY'S FUTURE SUCCESS IN LIFE

THIS SPELL ENSURES THAT AN INFANT WILL ATTAIN GREAT HEIGHTS IN the future.

As soon as is feasible after birth, carry the newborn (cradle and all) to the highest place inside your home. Position the cradle on the floor in the center of the room, and encircle it with coins, candles in holders, and a key. Place a saucer of table salt on the baby's belly, and intone the following Romany Gypsy incantation:

"This, for myself, I have not done,
But for love of this little one.

Not because (her/his) family
Great or wealthy chance to be.

But that (she/he) may rise, have I
Brought (her/him) to this room so high;

Thus may (she/he) by talents thrive,
And be the greatest (woman/man) alive!"[67]

Move away and watch the babe from a vantage point near the closest doorway. (The olde way was riskier—to leave the baby briefly unattended so the God/esses could enter and do their work.) Return after several minutes and hug the charmed cherub.

Spell Origin: Romagnan Italian magic

[67] *Adapted from "The Spell of the Cradle,"* Etruscan Roman Remains in Popular Tradition, *by Charles G. Leland (Phoenix Publishing, 1892), 307.*

SPELL TIMING: as soon as possible after an infant's birth
INGREDIENTS: coins, candles in holders, a key, a saucer of table salt
AMBIANCE: your home's highest point; for example, upstairs, or in the attic
MAGICAL THEORY:

> **SYMPATHETIC MAGIC:** Physically elevating the baby to the highest pin-
> nacle of your house ensures that the child will attain the height of success
> in the future. Coins symbolize adequate income, candles help the child
> magically navigate challenges, the key equates with wisdom and the ability
> to open doors of opportunity, and salt represents a steady salary and abun-
> dant food—all someone who loves a child wishes for him or her.

TO PROTECT A CHILD

NON-INTRUSIVELY PROTECT NEGLECTED NEIGHBORHOOD KIDS, SHIELD
youngsters you know from the often-cruel consequences of their own frustrated
outbursts, or proactively reduce a problem child's penchant for violence.

On a Monday at midnight, fashion a pale green wax poppet of the child in
peril. The completed figure should be about the size of your open hand. Melt
wax to use as binding glue; then apply either a lock of the child's hair atop, a
baby tooth that you saved or were given to the mouth area, or a clothing swatch,
or snippet of the child's baby blanket to serve as clothing. If you possess a photograph of the child, cut the face section into a roundel and affix it in the facial
area of the effigy. (Substitute a photocopy or computer-scanned print of the
photo if you don't want to sacrifice the original.) With a boleen, bigrave descriptive details on the ding-ding darling doll—perhaps even, the child's name in
Theban. (See Magical Alphabets, page 193.)

When the poppet has completely air-dried, cradle it lovingly in your hands.
Enliven the shadow child by blowing your breath into its mouth. Gaze fondly
at it—coo and soothe it as you would a newborn. Appeal to the child-protecting
Goddess Artemis, ardently explaining the child's dire situation. Charge the
Goddess to use her astral arrows to provide adequate food for the child in times
of want, and to thwart predators and pedophiles who could harm the child.

When done, wrap the poppet in a black cloth and hide it in the North.
Fervently thank Artemis for guarding the youth at your request. In salute of the

Goddess's notable hunting skills, eat jerky (or a suitable substitute if you're vegetarian).

When the danger to the child wanes, cast a circle and formally release Artemis from her appointed task. Verbally dispirit the poppet, severing all its previous spiritual connection with the child. Gently pulverize the now-soulless vessel and return the remnants to Mother Earth.

SPELL ORIGIN: Grecian and Italian *Strega* magic
SPELL TIMING: as needed, but preferably during the Witching Hour on a Monday
INGREDIENTS: pale green wax, a double-boiler setup, water, scissors, a photo of the child and a lock of the child's hair, a baby tooth or a swatch of clothing, a baby blanket, or so forth, a boleen, black cloth, and meat jerky or a vegetarian substitute
AMBIANCE: alone in moonlight or candlelight amidst sandalwood or white sage incense
MAGICAL THEORY:
  SYMPATHETIC MAGIC: A poppet with a bit of a person's hair or clothing is the person magically, in absentia.
DEITY TO INVOKE: Artemis, Greek Goddess who protects children

TO CREATE FAMILY HARMONY

SILENTLY AVOID OR RESOLVE FAMILY FEUDS WITHOUT BECOMING unduly involved—wear a gemstone that addresses the crux of the continual contention, such as:

* *lapis lazuli*—to promote tenderness and sympathy
* *sapphire*—for love, loyalty, and wisdom
* *turquoise*—for friendship
* *topaz*—for fidelity and forgiveness
* *chrysolite*—for happiness
* *alexandrite*—for luck, prosperity, and contentment

Insist on civility during tense times—make a powerful harmony wand and rely on it to keep contentious family discussions from devolving into loud screaming matches.

During the new or waning Moon or while the Moon is in Libra, use a boleen to harvest a branch from an apple tree. The wand should be about 13 inches long.

Prevent the wood from bowing by air-drying the piece flat.

Speed-cure the branch by immersing it for a time in water-diluted apple juice then removing it and wiping it dry.

Daily observe the wood's integrity for signs of mold. If some develops, don gloves and a face mask and sand it off adoors.

When you can easily pry the outer bark from its inner pith with a fingernail, whittle off the bark, then sand smooth the white wood beneath it.

Using copper or silver craft wire, attach tiny, anger-dispelling bells, or dig out natural wood knots and inset with clear epoxy glue any kind of concord-connoting gem chip.

Top the tool with an inset peace-promoting peach moonstone.

The wand works like a Native American talking stick; the holder has the right to speak for a pre-agreed time limit and can shake it to silence anyone who dares interrupt. When the person's talking time is up, he or she passes the wand to another speaker.

SPELL VARIATIONS

- Foster feelings of familial friendship on Fridays, the time when Venus's love abounds and pervades.
- Cleanse your home of hostility and promote peace by adding a few drops of cypress oil or lavender to mop water. Alleviate animosity with an arrangement of sky-blue aster flowers.
- Avoid bickering on Tuesdays—arguments are prone to degenerate into violence on this weekday sacred to Mars, the God of war.
- Avert fights by infusing the air with apple essence. Simmer slices in water on your stove, or purchase apple-scented oil, daub it on lightbulbs with a cotton swab, then turn the fixtures on to diffuse the fragrance throughout your environment.

- Calm folks following fights by brewing passionflower tea. For each drinker, steep ½ to 1 teaspoon of the flowers in 6 to 8 ounces of boiling water for three to five minutes. Strain, and then chill the liquid in your refrigerator. Add ice cubes to individual glasses and serve cold.

SPELL ORIGIN: European and Roman magic, Victorian gemology, and herbalism

SPELL TIMING: as needed or on a Friday after sunset—harvest the apple wood for the harmony wand during a new, waning, or Libra Moon

INGREDIENTS: a gemstone amulet; a boleen, a whittling knife, a 13-inch length of an apple tree branch, water-diluted apple juice, small-grained sandpaper, copper or silver craft wire, tiny bells, a peach moonstone gem chip, and clear epoxy glue

    FOR THE VARIATIONS: cypress oil or lavender, water; sky-blue aster flowers; apple slices, water, a heat source, or apple essential oil, cotton swabs and lightbulbs; ½ to 1 teaspoon of dried passionflowers per person, 6 to 8 ounces of hot water per person, ice cubes

AMBIANCE: your most serene surrounding

DEITY TO INVOKE: Harmonia, the Roman Goddess of harmony

TO PREVENT DRUNKENNESS

WITCHES LOVE TO CELEBRATE THE SABBATS BY INGESTING SPIRITS BUT loathe suffering the morning-after symptoms. We thank the God/esses that we have centuries of lore to draw on to help us prevent the phenomenon.

Water signs provoke tides of tears and incline folks toward seeking solace in fluid form. Therefore, avoid alcohol when the Moon is waxing in emotional signs such as Pisces, Cancer, and Scorpio. Rather, drink during a waning Moon—it's harder to get tipsy when la Luna is in a stable Earth sign, such as Taurus, Virgo, or Capricorn.

Immunize yourself from inebriation prior to imbibing by donning an amethyst necklace or keeping one of the grape-colored gems in the bottom of your drinking horn, ale stein, goblet, or wine glass.

To avert intoxication on an ongoing basis, obtain a slice of hazel tree at midnight on Samhain and wear it as a temperance talisman.

SPELL VARIATIONS

- Because alcohol dehydrates the body and brain, before going to bed drink as much water as you did spirits.
- To sober up fast, drink tangy orange peel tea or eat a lot of lettuce, which minimizes morning-after headache.
- If you occasionally imbibe in excess, prepare a palliative potion in advance—Oldenwilde's hangover tincture:[68]

Into a large, clean jar, put equal handfuls of powdered slippery elm bark (stops stomach cramps), willow bark (halts headaches), fresh, dried marshmallow (coats and soothes the stomach), St. Johnswort (elevates the mood), chamomile (becalms and eases body aches), and feverfew (prevents or palliates headache).

Fill the jar to the rim with moonshine or vodka. Cap, shake thoroughly, and store the herbal medicine in darkness. Whenever you remember to, shake the extraction three times.

After 21 days, transfer the potent, amber-colored liquid into an empty tincture bottle.

When needed, squirt three to four droppersful beneath your tongue and swallow it whenever you can—despite its raw taste, you'll cease feeling queasy and be clear-headed within minutes.

SPELL ORIGIN: Irish magic and Coven Oldenwilde herb craft

SPELL TIMING: as needed

INGREDIENTS: an amethyst necklace or a grape-colored gem; a hazel tree slice cut at midnight on Samhain

> **FOR THE VARIATIONS:** water; orange peel tea or lettuce; a large, clean jar; moonshine or vodka, equal amounts of powdered slippery elm bark, willow bark, marshmallow, St. Johnswort, chamomile, and feverfew, and one dark tincture bottle with rubber-topped dropper

AMBIANCE: surrounded by friends during a Sabbat; alone, adoors, near a hazel tree on Samhain; content in your kitchen

---

[68] *The potion powder is so powerful that you'll probably be able to concoct three batches recycling the original herbs. When you run out of your initial supply of liquid medicine, simply douse the herbs with more moonshine or vodka. Stop using the originally crushed herbs when the fluid stops turning amber-colored after 21 days.*

Magical Theory:

> Sympathetic magic: Water is the principal element that corresponds to alcohol. "Firewater" also corresponds to Fire—hence its dehydrating effect.
>
> Antipathetic magic: Earth signs are opposite the Water signs on the zodiacal wheel of the year.
>
> Inversion magic: The grape—which can intoxicate—can also sober. The Greek word *amethystos* means "not drunk."
>
> Like cures like: A purple (grape-colored) stone tricks the body into believing it is already inebriated, thereby affording you sobriety.

Deity to Invoke: Saturn, the ruler of boundaries and restraint

TO STOP SOMEONE FROM CAUSING HARM

At midnight when the Moon is waning or new, place sands of two different colors and some black Witches' salt (pulverized jet) in separate saucers. If you don't have varying shades of sand, substitute wild birdseed, dried herbs, or food-coloring dyed table salt, raw rice, shredded coconut, or so forth.

Cast a circle ayenward. Face the North, and sit cross-legged on an uncarpeted floor. Meditate on precisely how the person has harmed you or others. Consider the person's motives, mind-games, or manipulative ways of thinking or operating. Consciously reduce the problem to its simplest symbol. For instance, if the chaos the person has been causing is hurting folks' feelings, visualize a broken valentine-style heart and concentrate on stopping the heartbreak.

Half-fill your palm with the palest shade of sand, grip the grit in your palm, then slowly and steadily release it onto the floor in the shape you've visualized. Refill your palm as needed until you complete the design. If you suffer from arthritis or feel uncomfortable with your hand muscle control or design precision, fill recycled plastic bags each with a different-colored sacred sand. For each baggie, remove any excess air, press its top closed, turn it upside down, and snip a tiny opening in one of the bottom corners. Use it like a cake-icing bag, relying on the opening to control the flow of the sand.

Next, select the darker sand, focus on the harmful person, and repeat the process, this time encircling your design sunwise with the sand. To prevent further harm, take up the black Witches' salt and make an X over, and an ayenward circle around, the entire glyph.

Mentally condense all your goodly hopes for a positive outcome; then splay your hands just above the glyph and magically empower it with your strongest Witchy will. With your besom, sweep up the grains and keep them in a handkerchief, scarf, or mojo bag. Afterward, whenever you feel inclined, grasp the container and mentally re-impress your banishing spell.

When the harm has stopped, open the bag and let the wind waft away its contents.

SPELL VARIATION

- Put harmful folks on ice—make an ice-cube poppet to prevent them from causing further harm:

  Half fill with water a single mold in an ice-cube tray. Freeze it.

  Atop it, place a thumbnail-sized sketch, photograph, or similar representation of your adversary's face. Secure it with a tiny bit of water, then refreeze it.

  Add more water until the mold brims full. Then freeze it for a third time.

  When the poppet is fully frozen, pop it out, house it in its own labeled and dated container, and store it in the freezer.

  When the person's ill intent abates sufficiently, cast the poppet into a stream or river and let it naturally melt any remaining negativity the person may harbor.

SPELL ORIGIN: Navajo and modern European magic

SPELL TIMING: at the Witching Hour when the Moon is waning or new

INGREDIENTS: two shades of sand or acceptable substitutions (listed above), black Witches' salt, an uncarpeted floor, a besom, and a handkerchief, scarf, or mojo bag

　　FOR THE VARIATION: an ice-cube tray, water, a representation of the harmful person, a pen, a freezer-compatible container, a coursing body of water

AMBIANCE: engulfed in billowing clouds of a banishing incense, such as dried mugwort or asafetida

MAGICAL THEORY: The sand glyph you make is a sigil. (See Making Sigils and Seals, page 200.)

MACROCOSM = MICROCOSM: Black Witches' salt (crushed jet) is a banishing/binding magical component that corresponds with Saturn.

SYMPATHETIC MAGIC: The frozen ice-cube poppet immobilizes the person, who can then cause no harm.

TO BIND ILL FROM ENTERING

PREVENT THIEVES, VIOLENT EX-SPOUSES, AND INTRUSIVE TYPES FROM entering your domain. Go adoors at noon and circumnavigate sunwise once or thrice the place you want to protect. See the area as the dastardly do—ripe for theft, scam, or harassment. Reflect on the kinds of people who seem attracted to your premises. Focus your mind like a laser beam and concentrate on thwarting thieves, solicitors, and emotionally draining, depressing, or disruptive sorts who try to breach your sacred bounds. Empower the entrances to serve as a magical placenta allowing entrée to kindly kith and kin, but perpetually barring all with ill intent.

Use your left middle finger to make banishing pentagrams with dragon's blood oil[69] in the extreme left corner of each window. Begin drawing at the Earth point of the pentagram on your lower left and draw ayenward toward the uppermost right hand point, where your pentagram should end, before encircling it ayenward. Anoint in like manner your doorknobs and keyholes.

Follow up the inside treatment with an outside one: Go adoors at the Witching Hour and sprinkle a demarcating line of black Witches' salt in front of each of your entrances and exits. Don't sweep up the Witches' salt—let nature waft it away at will.

Properly performed, none shall pass without your consent.

SPELL VARIATIONS

• If you don't possess or can't find or afford dragon's blood oil, brew your own, equally goodly mugwort or asafetida oil.

Extract the power of the plants by half-filling a Mason jar with either dried herb.

---

[69] *Available from occult or magical supply shops.*

Fill the jar to the rim with moonshine or vodka. Cap, shake, and ferment the material in darkness for 21 days. Shake the contents every few days.

Strain and drain the liquid into an amber or a cobalt-colored vial, and add a few drops of olive oil until the solution achieves an appropriate viscosity.

Cork and label and date the contents.

- Make and affix skull-bead talismans above doors, vents, chimneys, and attic and basement entrances.

Obtain silvery craft wire and handfuls of rounded, bone skull beads and reflective hematite spheres.

On each wire talisman, string a hematite bead, a bone skull bead, and a second hematite bead, for a total of three beads on each fetish.

Bend each into an elongated loop so that it will hang in a stable manner; then twist its top closed with your fingers. You may use pliers to bend down scratchy edges or shears to snip off any excess wire, although magically such pointy jags can only aid in opposing burglars. Use small carpentry finishing nails to suspend the talismans in plain sight.

Heed how the skulls appear to you at any time—their grinning or scowling countenances accurately predict whether the next person to cross your threshold will be a friend or a foe.

- Blatant Paganism tends to repel untrustworthy types, so suspend a door harp on the outside of your main door, hang pentagram wind chimes from eaves, or affix a pentagram decal to a prominent front window.

In two shakes of a satyr's tail, your sanctuary will be protected from ill-meaning folk.

SPELL ORIGIN: European magic and Coven Oldenwilde practices

SPELL TIMING: optimally, during Saturnalia from December 17–19; noon and midnight during a waxing or full Moon

INGREDIENTS: dragon's blood oil and black Witches' salt

FOR THE VARIATIONS: a Mason jar, dried mugwort or asafetida leaves, moonshine or vodka, an amber or a cobalt vial, a cork, a label; silvery craft wire, round, bone skull beads, spherical hematite beads, and finishing nails; a door harp, pentagram wind chimes, or a pentagram decal

AMBIANCE: usually alone, inside during the day, then adoors at midnight; in your comfy kitchen

MAGICAL THEORY:

SYMPATHETIC MAGIC: Marking your territory with a pentagram affords it the protection of Air, Fire, Water, Earth, and Spirit. Dragon's blood oil is powerful and is often used to strongly repel negativity. Your longest, middle finger is sacred to Saturn, the planet that binds, constricts, and constrains. By drawing pentagrams with your left finger, you signal that the activity is magical. Drawing on the extreme left of a windowpane signifies that you are targeting the spell to impede sinister types.

ANTIPATHETIC MAGIC: Whereas you protect in an obvious way during daytime, you should also follow up at night using black Witches' salt. White salt attracts; black salt repels. Mugwort and asafetida are pungent banishing herbs.

BETWEEN THE WORLDS: Anointing keyholes prevents folks from having keys made, using old ones to enter the premises, or using a wire to bypass your defenses. Doorknobs are a vulnerable mode of entry, so they must be charmed to prevent them from being (literally) turned against you. Places must be protected night and day or they're only half protected.

DEITIES TO INVOKE: Saturn, the ruler of boundaries, constriction, and constraint; Janus, Roman God of doorways and thresholds

TO CONFUSE YOUR ENEMIES

ELUDE PURSUIT, CONFOUND CHALLENGERS, AND CONCEAL THE NATURE of your spellwork by intoning the following Barbarous Words of Power:

Aglaria Pedhel
Garia Ananas
Q'epta

(ah-GLAH-ree-ah PEH-dhel
GAH-ree-ah AH-nah-nahs
KEHP-tah)

The Aglaria Pedhel spell is so olde that its origin is unknown. Properly chanted, it misdirects those who mean you ill, thereby affording you safe escape, invisibility, and privacy.

Reinforce the spell by inconspicuously making a downward-pointing *mano cornuta* gesture with either hand.

SPELL ORIGIN: traditional European magic, origin unknown; Italian *Strega* gesture

SPELL TIMING: as needed for a long-term problem, best when the Moon is in Pisces or in a hard aspect with Neptune

MAGICAL THEORY: Composed of vowels and consonants that have multiple magical correspondences, Barbarous Words of Power are innately mighty. Because they're of ancient derivation, their power has accrued over time.

SYMPATHETIC MAGIC: Pointed downward, the gesture of protective horns reinforces your diversion and distracts a pursuer's attention.

TO MAKE AND BIND A POPPET FOR PROTECTION

LONG-TERM PROTECTION FROM HARM NECESSITATES THAT ADVERSARIES view you in a goodly light. Therefore, employ the following binding charm to keep them from initiating scandal, working mundane or magical harm, and praying against you. Best of all—compel them to leap to your aid or defense!

We like to call this kind of poppet a "mum moppet." During Moondark, use a double-boiler setup to melt down several used, dark-colored candles. Remove wicks and any metal stabilizers, then pour the liquid into a shallow, waxed-paper-lined baking pan. Allow the wax to cool until you can fashion a figure from it with your bare fingers. Form a crude five-pointed star, and then refine the poppet's features (head, arms, and legs). Either impress or bigrave onto the poppet a representation of the person, such as a picture of the face, or a bindrune of their name. When dry, peel off any adhering wax paper. Enter your ritual room, place the poppet in the North, and light black candles and burn asafetida or mugwort as banishing incense.

Cast an ayenward circle, and address the poppet by name. Descending from head to toe, affix strands of black hemp or undyed twine around its body. As you tie each knot, intone its corresponding rune:

To see me well, I bind thine eyes.
I bind thy tongue to tell no lies.
I stay thy hands from working ill.
Thy knees shall bend against me nil.
Thy feet shall seek but help for me.
As (I/we) do will, so mote it be!

Wrap the mum moppet in black silk and hide it somewhere in the Earth Quarter. When the person ceases to be a threat, pulverize the wax and bury the remains.

SPELL ORIGIN: European magic, Coven Oldenwilde charm

SPELL TIMING: as needed, during Moondark, or during Saturn's day or hour

INGREDIENTS: several previously burned brown or black candles, chopsticks for removing wicks and stabilizers, wax paper, a baking pan, asafetida or mugwort, black hemp or undyed twine, black silk

AMBIANCE: alone in your kitchen and amidst clouds of asafetida or mugwort incense in your ritual room

MAGICAL THEORY: The mum moppet works by the principles described in Making Healing Poppets, page ooo. Preventing or eliminating harmful behavior is akin to healing an illness.

> **SYMPATHETIC MAGIC:** A brown or black poppet is composed of colors and wax that correspond with silent Earth. Asafetida and mugwort are potent banishing incenses that silence or repulse threats. Black hemp and undyed twine correspond with restrictive Saturn. Black silk calms the poppet and prevents its detection. Similar to "burying the hatchet," burying spell remains enables a future friendship between you and your former adversary.

> **MACROCOSM = MICROCOSM:** Because the poppet is a simulacrum of your adversary, your spell target will be similarly silenced.

DEITY TO INVOKE: Saturn, Roman God of binding and restriction

TO SEVER A BOND

...AUMA, AN ABUSIVE RELATIONSHIP, OR A
...o the point of obsession—secure your bliss by per-
...luences' attachment to you.

...double symbol that represents your situation,
...ce places. For instance, if you feel ungoodly bound
...r person, you'd fashion twin paper dolls attached at the
...d feet.

...se magical energy by talking aloud about the tie that binds you. When
...ou feel compelled, repeat this olde charm:

Once I cut—to break the tie.

With your fingers, tear in twain your symbol's top-most connection.

Twice I cut—for pain to fly.

Tear apart your symbol's middle connection.

Thrice I cut—the bond to cease.

Rip your symbol's lowest connection. When you feel properly empowered,
cement your spell by saying:

*As I will it,
so mote it be!*

In so doing, you initially break the constrictive bond; secondly, stop the
pain it's caused you; thirdly, sever the connection again; and finally, conjure closure on the subject.

SPELL ORIGIN: European magic
SPELL TIMING: As needed; preferably on a Friday during Moondark or when
    the Moon is waning

INGREDIENTS: parchment or paper and scissors

AMBIANCE: alone in a ritual setting adoors or inside

MAGICAL THEORY:

SYMPATHETIC MAGIC: The double paper poppet represents you and the problem that oppresses you. Severing the two psychically and physically negates any previous bond.

TRIPLICITY: The person who exerts a damaging constraint on you must be severed with at least three magical tears to break his or her power over you.

TO AID EARTH'S ENVIRONMENTAL RECOVERY

ALTHOUGH HISTORICALLY BLAMED FOR BLIGHTING CROPS AND KILLING livestock, Witches actually spell throughout the year to maintain seasonal weather patterns and oppose species eradication. Many share our compulsion to prevent nature's destruction, but few are aware that Earth's very name derives from Hertha, a German Goddess to whom medieval Witches were particularly devoted.

On a full Moon Friday during the Witching Hour, go adoors and commune with the Great Mother. Make intimate contact by sitting on the ground in a relaxed position, cross-legged or lotus-style. Mentally take the planet's temperature, so to speak—let your mind traverse the globe to get an overall picture of both Earth's splendor and her crying need.

From the slew of environmental plights you'll desire to address, select the one that you feel most urgently requires remedy; then stand and cast an ayenward circle. Direct your inner energy outward to increase the elements' powers.

Summon Fire, Air, Water, and Earth at their respective Quarters and demand that the Four Elements defy their human oppressors. Visualize stones rebelling at construction sites, water refusing redirection and crashing through constraining dams, and plants resisting pesticides and genetic manipulation and thriving with immutable vigor. See folks freed from toxic tyranny, basking in the glow of a planet restored to pristine status.

Passionately appeal to Hertha to make it so; then spin ayenward with outstretched arms for some time. Concentrate on undoing damage done by others. Spin until you collapse in a satisfied heap.

You'll have turned back the countdown clock of desertification and reiterated that the God/desses are not alone in their love of unbridled beauty.

SPELL VARIATION

- Keep a goodly rapport with wild animals—drum at dusk on logs with a stick or staff.

Coven Oldenwilde discovered this power of Orpheus, the legendary musician who spoke with the beasts through his lyre, at a Lammas Sabbat when we were camping adoors in a favorite area. Though off the beaten path of nearby hikers and hunters, the wildlife had always kept itself well concealed. With a crooked beater stick, *Diuvei began playing rhythmically on several firewood logs. About an arm's-width in diameter and of varying lengths, propped up on one end, they made resonant tones approximating a major chord. Our Third Degree Rowan Greenleaf joined in and played a steady beat on the ground with his staff.

Suddenly a flock of screech owls began making eerie sounds like the neighing of a ghostly herd of horses. They flew closer and closer and then began whinnying ecstatically just a few yards away, though remaining invisible in the tree cover. They continued answering whenever we drummed, for five or ten minutes. Shortly afterward, a pair of wildcats began mating exceedingly close to our campfire, replete with distinctive loud purring.

When we'd recovered from our astonishment, *Diuvei and Rowan resumed drumming. The male wildcat began making a slow, loud circuit around us and continued as long as the men drummed. Far from being hostile, the wildcats seemed by their singing to be celebrating the Sabbat with us.

SPELL ORIGIN: European magic, Coven Oldenwilde practice

SPELL TIMING: midnight on a Friday closest to a full Moon; during a Sabbat or an overnight camping trip

INGREDIENTS FOR THE VARIATION: a stick or staff and several logs of varying thickness that make various tones when struck

AMBIANCE: alone, adoors in moonlight, communing deeply with Mother Earth (replete with ritual tools and incense if desired); sitting around a balefire in a forest with friends

MAGICAL THEORY:

> ANTIPATHETIC MAGIC: To banish environmental destruction, cast (and move within) a circle ayenward.
>
> SYMPATHETIC MAGIC: To palliate the planet's ills, you must invoke a Deity known to have a marked affinity for the world.

DEITY TO INVOKE: Hertha, a German Goddess. Gaia or Ge is her name in Greek, and Terra is her Latin name.

TO PROTECT FOREST, FIELD, AND STREAM

PREVENT FOLKS FROM FELLING FORESTS, DEVELOPERS FROM PAVING wetlands, or corporations from mining and contaminating pristine locales—create and command a *fetch* (a mentally formed, magically animated entity) to perpetually patrol and protect a vulnerable magical environment.

During a waxing or full Moon, quietly walk to the endangered place. Sit lotus-style and consider the types of threats that imperil the habitat and ways to prevent its destruction.

Mentally fashion the fetch—something ghostly and intimidating. Conjure the entity as you wish it to appear to others. Make it mirror nefarious folks' darkest fears, for instance. Create a drawing, painting, or sculpture to help you visualize it, or depending on your talents, compose a conjuring song that activates it. Picture it glowing eerily or gliding spookily sans feet. Make it materialize silently with a penetrating glare, or have it howl, wail, keen, or screech in a frightening manner. Arm the spirit with wit for weapons—empower it with the magical ability to break chainsaws and backhoes, spill buckets of nails, or confuse construction workers. Give it an appropriate name to help you summon it should the need arise, and then bid it to wander the wilds and duly horrify anyone who means the land ill.

You'll soon hear tales about a mysterious haunt scaring environmental destroyers by suddenly materializing with a menacing grimace.[70]

---

[70] *Janet and Stewart Farrar,* A Witches Bible Compleat, *vol. II (New York: Magickal Childe Publishing, 1984), 242–243. The authors describe a fetch named Mara that their coven created to protect two islands off the coast of County Mayo from local fishermen who were killing seal pups delivered there. Their creation was both effective and just—in later years, sailors told them the spirit had warned them away from the islands' dangerous rocks.*

To guard a garden or ensure a field's fertility, summon the protection of Mars and appeal to helpful rural ancestral spirits (*Lases* or *Lares*). Chant the following Barbarous Words of Power while you sow or tend plants:

The Enos Lases Iuvate[71]

Enos Lases Iuvate, (Intone thrice.)	*Help us, O Lares.*
Neve Lue Rue Marmar *Sins Incurrere In Pleoris,* (Intone thrice.)	*And thou, Marmar,* *suffer not plague and ruin to* *attack our folk.*
Satur Fu, Fere Mars, *Limen Sali, Sta Berber!* (Intone thrice.)	*Be satisfied, O fierce Mars,* *leap over the threshold, halt* *here, here!*
Semunis Alterni *Advocapit Conctos.* (Intone thrice.)	*Call in alternate strain* *upon all the heroes.*
Enos Marmor Iuvato. (Intone thrice.)	*Help us, O Marmor.*
Triumpe! (Intone five times.)	*Triumph!*

SPELL VARIATION

- When next the Moon waxes full, walk quietly into a wood. Invoke Ardwinna or Herne, wildwood avenger God/desses, or Flidais, a Goddess of wildlife. Ardwinna exacts a fine for every animal killed in her realm and often appears astride a boar. Herne historically manifests himself as a longhaired

---

[71] *From the "Song of the Arval Brothers," an ancient Roman invocation to the* Lares *(ancestral spirits of the land) and Mars (Marmar) in his earliest, agricultural guise to produce and protect crops and flocks. Leland gives one version in* Etruscan Roman Remains. *Our version, dating from the fourth century B.C.E., is from "Carmen Arvale," electronic version by Ulrich Harsch, at Bibliotheca Augustana (**http://www.fh-augsburg.de/~harsch/arv_intr.html**), 1997/2003.*

horseman, though *Diuvei has experienced him as a mountainous, august God of luminous darkness, like the deepest depths of an old-growth forest, with an air of ancient wisdom that inspired profound reverence.

Vow to find ways to physically prevent the destruction of magical places. If you remain motionless and respectful, the God/desses may grace you with their presence and provide you with a guiding omen or insight regarding a solution. In gratitude, plant an acorn or unwind a vine that's choking a seedling. Leave when sunset silhouettes the tree trunks against the sky.

Follow the rite by taking physical measures—join an activist group, boycott companies with unconscionable ecological records, recycle, or clean littered thickets with friends.

SPELL ORIGIN: European, Celtic, and Irish Craft

SPELL TIMING: during a waxing or full Moon

AMBIANCE: immersed in nature

MAGICAL THEORY:

MACROCOSM = MICROCOSM: Like demigod/desses, protective entities are unrestricted by the conventional laws of physics—they're immanent and, within their realm, omniscient.

TRIPLICITY: Mars is thrice invoked through three variants of his name. The invocation calls on him to not only spare the fields from harm, but also to stand and guard them—"leap over the threshold, halt here, here!"

SPIRITS AND DEITIES TO INVOKE: *Lases* (helpful ancestral spirits); Mars in his earliest aspect of agricultural God; Ardwinna and Herne, Celtic woodland God/desses; Flidais, the Irish stag-mistress who protects all flora and fauna

· Attraction Spells ·

"And of all necessitation, that which comes from a soul endowed with intelligence is for the mightiest, seeing she imposes her law as a sovereign who is subject to none, and when a soul has decided for the best with fault-less wisdom, the utterly irreversible result falls out entirely to its mind."

—PLATO

Epinomis

*M*any folks feel that the deck of life is stacked against them: You've got to be born lucky to be lucky; it takes money to make money; only beautiful people marry. However, myriad spells have survived that can accord you the ability to attract your perfect mate or dream home, ensure business success, or even elicit justice from the most resistive "kangaroo court." Don't wait for luck or love to find you—learn how to find buried treasure, get Brownies to do your chores, win at games of chance, and make your wishes come true.

TO APPEAR BEAUTIFUL

PERFORMING THE FOLLOWING SPELL AND WEARING ITS ATTENDANT amulet will not only confer comeliness on you, but also impart to you the powers:

> *". . . to bless or curse, to converse with spirits, to find hidden treasures in ancient ruins, to conjure the spirits of priests who died leaving treasures, to understand the voice of the wind, to change water into wine, to divine with cards (cartomancy), to know the secrets of the hand (palmistry), to cure diseases, and to tame wild beasts."*[72]

Just before the Witching Hour on a Friday during a full Moon, travel to a secret wood or outdoor field. Place three vials—one each of water, wine, and salt—close at hand.

Cast a circle sunwise. Fill a red talisman pouch with salt, tie it shut with a red string, and clasp the bag firmly in your left hand. Adore the Moon, herself a mesmerizing Goddess of beauty. Honestly assess your physical attributes. How do you appear to others? How would you classify your style of movement? Do friends remark that you seem to glide gracefully through life, or are you often embarrassed when they note your marked degree of clumsiness? Contemplate physical changes you could make that might help you spiritually; for example, shy folks often overcome their detrimental body consciousness and increase their trust by working magic skyclad with others. Visualize physical actions you could take to alter your appearance for the better.

[72] *Leland,* Aradia: Gospel of the Witches.

Slowly begin summoning Aradia with the following spell. Emphasize the incantation's repetitions, and follow the spell's dictates as they occur. For example, when it's time to say, "I bless myself," anoint your forehead or the area above your heart with the water and wine.

Thus do I seek Aradia!
Aradia!
Aradia!

At midnight—
At midnight I go into a field.

And with me, I bear water, wine and salt.

I bear water, wine and salt—and my talisman—
my talisman—
my talisman,

a small red bag which I hold in my hand . . .
In it,
In it, salt.
with salt in it.

With the water and wine I bless myself—

I bless myself with devotion
to implore a favor from Aradia.

Grasp your talisman even more tightly. Picture yourself becoming infused with rosy life; enjoying abundant, warm blood flow from within, and taking on a healthy hue—an inner, mysterious glow. Mentally create a shimmery sheen of glamour just above your face and body. Empower your projection to be able to reshape any facial features you don't like—recalibrate the distance between your eyes, for instance.

Dance to increase the power of your spell. When you feel you've raised enough energy, chant to activate the incantation at will:

Aradia!
Aradia!

I implore Thee—
by the love which your mother, Diana, bore for Thee!

And by the love which I, too, feel for Thee!

I pray Thee grant the grace which I require!

And if this grace be granted,
May there be one of three signs distinctly clear to me:

The hiss of a serpent—
The light of a firefly—
The sound of a frog!

Whenever you feel compelled to, discharge your will to be beautiful directly through the fingers clasping your talisman. If your spell is taking hold, it should feel as though your power has sunk deep into the bag's contents without your having touched them. Thank Aradia for bestowing enchantment on you, and then close circle. Watch for the omens that you requested to manifest themselves within three to nine nights.

Wear your red pouch as a necklace mojo bag, or carry it hidden in your purse or pocket. You will appear to others as infused with a rosy glow by day, and irresistibly enchanting at night.

To keep your glamoury intact indefinitely, magically charge your talisman once a month by the light of the full Moon. Should you ever need or desire to dispose of your talisman, throw its contents into water flowing away from you. Shred the bag itself into bits with shears, and respectfully return them to Mother Earth.

SPELL VARIATIONS

- To become as gorgeous as a Goddess, stealthily slip adoors just before dawn on Beltane (May 1) and bathe your face in flower dew. Maintain your beguiling beauty by repeating the rite each year.
- For a luminous visage, grow damask roses.
- To have ever-renewing beauty, cultivate China roses.

SPELL ORIGIN: Italian *Strega,* Celtic, and European magic

SPELL TIMING: Friday at the Witching Hour during a full Moon

INGREDIENTS: three vials—one filled with water, one with wine, and one containing white table salt, a red, necklace-style talisman bag, and red string

    FOR THE VARIATIONS: Beltane flower dew; damask roses; China roses

AMBIANCE: alone in a field or forest

MAGICAL THEORY:

    SYMPATHETIC MAGIC: To attract beauty, you must project grace.

    A basic form of matter and a natural preservative, salt has been used in spells throughout history to represent stability, endurance, and preservation. In this spell, salt represents the element Earth. Matter and Earth equate magically with the body; therefore, the salt inside your talisman bag can preserve your body (for instance, you will age slowly), or magically alter your body's configuration into a prettier form.

    Red is associated with the blood and blush of life, as well as the Goddess in her fertile mother aspect. Colors influence by proximity; the more you wear your red talisman bag, the more it will infuse you with a rosy, mesmerizing glow that's irresistibly appealing to others.

    Three is an odd, therefore magical, number that in this case represents the archetypal prettiness of the Maiden, the ripe beauty of the Mother, and the wild strikingness of the Crone.

    Fourteenth-century Italians described Aradia as *bella,* "beautiful," calling her *la Bella Pellegrina,* "the Beautiful Pilgrim."

    ART OF CORRESPONDENCES: Rose petals' texture resembles soft baby skin, and people often use them to concoct herbal face washes.

    Victorians often sent blooms to convey messages. In that language of flowers, damask roses symbolize a clear complexion, and China roses, renewing attractiveness.

DEITY TO INVOKE: Aradia, mythically the mortal daughter of the Greek
Goddess Diana; historically, an Italian Witch who taught peasants Witchcraft during the 1300s

TO ATTRACT WITCH FRIENDS

THIS SPELL CUTS THROUGH BOUNDARIES LIKE BUTTER — FOLKS WILL
heed your call even if they reside in foreign countries! After you've done the rite
and Pagan friends duly enter your realm, they typically come bearing tales of
having felt utterly compelled to move to a place of which they had never previously heard. You'll experience what this olde proverb describes:

*"Witches and warlocks
without any bother,
Like gypsies, on meeting
well know one another."*[73]

Craftily collect cobwebs from your home, workplace, or other frequent
haunt. On a Friday at the Witching Hour during a waxing or full Moon, don
Witchy garb (black silk, wool, hemp, or cotton) and silver jewelry (preferably,
a pentagram or crescent Moon). Appear as alluring as possible. Place the cobwebs
in the center of your spellworking space as a focal point to remind you of your ritual intention. Cast your circle sunwise in the names of Hecate and Mercury. When
the air fairly crackles with an invisible charge, close your eyes and begin the rite.

Consider why you yearn for Witchy friends. Fantasize about sharing your
magical experiences with other Hidden Children (Witches) who would appreciate them and support your spiritual path. Think of ways you could all pool
your resources and help one another in times of need. Consider your likely similarities and antipathies.

Pray aloud, extolling Hecate's virtues and attributes. Appeal to her in a
heartfelt manner, specifically listing the characteristics you want your future
friends to possess, and meticulously excluding character flaws you don't want
them to have. Visualize the many modes of travel such friends may have to use

[73] *Leland,* Gypsy Sorcery and Fortune-Telling, *197.*

to reach your vicinity. Supplicate Mercury, humbly asking that he ensure their safe transport and timely arrival.

Inflame your inner passions—dance or similarly raise emotional and physical energy toward the fulfillment of your desire. When your magical energy peaks, direct the power by pointing with your left index finger—first at the cobwebs, then toward the universe (immanent throughout your circle, but typically skyward). Ask that folks of like mind appear to you in such a manner that you'll easily recognize them. For instance, you might tack on a couplet such as "Friend in black—foes will lack" to help you distinguish the Wise from the wicked, and the precious from the posers.

Close your circle by expressing sincere gratitude to Hecate and Mercury for alleviating your isolation or loneliness. Hang the cobwebs adoors, in midair, such as in a tree.

SPELL VARIATIONS

- Cut a long piece of household string or embroidery floss, and tie the ends together. While rocking back and forth, make cat's cradle designs with your hands, indicating your yen for Pagan friends.

When the spell is complete, put the string or floss into either a pink or a turquoise pouch. Wear the pouch as a mojo bag around your neck, or secrete it in your purse or pocket until you've attracted enough Wiccans. Use the pouch as needed for friendship matters, or to evoke general goodwill. Dispose of spent string or floss by burial when you feel inclined.

- Vertically set individual sticks or tree limbs into the ground approximately 1 to 2 feet apart, forming a circle large enough for you to be able to walk around inside. Using two skeins of undyed cotton clothesline (approximately 200 feet), weave an oversized dreamcatcher. The branches you erected dictate its basic form and must support its weight.

As you weave, sing or dance about to incline friends your way. When finished, remove the dreamcatcher from the tree-limb pegs and hang it on a wall in your home. Let it remain there undisturbed until you're fully satisfied with the number and caliber of magical friends you've attracted; then return the spent dreamcatcher to Mother Earth via burial.

SPELL ORIGIN: European magic

SPELL TIMING: a Friday at midnight during a waxing or full Moon

INGREDIENTS: cobwebs

> FOR THE VARIATIONS: string or floss and either a pink or turquoise pouch; undyed cotton clothesline, sticks or tree limbs

AMBIANCE: alone, either adoors or inside

MAGICAL THEORY:

> SYMPATHETIC MAGIC: Similar objects have a magical affinity for each other, and therefore tend to attract each other. For example, cobwebs are sticky, natural lures that act magically to trap and contain your desires so they can be used to catch friends.
>
> Friday is sacred to Venus, the Roman Goddess of Love. Witches have always met on Friday nights because at such times, Venus imbues all with friendliness and kinship.
>
> Hanging spell cobwebs in a tree activates the element Air, which rules communication and therefore aids Mercury to procure Craft friends for you.
>
> Pink signifies platonic love, and turquoise promotes friendship.

DEITIES TO INVOKE: Hecate, Goddess of the Hidden Children; Mercury, the Roman God associated with summoning and travel

TO CONJURE ABUNDANCE

SIMPLY ACQUIRING MORE MONEY ONCE RARELY ALLEVIATES THE CHRONIC LACK thereof. Rather, ongoing, oppressive material needs are best met by your conjuring a pervasive providence that helps you flourish in multitudinous ways.

To prevent poverty, make an arrangement of dried alfalfa and keep it in your home.

Another way to prevent penury is to carry an abundance charm, such as a shamrock. Each clover leaf bestows a gift to promote a happy life—the upper left leaf wafts you wealth, the upper right leaf elicits you love, the bottom right leaf grants you health, and the bottom left leaf favors you with fame.

Faced with insufficient funds to replace our covenstead's roof, Oldenwilde recently employed an olde *Strega* spell for abundance. The spell called for us to stick a lemon, which represents the Moon, with color-tipped straight pins (except black) and suspend it with hemp or thread in some out-of-the-way corner. We circled with our covenmates and took turns inserting the pins as deeply as the rind would allow, initially covering the lemon's surface with pinheads of various colors. We then used only green-tipped pins to demarcate a runic *F* to signify the Feoh sign that represents material goods. (You could substitute a bounty-bringing square, Earth's ancient magical symbol.) We duly received an unexpected donation that enabled us to replace our leaky old roof with a goodly new one.

A different abundance rite begins with a sweeping spell attributed to a wealthy Irish Witch of the 1300s named Dame Alice Kyteler.

Shortly before midnight on a Thursday during a waxing or full Moon, take your besom in hand and sweep sunwise toward the center of your circling area, muttering your own personal adaptation of Dame Alice Kyteler's incantation. In the first line, substitute the name of the person for whom you're conjuring wealth. In the second line, say the appropriate designation, such as my (self), my (mate), or my (daughter), and so forth. At the charm's fourth and final line, supply the name of the town you live in or nearest to.

> *To the house of (William),*
> *my (son)—*
> *Hie all the wealth*
> *Of (Kilkenny) town!*

Improve your ritual area's decor and ambiance to augment your ability to attract abundance—light, earthy, emerald-colored candles and so on. Cast a circle sunwise to initiate the increase magic. Sit and recall times when miraculous luck and divine favor graced you. Picture yourself provided with plentitude.

Whenever you're ready, make lucky "fixed rice." Put approximately 3 cups of raw rice into a glass bowl. Drip green food coloring on top of the grains with your right hand, and then stir sunwise with a chopstick or silver spoon to evenly dye the rice. Stare deeply into the bowl and fervently invoke the God/desses Copia, Gaea, and Jupiter to empower the green grains to draw prosperity to you and yours from every direction and dimension.

When your fixed rice has dried and you feel duly inspired, fling handfuls of the grains high into the air! The more you toss, the more you'll be inundated with serendipitous showers of the God/desses' largesse. Sweep the rice up with your besom, store it in an airtight container for future use, and label and date its contents.

Henceforth, whenever you need funds, use an appropriate amount of the lucky fixed rice in a spell to relieve your need. Minor monetary matters require minimal rice, whereas the brink of bankruptcy requires a copious quantity.

Coven Oldenwilde's Third Degree hive-off High Priestess Lady Cassandra-Shine first used her lucky rice to obtain cheap tickets to visit holy sites in Mexico. The components worked so well, she used them again to draw food during a prolonged period of unemployment. That worked so successfully that she used her lucky fixed rice a third time and landed her dream job.

SPELL VARIATIONS

- To attract money on an ongoing basis, carry a few grains of green prosperity rice in your wallet, coin purse, or checkbook.
- Leave an offering of fixed rice for Gaea or Hertha at the base of a plant or tree.
- Put a goodly amount of lucky green rice on a tray, or spill a goodly quantity on the floor. With your forefinger, draw designs that symbolize your need.

  After you empower the rice to attract your desire, fill a mojo bag or necklace pouch with it, and wear the bag until your wish is fulfilled.

  To keep abundance flowing your way, charge your amulet once a month during the full Moon.
- Don't throw your luck away—whenever you sweep or rake anything, stroke inward toward the center of your house or property.

SPELL ORIGIN: Voudon, Italian *Strega,* Irish, and Santerian magic

SPELL TIMING: midnight on a Thursday during a waxing or full Moon

INGREDIENTS: dried alfalfa; a lemon, color-tipped (but not black) straight pins, and hempen string or thread; a besom; green candle(s), 3 cups of raw rice, a glass bowl, green food coloring, a chopstick or silver mixing spoon, and an airtight container

AMBIANCE: alone, indoors, in a private magical space

MAGICAL THEORY:

SYMPATHETIC MAGIC: Although a lime might seem to symbolize more aptly the emerald Earth, "The Conjuration of the Lemon and Pins" in *Aradia: Gospel of the Witches* equates a lemon with the Moon (magic) and an orange with the Sun (health).

La Luna is a luck-bringer who can take away your poverty during the low tide she creates, or inundate you with plenty during her full phase.

Lush Earth offers everyone infinite options for opulence. Dyeing green a crop that much of the world depends on for sustenance directly attracts Gaea's bounty to your daily life.

The Goddess Copia (of cornucopia fame) has the power to bestow "copious" abundance.

Because plants grow in all directions, luck will similarly come to you from everywhere if you leave an offering to an Earth Goddess at the base of a plant or tree.

Thursday is Jupiter's day. The largest planet in our solar system, Jupiter is the astrological ruler of abundance and good fortune. In chiromancy (palmistry), Jupiter rules the forefinger.

Sweeping or raking outward disperses your prosperity to others. Dirt, grass clippings, and leaves are organic, so by sweeping toward your property, you not only maintain your household's prosperity, but replenish your land's fertility as well.

DEITIES TO INVOKE: Copia, a Roman Goddess of bounty; Gaea and Hertha, Greek Earth Goddesses; Jupiter, a Roman God of expansive abundance

TO BE LUCKY AT GAMES OF CHANCE

" . . . the divine witchcraft of fun and the sublime sorcery of sport, . . . are just as magical and wonderful in their way as anything in all theurgia or occultism. . . ."[74]

Games typically involve a prescribed number of moves, spins, turns, rolls, guesses, or dealt cards. Magical folk can "stack the deck" in their favor by employing ancient magic squares composed of numbers called constants.

[74] *Leland,* Gypsy Sorcery and Fortune-Telling, *222.*

On a Thursday night during a waxing or full Moon, set an appropriate ambiance with candles and incense. Cast a sunwise circle in the name of the Goddess Felicitas. Call the Four Quarters and accord marked reverence to the Element Earth, which rules fortune. Bid hail to the Four Elementals, particularly the earthy Gnomes, treasure-loving leprechauns.

When you're properly expectant, construct a hinged magical seal on which you'll ink mystic signs and sigils to lure Jupiter's luck. Throughout the process, never cast your shadow on the seal.

Fold a piece of paper in half. In the center on the left-hand folded side, leave approximately ½ inch of the fold intact, and snip with scissors both sides of this ½ inch measurement about ½ inch toward the paper's open side. Use the end of one of the two snips as a starting point; then cut a circle approximately 3 inches in diameter. You should end up with two overlapping circles connected paper-doll style.

Lay the roundels atop the God Jupiter's magic square, below. Note that the numbers add up to 34 horizontally, vertically, and diagonally.

SQUARE OF JUPITER

4	14	15	1
9	7	6	12
5	11	10	8
16	2	3	13

Lift your hinged circle's top flap to reveal the image of Jupiter's number square beneath the parchment. On the inside of the bottom circle, trace the square's lines in black ink. Fill in the numbers inside the boxes with red ink. Allow the seal to air dry.

Close the seal as you'd close a compact, flip it over, and place it atop Jupiter's planetary sigil.

SIGIL OF JUPITER

Open your seal. Note that the sigil visible beneath it includes each box that composed the previous numerical square. Trace the sign with blue ink. Sketch the four corner circles first, then make an X to connect two at a time to their cross-quarter opposites. Last, copy the large center circle. Allow your roundel to air dry, then close the seal again.

Sum up your desire in one symbol ($, for instance), and ink it in black on the blank top of your seal. You may also elect to distill your wish into a succinct phrase, such as *lucky at games,* convert its letters into a magical alphabet, and ink it around the periphery of the seal's top circle. Finally, ink your magical name (perhaps in Theban) on the blank bottom of your seal.

When your seal is dry, fold it in half, then once more—thrice in all, from the beginning to the end of the spell. When properly folded, your finished seal should resemble a piece of pie. (You may also simply roll the talisman into a tube and secure the scroll with string.)

Grasp your seal in your left hand, and consecrate it with censing and spurging: Pass it through incense smoke, then flick it with either salt water or essential oil.

Earnestly appeal to Felicitas and Jupiter for future goodly fortune during games of chance. Thank them in advance for granting you abundant luck. Place your talisman in a pouch, or wear it beneath your clothes whenever you play a competitive game.

Never brag about or show off your secret weapon—such base exposure offends the animated talisman, and it will likely cease charming for you.

SPELL VARIATIONS

- Illustrated below is a dice sigil that will bring you good luck whenever you throw dice.

*Diuvei devised it by arranging in their natural order all the possible throws of two dice. An aficionado of backgammon, he originally drew this aleatory matrix to understand which throws are most probable (those closest to the center horizontal row). He soon discovered that this cosmological diagram also has magical and divinatory properties. (No disrespect to Einstein, but if the Gods *do*

ALEATORY MATRIX

This seal represents all possible rolls of two dice.

play dice with the universe, the aleatory matrix likely serves as the model for the hyperdice they use.)

Draw, copy, or bigrave the dice sigil on a small piece of parchment or metal. On a Thursday during an hour of Jupiter, cense it with the smoke of burning clove, nutmeg, or allspice. Appeal to Jupiter to grant you power over dice with the aid of this device.

Carry the talisman with you when you are going to play a dice game. If possible, touch the dice to it before you roll; otherwise, hold it in one hand while you roll with the other. Focus intently on the dice roll you desire; then let go when you feel compelled to and allow it to happen.

- Increase your luck by sticking a crooked pin in your lapel, or bathing in Jamaican ginger tea before going out on gambling adventures.
- To avert a reversal of fortune, sit facing the door, and don't cross your legs, sing, or lose your temper while gaming.
- Change your luck for the better—crush khus khus (vertiver) with a mortar and pestle and steep 1 teaspoonful of the herb in 6 to 8 ounces of hot water for three to five minutes. Pour the tea into your bathwater and bathe in it. Wash in such an additive on nine consecutive days.
- Acquire one or more lucky fetishes. Effective examples include a wheel (of fortune) charm, a money symbol ($), a necklace strung with seven golden rings, a silver coin, a rabbit's foot, or a hag stone (a rock with a natural hole in it).

Cleanse and consecrate your lucky charms by passing them through all Four Elements (salt water, incense, and candle flame). Bless your fetishes by anointing them with money-drawing oil or ground allspice dissolved in tap water.

Construct a pile of all the cash and coins you have on hand, and place your lucky charms in its center. Charge the fetishes by firmly, verbally insisting that you want them to attract only stellar and stable luck, not capriciousness. For instance, you expect them to help you win money, but won't brook any setbacks or reversals.

House your fetishes in a mojo pouch, and wear it touching your skin during your next gambling outing. If you decide to keep your fetishes in your pocket, fondle them inconspicuously at pivotal moments during a game, such as before rolling a die, or when your hand is being dealt.

Periodically re-empower your fetishes with renewed vigor by charging them once a month in the rays of the waxing or full Moon. When they've helped you consistently beat the odds, cleanse them of your personal energies and pass them on to another needy person.

- Practice astragalomancy and cartomancy (divination by dice and by cards, respectively) whenever you have time and a peaceful, conducive environment in which to properly concentrate.

    Begin by holding a pair of dice or a deck of cards in your left hand. Focus intently on each dice roll or card lay until you're consistently able to psychically predict which number the dice will land on or which card will be dealt next.

    Start simply, and progress in complexity over time. For instance, prior to a dice roll, intuit whether the outcome will be the number *3,* less than *3,* or more than *3.* Sense basic die shapes; for example, a box image portends the "boxcar," or six dots. Similarly, if you're psychically scanning cards, will the one about to be dealt be black, red, or a face card?

    Categorize the mental images you receive with respect to "many" or "few"—busy with pictures, or radiating minimal imagery. The ten of spades, for example, has multiple curvy and linear graphics that cover much of its available surface area; therefore, you will intuit it differently than you would an ace or a face card.

    Cease practicing whenever you begin to feel mentally drained—often, whenever the dice or cards inexplicably start to "cross you" so that you're able to sense only their opposite values. (You're sure the next card's an ace, for instance, but it turns out to be a king.)

Should diligent practice convince you that you're simply not gifted at astragalomancy or cartomancy, appeal for help from the Goddess Fortuna.

- Crafters delight in using telekinesis to produce desired dice rolls and card deals.

To accomplish such a wondrous feat, don't stress out over the difficulty of the prospect or try to calculate mathematical probabilities. Instead, ease yourself into "the zone" wherein psychism flows from you, to the cards, and back to you again. Psychically push hard regarding your desire for about a minute; then relax and allow it to manifest itself the next.

- When you've mastered basic astragalomancy and cartomancy, up the ante by testing your psychic prowess against that of an opponent or other players. Record each player's psychic "hits" throughout the game. Tabulate the results and award the most accurate psychic a magical prize.
  - Practice mentally manipulating the rolls and deals to be what you want them to be. Decide which dice numbers you want to roll or which card you want dealt, declare it aloud, and then magically will it to occur by sheer mental force.

When all are well satisfied (typically, when ability wanes), tabulate the results and give a magical prize to the most accurate telekinetic.

SPELL ORIGIN: Voudon herbalism, Babylonian numerology, European magic

SPELL TIMING: a Thursday night in an hour of Jupiter during a waxing or full Moon—preferably when la Luna is in a good aspect with Jupiter, or in one of his signs (Sagittarius and Pisces)

INGREDIENTS: a feather or porcupine quill pen, parchment or paper, scissors, black, red, and blue ink, a Jupiter number square and planetary sigil, and a mojo bag

FOR THE VARIATIONS: an aleatory matrix and a pair of dice; a crooked pin; 1 teaspoon of Jamaican ginger, 6 to 8 ounces of water, bathwater; a mortar and pestle, 1 teaspoon of khus khus (vertiver), 6 to 8 ounces of water, bathwater; lucky charms, money-drawing oil or

WHEN MONEY IS INVOLVED, however, you start stepping into ethical quicksand. In general, if you employ telekinesis while gambling with friends, you'll quickly lose them. In that kind of game, the odds are supposed to be equal among everyone, and the fun involved is intended to derive from the skill you display in managing the hand fate deals you. Even if the other players think that you're just uncannily lucky, the bottom line, with very few exceptions, is this: It's cheating to use your magic to manipulate a game process that's intended to be random. Exceptions include when you're gambling in a casino wherein you're simply evening up the house's heavily stacked odds, or when you're playing against a card-counter, another telekinetic, or an arrogant boor who deserves to be humbled.

ground allspice and water, the Four Elements (salt water, incense, and candle flame), cash or coins, a mojo pouch; a pair of dice or playing cards

AMBIANCE: alone in a private circling space (typically indoors); gaming or gambling with an opponent or friends

MAGICAL THEORY: Witches are luckier than most because we actively appeal to God/desses of fortune and encourage luck to manifest itself.

MACROCOSM = MICROCOSM: Most games of chance are based on underlying number patterns; a magic number square or an aleatory matrix helps you tap the powers that govern these patterns.

SYMPATHETIC MAGIC: If you would be lucky at games, invoke a God/dess known for possessing and bestowing the nebulous quality. You can receive a planetary God/dess's aid if you trace over his or her numerical magic square and planetary sigil. Wearing their talisman close to your skin transfers their power to you by virtue of proximity.

DEITIES TO INVOKE: Felicitas, the Roman Goddess of goodly fortune; the Roman God Jupiter; Fortuna, the fate Goddess who spins the Wheel of Fortune

TO ATTRACT FAIRIES TO YOUR YARD

CRAFTERS LIKE TO ATTRACT FAIRIES—ALSO CALLED DEVAS OR NATURE spirits—to our yards and gardens because we love all creatures of nature. These intelligent Beings, which appear to exist partly in the material and partly in the spiritual realms, are always associated with a thriving, diverse ecosystem. Their presence adds daily magic and wonder to Witches' lives.

Like the God/desses, fairies are real Beings with a long history of interacting with humans. Species run the gamut from tiny, ethereal lights, such as Will-O'-the-Wisps, to tall types that manifest themselves in corporeal form. For example, Oberon once detached himself from the trunk of a tree, rendering Lady Passion mute by his utter immensity. The King of the Fairies stood 10 feet high with glistening reptilian skin, piercing yellow eyes, and a barrel chest so massive that it resembled the hull of a ship.

Fairies have many modes of defense. Airy fairies stay safe by mimicking the forms, flight patterns, and life cycles of insects. Other species reside in planes of existence far different from our own, and appear only when magically lured or they feel compelled to express their displeasure regarding something you've done or are in the midst of doing. Some pixies occasionally help humans—others are downright capricious, suspect human motives, or may chide you with words or withering looks if you act thoughtlessly.

Fireplaces and adoors fire pits attract Fire fairies. They frequently buzz and manifest themselves in a frenetic or slightly agitated manner. Fire elementals called Salamanders often slither like lizards among hot coals or flicker within or atop flames. To conjure Fire fairies:

Half-fill a cauldron with Epsom salt. Pour atop the crystals an entire bottle of 70 percent isopropyl (rubbing) alcohol, and ignite the liquid. The ingredients produce animated azure flames that are often cold enough for you to play with by hand. Whenever the fire wanes, stir the salt with a stick to keep it lit longer.

To lure winged Fey to your yard, provide them with close, protective shelter in which to live and breed by gently weaving pliant plants, such as honeysuckle, ivy, or morning glory, into tight, convoluted shapes. Approach the exercise as a Wiccan form of meditation similar to Chinese bonsai-tree trimming, minus the scissors. Weave a bit every few days from Ostara to Samhain, allowing the vines to rest throughout the winter months. At our covenstead, blue-white fairies that resemble flying wedding gowns bide in some lilac bushes that Lady Passion rescued from suffocation by trumpet vines. Attract Airy elementals called Sylphs by hanging many different kinds and tones of wind chimes near your front and back entrances. Sylphs range in form from blurry white things that occasionally dart past your peripheral vision, to friendly, inquisitive entities resembling butterflies.

Entice water-dwelling Naiads and sleek, silvery elementals called Undines by making a grotto out of any big bowl you have on hand. Decorate its bottom with coral, seashells, colored glass shards, pebbles, and silver coins. Stack bricks 3 feet high, place the bowl atop the stack, and fill the bowl with water. Set it adoors or inside in the Western direction.

Crotchety leprechauns and Earth elementals called Gnomes have skin that resembles leathery bark, so it's little wonder that they reside in rabbit holes or caves, or in or near trees or such plants as Scotch broom and deadly nightshade. They covet treasure, so attract these fairies by putting out shiny baubles or costume jewelry, or construct an open-air arbor of river cane or bamboo.

Try to acquire a species of cane that resists weathering. Set the poles 2 to 3 feet deep into the ground. Support the structure with itself—lock the cane's branches together as you fashion the framework. If needed, tightly lash poles together with a pliant vine, such as honeysuckle, or leather thongs. Rustically decorate the inside—hand-weave grass-mat curtains; use a large, flat stone as an altar, and split logs as primitive seating. When Coven Oldenwilde did this, Lady Passion planted and interwove twisty willow trees betwixt the arbor walls so they would replace the cane structure as it naturally deteriorated over time.

SPELL VARIATIONS

- Grow fairy-luring plants. Periwinkles, violets, yarrow, and berries of all sorts attract a wide variety of Fey species.
- Make an enchanting altar adoors, and leave ritual libations and fairy offerings on it. Decorate it with iridescent glitter, neon-blue woad, shiny coins, nut halves, dried herbs, cone incense, and handfuls of blue-green-pink fluorites, or fairy stones.

SPELL ORIGIN: European and Coven Oldenwilde practice

SPELL TIMING: in the cool of the day (early morning or just before sunset)

INGREDIENTS: a cauldron, Epsom salts, a bottle of 70 percent isopropyl alcohol, and a stirring stick; pliant vines; a big bowl, decorations such as coral, seashells, colored glass shards, pebbles, or silver coins, and water; shiny baubles or river cane or bamboo poles, vine or leather lashing, an altar stone, and half-round logs

FOR THE VARIATIONS: fairy-luring plants; a flat altar stone and shiny or natural decorations such as iridescent glitter, neon-blue woad, shiny coins, nut halves, dried herbs, cone incense, and fluorite gem chips

AMBIANCE: alone or with the assistance of family or friends, employing Fire, Air, Water or Earth elements to lure corresponding fairy species

MAGICAL THEORY: Nurturing fairies adds excitement and dimension to life and reminds folks that humans are not the only magical, sentient species on the planet.

SYMPATHETIC MAGIC: To lure fairies, use elemental correspondences associated with specific species. For instance, to attract water fairies, make a fountain, pond, or birdbath.

ENTITIES TO SUPPLICATE:

Salamanders (Fire elementals)

Sylphs (Air elementals) and Will o'-the Wisps (bodiless glowing fairies)

Undines (Water elementals) and Neriads and Naiads (fairies of river and stream)

Gnomes (Earth elementals), Leprechauns (land fairies), and Dryads (tree fairies)

TO BID BROWNIES DO YOUR HOUSEWORK

STERILE CLEANLINESS IS AN IMPOSED, PURITANICAL CONCEPT QUITE at odds with the natural order of life, so don't assume that your distaste for drudgery is some character defect on your part. By design, ceaseless chores can deter Crafters from accomplishing more important, magical tasks.

If you're tired of muttering, "There's dignity in all work, there's dignity in all work," stop, drop to your knees, and appeal for help from a Goddess who rules millions of minions who can do your housework while you slumber.

Summon the Queen of Elfame by shaking a wind-chime or ringing your altar bell. According to tradition, Titania is both inquisitive and protective. When conjured, she often initially watches events from behind shrubbery. If the Queen of the Fairies likes what she sees, she then reveals her form more fully. Titania stands about 5 inches tall and has sharp, delicate features and a pointed nose resembling a bird's beak. The Goddess has fair, porcelain skin and long blond hair, and wears a long azure, dark green, or beige dress. Her penetrating gaze plumbs your soul to discern your intent. She often points or stares, but if she deigns to speak, her voice resounds like underwater bells.

When you sense that Titania has manifested herself nearby, passionately intone thrice to nine times:

*"God/dess grant
that the Fairies put money in my shoes,
and keep my house clean."*[75]

[75] Adapted from Leland, *Gypsy Sorcery and Fortune-Telling,* 202.

Offer the Queen of Elfame a dish of shiny baubles.

Brownies are reputedly brown-skinned elves. To prevent the Wee Folk from pilfering your goods while they sweep and scrub, offer them fairy food in a different room, in their own separate dish. Traditionally, there are two types of fairy food—wet and dry offerings. "Wet" offerings include water, wine, and cooking or scented essential oils. "Dry" offerings include salt, coins, gem chips, blossoms, seeds, dried beans, corn kernels, grain, rice, cornmeal, loose-leaf tobacco, or resin incense. Ensure that your offering is of sufficient quality and quantity to keep the Brownies satisfied.

Leave the offerings in both dishes utterly undisturbed. Over the next several days or weeks, the Queen's crew may blatantly announce their presence by inexplicably rolling things off tables or moving trifles from their normal location. Not to worry—this simply means you've properly primed the diminutive domesticians to do specific tasks for you.

Solidify your relationship with them by talking to the fairies in soothing, appreciative tones, as you would plants. The Brownies will reciprocate by cleaning and arranging things to your liking overnight or while you run errands.

SPELL ORIGIN: Romany and European magic

SPELL TIMING: when chores overwhelm

INGREDIENTS: Goddess offerings, fey food, and two saucers

AMBIANCE: in private at home

MAGICAL THEORY:

> **SYMPATHETIC MAGIC:** To attract the Queen of Elfame and her Brownies, use spell components traditionally associated with fairies, such as bells, baubles, and the foods to which they're partial.

DEITY TO INVOKE: Titania, a Roman Moon Goddess invoked in modern times as Queen of the Fairies

TO LEARN DIFFICULT SUBJECTS

FOR DIVINE HELP LEARNING ANYTHING, FASHION A PARAFFIN OR white wax statuette of one of the nine Grecian Muses:[76]

---

[76] As described by David Fideler at **www.cosmopolis.com**.

- To comprehend astrology, sculpt Urania holding a zodiacal globe.
- To understand history, depict Clio holding a scroll.
- To master music, make Euterpe holding a flute.
- To learn how to dance, depict Terpsichore dancing, holding a harp.
- To write love poetry, fashion Erato holding a lyre.
- To succeed in all projects involving writing, pose Calliope, the Muse of epic poetry, holding a writing tablet.
- To write or memorize sacred songs (such as chants), show Polyhymnia looking pensive.
- To master comedy, form Thalia wearing a comic mask.
- To deal with human suffering (sing blues, practice psychiatry or medicine, and so forth), sculpt Melpomene wearing a tragic mask.

To retain what you learn, invoke the aid of the Muses' mother, Mnemosyne, the Goddess of memory, by converting dull data into memorable rhymes, or *mnemonic* devices.

Throughout the learning process, keep your statuette standing near where you study. Your Muse will boost your creativity and inspire you to excel. Because she is magically animated, occasionally scrutinize her expression for guidance. She may nod, for instance, when you're progressing, or look away if you've gotten off track.

When you complete the project or master the skill, thank your Muse and reunite her, intact, with Mother Earth via burial.

SPELL VARIATION

- Construct a crystal concentration crown, and wear it whenever you must study or absorb arbitrary facts.

    Braid three long lengths of silver craft wire. Approximately halfway through your braiding, twist the wires 360 degrees around with needle-nosed pliers, then slip one or more drilled, clear crystal beads or gem chips onto the middle strand. Twist the wires again 360° to secure the crystals, braid the second half, form a hook-and-eye closure, and then form the completed braid into an oval that fits around your head.

SPELL ORIGIN: Greek magic, Coven Oldenwilde practice, and gemology

SPELL TIMING: preferably during a waxing or full Moon (memory is minimal during Moondark)

INGREDIENTS: a double-boiler setup, paraffin or white wax, sculpting tools

    FOR THE VARIATION: silver craft wire, 1 or more clear crystal bead(s) or gem chip(s), and hemostats or needle-nose pliers

AMBIANCE: a calm, well-lit reading area or kitchen; a dimly lit ritual room

MAGICAL THEORY:

    MACROCOSM = MICROCOSM: For every need, there's a God/dess or magical Being or entity that rules it and can therefore help you with it.

    A crystal over your forehead (atop your "third eye") will help you concentrate, intuit, and retain information.

    Because silver is a lunar metal, a silvery Moon crown can help you understand a subject on an instinctive level.

    CONTAGION: Once you intimately form and animate your Muse, she'll remain at your disposal—especially if she is in close proximity to where you most need her aid.

DEITIES TO INVOKE:

    Mnemosyne, the Greek Goddess of memory, or one of her nine daughters:

    Urania ("the Heavenly"), the Muse of astrology

    Clio ("the Proclaimer"), the Muse of history

    Euterpe ("the Giver of Pleasure"), the Muse of music

    Terpsichore ("the Whirler"), the Muse of dance

    Erato ("the Lovely"), the Muse of love poetry

    Calliope ("the Fair Voiced"), the Muse of epic poetry

    Polyhymnia ("She of Many Hymns"), the Muse of sacred poetry

    Thalia ("the Flourishing"), the Muse of comedy

    Melpomene ("the Songstress"), the Muse of tragedy

TO MAKE WISHES COME TRUE

THE UNIVERSE AUTOMATICALLY GRANTS ALL WISHES MADE WHILE eating new potatoes for the first time in the year.

    If your want is urgent and you feel that you can't wait for an auspicious time in which to conjure it, write it on onion skin, then intone it aloud while you burn it, and your boon will be granted.

Common coins have been used for centuries to make unspoken wishes come true. To ensure that your hopes are fulfilled, pick up coins you find lying heads up on the ground, and then wish on them. Wish and throw a coin into a fountain or coursing water, or turn over a silver coin in your pocket whenever you behold a full Moon.

An olde Gaelic spell to ensure that your wishes will be granted involves concocting wish-powder well in advance of your need:

When the Sun is in Leo (July 21 to August 21, give or take a day or two), harvest a handful of garden sage leaves.

Dry them, and then grind them into a powder with a mortar and pestle.

Place the powder in a covered pot, and bury it in your compost pile or a dung heap for 30 days.

Dig the pot up, and burn between two bricks the "worms" into which the powder has been transmuted.

Sprinkle the resulting dust at your feet whenever you make a wish, and it will come true.

SPELL VARIATIONS

• Make a Japanese wish pot to store your dreams in until they're fulfilled.

Sculpt a palm-sized jar from self-hardening clay.

Form the top opening so that it will fit around a recycled champagne-bottle cork.

Allow the pot to air dry.

Decorate its exterior with glistening stars and so on, and cap the container with the cork.

House it in the Eastern direction.

Write each wish on parchment, and store in the wish pot. When fulfilled, burn the paper in thanks to the God/desses.

- Brew 1 teaspoonful of dried buckhorn brake fern in a cup of hot water, and sprinkle the liquid in a circle during the full Moon.
- Many people think a wish will come true if they blow on a shed eyelash, but a superior spell is to place it delicately on the back of your left hand, cover it with your right, and make a heart-felt plea. The God/desses will grant your wish if the lash clings to your right hand.
- Blow all the seeds off a blooming dandelion while wishing.
- Ask the Goddess Venus to grant your desire—wish on the morning or evening star when first you see her.

Spell Origin: Irish, Japanese, European, Voudon, and Greek magic

Spell Timing: as needed, during the full Moon; in the evening at the beginning of a new year (for Witches, during the Samhain Sabbat); when the Sun is in Leo

Ingredients: new potatoes; onion skins, charcoal, and matches; coins; a handful of garden sage leaves, a mortar and pestle, a covered pot, a compost pile or dung heap, two bricks, a fire, and a container

For the variations: self-hardening clay, sculpting tools, decorations, parchment, quill pen and ink; 1 teaspoon of dried buckhorn brake fern, 6 to 8 ounces of hot water, a teakettle; an eyelash; a dandelion top that's gone to seed

Ambiance: alone in your kitchen or ritual room, while out and about, or in your garden

Magical Theory:

Macrocosm = microcosm: Potatoes are round and white and, therefore, lunar. By eating them, you absorb the Moon's ability to grant wishes, so your own will come true.

Onions are similarly lunar—by writing on, and then burning the parchment-like skins, you are conveying your wish to the Moon.

Being round and reflective, coins represent planets: Silver coins resemble the Moon, gold coins equate with the Sun, and copper coins correspond to Venus.

The strong Sun is doubly strong when it's in Leo, the sign it rules. A dandelion bloom resembles the Sun.

Fertile Venus can make your desire fruitful.

SYMPATHETIC MAGIC: Fairies bide in fern stands, so brewing buckhorn brake fern tea and spurging a circle with it beneath a full Moon compels them to grant your wish.

Wishes are ethereal, like dainty eyelashes, so to make something small but important manifest itself, use a small spell component.

CONSTELLATION AND DEITY TO INVOKE: Leo and Venus, though the planet Jupiter and wish-granting Goddess Hecate are also goodly for manifesting wishes.

TO ATTRACT AN OBJECT

ALONE IN YOUR PRIVATE CIRCLING SPACE ON A WEDNESDAY DURING the Witching Hour, place your spell ingredients before you, including a representation of your desire—a tangible sample, photograph, drawing, or symbol of the item. Set an appropriately delicious mood. Light candles and incense, play Pagan music, and so on.

Concentrate intently on the representation. Consider in minute detail exactly why you want it. If your goal is more of a need than a desire, mentally review all the reasons getting it is a must. Fantasize about having its every molecule materialize in precisely the way that would make you happiest. For instance, don't envision the boxy symbol you might have drawn to represent your dream car, but rather, the rose-red Rolls that you have your heart set on.

When you've properly inflamed your inner passions about the subject and feel restless frenzy welling up, prepare your glue. If you brought gum to circle, chew it until it's soft, and then stick it on your desire symbol. If you chose to work with copal resin (or pine tree sap), melt a chunk in a silver spoon over a candle flame, let it cool slightly, and use a cotton ball or swab to apply it to the representation. Your chosen bonding agent attracts your desire toward you.

Roll your glued representation into a ball, and hold it tightly between both palms. Appeal to enchanting Circe to compel your desire to you. Secrete the attractor away until your want has manifested itself to your satisfaction; then dispose of it by burial.

SPELL VARIATIONS

- Apply a likeness of, or write your spell desire on, the ball of an inexpensive elastic-stringed paddleball toy.

    On the side of the paddle where the ball is attached, write *Mercury,* in yellow or gold, if possible. On the opposite side of the paddle, write *Gaea,* preferably in green.

    Play with the toy until you achieve a consistent rhythm; then concentrate hard on your dream goal. As the elastic springs the ball ever back to the paddle, so the cosmos bring your desire to you.

- Acquire or barter for two lodestones—one rough, "male" stone, and one smooth, "female" type.

    Feed your lodestone couple iron shavings—they'll magnetically attract ("eat") the filings. Verbalize your specific request; then firmly charge the stones to magically procure your desire.

    Stable luck will bless your life, dwelling, and pursuits if you continue to feed the lodestones each Friday after sunset, or once a month during the waxing or full Moon.

SPELL ORIGIN: European Witchcraft

SPELL TIMING: Wednesday at the Witching Hour during a waxing or full Moon; Friday after sunset; during Moonbright

INGREDIENTS: : a representation of your desire, a piece of chewing gum or copal or pine resin, a lit candle, a silver spoon, and a cotton ball or swab

FOR THE VARIATIONS: an elastic-stringed paddle-ball toy, yellow or gold and green ink or paint, and a pen or paint brush; two lodestones and iron shavings

AMBIANCE: alone in a private circling space, preferably inside

MAGICAL THEORY:

SYMPATHETIC MAGIC: Applied to your object's representation, sticky gum or melted sap cements your magical will to your desire, thereby forcing it to manifest itself concretely.

    Concentrating on your desire for the object compels the cosmos to meet your need.

Mercury communicates your desire to the God/desses, and Gaea can physically manifest it.

Two lodestones represent a needy couple with a mutual need, such as money for rent.

DEITY TO INVOKE: Circe, a Cretan Goddess known for her luring abilities.

TO RECOVER OBJECTS STOLEN BY HUMANS

WHEN A THIEF STEALS SOMETHING PRECIOUS TO YOU, THEY UNWIT-tingly create a three-way connection between you, the object, and themselves. Once you've determined who the thief is (see To Reveal the Identity of a Thief, page 407), you can use this bond to compel them to return the object—especially if you and the thief have had much contact.

There are many ways to accomplish this. For instance, you might verbally confront the thief from afar, bind him or her to return the object, vow magical reprisals if they fail to comply, or lay a compulsion curse on them that worsens until they return the object to you.

Folks' appreciation of Witches' efficacy persists to such a degree that there are those who'll steal anything a Witch has touched or used. We're still occasionally amazed when someone absconds with, say, a ratty plastic broom we used to clean a site after a public ritual. Most of the time, we let such trivialities go—if people are *that* needy, may the Gods bless 'em, right? But every once in a while someone dares to steal something dear.

For example, Lady Passion owns a deck of tarot cards that she highly values. Even more important to her than the cards themselves is the hand-painted silk bag she has stored them in for almost 30 years.

Once, when Coven Oldenwilde conducted a circle open to the public at our covenstead, a handsome, blue-eyed, articulate, and well-dressed fellow came who called himself Merlin. Before that night's rite, Lady Passion used the deck to illustrate a point to a long-time student—within Merlin's field of vision.

Later that evening, Lady Passion found Merlin lurking stealthily near where she kept the cards. After muttering a clumsy explanation regarding what he was doing there, he quickly excused himself and left. Two days later, we discovered that the silk bag and deck had been stolen. It didn't take long to narrow the list of suspects to Merlin.

Over the next couple of weeks, Lady Passion intuited that Merlin had no intention of returning her magical tools. She poured the raw energy of her righteous outrage into a curse on him and reiterated it again and again, day after day. The words she used didn't matter as much as the sheer force of her intent. Every time she cast the curse, she willed havoc and chaos to fill his life, constantly increasing and worsening unless and until he returned her tarot deck and silk bag.

Finally, on a Saturday night the High Priestess stood in our ritual room and focused all her power on binding the thief. She knew that by then the cascading curse had wreaked such misery in Merlin's life that it could shortly prove fatal—unless he lifted the curse by bringing her tools back on humbly bent knee that very night. Three times she pressed the charge on him—the final time straining so hard that she felt her innards fairly snap. Afterward, she confidently predicted to *Diuvei that the cards would appear on the covenstead porch before night's end.

At 4:20 a.m., Lady Passion abruptly awakened *Diuvei as she excitedly jumped onto the bed.

> *"Hey, *Diuvei, guess what time it is?"*
> *"Uhh, mmpf . . ."*
> *"Time to celebrate!"*

She threw a small object down beside his pillow. It was the silk bag with the Tarot deck inside—all in pristine condition and with every card intact. A little earlier, she related, she had been preparing for bed when she heard the telltale creak of a floorboard on our front porch. She knew what it signified, and after waiting a merciful interval, she opened the door and found her beloved tools returned.

SPELL ORIGIN: Italian *Strega* magic

SPELL TIMING: as needed; Saturday night or during the hour of Saturn

AMBIANCE: anywhere, but sacred space amplifies the spell

MAGICAL THEORY: A target can stop a worsening curse if they fulfil the terms specified by the Witch who laid it.

CONTAGION: Once you're in contact with or own an object, it retains a practically molecular memory of that connection, regardless of whether it is lost, stolen, inherited, or so forth.

SYMPATHETIC MAGIC: By stealing from someone, a thief inadvertently establishes a magical bond with the wronged party that a Witch can use to compel the robber to return the object.

REPETITION: Reiterated forcefully again and again, the curse snowballs until the thief can't ignore or escape it.

TO LURE PEOPLE TO YOUR WEB SITE

MYSTICALLY LURE FOLKS FROM AROUND THE GLOBE STRAIGHT TO your domain.

On a Wednesday when la Luna is waxing or full, open your Web site's source file. At the top, immediately after the <HEAD> and before the <HTML> command, type as asterisks the ancient geomantic glyphs that represent acquisition and conjunction, then enclose them in comment code (<!---->). Upload the change. The charm won't be visible on your site.

```
    * *          * *
     *            *
    * *           *
     *           * *
  Acquisitio   Conjunctio
```

Acquisitio will magically acquire visitors or cash-bearing customers for you; Conjunctio will encourage folks to seek out your Web site and easily access it. Together, Acquisitio and Conjunctio signify the magical command to "acquire connections."

SPELL VARIATION

• Make a silver scroll computer charm.

Obtain a pen with silver ink. If you have trouble finding a goodly one, try a Christian bookstore, where they're sold for underlining scripture.

Cast a sunwise circle.

On parchment, draw with the silver ink a simple, linear spider web no larger than 2½ by 2½ inches.

When the glyph is dry, add dots atop it in blue or purple ink to form the geomantic signs above, Acquisitio and Conjunctio.

Air dry the parchment again, roll it into a scroll, tie it closed with twine, and tape it onto or close by your laptop, keyboard, or computer monitor.

SPELL ORIGIN: Arabic magic and Coven Oldenwilde practice

SPELL TIMING: on a Wednesday during a waxing or full Moon, preferably when la Luna is in a good astrological aspect to Jupiter

INGREDIENTS: a computer, the source file for your Web site, and a word processor or an HTML editor

FOR THE VARIATION: a 2½- by 2½-inch piece of parchment, a silver ink pen, a blue or purple ink pen, twine, clear tape

AMBIANCE: a quiet setting conducive to concentration

MAGICAL THEORY:

INVERSION: What can foretell can also spell—geomantic figures can be used both passively for divination and actively for magic.

TO GET A BETTER JOB

SECURE A PROMOTION OR PREFERABLE POSITION BY CARRYING A PINCH of gravelroot or a piece of kava root in a green flannel bag.

If you are going to an interview, enter the place of business with your right foot forward and remember to offer a prayer for success at the moment you cross the threshold. If you stumble as you cross the threshold for the first time, it's an omen that this probably isn't the right job for you.

Following an interview, take the employer's business card or any paperwork home. If you have neither, pocket a pebble from the premises or some other signifying sample.

Once home, make Earth condenser oil, which concentrates the North's prosperous power and adds extra strength to your spells. Sprinkle a pinch of oregano into a clear glass vial of olive oil, add an emerald or malachite gem chip, cork the bottle, and bury it overnight in the Earth direction.

At high noon the next day, dig up the vial and take it to your sacred working space. Heat the tip of your boleen in a candle flame, then bigrave, in runic letters, a green pillar candle with the title of the job for which you're being considered.

When the wax is cool, set the candle in the North and anoint it with the Earth condenser oil. Begin at the center of the candle, spiral sunwise downward to the base, then return to the middle and wind upward to the wick. Place the business card, paperwork, or symbol and a silver coin beneath the pillar's base, and light the wick.

For five to 13 minutes, focus intently on your being hired. Invoke the coin Goddess Moneta, or Kubera, a God of riches. Burn the candle completely. Remain attentive for one of the God/desses' goodly omens to manifest within three days. For instance, it would be a favorable portent from Moneta if you found a rare or unusual coin during that time. Kubera's auspicious signs are:

a white, Lilliputian male riding a cow or chariot, carrying a purse;
yellow spirits wearing royal attire;
an ax, a banner, a club, a cup, a hook, or a trident.

You may recognize the omen in the form of a newspaper or magazine picture, or some such. One of Kubera's symbols may stridently assert itself in your thoughts, or you might experience it in a dream.

Similarity counts when it comes to interpreting portents—a short Caucasian farmer riding a tractor to market (carrying money) is magically the same as a white, Lilliputian male riding a cow or chariot, carrying a purse.

SPELL VARIATIONS

- Don't get lost in the shuffle—communication goes awry when Mercury is retrograde (orbits backward), so inquire about job openings or mail your résumé when the planet is direct (moving forward in its circuit around the Sun).
- Schedule interviews for astrologically auspicious times—best is when the waxing Moon is in a good aspect with Jupiter. Your confidence and competence are strongest when the Moon is waxing in your Sun sign or rising sign.
- Keep an attraction amulet in your pocket during interviews. For example, a carbuncle (ruby cabochon) attracts success in business.

- Practice glamoury and magical gesture. Maintain open body language throughout interviews—keep your posture erect, arms akimbo, and legs uncrossed. Mirror the interviewer's speech style, and radiate an air of cordial competence.

SPELL ORIGIN: Voudon, European, and Roman magic; herbalism and gemology

SPELL TIMING: prior to applying for a position; at midnight after you've applied for a job, and at noon the next day

INGREDIENTS: a pinch of gravelroot or a piece of kava root in a green flannel bag; a business card or job symbol, a boleen, a green pillar candle, a pinch of oregano, an emerald or a malachite gem chip, a glass vial, a cork, a silver coin, and matches

FOR THE VARIATIONS: an astrological calendar; a carbuncle (ruby)

AMBIANCE: Bury the oil adoors at midnight; burn the candle inside your sacred space the next noon.

MAGICAL THEORY: Earth elemental and traditional prosperity correspondences

SYMPATHETIC MAGIC: The right foot equates with mundane matters, so going right foot forward inside a prospective job site encourages success. Oppositely, stumbling when you initially enter a building or room is an inauspicious omen warning of a future negative experience involving the place.

To conjure abundance, use a color that corresponds to lushness, such as green.

A condenser oil can be made from each of the Four Elements by exposing olive oil to the raw manifestation of each. When used as a spell component, the elementally imbued oil amplifies the spell's power.

CONTAGION: A piece from or a symbol of a place can serve magically as a poppet or simulacrum of the place from afar.

BETWEEN THE WORLDS: As you cross the physical threshold of a business, you enter its psychic realm as well.

DEITIES TO INVOKE: Moneta, the Roman Goddess of the mint; Kubera, a Hindu wealth God

TO MAKE YOUR BUSINESS BRISK AND SUCCESSFUL

TRADE HAS ALWAYS BEEN A MERCURIAL AFFAIR, DEPENDENT ON factors as variable and risky as the winds that drove a merchant ship to safe port or the seafloor, or the whims that whip the stock market up or down.

Spells to make a business stay in the black have been practiced in the marketplaces of every nation. Below are two that come down to us from the shopkeepers' stalls of ancient Egypt.

The Egyptian God Thoth and the Greek God Hermes equate with Mercury. If you want customers calling in droves, appeal for their favor using the following ancient spell.[77]

Dedicate your store or office to Hermes by saying his "olde" names:

Phthoron Phthione' Thouth

Next, get his aid year in and year out by saying his "great" names, followed by the number of days of the year you want his favor:

*Iao' Sabao'th Ado'naie
Ablanathanalba
Akrammakhamarei
365*

Cement your solicitation by saying his "barbarous" names:

Pharnathar Barakhel Khtha

Finally, passionately intone this invocation:

*Give Thou
business, favor, elegance, prosperity
to (your name) and to my work.
Nun! Nun! Ede! Ede!*[78]

[77] *Possibly compiled by the ancient magician Astrapsoukos, this spell is abridged from lines 1–63 in the PGM, VIII, 122, Longdon Papyrus.*
[78] *Means "Now! Now! Quickly! Quickly!"*

A different spell for continuous business[79] involves making a waxen statue of Psentebeth, an Egyptian God of commerce. Mix melted and cooled orange wax with juice from the aeria plant (mistletoe) and ground ivy; then fashion a hollow God figurine with a herald's wand in his left hand, and a small bag in his right.

Write on parchment the following:

Chaio'chen Outibilmemnouo'th Atrauich

*Give income and business to this place,
because Psentebeth lives here!*

Put the parchment inside the figure; then fill in the hole with leftover melted wax. Crown his head with a golden ribbon and deposit it inside a wall of your business place, or stand him in some inconspicuous corner. Eat chicken in Psentebeth's honor, offer him a libation of white wine, and light a lamp that is not colored red.

SPELL VARIATIONS

- To quickly increase business, sprinkle the place's floor with Irish moss tea. Steep 1 teaspoon of dried Irish moss in 6 to 8 ounces of hot water for three to five minutes. 'Twill lure the luck of the Irish to your door.
- If you build a new structure for your dream business, place an intact, uncooked egg in the foundation.
- Tolerate a territorial spider in the corner, for its web will catch customers for you.
- Cultivate a personal helper spirit, such as your ancestral *Lasii,* who can aid you on behalf of your lineage, or Teramo, an Etruscan spirit who supports vendors.
- Placate any fairies that frolic in your foyer to keep the Wee Folk from pilfering stock, documents, or money when you're at home at night. Brownies will clean up in your absence, and cluricauns keep taverns' kegs full in exchange for slurps of spilt ale.

---

[79] *Adapted from* PGM, *IV, 2359–72.*

Spell Origin: Egyptian and Grecian magic; Irish and Voudon herbalism; European Craft; Etruscan (proto-Italian) magic

Spell Timing: preferably on a Wednesday when the Moon is waxing or full

Ingredients: a double-boiler setup, orange wax, mistletoe juice, ground ivy (*Nepeta hederacea*), pen, ink, parchment, cooked chicken, a libation bowl, white wine, a non-red lamp

For the variations: 1 teaspoon of dried Irish moss, a teakettle, and 6 to 8 ounces of water; a raw egg; a living spider; a cultivated personal helper spirit or fairies

Ambiance: alone where you conduct business; alone in your ritual space; with friends when you begin construction; on an ongoing basis

Magical Theory:

Sympathetic magic: Knowing and saying God/desses' ancient, true names inclines their favor and imbues the invoker with some of their power, as in the fairy tale "Rumpelstiltskin."

For ongoing divine aid, specify the duration of your need; saying the numbers *365* is the same as requesting 24-hour coverage.

A freshly laid egg is not fragile, but rather, remarkably strong. If put beneath a cornerstone, it will magically prop the building up. Placed elsewhere, the egg will make a structure magically sturdy.

Orange wax is the color of the Sun, who can make your business healthy. The gold ribbon crown also equates with the Sun, as does eating chicken (cocks crow at sunrise).

The aeria plant (mistletoe) is associated with the element Air and Mercury, a God with winged feet.

Ivy creeps (expands) and is tenaciously resilient (desirable qualities for a business). God/desses (figures) and fertility objects (unbroken, raw egg) bless where they bide.

Triplicity: Hermes is invoked by three different sets of his names. These are also linked to the Sun God Abrasax (see Break a Fever, page 268).

Antipathetic magic: To avoid business hardship—associated with Mars and, therefore, the color red—don't magically light customers' way to your business with a red-colored lamp.

Properly propitiating the fairies traditionally associated with your enterprise can prevent them from being pesky and actually help your business thrive.

DEITIES AND SPIRIT TO INVOKE: Mercury, the Greek Messenger of the God/desses; Thoth, the Egyptian God of truth; Hermes, the Greek God of purveyors; Psentebeth, an Egyptian God of commerce; Teramo, an Etruscan spirit who supports vendors

TO WIN IN LEGAL MATTERS

YOUR CAUSE IS JUST, BUT YOU ARE POOR—AND AS WE ALL WELL know, the scales of justice all too often tip toward the side of the wealthy and elite. Nevertheless, even an army of overpaid lawyers lacks the potent weapon you possess: magical wits.

No matter how dauntingly complex or foregone a legal entanglement may appear, it simply involves a basic conflict—a duality—between a plaintiff's and a defendant's divergent points of view. Like a seesaw, such situations can easily be tipped in *your* favor.

It's important to remember, of course, that magic alone won't help you if you neglect the mundane. If you forget to show up at your hearing, skip out on a bond, fail to pay child support, neglect to consult with a lawyer or do your own legal research, or really *are* guilty of the charge, then even the best spell probably won't bail you out.

But if your cause is just and you want to win a legal wrangle, first gather two spell components: one that symbolizes the opposition's error, and one that signifies your righteous stance. Cast a sunwise circle on a Thursday night during a waxing Moon. Recall how your opponent has maligned you during the long legal process. Inflame your passions regarding his or her needless meanness. Physically cover your opponent's representation with your own. Vehemently verbalize why your opponent should not win, cannot win, must not win, will not win. Appeal for aid for you and your attorney from the Greek Goddesses Themis and Nike. Burn the token that represents the flaw in mundane law that has harmed you. Safeguard your own righteous representation in the East if you want your opinion to prevail, in the West if you want to mercy from the judge and jury, or in the North if you want the case to be dismissed or get lost in the shuffle.

Perform spells that necessitate a bit of derring-do. Before a court appearance, brew a tea of cascara sagrada and sprinkle it around the perimeter of the courthouse in which you're scheduled to appear. Masticate chewing john root in the courtroom and discreetly spit the cud into a handkerchief before proceedings.

Protracted suits often require multiple magical measures and may necessitate repeated mental impressions of your Witchy will. For example, Lady Passion won a six-year long case against a mega-corporation by using magic seals, wearing clothes of specific colors to please the jury, and explaining her side to Web photos of state supreme court members who then duly ruled in her favor.

SPELL VARIATIONS

- To promote a favorable decision, burn several pinches of a banishing incense—black candle tobacco mixed with table salt.
- Two weeks before a hearing, burn a piece of galangal (chewing john root) on 14 consecutive nights, save the ashes, and carry them in a green flannel bag to court.
- The day of trial, brew and bathe in lovage root tea.

    Chop ½ teaspoon of the root, steep it in 1 cup of hot water for three to five minutes, cool until tepid, and add the strained liquid to your bathwater.

    Afterward, sip sassafras tea—1 teaspoon of bark steeped in 1 cup of hot water for three to five minutes.
- To win a very difficult case, pocket a piece of snakeroot and fondle it during court.

SPELL ORIGIN: European, Voudon, and Greek magic; herbalism

SPELL TIMING: after sunset on a Thursday (Jupiter day) during a waxing Moon; prior to any legal proceeding; as needed

INGREDIENTS: two different representations, matches, a teaspoon of cascara sagrada herb, a teakettle, and 1 cup of hot water, and a piece of chewing john root

FOR THE VARIATIONS: several pinches of black candle tobacco, table salt, charcoal, and matches; burned galangal (chewing john root) ashes and a green flannel bag; ½ teaspoon lovage root, a teakettle, 1 cup of hot water, bathwater, and 1 teaspoon of sassafras bark brewed into a cup of tea; a piece of snakeroot

AMBIANCE: alone in a private circle (usually indoors); surreptitiously around or in a courthouse; in your kitchen or bathtub

MAGICAL THEORY:

ART OF CORRESPONDENCES: Thursday is the day of Jupiter, who rules Sagittarius, which in turn rules legal matters.

SYMPATHETIC MAGIC: Because your representations stand in stead for you and your legal opponent, asserting your Witchy will toward your desired outcome overwhelms your opponent's stance and attracts good will toward you.

Green is Venus's color, a lucky color (that of a four-leaf clover) and a color of prosperity (the color of American "greenbacks"). Therefore, carrying a green pouch can compel the Goddess of love to make judge and jury love you and lure legal luck and goodly financial settlements.

As someone involved in a legal matter, you want to speak the truth; the herbs chewing john root and tobacco suggest mouth imagery.

Snakeroot, an herbal cure for snakebite, helps you slide through the justice system's caprice without getting "snake bit."

DEITIES TO INVOKE: The Greek Goddesses Themis, who holds social contracts inviolate, and Nike, Goddess of victory; Jupiter

TO MEET YOUR PERFECT MATE

TO MEET YOUR MATCH OR FIND YOUR BETTER HALF, CONCOCT LADY Passion's Infallible Love Oil on a Friday during the Witching Hour under a full Moon.

Blend equal parts (39 drops each) of civet cat musk or amber essential oil, and ambergris or patchouli essential oil. Add 19 drops of either lotus or eucalyptus essential oil. Fill a dark glass bottle with the blend, cap it closed, and then thoroughly shake the contents with your left hand.

Wear the potion every Friday. Resist being annoyed by the sudden swirl of potential mates it will attract like bees to hibiscus. Instead, revel in your myriad choices!

If you're a woman and already have a man in mind, perform a Gypsy spell popular in the 1800s. Collect dust from within the outline of his footprint, and bury it beneath a willow tree, saying:

> *"Many earths on Earth there be,*
> *Whom I love my own shall be,*
> *Grow, grow willow tree!*
> *Sorrow none unto me!*
>
> *He the axe, I the helve,*
> *He the cock, I the hen,*
> *This, this (be as) I will!"*[80]

To divine whether you'll get your heart's desire, slice an apple in twain—your wish will be fulfilled if the knife doesn't knick a seed.

SPELL VARIATIONS

- You can have your choice of mates if you:
  can eat sour fruit, such as a crab apple, without frowning;
  have curly hair;
  cut your nails on nine consecutive Sundays.
- Get the beau or beauty you've been pining for—during a full Moon, walk skyclad around a field or house, casting table salt behind you with every step.[81]
- If you know your target's mundane name, bond the person to you using two sewing needles. One needle poppet signifies you; the other, your intended. Bless each individually, and bestow on them their proper names. This animates the needles, magically transforming them into real people. Insert the designated "masculine" needle's point into the designated "feminine" needle's eye. Bind them together with red hemp, string, or thread. Secrete the poppet couple to avoid their detection.

---

[80] *Leland,* Gypsy Sorcery and Fortune-Telling, *112.*
[81] *Leland,* ibid., *19.*

- Decorate yourself with an alluring amulet.

     Women should wear passionate red, orange, or pink gems, such as rubies, red coral, garnets, carnelians, amber, rhodocrosite, or rose quartz.

     Men should wear comforting colors, such as green tourmaline, malachite, variscite, or moss agate stones.

     If such gemstones are set in metal, it should preferably be copper.

- A less expensive but no less goodly lure both sexes can wear is a green mojo bag containing two whole cloves and powdered white orris root, readily available in grocery stores.

- Eat love-attracting foods, such as apricots, Brazil nuts, ginger, licorice, peas, raspberries, rhubarb, and strawberries.

- Grow a living passion beacon—plant an enticing flower box filled with asters, pansies, poppies, roses, thyme, tulips, or violets.

- Entice your sweetie to become physically intimate with you.

     Fashion a love ball of 2 handfuls of melted beeswax; three of the person's hairs; and 1 teaspoon each of powdered dove's blood (dried, crushed spotted geranium petals) or dove's blood incense from an occult supplier, dried straw (or grass), rose petals, and rosemary or marjoram.

     Secure the dried, round poppet in a pouch, and wear it over your heart until consummation.

- Inspire requited love.

     When you and your beloved are together, warm mint between your palms, or dip your hands in vervain juice, air dry them, and then silently caress your target for a full ten minutes.

- To sharpen your sweetheart's love pangs, secrete an empty, dried wasp's nest in your clothing.

SPELL ORIGIN: European herb craft and Romany and Irish magic

SPELL TIMING: on a Friday at midnight during Moonbright; plant the love-luring flowers during Moondark

INGREDIENTS: one dark-colored bottle with an eye-dropper cap, civet cat musk[82] or amber essential oil, patchouli or ambergris essential oil, and lotus or eucalyptus essential oil.

---

[82] *Because civet musk and ambergris come from endangered species, most of what you can acquire is synthetic, but will work magically as well as the real thing after being duly consecrated with the Four Elements.*

For the variations: several handfuls of table salt; two needles and red twine; specific alluring gems; a green pouch, two whole cloves, and powdered orris root; attracting foods; attracting flowers and a clay container; two handfuls of melted beeswax, three of your target's hairs, and 1 teaspoonful each of powdered dove's blood (dried geranium petals) or dove's blood incense, straw or grass, rose petals, and rosemary or marjoram; several fresh mint leaves or some vervain juice; an empty, dried wasp's nest

Ambiance: alone in a private circle, amidst provocative ambiance

Magical Theory:

Sympathetic magic: Civet cat musk and amber oil symbolize femininity. Ambergris and patchouli oil denote masculinity. Lotus and eucalyptus oil are clear, "high-note" scents that represent your spiritual bond with a future mate.

Employing odd numbers while measuring lets the ingredients know that you intend to use them in a magical way.

Because salt is the Earth element *par excellence,* throwing grains of it behind your every step transforms your thought or spoken desire into tangible reality.

Fiery reddish jewels convey the innate sexuality of the mating Mother Goddess. Earthy greenish gems evoke the rutting Horned God's magic.

Copper is sacred to Venus.

Inversion: In order to attract their opposites, the female, who represents Venus, wears the red color normally associated with Mars, and the male, who represents Mars, wears the green color that normally corresponds with Venus.

Deity to Invoke: Venus, the Roman Goddess of love

TO COMPEL AN ERRANT MATE TO RETURN

Employing Wicca's "do as thou wilt" philosophy, many Pagans tolerate their mates' philandering. The first half of that maxim, however, is "an it harm none." So if you're suffering from alienation of affection, compel your erstwhile mate to return to home and hearth by enacting the sexual union of the archetypal Perfect Couple—plunge an athamé (a masculine magical tool) into a filled chalice (a feminine counterpart).

A similar means to reunite with a wandering woman or meandering man necessitates that you obtain an oak acorn cup (a feminine symbol) and an ash tree pod with the seeds (or penile "keys") still intact. Secrete the couple components beneath your pillow, and sleep atop them on three consecutive nights, thrice repeating this traditional rune before retiring:

Acorn cup and ashen key,
bid my true love back to me!
'Tween the Witching Hour and sunlight,
bring them o'er the hills this night!

O'er the meadows,
o'er the moor,
o'er the rivers,
by the shore,
o'er the threshold
and through my door!

Acorn cup and ashen key,
bring my true love back to me!

Your petulant partner will soon return, likely apologize for his or her behavior, and reconcile your relationship.

SPELL VARIATIONS

- Compel your lover to remain forever faithful—turn a bluebell blossom inside out without tearing it.
- Be smart from the start—remember the rule "marry in May and rue the day," and don't get hitched that month!

   Rather, predispose your mate to faithfulness by wedding in June.
- To prevent a cheating mate from moving out and legally separating from you, write with lemon juice the following power-square numbers on a green leaf:

1	21	63	7
21	7	1	21
9	19	91	9
12	4	6	8

Hold the talisman in your left hand, gaze intently into your mate's eyes (or at a photograph of the person's face), and say only the top and bottom rows nine consecutive times.

SPELL ORIGIN: traditional European magic

SPELL TIMING: as needed—preferably on a Friday or Saturday night during a waxing or full Moon

INGREDIENTS: one white or English oak acorn and one ash tree pod with intact seeds

FOR THE VARIATIONS: a feather or quill pen, lemon juice, and a green leaf (optional—a photo of your mate); a bluebell blossom

AMBIANCE: your bedroom, amidst billowing clouds of rose incense

MAGICAL THEORY:

ART OF CORRESPONDENCES: Friday is the day of love; Saturday is the day of binding or compelling.

SYMPATHETIC MAGIC: According to the Craft saying, "As the athamé is to the male (penis), so the chalice (womb) is to the female. And so, conjoined, they bring blessedness."

May is the month of the Beltane Sabbat (May 1) when folks traditionally go greenwooding[83] with a one-night-only partner. The month of June is named for the Goddess Juno, whose Greek predecessor Hera perpetually compels her errant Zeus home.

DEITY TO INVOKE: Juno, the Roman Goddess of marital fidelity.

TO PURCHASE A HOME

TACK A PIECE OF STRING HORIZONTALLY ACROSS A CORNER OF WALL, and attach four clothespins. In a clear glass container, dissolve 3 to 5 pinches of

[83] *A Wiccan word for a couple's mating in the forest—a natural result of Sabbatic bliss.*

saltpeter in 2 to 3 ounces of water, stir the liquid with a chopstick, and submerge a piece of parchment in the solution. Remove the paper, and attach two corners of it horizontally to the string. To prevent the bottom of the paper from curling during drying, weight the two bottom ends down by attaching the remaining two clothespins. Allow the parchment to air dry; then remove it from the string and ink your desire on its surface—either in sentence form, or as a symbolic sketch. Include such details as the style of architecture you want, a preferred location, and its proximity to work and nearby amenities, such as a park, pool, or market.

Place your magical "flash paper" in a censer, light it, and scry its smoke. The smoke's pattern has magical meaning. It may take the form of figures, such as that of a man or woman who will sell you the place; geometric designs that resemble its appearance; or a directional indicator. For instance, a westerly spin may presage that you'll find the perfect property on the west side of town. Record and act on the omens you receive.

Invoke Hestia, the Goddess of the hearth, by extolling her virtues aloud— for example, "She who creates comfortable, safe, and stable homes." First, tell her what you do want, such as a palace that's inexpensive, and then, what you *don't* want—hidden horrors such as termites or a cracked foundation. Charge Hestia to fulfill your wish within a specified time period. Thank her in advance with words of praise worthy of the mighty homemaker.

SPELL VARIATIONS

- It is goodly luck to move into your home during a waxing Moon. Bless your home by carrying bread and salt through every room.
- It is ill luck to move into a new home on a Friday or during a downpour. Worse still, moving on a Saturday hastens a loan default or a quick departure from the premises.

Spell Origin: Greco-European magic

Spell Timing: on a Friday at the Witching Hour—preferably with the Moon in Cancer, or when she's passing through your birth chart's fourth house

Ingredients: a piece of parchment or paper, 3 to 5 pinches of saltpeter, 2 to 3 ounces of water, a clear glass container, a chopstick, a piece of string, two tacks, four clothespins, ink, a censer, and matches or a lighter

Ambiance: alone, indoors, preferably by a fireplace or cauldron fire

Magical Theory:

Macrocosm = microcosm: Moving during a waxing Moon accords your new undertaking an auspicious blessing.

Saltpeter is flammable and helps you waft written spells through the air to the God/desses' ears.

Bread and salt equate with the element Earth and connote home life.

Deity to Invoke: Hestia, the Greek Goddess of the hearth

TO RELIEVE POVERTY

Families in magical cultures honor the spirits of their ancestors, who remain accessible after death to help their living relatives prosper. They also honor the spirits of the land—the home where their ancestors bide, which they view as being the same as, or a manifestation of, their ancestors.

The Etruscans and Romans called these ancestral spirits *Lares* or *Lasii* (see To Protect Forest, Field, and Stream, page 327) and depicted them as winged naked women similar to our modern representations of fairies. The worship of Lasii survived in Tuscany until relatively recent times. The spell we give below was used there only 100 years ago, and is still cast by some Italian *Strega* Witches.

In modern Thailand, every home or office building has a small spirit house in a corner of its grounds where no shadow can fall upon it, placed there at an auspicious time by a priest. A figure representing the spirit of the land is placed inside it, and the building's inhabitants regularly offer it flowers, incense, and food.

To obtain the aid of your *own* ancestral spirits, acquire a small wooden cabinet at a discount or arts-and-crafts store. In late June or July, when the Sun is in Cancer (the sign of home and ancestry), hang the cabinet on a wall in the lowest area of your dwelling (a place where no shadow will fall on it). Decorate the interior with pictures of fairies or photos or representations of beloved relatives who have crossed over into the Summerlands. Fill a saucer with traditional fairy food (for suggestions, see To Bid Brownies Do Your Housework, page 348, and put the filled offering dish on an inside shelf of the cabinet). Say encouraging words aloud to conjure the spirits into their home; then close the cabinet's door and vacate the premises without looking backward.

Ever after, when you want your Lasii to help you or your family through tough times, work the following spell before their shrine.

> *"Lasii, Lasii, Lasii!*
>
> *Here I present myself*
> *bearing three candles.*
> *Three candles lighted,*
>
> *Three cards—*
>
> *The Ace of Spades,*
> *And that of Clubs,*
> *And that of Diamonds.*
>
> *I fling them in the air,*
> *that You may see them plainly before you,*
> *here just at midnight.*
>
> *In the air I throw them!*
>
> *If you grant me a favor,*
> *Cause me to find the Ace of Clubs plainly.*
>
> *If 'tis the Ace of Spades,*
> *'tis a sign That you will not grant me the favor;*
>
> *But if you make me find the Ace of Diamonds,*
> *then 'tis a sign that my wish will be granted."*[84]

The first card that lands face-up is your answer. In the unlikely event that two or all three settle faceup, the card that is closest to you reveals all. (Note that

---

[84] Leland, *Etruscan Roman Remains, 87. Only after some delay.*

this spell doesn't contain the oft-dreaded "maybe" response so common in other divinatory methods.)

If the result is unfavorable, cultivate the Lasii's goodwill by verbally praising your ancestors' accomplishments, or adding more (or perhaps different) shrine offerings until they seem appeased and inclined in your favor.

To ensure that enough offerings remain inside to delight and sustain your Lasii, inspect your propitiating shrine at least once a month. Replace disturbed, missing, or depleted ingredients as needed. Cease offering them substances for which they show lack of interest or abject disdain. Because they won't consume those types of offerings, you'll notice that those materials never seem to need restocking.

SPELL VARIATIONS

- Send a financial distress call to your Lasii—burn a pinch of the money-attracting herb rue as an offering to them.
- Make a poverty-preventing poppet.

   Using a double-boiler setup, liquefy several handfuls of paraffin or wax, then carefully pour it onto a flat, cool surface. Before it fully hardens, finger-form the wax into a figure resembling an Entity (use your creativity here).

   When your poppet is dry, cast a sunwise circle and magically animate it with Life Force so it will be able to act invisibly on your behalf. Hold the poppet in both hands, up close to your face. Breathe into its mouth. Tell it *exactly* how you want it to relieve your money woes. Specify any ethical clauses you don't want it to breach—for example, no profiteering in your name.

   Give your poppet a name that represents your ongoing need, such as Bill Money.

   Secrete your poppet from all eyes—finders could work money magic against you.

   Your poppet will magically scan the world for hidden or obscure financial opportunities, make you aware of them, and thereby accord you or your family every goodly means to thrive.
- Make a green prosperity root-and-herb bag.

Use flannel, fabric, or dyed leather to fashion the pouch. Inside, sprinkle pinches of any of the following mystical poverty-relieving herb charms:

myrtle
juniper
heather
bayberry
cinnamon
heliotrope
gold coin grass
lucky hand root
High John the Conqueror root

Wear the mojo bag until your money woes have been completely vanquished; then dispose of the bag and its contents in water coursing away from you.

- To conjure money or convert base metals into gold or silver, inscribe in ink with a quill pen the following power-square numbers and letters on parchment:[85]

1	5	8	A	O
7	9	1	O	A
1	8	5	O	O
8	5	1	O	A

Carry the talisman in your wallet, pocket, or purse. Money will gravitate toward you and your pennies will turn into more-valuable coins.

- To ensure loan or credit approval, wear petunia essential oil, or anoint a job application with the scent.

SPELL ORIGIN: Etruscan, European, and Voudon magic

SPELL TIMING: at the Witching Hour, preferably with the Sun in Cancer; give Lasii offerings after sunset, or any time you need emergency aid

INGREDIENTS: a small cabinet, a saucer or an offering dish, three candles (no color specified, but probably either white or green), an ace of clubs, an ace

[85] *Anna Riva,* Secrets of Magical Seals: A Modern Grimoire of Amulets, Charms, Symbols and Talismans *(International Imports, 1975), 55.*

of spades, an ace of diamonds, and traditional fairy/Lasii offerings. (See page 345.)

FOR THE VARIATIONS: dried rue, a censer and matches; a double-boiler setup, water, and several handfuls of paraffin or wax; a green pouch and pinches of poverty-preventing roots and herbs; a porcupine quill or feather pen, ink, parchment, and power-square numbers and letters; petunia essential oil

AMBIANCE: the lowest area of your dwelling

MAGICAL THEORY:

SYMPATHETIC MAGIC: Propitiating your family fairies inclines them to reciprocate and help you from the spirit world.

Myrtle attracts money. Juniper lures riches. Heather ensures long-term financial security. Bayberry puts money in your pocket. Cinnamon conjures money quickly. Heliotrope is sunlike and hence attracts gold. Gold coin grass—well, its function is obvious! Lucky hand root brings money from unexpected sources. High John the Conqueror root helps you overcome financial impediments.

ENTITY TO SUPPLICATE: a *Lar* (plural *Lares* or *Lasii*), an ancestral spirit who remains devoted to its familial lineage

TO BECOME FERTILE

BECAUSE IT'S PERFECTLY NATURAL TO WANT TO PERPETUATE LIFE, many olde spells exist to help a couple conceive. Such spells are based on tried-and-true ingredients that correspond with fertility.

The first spell we present is for a woman to work alone; the second, for a man to perform in private. The first spell variation requires a partner; the second, a couple with friends.

FOR A WOMAN WHO WANTS TO CONCEIVE

SHORTLY BEFORE MIDNIGHT ON A FRIDAY DURING A FULL MOON, assemble your ingredients and light a red candle in the center of your circling area or a caldron Witch fire (see To Induce a Trance for Scrying, page 399.) Create an evocative ambiance, and cast a circle sunwise.

Sit and meditate, letting your mind and body fully relax, lulled by flickering flame. Consider which sex you want your baby to be. If you have a mate, intensely remember every parental characteristic he has ever displayed in your presence. Does he seem to soften when he encounters children in public? Is he good at playing with youngsters? Fantasize about how you'd like to progress along these lines as a couple.

When you feel inclined to, begin eating the hard-boiled egg or cooked bacon. Savor it, then invoke Freya, a Norse fertility Goddess. Pray that she grant you a quickening womb.

When you grow restive, move to the outside edge of the circle. Mount your besom as if it were a child's toy hobbyhorse—straddle the pole between your legs, with the brush portion on the floor behind your feet. Hold onto the pole with both hands and hop-skip sunwise around your ritual area. This dance may take 20 minutes or more (magic takes as long as it takes, so don't rush this part). Slowly spiral inward toward your candle or cauldron fire until you stand before it.

Cast your broom aside, condense your Witchy will like a ball into your belly, wish for the baby of your dreams with every fiber of your being, and then jump over the fire. Wish and leap repeatedly until you're sure the spell has taken hold. Then relax and promote egg implantation by eating seed-filled grapes. End the rite by sincerely thanking Freya and giving her an offering of grapes and bacon.

Afterward, wear a fertility amulet of cowrie shells, or a round, brown, horizontally black-striped "sea bead."

FOR A MAN WHO NEEDS TO UNJINX HIS NATURE IN ORDER TO BE VIRILE

WHEN YOU CAN'T HELP YOUR MATE CONCEIVE BECAUSE AN ANGRY ex cursed you with impotence, break the spell by breaking bread.

Buy frozen bread dough. Knead in white sesame or mustard seeds. Shape the dough into a loaf resembling a penis. Bake until golden brown, cool the bread, and place it on a plate.

On a full Moon Friday before the Witching Hour, create a magical mood with candles and incense. Cast a circle ayenward, and then sit in the middle of it. Hold a vine or string with both hands—one hand holding one end, and the other hand holding the opposite end. Study its linearity intently, for it represents the solution to your potency problem.

Think about the difficulties the hexing of your nature has caused—how it erodes your self-esteem, affects your sense of identity, and impedes your ability to maintain an intimate relationship. When you feel justifiably angry about the situation, tie a knot in the center of the vine or string. Stare at the knot intently, for it is a microcosmic representation of your problem (your member is figuratively tied in a knot, hence your impotence).

Next, focus on the future. How virile would you like to be? Fantasize about how much better things will be when you are no longer plagued by temperamental performance.

Invoke the goat God Pan, and request that he grant you some of his notorious sexual prowess and stamina.

When you feel the time is right, untie your vine or string knot—you are healed. Immediately burn the vine or string in the southern direction. What's done is gone.

Stand up and walk or even dance about for a time. Breathe deeply and make your movements expansive and easy. Enjoy eating your fertility bread and knowing that as you do so, you increase the number of your own seeds by consuming those in the loaf. End your rite by thanking Pan for restoring your virility.

Afterward, wear an amulet that is a sharp pendant of some kind—a boar's tooth is traditional, but an arrowhead, a sea urchin spine, or a twisted horn charm also works well.

SPELL VARIATIONS

- Cook and consume with your partner a meal prepared with any of the following traditional aphrodisiacs: apple, artichoke, asparagus, cabbage, caviar, celery, clam, egg, leek, lettuce, oyster, parsnip, partridge, potato, tomato, or turnip.
- Have friends dance a Maypole dance[86] around you and your partner.

  First, construct the Maypole. Atop a tall straight wooden pole, affix a

---

[86] *Typically done during the Beltane Sabbat, annually on May 1.*

large, flower-bedecked circlet with brightly colored florist-style or fabric ribbons attached to it that trail down and a few feet along the ground.

Have everyone stand about 10 feet away from and encircling the Maypole. Alternate the sexes (male, female, male, and so on). The women should turn ayenward, the men face sunwise, and everyone grab a ribbon in the hand closest to the pole.

Clasp hands with your mate, walk beneath the raised ribbons, and stand with your backs supported against the phallic symbol.

When the dance begins, the women should bend beneath each man's ribbon and raise their own ribbons above the head of every woman they meet, producing a delightful in-and-out weave. The ribbons grow shorter the longer the dance lasts, bringing the dancers into increasingly intimate contact with one another as the ribbons weave a tight pattern onto the Maypole. You and your partner will eventually be gently pressed closer and closer together until you're both bound to the pole.

Magical conception swiftly follows the performance of this rite.

SPELL ORIGIN: European Witchcraft

SPELL TIMING: before the Witching Hour on a Friday during a full Moon (wear amulets until you or your mate conceives); erect a Maypole as needed, during spring, or during the Beltane Sabbat on May 1st

INGREDIENTS:

FOR A WOMAN WHO WANTS TO CONCEIVE: one red, lit candle or a cauldron Witch fire and either a hard-boiled egg or cooked bacon, a besom, seeded grapes, and a cowrie shell or "sea bead" amulet

FOR A MAN WHO NEEDS TO UNJINX HIS NATURE: vine or string, bread dough, small white seeds (sesame or mustard), and a phallic pendant

FOR THE VARIATIONS: aphrodisiac foods; a tall, smooth pole, a pole topper (a circlet of flowers), lots of long colored ribbons, and a shovel with which to set the Maypole in the ground

AMBIANCE: often, alone in a private, sacred space; some spell variations require a sexual partner or helpful friends; the Maypole dance should be adoors, amidst meriment and ribald double entendres

MAGICAL THEORY:

SYMPATHETIC MAGIC: Traditionally, the God of the fire will magically

impregnate a woman who jumps over one with the heartfelt desire to conceive. Fire corresponds with a man's Life Force; the round cauldron or fire
pit in which it burns resembles the womb and represents a woman. When
conjoined in a rite, the two can magically trigger parthenogenesis.

Brooms are composed of both feminine and masculine aspects—the
brush resembles a woman's bush, and the pole resembles a man's member.
Hopping around astride a besom mimics mating movements.

Friday is Freya's day. She is traditionally depicted riding a boar. Pigs
deliver frequently; therefore, eating bacon or pork can confer on you both
Freya's and pigs' innate fertility.

Bacon is high in fat; women normally ingest more fat during pregnancy to help adequately feed their fetuses. By eating bacon, you tell the
Gods you want to be pregnant.

Often termed "the staff of life," bread rises as it bakes. Ingesting some
can make a man's member rise to *amore*.

White sesame or mustard seeds resemble sperm, so by ingesting bread
topped by such seeds, a man can magically elevate his sperm count, thereby
facilitating fertility.

CONTAGION: The fertility of one species can be transferred to a different
species if a portion of the first is consumed by the second. A woman who
eats an egg, therefore, may soon swell with her own fetus.

MACROCOSM = MICROCOSM: A full Moon resembles both an egg and a
pregnant belly.

A translucent grape with a visible seed is magically the same as a pregnant woman's belly with an implanted embryo inside. Therefore, eating
grapes magically promotes embryonic implantation.

INVERSION: Tying a piece of vine or string mimics the effect of some types
of male infertility, such as contorted or occluded penile tubes. Therefore,
untying vine or string magically alleviates impotence.

DEITIES TO INVOKE: Freya, a Nordic fertility Goddess, and Pan, the Greek
satyr God

· Discernment Spells ·

"What joy to discern the minute in infinity!
The vast to perceive in the small, what Divinity!"
—JAKOB BERNOULLI
17TH-CENTURY SWISS MATHEMATICIAN

itchcraft is aptly called the Craft of the Wise because Witches actively develop discernment—the ability to distinguish fact from fiction, to distill the truth from a lie. This survival skill helps us dismiss propaganda, exercise goodly judgment, anticipate cultural and political changes, and divine future events.

Although some folks resist inquiring about unknown things because they fear negative answers, spellcrafters know that possessing information in advance affords us the chance to magically alter any currently negative trend in order to produce a positive outcome.

Discernment spells concern matters many people want to know about—the origin of a rumor, the contents of a secret, the identity of a thief, a future mate's name, a child's future career, where best to relocate, and how to get out of a seemingly impossible situation.

As you perform the following discernment spells, take courage from the truism that "to be forewarned is to be forearmed."

TO DETERMINE WHETHER THE GOD/DESSES FAVOR YOUR SPELL

MAKE HAG'S TAPERS TO SEE IF A RITE YOU PERFORMED PLEASED the God/desses.

Before a mullein plant goes to seed, harvest several long, plump stalks (strip the leaves off). The spell requires two, but make extras for future use. Suspend the stalks upside down, and allow to air dry for several days.

When you're ready to work the spell, fry bacon, let the grease cool, and then thoroughly coat the stalks with it. Leaving an inch or so of space between each stalk, place the stalks on a paper plate to dry fully in front of a window that receives goodly sunlight. Turn the stalks once daily for up to two weeks to ensure tight, even drying. Replace the paper plate as needed to prevent molding throughout the drying process.

When your stalk candles seem properly dried and stiff, tenderly wrap the top and bottom of one goodly specimen with undyed hemp or string. Repeat the process with another stalk, using black or dyed twine.

On a Monday night just before midnight, cast a sunwise circle. Set both Hag's Tapers in separate, sand-filled censers. At the stroke of the Witching Hour, light both and scry their smoke for the appearance of phantasmic forms or omens.

If the candle wrapped in undyed hemp ignites easily and burns brightly, the God/desses heartily endorse your magical efforts. However, if the black-tied taper flames with more vigor, the spell in question will likely fail, owing either to contrary planetary influences, or to the God/desses' disapproval of your motives or methods.

SPELL ORIGIN: Roman magic

SPELL TIMING: at midnight on a Monday

INGREDIENTS: two or more mullein stalks, bacon grease, a paper plate or two, thread, a length of undyed hemp or string, a length of black or dyed twine, a sunlit windowsill, two sand-filled censers, matches

AMBIANCE: a private sacred space, surrounded by enchanting accoutrements

MAGICAL THEORY:

SYMPATHETIC MAGIC: The white-wrapped Hag's Taper represents maidenlike purity and divine approval of your previous spellwork.

The black-wrapped candle symbolizes death and deafening divine disapproval of your spellwork motives or methods.

Mullein's common name is lamb's ear; in this spell, your question—"Did my magic please the Gods?"—is wafted to their ears by the smoke of the lamb's ears.

TO ASCERTAIN WHETHER SOMEONE GRAVELY ILL WILL RECOVER

THE MEDIEVAL GRIMOIRE *ARS NOTORIA* GIVES THIS SPELL TO DETERmine whether an extremely sick person will recuperate.

Stand before the patient and thrice reverently recite the following:

Ancor, Anacor, Anylos, Zohorna, Theodonos, hely otes Phagor,
Norizane, Corichito, Anosae, Helse Tonope, Phagora
Elleminator, Candones helosi, Tephagain, Tecendum, Thaones,
Behelos, Belhoros, Hocho Phagan, Corphandonos
Humanæ natus et vos Eloytus Phugora

Afterward, ask the person how he or she feels.

If the response is one of relief or of being "on the mend," the person will probably recover. However, if the person reports feeling worse, he or she is likely to succumb and cross over into the Summerlands.

SPELL VARIATION

- Another way to discern whether someone at death's door will improve involves removing nine smooth stones from a running river, tossing them over your right shoulder, then leaving them overnight in a fire.

  If the medical problem is destined to make the person a shade, the rocks will emit a distinctive death knell when you strike them together the following morning.

SPELL ORIGIN: European and Irish magic

SPELL TIMING: as needed. Collect the river stones during the day, burn them during the night, and strike them together the next morning.

INGREDIENTS FOR THE VARIATION: nine smooth stones plucked from coursing water and an overnight fire

AMBIANCE: calm, by the sickbed; adoors near a running river, then later near a comforting fire pit or fireplace

MAGICAL THEORY: Intoned Barbarous Words of Power provoke a response that can be interpreted to reveal future events.

SYMPATHETIC MAGIC: The coursing water represents the course of the disorder from which the patient suffers; the fire represents any fever the person may have; together, the water and fire represent the battle between health and death that is being waged within the patient.

Nine is the highest magical number under 10 (the number of completion), so to determine whether a loved one is nearing the end, use nine spell ingredients. Stones equate with the element Earth, which symbolizes matter and, therefore, the body, so nine stones are necessary to determine whether someone will live or die (return to Mother Earth).

TO DISCOVER WHERE YOU SHOULD RELOCATE

AFTER SUNSET DURING THE WANING OR NEW MOON, CAST A SUNWISE circle, light white candles, and burn several pinches of powdered sandalwood incense. Stand before each of the Four Quarters and meditate on your needs and desires. Record your impressions. Close circle, and then acquire maps of the directions that lured you most.

Within a day or two at dusk, choose a map to scry and spread it out flat on the floor. Place a clear shot glass or video camera lens atop it to serve as a *planchette* (a viewfinder through which you scry).

Close your eyes, and begin moving the glass across the middle of your map Ouija board in a smooth, continuous infinity symbol (a horizontal, elongated number *8*). Gracefully sway from side to side in time with your breathing. When you've established a relaxed rhythm, pose your relocation questions, such as "Where will I fare best moving to?"

Whenever the planchette suddenly sticks, slows, or consistently favors a specific area, write down the names of cities that show beneath the glass. Repeated passes will reveal optimal choices, possible routes, and future relocation sites.

SPELL VARIATION

- Place your left elbow in the lower left corner of a map. From the middle finger of your left hand, suspend a clear crystal pendant. Dangle its point over the center of the map.

Move your pendulum about from time to time; it may also spin, arc, or lurch from side to side of its own accord. Note the movements it makes, and the names of the cities beneath where the crystal point is when such happens.

Places your pendulum points to, pulls to, or spins sunwise over indicate goodly places to move to. Oppositely, don't move to areas your pendulum avoids, moves erratically when near, or spins ayenward over.

SPELL ORIGIN: European magic

SPELL TIMING: at twilight when the Moon is waning or new; after dark within a day or two after meditative inquiry.

INGREDIENTS: white candles, several pinches of powdered sandalwood incense, maps, a flat surface, a transparent shot glass or video camera lens, a pen, parchment

FOR THE VARIATION: a clear, pointed-crystal necklace and a map

AMBIANCE: a quiet circle lit with white candles, surrounded by clouds of sandalwood incense

MAGICAL THEORY:

SYMPATHETIC MAGIC: Moondark is the best time to perform discernment spells because the dark night is similar to using a black mirror to scry the future.

An electromagnetic conductor, crystal can detect magical ley lines and geographic power places. It also promotes mental clarity when deciding where to move.

White candles evoke the eastern Power to Know.

BETWEEN THE WORLDS: Twilight is a transitional time, and a goodly hour to set a future course.

DEITY TO INVOKE: Gaea, the Greek Goddess of Earth

TO MAKE A DIFFICULT CHOICE

ACQUIRE OR MAKE A SIMPLE PENDULUM. ALTHOUGH THE BEST pendulum is an aqua apatite stone ring strung on a silver chain, you can use any weighty object tied to the end of a flexible line as long as neither is plastic. Practice with whatever weight and line you devise to determine what constitutes the pendulum's yes and no answers. What feelings do its back-and-forth rhythms versus the pendulum's side-to-side motions evoke in you—similar to a head nodding yes or shaking no? Note the unique dichotomies of movement your pendulum may display.

Then, whenever you can't decide which of two options would constitute the right choice for you, grab your pendulum and stand in the threshold of a doorway. Slip your left forefinger into the loop of the chain, let the pendulum dangle freely, and concentrate on your question. Your pendulum's movements will answer yes or no questions you ask either mentally or aloud and help you eliminate the wrong choice.

If, however, you feel your divination was inconclusive, stay beneath your front doorway and verbally ask the God Janus to send you an instant omen. Tell him about just one of the possibilities, and then ask whether he thinks that's the correct course for you. Wait in silence for a minute or so for a positive or negative omen to occur. For example, you should consider hearing the sounds of a screeching ambulance or two animals fighting to be a bad omen. A laughing child riding a bike or sunlight breaking through the clouds is a goodly omen concerning the question you asked.

SPELL ORIGIN: traditional dowsing practice and Roman magic

SPELL TIMING: as needed. Janus is best invoked during transitional times, such as twilight, noon, or midnight.

INGREDIENTS: an aqua apatite ring and a silver chain or anything that can serve as a pendulum, such as eyeglasses you can dangle from a temple piece

MAGICAL THEORY:

SYMPATHETIC MAGIC: The aqua apatite gem is renowned for inducing psychism.

MACROCOSM = MICROCOSM: Your intuition, the flow of the universe, and the God/desses' insight concerning your inquiry animate the pendulum and make it sway.

BETWEEN THE WORLDS: Just as you stand on the verge of deciding between two choices, so also is a threshold the midpoint between two opposite realms (adoors versus indoors).

DEITY TO INVOKE: Janus, the two-faced Roman God of past and future, thresholds, and choices

TO RESOLVE A DILEMMA

A DILEMMA IS DAUNTING BECAUSE IT MAKES YOU FEEL AS IF YOU have only an either/or option (stay or leave, take abuse or retaliate, and so on). Yet the solution often lies not in settling for the middle ground between two extremes, but rather in deducing an entirely different, third way out of your quandary. The following spell employs *cleidomancy,* a system of divination using a key.

Acquire an antique key and string it onto a silver chain. Next, find a Hecate crossroads (a place adoors where three paths converge). An hour before midnight on a Wednesday during Moondark, don the key like a necklace and hasten to the triple crossroads.

When you arrive, stare neither right nor left, but straight at the center path. Whisper your plight and request divine inspiration from mighty Hecate. Clutch the key in your left hand, and then hold it against your forehead.

Avoid obsessing between two equally unsatisfactory choices—instead, consider your circumstance in unconventional terms. Ask yourself "What if?" questions. Fantasize freely about how you'd like things to be. Let your mind run wild with preferences and plans. The Goddess will likely disclose a way out of your dilemma within minutes.

When you're ready to go, turn around and don't look back as you leave Hecate's haunt.

When your quandary is resolved, thank Hecate for aiding you—return to the site and leave her an offering of food or *katharmata* in the center of the crossroads. (Katharmata are remains from a previous ritual—candle stubs, leftovers from Cakes and Wine, and half-burnt incense, for example—sacred to Hecate in her aspect of wizened Crone.) Depart without looking backward.

SPELL ORIGIN: European magic

SPELL TIMING: after sunset

INGREDIENTS: an old key, a silver necklace-type chain, a triple crossroads, and an offering of ritual remains

AMBIANCE: silent, adoors, standing before a triple crossroads (avert detection by wearing dark clothing or a black cloak)

MAGICAL THEORY:

TRIPLICITY: Seek a third option rather than being forced to choose between two equally unsatisfactory outcomes.

This spell requires a triple crossroads (a point where two roads intersect a third).

Further, you appeal to Hecate *Triformis,* the Goddess who manifests herself as a young maiden, a mature mother, and a wizened crone, representing your past experience, the present problem, and your hope for the future.

INVERSION: Unlike most spells, which encourage intimate contact with the God/dess you invoke, this spell requires you to appeal, then leave without looking backward—what's done is done. Hecate is mighty, and Witches know it's best to treat her with the most solemn reverence. Not only should you avoid expressing Orpheus-like doubt (see The 24-Hour Rule, page 264), but if you did look back, you could be terrified by what you see.

DEITY TO INVOKE: Hecate Triformis, the Greek Goddess of Witches, who is often depicted holding a key symbolizing her ability to unlock hidden mysteries

TO REVEAL THE NAME AND OCCUPATION OF YOUR FUTURE MATE

ON WALPURGISNACHT, (MAY EVE, THE NIGHT BEFORE THE BELTANE Sabbat on May 1), hang a linen or sheer white handkerchief outside overnight. Scry it for marks the next morning—the dew will have formed your future mate's initials on the fabric.

Note the first spring flowers you see—the letters their common names start with predict either your future mate's initials, or are contained within his or her name. For instance, should the first three flowers you see be a crocus, a daffodil, and a violet, your future mate's monogram will be C. D. V., or their name might be Vincent Daniels or Carmen Vandross or something similar.

To see a manifestation of your future mate, sit silently from midnight until one in the morning with someone of your sex. During the hour, pluck as many hairs from your head as you are old, and place them in individual linen cloths, each with a pinch of your choice of differing herbs.

At precisely one o' clock, burn them and say:

I offer this, my sacrifice
to (her/him) most precious in my eyes.

I charge thee now
come forth to me
that I this minute
thee may see!

Their face may appear as a reflection in a mirror, or briefly manifest as a vision.

A different spell to conjure a peek at your future mate advises that you go to a crossroads on Ostara (Easter) night, comb your hair backward, and prick the pinky on your left hand.

While three drops of blood fall on the ground, say:

I give my blood
to my loved one,
Whom I shall see
shall be mine own!

The form of your future mate will materialize, then slowly dissipate. Dispose of the bloody dust by casting it into a stream or river.

To have a dream about your potential partner, place your shoes beside your bed in the shape of the letter *T* on Midsummer Night's Eve (the night before the summer solstice), and intone the following rhyme:

Hoping this night
my true love to see,
I place my shoes
in the form of a T.

Your dream may reveal your future mate's occupation as well.

SPELL VARIATIONS

- Having annoying tinnitis, or ringing in your ears, actually has an up side—it's an opportunity to divine your future mate's identity.

  Whenever your ears ring, ask someone else in the room to randomly pick a number no higher than *26* and say it aloud. Match the choice with its corresponding alphabetical letter (*1=A, 2=B,* and so on). For instance, if they say the number *5,* you'd quickly surmise that your future mate's name will begin with the English letter *E* (for Ethan or Elaine, perhaps).

- Intone the following incantation while harvesting ivy to wear:

Ivy, Ivy,
I thee pluck.
And in my bosom,
I thee put.

The first young (woman/man)
who speaks to me
my own true lover
(she/he) shall be.

The first person to engage you in discourse could be your soul mate.

SPELL ORIGIN: Irish and traditional European magic

SPELL TIMING: on Walpurgisnacht (May Eve); Midsummer Eve (the night before summer solstice); as desired, but preferably on a Wednesday or Friday during Moondark

INGREDIENTS: a linen or sheer white handkerchief; hair, linen cloths, pinches of your favorite herbs; a crossroads, a comb, a needle; a pair of shoes

FOR THE VARIATIONS: a randomly spoken number; a bit of ivy

AMBIANCE: close to home, in a cast circle, or in your bedroom or garden

MAGICAL THEORY:

SYMPATHETIC MAGIC: The Mayday morning dew is a magical ingredient in many an olde love and beauty spell.

Little in life is truly random; therefore, even the first letter of a spring blossom you see at Beltane betokens a message you should consider.

Plucking hairs and matching them with your age signifies you in a spell. Combining that with an herb gives you the power of Earth, which corresponds to hearth and home (or mating or marriage). Burning both represents your desire for love and passion.

In palmistry, the pinky finger equates with the planet Mercury.

Folks don't normally place their shoes precisely, so taking time to do so implies strong intent. Because a mated pair of shoes corresponds to a mated human couple, placing one shoe in front of the other so that one shoe can fully "see" its mate enables you to see yours in a dream state.

The universe knows who your future mate should and will be. By restricting its responses to alphabetical letters you recognize, you improve your chance that you will recognize the person when the two of you meet.

Ivy is a vine that binds lovers together in many love spells, and is traditionally used to tie lovers' hands together during a Handfasting.

DEITIES TO INVOKE: Aphrodite, the Greek Goddess of love; Adonis, an affectionate Greek God

TO LEARN A CHILD'S FUTURE OCCUPATION

TO DIVINE A CHILD'S FUTURE FIELD OF WORK, SCRY AN EGG FOR revealing images. At noon on a regular weekday in summer, fill a new, clear glass with clear water. Take an egg freshly laid by a black hen, crack it open, and add the yolk to the water. Place the glass in the sunlight. Stir the water and yolk with your index finger, and let the viscous contents settle for a moment.

Without touching the glass, look through it to see images or symbols related to the child's future occupation. These might include a cross if the child is destined to practice medicine, or spidery lines that spell out indicative words or initials, such as D.D.S. for a future dentist, or C.P.A. for a budding certified public accountant. For instance, seeing the letters *L, W, Y,* and *R* could denote a future lawyer.

SPELL ORIGIN: unknown, but probably European magic
SPELL TIMING: at noon during summer
INGREDIENTS: a black hen's egg, a new, transparent glass, and water
AMBIANCE: a sunny room or adoors

MAGICAL THEORY:

> MACROCOSM = MICROCOSM: The yolk is a microcosmic representation of a child.
>
> SYMPATHETIC MAGIC: The forms you see in the glass (a primitive crystal ball) are omens regarding the child's occupation.
>
> The color black corresponds to Moondark—the best time to divine.

DEITY TO INVOKE: Fate, the Greek Goddess who knows children's future

TO DETERMINE WHETHER SOMEONE IS A VIRGIN OR YOUR MATE IS FAITHFUL

TO KNOW WHETHER SOMEONE HAS GONE GREENWOODING, SO TO speak, or your partner has loved another, repeat the egg spell above.

If the yolk floats to the top of the water in the glass, the person in question remains a virgin, or your mate has not had a sexual affair.

If, however, the yolk sinks to the bottom of the glass, the person you're scrying about is no longer virginal, or your mate has, indeed, made love with another.

SPELL ORIGIN: paraphrased from the *Grimorium Verum*

SPELL TIMING: preferably at noon on a weekday during the summer; as needed

INGREDIENTS: a black hen's egg, a new, transparent glass, and water

AMBIANCE: indoors, in private

MAGICAL THEORY:

> SYMPATHETIC MAGIC: A floating yolk implies levity and spiritual inclination and, therefore, virginity or fidelity; a sinking yolk symbolizes gravity (i.e., pregnancy) and, therefore, carnal experience or infidelity.

DEITIES TO INVOKE: to inquire about a woman's sexual status—Aphrodite; to ask about a man's sexual status—Dionysus; to determine whether your mate is faithful—Hera

TO KNOW HOW FARAWAY LOVED ONES ARE FARING

USE A PIECE OF HEMP TO SUSPEND A SPRIG OF SAGE IN YOUR KITCHEN. Uniform drying without molding or mishap, such as falling leaves, means all is well. A cutting that withers portends an ill or unhappy loved one.

To converse with distant or estranged loved ones, fast from dawn until dusk for a week. On the eighth day, cast circle after sunset, burn eucalyptus incense, and intone the following power-square numbers seven times seven (say the numbers in both lines 49 times consecutively).

1	9	2	5	4
9	6	5	3	3

Each time you repeat both lines of numbers seven times in succession, turn your head in a different direction to repeat the next batch of numbers (for a total of seven times).

Think about your faraway loved one. Speak as if the person is present, and ask what you will. You will feel the person's rapt attention during this spell, and he or she will hear your concern regardless of how vast the physical distance is.

The person will likely contact you and relate the conversation as having occurred in a dream about you, or confess a strange compulsion to call you.

SPELL VARIATION

- Make an amulet that acts as a de-facto telephone whenever you want to connect with far-flung friends or relatives.

   Acquire a blank, pewter, pendant-style roundel about 1½ inches in diameter. Using an awl, bigrave it with the power-square numbers above. Consecrate the talisman by immersing it in all Four Elements; then wrap it in a white handkerchief or white silk scarf.

   When you want to contact someone far afield, hold the disk in your left palm, gaze on its inscription, visualize your loved one's visage, verbally repeat the numbers as in the spell above, then speak to the person in absentia.

You will sense that your friend can hear and understand you during the magical working. You may even hear the person respond to your questions or comment in his or her customary manner.

The person will likely get in touch with you soon, say that he or she has been thinking about you, and actually inquire about how *you're* faring.

SPELL ORIGIN: English and Ceremonial magic

SPELL TIMING: as needed, but preferably during Moondark

INGREDIENTS: a clipping of garden sage, hempen hanging string, a tack or cup-hook, power-square numbers, and eucalyptus incense

> **FOR THE VARIATION:** a pewter roundel, an awl, power-square numbers, the Four Elements (salt water, incense smoke, and candle flame), and a white handkerchief or silk scarf

AMBIANCE: in your kitchen or home; alone in your ritual space, engulfed by clouds of Air incense (such as eucalyptus), Witchy music, and so forth

MAGICAL THEORY:

> **SYMPATHETIC MAGIC:** An alloy, or mixed metal, pewter is sacred to Mercury, the God of communication. Eucalyptus is a clean Air scent that corresponds to the East, and hence, communication.
>
> The herb sage corresponds to longevity, so watching sage dry reveals whether your loved ones are healthy and faring well. If it rots, they may be ill, having financial woes, or experiencing some kind of crisis.
>
> Seven is a magical, lucky number, so intoning the spell seven times seven increases the odds that you'll make contact with faraway loved ones.
>
> Power-square numbers are ancient and steeped in magical might from repeated use. Because some sets are composed of odd or even numbers that correspond to the content of your spell desire, it is easy to figure out why and how they work. Others are more obscure but no less traditionally effective, so Crafters continue to use them even if their original meanings have been lost in the sands of time (as with this spell's numbers).
>
> **MACROCOSM = MICROCOSM:** Intoning the spell seven times compels the Seven Planets to favor your desire.

DEITY TO INVOKE: Mercury, the Greek God of communication

TO TRAVEL ASTRALLY OR COMMUNICATE PSYCHICALLY OVER VAST DISTANCES

ASTRAL TRAVEL IS AN EXCITING ADVENTURE FOR ANY SPELLCRAFTER. It's also very useful if you are unable to travel conventionally—if you are physically limited or confined to a prison cell, for example.

Our true tale of a spell for sending a message via the full Moon reflects the romance of real magic from the olden days of knightly mages' derring-do, to a recent test of a Wiccan coven's love and courage.

TO TRAVEL ASTRALLY

DEFY DISTANCE AND BORDER BARRIERS, AVOID TERRORIST THREATS AND security searches—don't "go Greyhound"; go astral!

You won't have access to a map or an atlas while you travel in spirit form, so before setting out, familiarize yourself with the route you want to take "as the crow flies" (as a bird would fly it). When you're confident of the course, don a calming green kyanite amulet, and lie on your back on a mat or bed.

Close your eyes and meditate. Incrementally slow and deepen your breathing pattern. Your mind may initially race with mundane details of the day, but resist the temptation to fight such phantoms—you will relax in time. (Beginners may note that this process can take an hour or longer; with diligent practice, however, you can shave this down to mere minutes.) Lady Passion's favorite relaxation technique is to picture herself lying on a matress afloat on a serene sea.

When your body feels heavy, let your spirit quit its bodily constraint, detach, and float just beneath the ceiling. Enjoy the liberating sensation of rising upward—it may even tickle as if butterflies were dancing ballet in your belly. Look around and mentally acknowledge that you're in the air. Then, when you're ready, float through your roof and out into the weather.

Skim just above the treetops, and use their tips as landmarks to help you keep your bearings along the way. When you reach your destination, you'll be able to stay adoors and converse with someone at a door or window. Don't allow physical contact, however, or the person will receive a slight electric-like shock. Return the way you came, and then sleep deeply with satisfaction.

TO COMMUNICATE PSYCHICALLY

MIRROR A MESSAGE ON THE MOON TO COMMUNICATE SECRETLY WITH a faraway friend or loved one.

Agrippa describes this as an "art of declaring secrets ... very profitable for towns, and cities that are besieged"[87] that he used himself. Apparently, this occurred in the course of a gloriously doomed chivalrous adventure he undertook on behalf of a fellow noble in 1508, the year before he penned the *Three Books of Occult Philosophy*. Agrippa and his cohorts probably used this spell to aid their mystifying escape from a heavily besieged house following their daring but short-lived capture of the Black Fort of Tarragon.

At a time you've prearranged with the person who is to receive your message, take an image or letters you've drawn and go adoors on a clear night beneath the rays of a full Moon. Hold them up so they reflect la Luna's rays straight back at her. Your message will bounce off the Moon much like a telecommunications signal bounces off a satellite. The person you've told to look up for the message "at a long distance sees, reads, and knows [it] in the very compass, and circle of the Moon," wrote Agrippa. Your images' "resemblances," he mentioned cryptically, will be "multiplied in the Air."

Coven Oldenwilde's experience with this spell, in a dire situation that befell us the year before we began writing *The Goodly Spellbook,* was as effective for us as it was for Agrippa. Forced to elude bigoted local persecutors, Lady Passion and her daughter spent several months in hiding in a tolerant region on the West Coast. Her covenmates greatly desired to communicate with the High Priestess and let her know that they loved her and missed her dearly, but because her whereabouts had to remain secret, Lady Passion's covenmates could not talk openly with her by telephone. However, *Diuvei managed to inform her that during the next full Moon, she should gaze at la Luna at a certain time to receive a message.

At the next coven meeting, members jointly made a round white parchment seal 9 inches across. On the back, in red ink, they inscribed a pentagram. On the front, in silver ink, they drew a large runic letter *O* (the Odal rune, sig-

---

[87] Agrippa, *"Of the Wonderful Natures of Water, Air and Winds," in* Three Books of Occult Philosophy.

nifying homestead or, in our case, the covenstead) surrounded by the words *Home, Land, Free.* Everyone charged the seal by dancing around it and chanting the three words. At the appointed time, they went adoors and held it aloft beneath the Moon. Meanwhile, across the continent, Lady Passion stood and beamed a smile of love and perseverance toward the dazzling orb.

When Passion and her covenmates reunited, they inquired of one another what had transpired during the spell. Several covenmates reported seeing Passion's smiling face across the Moon's surface, which mirrored her features to them in complete detail. Lady Passion clearly saw the shape of the Odal rune, not only in the Moon's circle, but also "multiplied in the air" everywhere—in the interlacing of tree branches, in a shadow cast by a twisted telephone cord, and so on.[88]

Proving in such a way that distance, persecution, and secrecy were no impediments to magical communication heartened everyone.

SPELL ORIGIN: European magic; Coven Oldenwilde practice

SPELL TIMING: after sunset during Moonbright

INGREDIENTS: a mat or bed and a kyanite stone; a parchment roundel, two pens, one red and one silver, and a devised message or symbol

AMBIANCE: lying comfortably on your back; while adoring la Luna adoors

MAGICAL THEORY: Witches' Power to Will involves physical, magical, and psychic practices as well.

   SYMPATHETIC MAGIC: The Moon reflects light at night and therefore makes an excellent screen on which to project an image (with her permission, of course).

DEITY TO INVOKE: The Goddess Luna

TO INDUCE A TRANCE FOR SCRYING

FOR A GOODLY HYPNOTIC EXPERIENCE, LIGHT A WITCH FIRE AND SCRY its flames to determine future events.

Set the mood by burning some darkly mysterious incense, such as musk or myrrh. Then make a fire in your cauldron.

---

[88] *Ham-radio operators who bounce their transmissions off the Moon report an uncannily similar "scattering" effect on the signal.*

- Half fill it with one ore more boxes of Epsom salts.
- Pour one or more bottles of 70 percent isopropyl (rubbing) alcohol over the crystals.
- Ignite the liquid, plunge the room into darkness, and then sit in meditative repose before the blaze.

Stare raptly at the animated flames—the way they act has divinatory bearing on your life. Note whether the fire appears lively and burns tall and straight-flamed (good omens), or seems sluggish, pops, or hisses (negative portents). Ponder the images the flames form.

Ask aloud any questions you have about current or future events, and consider the fire's responses. Sudden brilliance or flame elongation means *yes;* frenetic flickering or abrupt dimness means *no.* The direction in which the flames slant typically indicates that a particular Quarter power is operative, and hence must be propitiated regarding the matter.

As the alcohol evaporates, the flames will begin to wane. You can extend your trance by stirring the salt with a stick, which will produce additional enchanting images for you to scry.

Spell Origin: Coven Oldenwilde practice

Spell Timing: preferably after sunset during Moondark; as desired

Ambiance: alone or with friends in ritual space (inside or adoors) amidst Witchy incense and at a safe distance from flammable objects

Ingredients: incense (such as musk or myrrh), a cauldron, one or more boxes of Epsom salts, one or more bottles of rubbing alcohol, and a stirring stick

Magical Theory: Stressing about things won't assuage your concerns, but you can find answers if you go into trance and seek divine insight.

    Like attracts like: To divine about a matter that could change over time, scry a mutable element such as Water or Fire.

    Macrocosm = microcosm: The cauldron fire not only contains universal wisdom concerning your problems, but also represents yourself, your circumstances, and future life events—just as a teacup does during tasseography (tea-leaf reading).

Deity to Invoke: All-seeing Hecate, who opens the doors between worlds

TO GAIN SECOND SIGHT

To envision future events,[89] pour transparent scented oil, such as eucalyptus, into a bronze or brass cup. Anoint your third eye (or psychic center in the middle of your forehead) with it and your body also, if you wish. Next, anoint your right eyelid with water from a shipwreck. If you lack this ingredient, substitute liquid bailed from a submerged wicker basket, seawater or, least desirable, salt water. Finally, anoint your left eyelid with a mixture of the same water and kohl.

When you feel ready, request foresight from the Sun God by chanting his Gnostic name—Ablanathanalba—included in the following ancient incantation:

Eeim To Eim
Alale'p
Barbariath Menebreio Arbathiao'th
Ioue'l Iae'l Oue'ne'iie
Mesommias

Let the God who prophesies to me come
and let Him not go away until I dismiss Him

Ourna Our
Soul Zasoul
Ougot Nooumbiaou
Thabrat Beriaou
Achthiri Marai
Elpheo'n Tabao'th
Kirasina Lampsoure' Iaboe
Ablanathanalba
Akrammachamarei!

---

[89] PGM, V, 54–69.

SPELL VARIATIONS

- To increase your psychism, bathe in several handfuls of dried buchu leaves.
- Purchase star anise from a grocery store, and burn a pulverized ½ teaspoon of it whenever you tell fortunes.
- To excel when practicing your psychic skills during Moondark, pop a moonstone into your mouth.
- Convert a moonstone necklace into a diadem that fits around your head, and wear it over your brow whenever you want to divine the future.
- During Moondark, sit beneath a bay or mimosa tree and inhale its bewitching perfume. You will likely experience immediate foresight.
- To receive prophetic dreams, gather several handfuls of fresh bay leaves or mimosa blossoms, and sleep with them beneath your pillow.
- To become a Pagan prophet/ess, appeal for help from the Goddess Nyx.

SPELL ORIGIN: Egyptian, European, and Voudon magic

SPELL TIMING: at the Witching Hour on a Monday or Wednesday during Moondark

INGREDIENTS: some eucalyptus or a similar transparent oil, a bronze cup, kohl, several ounces of water in which a ship or skiff has wrecked, or water from a submerged woven basket, seawater, or salt water

FOR THE VARIATIONS: several handfuls of dried buchu leaves; star anise, a censer, charcoal, and matches; a moonstone gem; a moonstone necklace; a bay or mimosa tree; several handfuls of bay or mimosa leaves and a pillow

AMBIANCE: in minimal candle light while facing the eastern direction

MAGICAL THEORY:

SYMPATHETIC MAGIC: To become psychic, appeal for help from a prophetically powerful God/dess.

Black star anise is associated with secrets and the wisdom of the heavenly bodies.

The mutable Moon has been associated with magic and prophecy since ancient times; thus, keeping a moonstone in your mouth can enable you to know and speak future's truth.

The third eye (the area between the brows or in the middle of the forehead) has long been associated with the forebrain, or one's highest ideals or knowledge.

Voudon spellcrafters use buchu leaves to induce psychism.

For eons, folks have had precognitive dreams while asleep beneath bay and mimosa trees.

INVERSION MAGIC: A shipwreck is a traumatic event that psychics have traditionally sought to foresee and help folks avoid.

DEITIES TO INVOKE: Ablanathanalba, the Gnostic Sun God; Nyx, a Grecian night Goddess who bestows the gift of prophecy

TO SEE FAIRIES

ON A SATURDAY NIGHT, IN THE LIGHT OF A FULL MOON, LAY SEVERAL broom straws on a table by an open window and chant:

> *Straw, draw, crow, craw,*
> *By my life I give thee law.*

The "straws will become fairies and dance to the cawing of a crow who will come and sit on the ledge of the window."[90]

To talk with the tiny ones, stand by a fern an hour before midnight on Midsummer's Eve (the night before summer solstice) and say:

> *I ask the God/desses*
> *that the Spirits with which I wish to speak*
> *will appear at precisely midnight.*[91]

Then, fifteen minutes prior to the Witching Hour, chant the following exactly nine times:

> *Bar, Kirabar,*
> *Alli, Alla,*
> *Tetragrammaton.*

---

[90] *Leland,* Gypsy Sorcery and Fortune-Telling, *31.*
[91] *Adapted from* Le Grand Grimoire, *bk. II, by Antonio Venitiana (Paris, 1845).*

One or more of the Wee Folk will physically appear and either converse or psychically communicate with you in some way. If the fairies choose to speak, you'll find their voices have a reverberating, bell-like quality, sound like underwater garble, or resemble a porpoise's squeak. Their bodies may seem stacked—one atop another—in a way that humans' aren't. They are typically attired in ancient, olde, or woodsy-practical fashion.

You may feel either a chill or an odd warmth when you encounter them, and experience slight dizziness or the certainty that time is passing too swiftly or too slowly. You will likely be reluctant to move and break the spell because the moment seems so fragile and profound. Trust your feelings, for these days fairies typically keep folks they enchant for only a while, then tend to release them back to their own timeline.

SPELL VARIATION

- As deeply in nature as you are able to hike (in a wood, glade, marsh, or cove, for instance), bathe in moonbeams and nip alcoholic spirits on Midsummer's Eve. Depending on your particular climate, you're likely to observe gnarly Gnomes, crotchety leprechauns, and diverse spirits frolicking hither and yon.

  For example, our coven looks forward all year long to camping during the Litha Sabbat (summer solstice) and watching Will-o'-the-Wisps—azure orb-shaped entities that fly around at night with true intelligence. Nineteenth-century Gypsies called them *mullo dudia*—dead or ghost lights.

  Be motionless, make no utterances, and remain reverent throughout. Resist the temptation to approach them—do not spook or encroach on them in any way. Simply be grateful for any interest they may show in your presence, or any assistance they may provide (if you're lost and scared, for instance).

  Don't follow their ramblings, or you'll become hopelessly fairy-led into their ethereal realm, and possibly ne'er beheld by human eyes again.

  If they nonetheless bewitch you, break their enchantment by refusing to follow them inside a hillock, refusing to step inside their mushroom fairy ring, and turning your shirt or jacket inside out.

  Whenever you have been blessed to witness real fairies, always leave them a shiny stone, bejeweled trinket, or tobacco offering in gratitude.

SPELL ORIGIN: Romany, Persian, and European Craft; Coven Oldenwilde practice

SPELL TIMING: a Saturday night during a full Moon, or an hour prior to midnight on Midsummer's Eve (the night before the Litha Sabbat or summer solstice, annually June 21 or 22)

INGREDIENTS: several natural broom straws, a moonlit table, and a windowsill; a stand of woodland fern

FOR THE VARIATION: alcoholic spirits, a wild, natural space, and fairy offerings (a found shiny stone, jeweled trinket, or pinch of tobacco)

AMBIANCE: in front of a windowsill with the full Moon shining on a nearby table; amidst fern fronds at night during the Litha Sabbat

MAGICAL THEORY:

SYMPATHETIC MAGIC: Traditionally, Fairies live in straw tubes.

The Fey also traditionally inhabit fern, so in effect, you're knocking at their very door.

Crows are notorious messengers of the God/desses, and reveal omens to humans in the number, intensity, and direction of their caws.

Fairies frolic during the season of the Sun's zenith.

Leaving forest fairies an offering keeps you on their good side and encourages them to manifest themselves more often.

TO REVEAL THE CONTENTS OF A SECRET

- Compel folks to confess all—wear frangipani oil or burn dried frangipani flowers as incense in their presence.
- Emeralds reveal secrets to their possessors, so if you want people to divulge what they're hiding, wear one of the green gems whenever you are in close proximity to them.

SPELL ORIGIN: Voudon magic; gemology

TIMING: as needed, but preferably at midnight during Moondark

INGREDIENTS: frangipani essential oil or approximately 1 teaspoon of dried, crushed frangipani flowers, a censer, and matches or a lighter; an emerald gem chip

AMBIANCE: in calm control in the presence of someone secretive

MAGICAL THEORY: Frangipani flowers and essential oil exude a comforting, lulling scent that induces folks to verbal largess, braggadocio, and the confession of secrets.

SYMPATHETIC MAGIC: Frangipani oil corresponds magically to the Sun, thereby exposing a secret to scrutiny or "the light of day."

INVERSION: Green emeralds are sacred to the North, the Quarter whose correspondences include imparting Witches with the Power to Be Silent, and Venus, the Roman Goddess of love. Secrets are hard to keep from Mother Earth (who knows all) as well as from loved ones; thus, wearing a green emerald induces folks to divulge secrets.

TO REVEAL THE SOURCE OF A LIE OR RUMOR

IF YOU WISH TO KNOW THE NAME OF THE ORIGINATOR OF A LIE OR rumor, appeal for revelation from the constellation Ursa Major by facing North adoors at midnight and intoning the following incantation:

*"Komphtho
Komasith
Komnoun*

*You who shook and shake the World,
You who have swallowed the Ever-living Serpent
and daily raise the Disk of the Sun and of the Moon*

*You whose Name is
Ithioo' E'i Arbathiao' E'*

*send up to me, (your name), at Night
the Daimon*[92] *of This Night
to reveal to me
concerning the (supply specifics) thing."*[93]

---

[92] *Though Christians attached diabolic connotations to the word,* daimon *originally meant the spiritual essence of an object or a life-form.*

[93] PGM, *IV, 1323–1330.*

The Mother Bear Goddess will defend you by revealing the rumormonger's name to your mind.

SPELL ORIGIN: Egyptian magic
SPELL TIMING: at the Witching Hour during Moondark
AMBIANCE: alone, in a private adoors circling space, surrounded by sky and stars
MAGICAL THEORY:

SYMPATHETIC MAGIC: Appealing to Ursa (Arbathiao'e) makes her the arbiter in a dispute regarding the truth.

In most of the Northern Hemisphere, Ursa Major never rises nor sets, but is perpetually visible circling the North Pole—thus, the liar or rumormonger cannot hide from her scrutiny.

DEITY OR CONSTELLATION TO INVOKE: the Mother Bear Goddess, Ursa, in the form of the constellation Ursa Major

TO REVEAL THE IDENTITY OF A THIEF

FIND OUT WHO STOLE FROM YOU—TAKE UP THE BLACK FAST:

"Who has been robbed and wishes to find the thief should take a black hen, and for nine Fridays must with the hen fast strictly; the thief will then either bring back the plunder or die."[94]

There's an easier and no less traditional way to unmask a mischief maker. Should you have several suspects, consider each in turn, and then carve each person's initials in a separate apple with a boleen. The fruit that withers the fastest bodes the bandit.

If you have no inkling of a thief's identity, cast a sunwise circle and ask for avenging justice from the Goddess Nemesis, who will duly mark the thief with some temporary, but obvious, sign of guilt.

A student of ours used a second "mark-the-thief" spell from the *Key of Solomon*.[95] Her boss had requested that she use magic to determine which employee had absconded with the business's grand-opening earnings.

---

[94] *Leland,* Gypsy Sorcery and Fortune-Telling, *137.*

[95] *S. Liddell Macgregor Mathers, trans., ed.,* The Key of Solomon the King *(York Beach, Maine: Red Wheel/Weiser, Weiser Books, 1972), chap. 9, 48–50, 1203 Lansdowne manuscript.*

The spell employs the divinatory method of *coscinomancy,* which is practiced with a sieve and shears. First, suspend a sieve by a piece of hemp (originally, "a cord wherewith a man has been hung") fastened around the circumference of its rim. At each Quarter on the inside of the sieve's rim, write with dragon's blood ink these characters:

Then fill a clean brass basin with water from a fountain and intone this incantation:

Dies Mies Yes-chet
Bene Done Fet
Donnima Metemauz

Spin the sieve with your left hand. Simultaneously stir the basin water in a contrary direction with a twig of green laurel in your right hand. When the water becomes still and the sieve no longer whirls, gaze fixedly into the water, and you will see the form of whoever has committed the theft. Cut a sign, such as an arrow or lightning bolt, into the water with your athamé. The next time you see the thief, he or she will be sporting the mark in the form of a sore, a scratch—even an infected boil—on their face.

The day after she performed this spell, our student identified the robber with ease when he came to work afflicted with a telltale facial sore. Her boss phoned the cops, who subsequently questioned the man. He readily confessed and promptly returned all the money.

SPELL VARIATION

- To hone your psychism and help you deduce a robber's identity, burn a handful of linseeds in a censer. The seeds will pop around and form the culprit's initials.

SPELL ORIGIN: Transylvanian, European, ceremonial, and Voudon magic

SPELL TIMING: during Moondark or Moonbright; as needed

INGREDIENTS: a black hen; as many apples as suspects, a boleen, a sieve, hempen string, dragon's blood ink, a brass basin, fountain water, a twig of green laurel, and an athamé

> **FOR THE VARIATION:** a handful of linseeds, a censer, charcoal, and matches

AMBIANCE: your private circling space, surrounded by candles and permeated with incense

MAGICAL THEORY:

> **SYMPATHETIC MAGIC:** Because an apple represents an individual on a microcosmic level, you can use it as a magical poppet to represent each suspect.
>
> As you mark the thief's image in the water, so you mark his or her actual face.
>
> Laurel has been associated with prophecy since ancient times.
>
> To expose a thief to the light of day, cast circle sunwise.

INVERSION: While pulverized linseeds make oil as slippery as a thief, in this spell, the intact seeds are poppets of the robber, so burning them actually compels the thief to "confess" his or her identity by forming the thief's initials.

DEITY TO INVOKE: Nemesis, an Attic Goddess who avenges injustice

Concealment Spells

"Mind the way to magic might—
Dress and act as dark as night.
Place a log inside your bed.
Pull your hood atop your head.

Slip adoors, and silent be.
Disappear behind a tree.
Spell as silent as a stone—
by the cock crow, back at home."
—Lady Passion

As a spellcrafter, you have the right—perhaps even the spiritual duty—to discuss your magical beliefs proudly and publicly. When you practice, however, you'll usually need protection from prying eyes. After all, spellcrafting isn't a spectator sport.

In medieval times Witches used to conceal their nocturnal spell and Sabbat frolics by putting a log in their bed. Asked the next morning how they slept, they would slyly reply, "Like a log!"

Modern Witches' occasional need for privacy is reflected in our penchant for wearing black woolen cloaks. We wear capes for two reasons: in honor of our Burning Times ancestors, who did so to disguise their identities while traveling afoot to Sabbats (a cloak's amorphous fabric obscures features such as the wearer's age and sex), and because when it comes to working magic, discretion is the better form of valor.

Concealment spells are an essential application of Witches' Power to Be Silent. Such workings come in many guises—from magically muting a noisy party, to thwarting thieves, to making yourself or your ritual site invisible.

TO PROTECT OR MUTE A NOISY PARTY

PERFORM A SPELL THAT PLANTATION SLAVES IN THE AMERICAN South often used to protect a forbidden party or religious rite from detection by their masters. Turn a large pot, preferably a cauldron, upside down, either in the direction from which you anticipate trouble, or on your front porch.

SPELL VARIATION

- If you want loud houseguests to quiet down, surreptitiously overturn an empty drinking cup—ideally, one that the most boisterous person present previously used.

SPELL ORIGIN: African-American folk magic; modern variation derivative
SPELL TIMING: as needed, but works best when performed during a waning or new Moon
INGREDIENTS: a cauldron or a large pot
  FOR THE VARIATION: a used drinking glass
AMBIANCE: calm amidst a cacophony
MAGICAL THEORY:
  SYMPATHETIC MAGIC: The overturned cauldron traps sound and prevents it from escaping the property.
  ANTIPATHETIC MAGIC: Because a filled chalice often instigates intemperance, a drained vessel will promote subdued sobriety.

TO DODGE DANGER WHILE DRIVING

TO PROTECT YOUR CAR OR OTHER MEANS OF TRANSPORT FROM needless scrutiny by thieves, carjackers, over-aggressive cops, and so forth, make it invisible—add eucalyptus oil to water and wash your vehicle with the potion at night during a waning or new Moon.

Before hitting the road, reinforce the magical cloak by mentally projecting a shimmery sphere of glamoury around your ride.

To elude dangerous traffic situations and unwarranted police attention, attach to your dashboard clean vertebrae from a snake that died of natural causes.

SPELL ORIGIN: European magic and Coven Oldenwilde practice
SPELL TIMING: as needed, though the spell is particularly effective when performed at night during Moondark

INGREDIENTS: eucalyptus oil, rags, a bucket of water, adhesive, and vertebrae from a snake that died naturally

AMBIANCE: proactively protective while washing your ride adoors at night; determined before a journey

MAGICAL THEORY:

ANTIPATHETIC MAGIC: Eucalyptus oil's pungency repels the Evil Eye.

SYMPATHETIC MAGIC: Eucalyptus oil's clarity confers invisibility. The vertebrae of a snake impart its stealthy slipperiness and hypnotic powers to the possessor, thereby helping you to slip through traffic jams, evade speeding tickets, and so forth.

DEITY TO INVOKE: Aradia, a deified 14th-century Italian Witch who successfully used disguise to evade her inquisitors, thereby enabling her to teach magic far and wide

TO CONCEAL MAGICAL VALUABLES FROM THIEVES

PLACE A PENTAGRAM ATOP YOUR BOOK OF SHADOWS AND MAGICAL valuables.

Individually wrap your power pieces in black silk, and then bind the covering closed with black hemp.

Store your sacred tools in a lockable strongbox, and disguise it on the outside with something drab and inconspicuous, such as an old, crinkly brown paper bag. Hide the lockbox so inaccessibly that curious people will expend inordinate physical effort in a vain attempt to find it.

SPELL VARIATION

• Thwart theft by placing an onyx, a black tourmaline, or a hematite atop your mystical treasures.

SPELL ORIGIN: European magic; gemology

SPELL TIMING: prophylactically or as needed

INGREDIENTS: a pentagram charm, black silk, black hemp, a lockable strongbox or storage container, and innocuous wrapping

FOR THE VARIATION: an onyx, a black tourmaline, or a hematite

MAGICAL THEORY:

SYMPATHETIC MAGIC: The ancient Egyptian hieroglyph for night was the five-pointed star. Night corresponds to concealment and secrets.

Wrapping items in black helps hide them from prying eyes.

Natural silk is the traditional material for protecting magical items because its light, breathable fibers don't impede the energy of the object it conceals.

Onyx and black tourmaline absorb light like a black hole, and therefore obscure objects. Hematite repels intruders with the strength of inner iron and a mirror-like reflectivity.

MACROCOSM = MICROCOSM: Because the pentagram represents a hand outstretched in a gesture of warding, and its points symbolize the power of the Four Elements plus Spirit, Witches use it as the ultimate protective symbol.

Black hemp corresponds to Saturn's rings, which symbolize binding, and therefore magically prevent trespass or theft.

DEITY TO INVOKE: Saturn, the ruler of boundaries and security

TO PREVENT DETECTION DURING SPELLWORK

MANY CRAFTERS WEAR BLACK, HOODED CAPES WHEN ADOORS CASTING spells. Before any need for it, imbue your cloak or ritual robe with the power to make you invisible on command.

At the Witching Hour on a Saturday during Moondark, go adoors, hold your cape aloft, and chant the following charm:

O thou my cloak, be strong as Oak!
Hide me from all hostile eyes—
inside your folds, my safety lies.

In deepest woods, and darkest night
protect me from all things that fright.

In city din or bright of day—
keep my enemies at bay.

On coldest night, pray keep me warm—
protect me from all things that harm.

While I breathe and when I'm buried—
ever be my sanctuary![96]

Wear dark clothing beneath your cloak. Avoid using reflective metal tools that might catch the light and evoke curiosity, or burning incense whose out-of-the-ordinary odor tends to lure folks from afar.

At night, don't build a balefire unless you're certain you're completely shielded from any nearby roads or prowling forest rangers. Don't employ artificial light, which attracts attention—light tiki torches or candles in jars that cast elusive shadows. You may also use a few fluorescent snap-stick lights, such as those divers, campers, and ravers use. Most present-day people are blind to anything that isn't bright, so as long as you avoid electric or gas-fueled light, you will avoid detection by unwanted onlookers.

The same admonition applies to sound, for pounding on a drum or blowing a shrill flute easily summons a curious crowd. If your risk of being overheard or interrupted is high, consider doing the spell silently—you can make much magic even if you're circling with others by simply relying on their psychic abilities, eye contact, and magical gestures.

If danger threatens, squat down as if you are a tight ball, pull your hood over your face, and conceal your entire body within your cloak's folds. Freeze and remain inert until the peril passes.

SPELL VARIATION

- Charm your cape against theft and flame licks—embroider in black the following rune[97] on the inside of the cloak's bottom hem.

---

[96] *Adapted from a charm by Third Degree Gardnerian Priest Rowan Greenleaf, a member of Coven Oldenwilde.*

[97] *Eihwas is an alternative spelling of the name of the 13th rune, iwaz, associated with the longest living European tree, the yew. The yew resists fire, so eihwas symbolizes protection, continuity, and endurance.*

EIHWAS

SPELL ORIGIN: Coven Oldenwilde and ancient European Witchcraft

SPELL TIMING: at the Witching Hour on a Saturday during Moondark

INGREDIENTS: a black, hooded cloak or ritual robe, dark clothing, tiki-torches and votive candles in jars or snap-stick lights

FOR THE VARIATION: black embroidery thread, a needle, and your cloak

AMBIANCE: alone, holding your cloak, whispering beneath a new Moon; cloaked in candlelight; adoors, alert to danger; in a sewing or crafts room

MAGICAL THEORY:

SYMPATHETIC MAGIC: Cloaks are loose garments that disguise wearers' features from behind.

Crafters wear dark clothes to help them disappear in darkness so they may work private night rites.

Flickering candlelight confuses pursuers.

DEITIES TO INVOKE: Hecate, Goddess of the Hidden Children; Herne, God of the darkest depths of the forest

TO SEAL A SACRED SPACE AGAINST INTRUSION IN YOUR ABSENCE

FEW THINGS ARE MORE DISPIRITING THAN TO RETURN TO YOUR favorite circling site and discover that some thoughtless thug has bruised its beauty.

Although you may be tempted to decorate your outdoor sanctuary with fancy statues and expensive baubles, the more obviously human-made objects you leave there, the more they may attract unwelcome attention from types who view pretty Paganism as being sinister Satanism.

Instead, let nature provide your sacred furnishings. Let a tree stump serve as an altar, a rounded boulder as a Goddess statue, a stang (a staff with a forked top) as a Horned God statue. Place flat stones beneath your candles to catch their telltale drippings. Use temporary, biodegradable decor, such as flower arrangements or vine garlands.

Before you bid the holy ground *adieu,* protect it from being desecrated, littered, or logged while you're away. Circumambulate the premises ayenward, carrying a censer of burning mugwort or asafetida incense. Afterward, beat a boundary into place by intermittently tapping a staff, limb, or strong flower stalk on the ground while you intone the following rune at will.

*Around this space, great walls do rise—
to keep away all prying eyes.*

*Beneath this place, bedrock be strong—
to keep out all who would do wrong.*

*Above this space, a dome doth grow—
to bar the way of any foe.*

*Should any come, for harm or harassing—
they'll be thwarted from trespassing.*

*But if a friend should pass this way,
then they may enter straight away.*[98]

You can also use this spell to protect a forest grove, a desert cave, or another wild, sacred place from being discovered and trashed by hunters or partiers or exploited by loggers, miners, or developers.

SPELL ORIGIN: Coven Oldenwilde practice
SPELL TIMING: prior to leaving a sacred site, preferably during a new Moon
INGREDIENTS: a staff, stick, or strong stalk, a censer, charcoal, matches, and pinches of banishing incense, such as mugwort or asafetida
AMBIANCE: beating a boundary while whispering, surrounded by billowing clouds of pungent incense
MAGICAL THEORY:
   SYMPATHETIC MAGIC: Five couplets equate with the two perfect pentacles (open hands with splayed fingers)—a warding gesture. Essentially, you're

[98] *Adapted from a charm by Rowan Greenleaf.*

preventing future irreverence or desecration via the vocal equivalent of two outstretched, barring hands.

Burning pungent incense and walking ayenward dispels and banishes all onslaught.

DEITY TO INVOKE: Herne, protector of wild spaces

TO MAKE YOURSELF INVISIBLE

ADOORS AT NIGHT DURING SUMMERTIME, SHAKE A FERN FROND WITH your left hand and collect—without touching it—a seed in a silvery bowl. (You may substitute an agate stone for a fern seed.) Carry the single fern seed and when you would be invisible, whisper:

Fall free, fall free
Where none shall see
And give the same
Great gift to me.

Use the Sun's brilliance to so bedazzle others that you're effectively rendered invisible. Form into a ball a night's sleep exudate from your eyes,[99] the oil of one unripe (green) olive, and any pungent resin incense you possess. Then intone this ancient invocation:

I adjure You by Your Great Name

Borke' Phoiour
Io' Zizia
Aparxeouch Thythe Lailam
Aaaaaa Iiiii Oooo
Ieo' Ieo' Ieo' Ieo' Ieo' Ieo' Ieo'
Naunax
Ai Ai
Aeo' Aeo'
E'ao'!

[99] *The original spell recipe in PGM, I, 222–231, requires the "Fat or an Eye of a Nightowl and a Ball of Dung." Our substitute symbolizes the closed eyes of sleep.*

Anoint your entire body with the mixture, then chant:

Make me Invisible, Lord Helios
Aeo' O'ae' Eie' E'ao'
in the Presence of Any Man until Sunset

Io' Io' O'
Phrixrizo'
Eo'a!

You will be able to go about unnoticed in broad daylight.

SPELL VARIATIONS

- The Roman naturalist Pliny the Elder recorded[100] that to make themselves invisible, spellcrafters in his time paired the stone heliotrope with the herb heliotrope, and repeated over the combination "certain incantations"—perhaps the very Barbarous Words we supply above.
- During a wintry new or waning Moon, bury seven black beans in the northern direction. After ten days, dig them up and immediately test each one's magical efficacy.

    While looking in a mirror, pop every bean, one at a time, into your mouth. Discard any that do not eradicate your reflection, and keep only those that result in your desired degree of invisibility.

    Whenever you would be invisible, suck one for the duration of your need.

SPELL ORIGIN: Irish, Egyptian, and European magic

SPELL TIMING: as needed; at noon or during daylight; during a wintry new or waning Moon

INGREDIENTS: a fern frond, a silvery bowl, a single fern seed collected untouched by human hand or an agate stone; sleep exudate from your eyes, the oil of one unripe (green) olive, and any pungent incense

FOR THE VARIATION: mineral heliotrope (translucent green chalcedony

---

[100] *Agrippa,* Three Books of Occult Philosophy, *41–42.*

with crimson spots similar to bloodstone) and a pinch of the herb heliotrope; seven black beans, a spade, and a mirror

AMBIANCE: preferably alone, adoors or inside

MAGICAL THEORY:

SYMPATHETIC MAGIC: Fairies dwell amongst fern fronds. Fairies are infamous for their ability to wink at will in and out of space-time. Ferns produce small seeds, so carrying one harvested without touching it can grant you fairy-like invisibility and immunity from human attention.

An agate's quixotic swirls render possessors invisible to someone with the Evil Eye and, by extension, to everyone else as well.

To blend with the night, use dark magical ingredients and correspondences, such as black beans, burial, Moondark, and winter.

INVERSION MAGIC: What Helios, the Sun God, can reveal in the light of day, he can also conceal.

ENTITIES AND DEITY TO INVOKE: Fairies; Helios, the Greek God of the Sun

· Repulsion Spells ·

"You the shot—
but I, the aim.

You, the sneer—
but I, the tain.

You, the lunge—
but I, the chain.

You, the foe—
but I, the friend.

You, the cut—
but I, the mend.

You, the start—
but I, the end."

—LADY PASSION AND *DIUVEI

*B*ound by an ethical code to "harm none," peace-loving Pagans prefer to prevent or rebuff menace rather than to retaliate.

Repulsion spells operate by such gentle-seeming magical techniques as:

- *averting*—preventing ill luck, such as jealousy or an undesired pregnancy
- *warding*—preventing harm, such as theft, vandalism, or ritual-site desecration
- *mirroring*—reflecting negativity back onto its sender
- *unhexing*—dispelling a curse
- *banishing*—expelling something that vexes you
- *negating*—nullifying dangerous weather, geologic disaster, or imminent peril

Make no mistake, though—these thwarting spells are shrewd, and succeed *because* of their apparent subtlety.

When you initially cast them, they may feel too mild to counteract a severe attack against you or your loved ones, but patience will prove that they erode their targets' resolve as powerfully as water carves canyons.

TO DISPEL A GHOST

SOMETIMES, DEPARTED SOULS WHOSE EMOTIONAL ATTACHMENT TO the physical world remains extremely strong refuse to move on to the spirit world. They might have died abruptly, perhaps by their own hand, without resolving whatever intense obsession still holds part of their consciousness in a kind of nightmare from which they cannot awake.

So to rid yourself of such a revenant, eliminate any distracting noises. Begin banishing the entity in the area it is haunting the most, usually the attic or basement. Establish your dominance by loudly shaking a rattle, banging cooking-pot tops together, stamping your feet, and so on. Boldly address the ghost as you would an ordinary person, and command it to leave and not return until it has fully counted every drop of water, every grain of sand, and every leaf on the planet.

Because water, sand, and leaves continually recycle themselves, your demand is an innately impossible task for the apparition to fulfill. It can never arrive at a final number, so the specter dutifully departs, never to return.

SPELL VARIATIONS

- Distract a ghost while you banish it—scatter seeds, raw rice, or beans on the floor. Spirits are fascinated by such minutiae, and feel compelled to count every one.
- Help the ghost cross over to its afterlife in the Summerlands—alert chthonic psychopomps Anubis, Hermes, and Charon that they have a soul to pick up.

   If the exorcise-it-yourself spells we supply above don't permanently banish a troublesome phantom, call in a Priest/ess experienced in ghost busting who can communicate with it and coax or compel it to release its death-grip on its previous life for the bliss that lies beyond.

ORIGIN: Italian *Strega* magic and Coven Oldenwilde practice

TIMING: as needed, but preferably during daylight

INGREDIENTS: a rattle or similar noisemaker

   FOR THE VARIATIONS: seeds, raw rice, or beans

AMBIANCE: preferably in the company of witnessing, helpful friends

MAGICAL THEORY:

   INVERSION: Ghosts like to be the ones making noise, so they are oddly disturbed by it if it doesn't originate from them. To get an apparition's attention, therefore, create a loud cacophony.

DEITIES TO INVOKE: Anubis, an Egyptian Underworld God; Hermes, a Greek psychopomp (soul guide of the dead); Charon, a Greek and Etruscan Underworld escort

TO SILENCE AN INCESSANT TALKER

BORED BY LOQUACIOUS ILK IN LOVE WITH THE SOUNDS OF THEIR OWN voices? Commit the following glyph to memory, and when you would impose silence, inconspicuously doodle it or trace its pattern using your fingertip. (Don't lift your pen or finger while drawing.)

SILENCING SIGIL

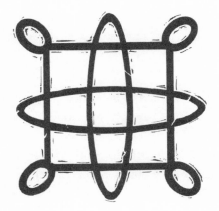

Ranters and pontificators typically cease talking within minutes. This spell silences noisy pets, too.

SPELL ORIGIN: unknown; Coven Oldenwilde practice

SPELL TIMING: as needed, although it works best when the Moon is waning or new

INGREDIENTS: a surface, pen and paper or your fingertip

AMBIANCE: amidst a crowd made restless by a droning speaker; when an incessant talker is monopolizing a conversation

MAGICAL THEORY:

SYMPATHETIC MAGIC: Tracing a continuous, convoluted knot pattern similarly ties your target's tongue in knots, and therefore prevents pontification.

MACROCOSM = MICROCOSM: Magically binding all eight directions (the Four Quarters plus the Cross Quarters) essentially gives talkers "no quarter," or no escape from silence.

The glyph itself first contains, then nullifies their speech.

TO GET RID OF UNWANTED GUESTS

FETCH YOUR BESOM OR A BROOM-PLANT BOUGH, AND BALANCE IT WITH the brush part skyward in the corner closest to the door your guests will most likely use as an exit. Although initially loath to leave, they nonetheless will within minutes. After they depart, restore your besom to its normal place and traditional, brush-down position.

Another silence spell involves appealing to Mercury to make your guests fly as if their feet had wings.

SPELL VARIATION

• Your guests will bolt as if they are barefoot on hot coals if you sprinkle down a drain a Wiccan hot-foot powder: three hot, red kitchen spices mixed together, such as cayenne pepper, chili powder, paprika, or cinnamon.

   You can also toss this powder in a yard to make someone move away, such as an obnoxious neighbor, an ex-spouse, or a stalker.

SPELL ORIGIN: European, Greek, and Voudon magic
SPELL TIMING: as needed
INGREDIENTS: a besom, a broom-plant bough, or a utility broom
   FOR THE VARIATION: three hot, red kitchen spices, such as cayenne pepper, chili powder, paprika, or cinnamon.
AMBIANCE: surreptitiously while amongst guests who have overstayed their welcome
MAGICAL THEORY:
   ANTIPATHETIC MAGIC: Because a brush-down besom implies domestic order, upending one informs the God/desses of your fatigue and need for their aid to restore tranquility.
   Although you are rubbed raw (or red) from excessive entertaining, putting red hot-foot powder down a drain quickly rids you of those who have so sorely taxed your energy.
   SYMPATHETIC MAGIC: Hot, red spices turn up the psychic heat on lazy loiterers.

TO REPEL JEALOUSY

JEALOUSY AND ENVY ARE OCCUPATIONAL HAZARDS OF SPELLCRAFT. As you become noticeably freer, stronger, more attractive, more creative, and more successful through magic and the God/desses' favor, acquaintances, co-workers, or family members may become jealous of your bliss.

To eliminate someone's spite, write the person's name on one side of a piece of green paper, and the following power-square numbers[101] on the opposite side:

666	848	938
811	544	839
111	383	839
273	774	447

Immediately burn the seal. You won't be further troubled.

SPELL VARIATIONS

- If someone's accusations or assumptions have sorely provoked your ire, thwart jealousy by wearing in the person's presence loose clothing in calming aqua, azure, or turquoise tones.
- To avert covetousness, activate the magical principle *similia similibus curantur* (like cures like)—string spherical blue lapis lazuli beads on sinew or black hemp, and suspend the dangles in your windows. (If you lack lapis, substitute similar items, such as blue wine bottles.)

These blue "eyes" will repel the Evil Eye cast by jealous folks.

SPELL ORIGIN: Latin and European magic

SPELL TIMING: at sunset on a Friday; as needed (hang ornaments after sunset)

INGREDIENTS: quill, ink, a piece of green paper, power-square numbers and a lit candle

FOR THE VARIATIONS: free-flowing blue clothing; scissors, several round lapis lazuli beads, hempen string or sinew, or blue items such as wine bottles

---

[101] *Riva,* Secrets of Magical Seals.

AMBIANCE: adoors or inside, usually alone, surrounded by becalming blue candles, amidst burning copal resin incense or its equivalent—dried, crushed pine tree sap

MAGICAL THEORY:

SYMPATHETIC MAGIC: Blue emotionally becalms others, and in *Strega* magic, repels the Evil Eye.

INVERSION MAGIC: Palestinian and Syrian women believe blue-eyed, clean-shaven men possess the Evil Eye, long associated with avarice. Because many folks' irises are colored blue, displaying blue in your windows will repel mean looks no matter what color the caster's iris is.

TO AVERT THE EVIL EYE

IN SUMERIAN TIMES, THE KINDS OF PEOPLE AUTOMATICALLY ASSUMED to possess the Evil Eye were those who were left-handed, or squinted, or had a cataract, an unusual eye color for their region, or a piercing gaze. There was more than a bit of truth to these presumptions, because folks who are physically different *do* typically possess psychic prowess; for example, many people who are "born Witches" have a "lazy eye."

The fact is, there is power in a glance, for the eyes truly are the windows of the soul. We do not simply passively take light in through our eyes—we also actively send energy out through them. Like a carrier wave, this energy communicates thought and emotion from one pair of human eyes to another, even when the additional cues of facial expression are absent, as is observable when someone wears a mask. The heart and will of the sender determine whether these soul-rays bear a blessing or a curse. The eyes of someone sane shine with a stable light noticeably absent from those of a delirious person, a soulless psychopath, or a corpse.

PIUS IX (1846–1878) AND Leo XIII (1878–1903) were both accused of the ability, and monks and priests in general were often viewed askance as possessors of the Evil Eye, as any free spirit who has been caught in the burning, condemnatory glare of a religious zealot can well understand.

Even today, most folks instinctively recoil whenever someone "shoots daggers" at them with their eyes, or studies their children or valuables with unnerving intensity. Whether popes or paupers, those who cast derisive glances abuse the normally noble mirror of the soul. Such steely-eyed stares—born of envy or longing—emanate a silent, withering curse capable of causing others real physical harm. Traditionally, being so "blinked" or "overlooked" can cause loss, illness, madness, and even death.

To avert the *mal occhio,* or Evil Eye, as you go about your daily life, carry a clove of garlic in your pocket, or a charm known to resist ill intent, such as a miniature horseshoe.

To protect your home from negativity from without, confuse malicious gazes by making a traditional talisman called a Witch's Ball:

* acquire a round transparent or slightly iridescent ornament;
* fill it with interlacing, knotted red ribbons and threads of various colors;
* display it in a window.

Burn an Evil Eye–averting incense, such as verbena, mugwort, or rue, or decorate your windows with gaze-distracting spirals and knot work.

Other magical ways to avert negativity include:

Hanging wind chimes, wearing fringe, suspending a bird's claw clutching a reflective orb from a window or two, having a frog fetish face your entrance, scattering agates around, or installing a golden, watchful Eye of Horus above your gable.

To quickly reverse the *mal occhio,* oppose contempt with your own—spit thrice in the person's general direction, or cast toward the person the appropriate magical gesture, or *gettatura.* To vex a hex with feminine force, form the *fare la fica,* or fig sign. To oppose spite with masculine might, discreetly make the *mano cornuta,* or horns sign. (See Magical Movement and Gestures, page 224.)

To nullify an ongoing curse, burn peacock feathers and scatter the ashes in a stream or river. You can also make an iron skeleton key into an amulet necklace, hold it between your eyes, and thrice softly say:

Kayn Ayn Ha'rah

SPELL VARIATIONS

* Protect newborns by decorating their rooms with any or all of the 13 symbols associated with the Italian *cimaruta* charm that traditionally protects infants:

a key
a fish
a dart
a hand
an eagle
a rooster
a serpent
a rue plant
a lotus bloom
anything silver
a horned Moon
a crescent Moon
a valentine-style heart.

(The dart should be safe, such as a rubber arrow.)

Be creative—employ paint, wallpaper, or pictures of the objects. Stuffed animals, figurines, and pets count.

- Bedeck older children's necks with coral beads and silvery bells.
- If you suspect that your child has been "overlooked," banish the Evil Eye right away. Borrow a silver coin from a neighbor, and then put it in the child's bathwater. The next morning, dress the child as usual, and make a game of turning him or her briefly upside down.
- To keep a stranger from coveting your goods, make discreet *fare la fica* signs either behind your back or in your pockets whenever you make a new acquaintance.
- The Evil Eye can affect not only the living, but inanimate objects as well. Therefore, to avoid catching penury from a previous possessor, spit thrice on your coins or bills when you first receive them.

SPELL ORIGIN: Italian herb craft; European, Irish, and Romany magic

SPELL TIMING: Avert the Evil Eye as needed; reverse it during Moonbright; banish it during Moondark.

INGREDIENTS: a clove of garlic or an Evil Eye–averting charm; a round iridescent ornament, knotted red ribbons, and variously colored threads; exorcising incense (verbena, mugwort, or rue); Evil Eye-averting decorations,

such as fringe, fetishes, agate stones, a frog statuette, or a golden Eye of
Horus symbol; peacock feathers, matches, a stream; an iron skeleton key

FOR THE VARIATIONS: 13 *cimaruta* symbols; a necklace of coral beads and
silvery bells; a silver coin borrowed from a neighbor and bathwater; spit

AMBIANCE: Although these spells are typically done alone so no one will know
all the levels of protection installed, families, friends, and roommates may
perform the spells together if desired.

MAGICAL THEORY:

ANTIPATHETIC MAGIC: Twisty, shiny, pointy, meandering, mutable, fringe-
like, dazzling, tiny, and iridescent things distract the straight-shooting
Evil Eye.

Displaying a sunny Eye of Horus thwarts a sinister Evil Eye.

LIKE CURES LIKE: An antidote for the non-verbal Evil Eye is a non-verbal
magical gesture.

DEITIES TO INVOKE: Diana Triformis, a Greek Moon Goddess; Horus, an
Egyptian Sun God

TO BANISH BAD LUCK

ON A MONDAY OR FRIDAY, NAIL A FOUND HORSESHOE TO YOUR MAIN
entrance and never let anyone touch it or take it down. Hang it points up—
tradition stipulates that only a blacksmith may hang a horseshoe with points
downward, over their forge.

Baneful spirits cannot strike with strife anything that primroses guard, so
grow the lovely flowers close to your home's entrance. Then whenever ill luck
looms, repel it by plucking one of the blooms before sunrise.

SPELL ORIGIN: traditional Irish magic

SPELL TIMING: on a Monday or Friday; when your climate permits planting
primroses

INGREDIENTS: a found horseshoe; cultivated primroses

AMBIANCE: adoors, alone or amidst family members

MAGICAL THEORY:

SYMPATHETIC MAGIC: Monday is associated with the Moon and magic, and Friday, with friendship (Witches traditionally work spells on Freya's day). Both days are auspicious for averting ill luck.

Horseshoes are sacred both because they are shaped like the crescent Moon, and because they represent an upturned cup to be filled with the God/desses' beneficence.

Medicinally, primrose is a diuretic and expectorant, so in this spell it is clearly used to magically expel ill luck.

INVERSION: Sharp, ill intent can be repelled by its own kind, or sharp things, such as rose thorns.

TO REPEL INTRUDERS

THWART INTRUDERS BY SUSPENDING AN AMULET OF AMETHYST OR chrysolite (olivine/peridot) beads near each entrance.

SPELL VARIATION

- Sprinkle red mustard seeds on the floor throughout your home.

SPELL ORIGIN: Irish and Voudon magic

SPELL TIMING: at moonrise during a waning or new Moon

INGREDIENTS: amethyst or chrysolite (olivine/peridot) beads

FOR THE VARIATION: red mustard seeds

MAGICAL THEORY:

SYMPATHETIC MAGIC: Tarot readers often put an amethyst gem chip atop their cards to prevent their theft. Amethyst confers temperance and hence, safety.

Chrysolite banishes night phantoms.

Red mustard seeds are likely an olde variation of the ingredients for the Wiccan hot-foot powder described in To Get Rid of Unwanted Guests, page 423.

DEITIES TO INVOKE: Kali Ma, a powerful, courageous Asian Indian Goddess; Jupiter Stator, "the Petrifier," an aspect of the Roman God so terrifying that he purportedly froze attackers in their tracks

TO EXPEL AN ENTITY INHABITING A DEVICE

A GHOST IN THE MACHINE — WHO HASN'T SEEN A MOVIE WITH THIS plot, heard tales of machines mysteriously acting out, or offered consolation when a friend's computer inexplicably crashed?

Machines fascinate entities, and gremlins (creatures blamed for mechanical failures) treat devices as their personal playgrounds if given half a chance. Somehow, they see such soulless golems as the perfect place in which to take up residence, as a hermit crab adopts an empty shell.

Indications that a spirit is squatting in your screen saver include: unusual noises emanating from your computer, its failure to heed your commands, undue difficulty logging onto the Internet, or a wiped hard drive.

Poltergeists also like to inhabit cars, clocks, light fixtures, mowers, appliances, radios, and many other household contraptions.

If a device performs erratically or seems broken when it shouldn't be, and you suspect that a spirit has taken up residence within it, repair the machine by laying an empty, uncorked wine bottle horizontally on a flat surface close beside it.

SPELL ORIGIN: American folk practice; traditional European Witchcraft

SPELL TIMING: as needed, although banishing works best during Moondark

INGREDIENTS: one empty, uncorked wine bottle

AMBIANCE: near your ailing or broken appliance, surrounded by purifying incense

MAGICAL THEORY:

INVERSION: The Crafter outwits the gremlin by using its curiosity against itself. The same natural inquisitiveness that compelled the entity to inhabit and impede your gadget becomes its undoing—it will crawl inside the wine bottle and remain quite content in its new home.

TO BANISH PESKY ENTITIES FROM YOUR LAND AND HOME

ALTHOUGH SOME SPIRITS THAT INHABIT PROPERTY PREDATE HUMANS, others were conjured. Both types can have so much power that they prove highly resistive to magical banishment.

Our regional Craft community has one of the former such entities. Legend credits Native Americans with having summoned a Fire elemental to guard a meadow where they held annual ceremonies to honor their dead. To the present day, folks who bide within a 5-mile radius of the pasture are routinely burned out of their homes.

When it comes to dealing with mighty spirits, it's wise to first avoid provoking their ire altogether. Instead, try to appease them and make them happy. For example, several years ago a woman phoned Coven Oldenwilde, distraught because angry red entities buzzing above a dry riverbed were suddenly menacing her country farm. Their attacks were so strident that none dared brave their onslaught long enough to empty the trash, much less plant a garden. Aware that the creatures fit the description of (normally neon blue) Will-o'-the-Wisps, Lady Passion ventured that she believed they'd turned crimson for want of water, and encouraged the caller to flood the gulch. The woman gratefully phoned back a day or two later and related that the entities duly responded by turning azure, and had already become dear family friends.

If you are pestered by creatures that spook your familiars, purchase a silver *fare la fica* or *mano cornuta* charm from a jewelry store and attach it to your pet's collar, dangle it from a birdcage, or add it to a fish tank, as the case may be.

If an entity is drying up your livestock, banish it by acquiring a horse brass[102] and suspending it adoors or wherever the entity is haunting, such as your barn or chicken coop.

If fairies are frustrating you, distribute rusted iron implements, such as candleholders, railroad spikes, and so forth around the premises.

Should you be uncertain what phenomenon you're dealing with, fumigate your surroundings with some noxious incense; then, with friends, create a

---

[102] *A charm in a traditional shape, such as a crescent or star, typically hung from a horse's tack to repel the Evil Eye.*

cacophony of noise to rout the specters. Mentally and verbally compel them to inhabit an innocuous inanimate object, such as a figurine or a closeable container.

SPELL ORIGIN: Italian, German, Celtic, and other European magic

SPELL TIMING: as needed, although such spells work best when the Moon is waning or new

INGREDIENTS: a *fare la fica* (a hand forming a sign resembling a fig) or a *mano cornuta* (a hand making the horns gesture) charm and craft wire; a horse-brass talisman and materials with which to suspend it; rusty iron items; noxious incense, charcoal, and matches; an inanimate object or closeable container

AMBIANCE: preferably with friends or family during daylight

MAGICAL THEORY: Before banishing an entity, first try to appease it by providing what it desires—a private home, food, water, attention, or whatever.

ANTIPATHETIC MAGIC: Applying a horse brass that has a traditional, protective shape such as a crescent (whose horns repel) or a star (with five averting points) protects magical familiars and livestock from pesky entities.

Legend has it that fairies fear iron because in antiquity, humans made iron weapons and forced the Fey to flee into hillocks in order to survive. Therefore, if capricious fairies plague you, scattering iron implements around will make them bolt for more-hospitable territory. Additionally, iron is ruled by Mars, and thus corresponds to hot-foot powder.

DEITY TO INVOKE: Epona, a Celtic horse Goddess

TO FORGET DISTRESSING MEMORIES

AT MIDNIGHT DURING A WANING OR NEW MOON, TAKE PARCHMENT and a pencil to circle. Create a serene setting. Smudge yourself with smoke from a burning sweetgrass braid; then burn the remainder in a censer in the Air Quarter (East). Face that direction and sit down.

Consider the memories that haunt you. List each event in detail, and why and in what ways they continue to hurt or impede you. For instance, if you've been traumatized, you might write *I was shocked,* followed by *which made me insecure.* To prevent decipherment of your private pain, skip every few letters or write in your own form of hieratic shorthand. For example, *shocked* might read *shkd* and *insecure* might read *nskur.*

When your list is complete, turn your back on the East (face West) and tear the parchment into micro-confetti. Toss the pieces into a running stream, or flush them down your toilet.

SPELL VARIATION

• Wear sweetgrass oil to assuage sad memories and initiate emotional healing.

SPELL ORIGIN: European and Voudon magic

SPELL TIMING: during the Witching Hour when the Moon is waning or new

INGREDIENTS: parchment or paper, a quill and ink or a pencil, a sweetgrass braid, and coursing or draining water

  FOR THE VARIATION: sweetgrass essential oil

AMBIANCE: supported by assuaging clouds of burning sweetgrass incense

MAGICAL THEORY:

  SYMPATHETIC MAGIC: Because memory is an intangible occurrence, it takes Air to alleviate an Airy phenomenon.

    Writing is an Airy magical act.

    Facing West, the direction of dusk, lets you put sad memories in their place (the past) and emotionally heal in the Quarter of feelings.

    Sadness corresponds to tears, and hence to the element Water; therefore, use a flowing river or draining water to take away your grief.

  ANTIPATHETIC MAGIC: Because painful memories are "dark" in nature, one way to ameliorate them is to expose them to the light of day by facing them openly in the East, the direction of dawn.

DEITY TO INVOKE: Mnemosyne, the Greek Goddess of memory

TO DISPEL INNER ANGER

ON A FRIDAY AFTER SUNSET DURING MOONDARK, CAST A CIRCLE ayenward to banish fiery Mars. Work in minimal candlelight. Begin resolving your pique by sitting or kneeling in the North Quarter of the circle. Sit on the floor for a while to ground your ire—the angrier you begin, the longer it will take to relax. Silently admit any adverse effect your anger might have had on your daily routine or magical obligations. Meditate on Mother Earth's restraint—although Hertha has cause to retaliate for the abuse she receives at humanity's hand, she rarely does so. Let her calm you with images of breathtakingly beautiful locales.

When you're less physically agitated, rise and walk ayenward to the West Quarter. Spritz a sea scent about, and allow the cooling mist to fall all over your body. If you feel compelled, cry with indignation until you can weep no more. Each time you need to banish the pain, twirl around ayenward three times. Continue the practice until your anger abates.

Walk ayenward to the origin of wrath—the South Quarter. Kneel and acknowledge how powerless the accusation or injustice has made you feel. Verbally rail about the situation until you exhaust your store of expletives and are utterly emotionally spent. Mentally review scenarios that typically enrage you. Examine your mode of reaction to help you avoid future meltdowns. Visualize yourself responding to future provocations from a stance of empowerment.

When you feel calm and strong, invoke Venus and ask her to manifest herself to you within three nights, in one of her traditional guises:[103]

> a dove
> flowers
> a camel
> a naked girl
> a female goat
> the herb savine
> a white or green garment
> a beautifully dressed maiden
> a king holding a scepter and riding a camel.

Thank Venus in advance with heartfelt terms of endearment.

You should feel more at ease at this juncture in the working, so walk ayenward to the East Quarter.

---

[103] *Agrippa,* Of Occult Philosophy, or Of Magical Ceremonies: The Fourth Book *(also known as* The Fourth Book of Occult Philosophy) *(ca. 1560; Robert Turner, trans., 1655; Twilit Grotto Esoteric Archives [**http://www.esotericarchives.com/agrippa/agrippa4.htm**]: Joseph H. Peterson, 2000). "Familiar shapes of the Spirits of Venus."*

Stand before your altar to Air and consider astrological aspects that might have contributed to the problem, such as miscommunication caused by Mercury's being retrograde, for example. Try to understand what caused your outrage. Consider rational solutions to resolve your ire. When you no longer seethe inside, ring your altar bell for a full minute, close circle, and exit the premises without a backward glance.

When the Goddess sends you an omen, recompense her care by doing an anonymous kindness for someone with whom you don't normally get along.

Spell Origin: European magic
Spell Timing: at dusk on Freya's day during Moondark
Ingredients: sea scent, a spritz bottle, list of Venus manifestations, and a bell
Ambiance: alone in your ritual room or circle adoors
Magical Theory:

Sympathetic magic: Match your magical actions with the attributes of the Four Quarters.

Ayenward movements banish.

Spraying a cooling scent becalms Fiery rage.

Repay kindness with kindness; if the Goddess vanquishes your anger, help a human do so.

In magic, an altar bell is often rung to distinguish ritual transitions, such as from working a spell itself, to enjoying the Cakes and Wine ceremony. In this spell, the bell is rung to formalize your change from inner ire to inner peace.

Deities to Invoke: Hertha, Mother Earth; Venus, the Goddess of love

TO NEGATE HATRED AIMED AT YOU

If you want to stop someone from acting hatefully toward you, work this spell for restraining their anger.[104]

Melt myrrh resin in a silver spoon over a candle flame, and use it to write this name of anger—CHNEO'M—on a piece of parchment.

[104] *Adapted from* PGM, XII, 179–181.

$$\boxed{\text{ΧΝΕΩΜ}}$$

Then hold the parchment in your left hand and say:

I am restraining the Anger of all,
especially of him, (angry person's name),
which is Chneo'm.

Chant the charm at will until you feel relieved about the situation. Close circle when you feel inclined.

SPELL VARIATION

- To stop an endless argument, use an olde spell that normally *creates* quarrels, then apply its antidote.

   In all Four Quarters, shout seven times each the following two words:

Roudmo
Pharrhua

Whisper the fighting folks' names, then exhort:

Fight, fight, Roudmo!

Lastly, assuage the anger by repeating the name in reverse:

Omduor

SPELL ORIGIN: Egyptian magic; spell variation source unknown
SPELL TIMING: as needed, but preferably on a Friday after sunset during a waning Moon
INGREDIENTS: a candle and a silvery spoon in which to melt a nickel-sized chunk of myrrh resin into ink, a quill (pen), and parchment
AMBIANCE: Perform bathed in the glow of soothing blue candles.

MAGICAL THEORY:

> **SYMPATHETIC MAGIC:** You're identifying a mad mortal with a God associated with the same emotion, and using the God's power to exorcise negativity.
>
> God/desses help those who summon them by their ancient names.
>
> **INVERSION:** You reproduce the fight, associating it with the rude name Roudmo, then reverse and end the conflict by saying the name backward.
>
> **HERBALISM:** Myrrh has purificatory and soothing qualities, which is why it helps cure toothache, too.

DEITY TO INVOKE: Chneo'm (origin uncertain)

TO UNJINX YOURSELF FROM A CURSE PLACED ON YOU

ADD ONE TEASPOON OF DRIED, CRUSHED BASIL TO YOUR BATHWATER;[105] then purge the curse down the drain.

Vexed by a potion or food additive? Dispel it by drinking tormentil tea. Steep one tablespoon tormentil in one cup of water for 30 minutes, strain, cool to tepid, and ingest by the mouthful throughout the course of a day.

Break all other hexes by scattering stinging nettle on your floors[106] or burning a pinch of African ginger, agrimony, ague weed, benzoin, betony, or bloodroot on charcoal in a censer as banishing incense.

Reverse a curse by burying a piece of Jezebel root in a jar on the sender's property, throwing several handfuls of twitchgrass into the person's yard, or nibbling a piece of chewing john root, and then casting it adoors in the direction in which the person lives.

Purify your home with an herbal brew. Go adoors, harvest a pine bough or branch of Scotch broom, and take it inside. Steep one teaspoon of angelica root in one cup of boiling water for five minutes. When the tea is tepid, submerge your aspergilum in the liquid and spurge every room (fling droplets around your premises).

---

[105] *Instead of basil, you may substitute one teaspoon of dried marjoram or curry powder to your bathwater; and instead of using conventional soap, you may lather up with the herb hyssop.*

[106] *To avoid skin irritation, sweep the plant up and away from yourself after some minutes.*

SPELL VARIATIONS

- Take prophylactic measures to prevent being jinxed:

    Fill a small necklace pouch with three, five, or nine balm of Gilead buds, a pinch of fennel seeds, or one or more devil's shoestrings, and wear the averting amulet whenever you feel malevolence loom.

- Other banishing, averting measures:

    - Burn a pinch of dill, vervain, ash leaves, or trefoil.
    - Grow garden sage near your doorways.
    - Grow bay in your kitchen.
    - Suspend St. John's wort in your windows.
    - Strew ground elderberries on your floors.

- A seventeenth-century spell that breaks hexes involves putting pins or needles and the victim's urine into a pot and boiling the lot.

SPELL ORIGIN: Voudon and European magic and herbalism

SPELL TIMING: as needed; take preventive measures during Moonbright, and unjinx during Moondark

INGREDIENTS: one teaspoon of dried basil, marjoram, curry powder, bathwater, and soap or hyssop; one tablespoon of tormentil steeped in a cup of water for 30 minutes; several handfuls of stinging nettles; a pinch of dried, powdered African ginger, agrimony, ague weed, benzoin, betony, or bloodroot, a censer, charcoal, and matches; a piece of Jezebel root and a jar, or several handfuls of twitchgrass or a chewing john root; a pine bough or Scotch broom aspergilum, one teaspoon of angelica root, and one cup of water

FOR THE VARIATIONS: a pouch filled with an odd number of balm of Gilead buds, a pinch of fennel seeds, or a piece of devil's shoestring plant; a pinch of dill, vervain, ash leaves, or trefoil, charcoal, censer, and matches; a garden sage plant; a bay pot plant; a string, tacks, and sprigs of St. John's wort; several handfuls of ground elderberries; pins or needles, urine, a pot, and a fire

AMBIANCE: alone or surrounded by supporters, maintaining calm amidst chaos

MAGICAL THEORY:

INVERSION: Sweet, benevolent herbs, basil and marjoram can nonetheless eliminate a dark hex.

Although tormentil tea sounds like it will *give* you torment, it actually soothes.

Stinging nettle can break a sharp hex using its own, needlelike projections.

Sympathetic magic: One way to remove a jinx is to let it drain away like bathwater.

Jezebel root resembles a barring hand, and twitchgrass resembles wiggling fingers—both equate with gestures for "Stop!"

TO RETURN BAD DEEDS TO THEIR ORIGINATOR

Has someone done you wrong? Defend yourself by reflecting the wrongdoer's ill intent and deeds back on himself or herself. Then the person will not only fail to harm you further, but also suffer thrice the amount of damage he or she tried to deal you.

Acquire a hinged wooden compact from a craft store. If it does not contain two opposite mirrors within, affix a couple with melted wax or resin. If you can't find a wooden version, substitute a magically de-plasticized cosmetic compact. (To de-plasticize an object, make passes over it with your left hand while mentally nullifying its negative properties.)

Before the Witching Hour during Moondark, assemble the perpetrator's personal items—hair, fingernails, a photo, or a swatch of sweat-soaked clothing. If you lack such ingredients, either make an ace of spades the wrongdoer's significator card, or translate his or her name (or as much of it as you know) into a magical script, and inscribe it in dragon's blood ink on parchment. Light black candles and cast a banishing, ayenward circle. Passionately summon the vengeance Goddesses Nemesis, Praxidike, and Andraste. Recount the culprit's baneful machinations toward you, and allow yourself to shake with righteous indignation while you relate the litany.

Place the personal items, ace, or parchment between the mirrors and forcefully close the compact. Seal it shut by dripping black candle wax around its periphery. Tightly grasp the poppet in both hands, and visualize your target being deluged with difficulty if he or she doesn't immediately cease their vendetta.

Secret the poppet in the Quarter that best suits your goal: for instance, in the East if you want an apology, in the South if you want vindication, in the West to elicit remorse, or in the North to never hear from the person again.

Pagans rarely hear a peep from wrongdoers after this rite.

SPELL ORIGIN: Coven Oldenwilde adaptation of a traditional European practice

SPELL TIMING: at midnight during the new Moon

INGREDIENTS: a hinged wooden or cosmetic compact with two interior mirrors, black candles, matches, and a wrongdoer's personal item(s), or an ace of spades or a parchment representation inscribed with a quill pen in dragon's blood ink

AMBIANCE: alone in an ayenward circle amidst minimal candlelight

MAGICAL THEORY:

CONTAGION: A body part or item that has been in intimate contact with a person retains the person's energy, and hence can be used as a poppet.

SYMPATHETIC MAGIC: Mirroring a person's representation and actions between two reflective surfaces bogs the person down with so many problems that he or she must quit attacking you, and instead deal with self-created misfortunes.

When employed in self-defense, black wax binds and constricts others to cease their counterproductive actions.

DEITIES TO INVOKE: Nemesis, an avenger Goddess; Praxidike, a Greek Goddess who blesses goodly folk and punishes bad ilk; Andraste, a Celtic vengeance Goddess

TO PREVENT PREGNANCY

ONE WAY TO PREVENT PREGNANCY IS FOR A COUPLE TO ABSTAIN FROM sex during the monthly time when the female is most likely to conceive. To know at a glance when she's most fertile, make, wear, and use an anti-pregnancy bracelet that beautifully, discreetly tracks her menstrual cycles.

Acquire 28 similarly sized beads in the colors listed below—large-holed "pony beads" are goodly. On a Friday at midnight during a waning or new Moon, assemble them and the rest of your ingredients and cast an ayenward circle.

On a length of red hemp or satin cord or craft "memory wire," string the following in the order specified:

> 1 crimson bead
> 7 rust-colored beads
> 11 fluorescent beads
> 9 dark pink beads

Each bead represents a day in an average woman's monthly menstrual cycle.

The crimson bead represents your pivotal first day of flow, and therefore represents a de-facto negative pregnancy test result. As you thread this bead, visualize yourself not getting pregnant in the foreseeable future.

The rust-colored beads signify the rest of your menstrual cycle, or the other days of the month when you're probably not pregnant. While you string these, strive to appreciate the merits of your monthly Moontime. Recognize that menstrual weight gain and pain are negligible compared to that attendant with pregnancy.

The fluorescent beads glow in the dark as a glaring reminder of when you're most fertile, and therefore are most vulnerable to getting pregnant. When attaching this set, vow to routinely abstain from intercourse throughout the time when you're most likely to conceive.

The dark pink beads denote your body's preparation for another menstrual cycle, characterized by a thickening of the vaginal walls. As you thread this final section, visualize yourself exercising caution during this time when you remain vulnerable to conception.

Together, the fluorescent and dark pink sections represent the days when the traditional "blanket rule" means of pregnancy prevention applies, wherein a woman abstains from sex from the ninth through the 19th day after her Moontime begins.

When you've strung all the beads, secure them by tying the two ends of the hemp or cord together, or fashioning a loop-and-knot closure if you're using memory wire. To cement the formula in your mind, thrice articulate aloud the bead sets' meanings (feel free to write them down and refer to your "cheat sheet" as needed).

Identify the bead that indicates your present position in your monthly cycle, and tightly tie a small piece of black goat leather or rolled sinew around the middle of it. If you're unsure about exactly where you are in your menstrual cycle, wait to calibrate your bracelet until the first day of your next period. Don your bracelet and dispel the circle.

Plot your cycles by moving the black marker once a day to the next appropriately colored bead in line.

SPELL VARIATION

- Sew pebbles into the hems of your clothing.
- A traditional herbal precoitus preventive is to brew into a tea equal amounts of dried parsley, sage, rosemary, and thyme, and cool until the liquid is tepid. Use the liquid as a vaginal douche before intercourse.[107] (If this foursome sounds familiar, it's because the herbs are prominently featured in the English folk song made famous by Simon and Garfunkel. "Going to Scarborough Fair" is an olde euphemism for making love.)
- This olde herbal contraceptive purports to prevent pregnancy for a year at a time.

    Procure the following liquid ingredients.[108]

    4 drams (1 tablespoon U.S.)[109] *Embelia ribes*
    2 drams (½ tablespoon U.S.) *Ferula asafetida*
    4 drams (1 tablespoon U.S.) *Piper longum*
    4 drams (1 tablespoon U.S.) borax

---

[107] *Parsley is an* emmenagogue *(a substance that promotes menstruation), and sage has been used to treat* dysmenorrhea *(painful menstruation).*

[108] *C. K. Atal, U. Zutshi, and P. G. Rao, "Scientific evidence on the role of Ayurvedic herbals on bioavailability of drugs," abstract, (National Library of Medicine, 1981). Embelia ribes (also called vavding) leaves, berries, and root bark prevent embryonic implantation. By increasing the iron in the bloodstream, Ferula asafetida can promote a miscarriage. The trikatu acid in Piper longum (long pepper) increases E. ribes's and F. asafetida's effectiveness by increasing a woman's ability to absorb them. Borax, derived from boron, an earthen deposit 12 to 18 million years old, makes women's uterine pH inhospitable to an embryo.*

[109] *An ancient apothecary measurement, the dram equates to ⅛ of an ounce.*

In the proportions listed in the recipe, transfer the liquids to a separate bottle, label and date the contents, then ingest it in equally divided doses for 22 days while abstaining from sex.

- For a morning-after herbal remedy, prepare in advance a high-proof alcohol extract of dried *Ferula asafetida* or *Ferula jaeschikaena*. Transfer the liquid into a dark, tincture-style bottle, and then store it away from light. After 21 days, ingest some within three days of lovemaking.

Spell Origin: traditional folk practices and herbalism

Spell Timing: on a Friday at the Witching Hour during a waning or new Moon

Ingredients: red hemp or satin cord or craft "memory wire," 28 similarly sized beads (see color and number requirements above), a small piece of black goat leather or rolled sinew, and scissors

For the variations: pebbles, a needle, and thread; water, a teakettle, equal amounts of dried parsley, sage, rosemary, thyme, and a douche bulb; four drams of *Embelia ribes, Piper longum,* and borax, and two drams of *Ferula asafetida*; high-proof alcohol (vodka, for example), *Ferula asafetida* or *Ferula jaeschikaena,* and a dark container

Ambiance: amidst candlelight in your ritual area, or in your kitchen or sewing room

Magical Theory:

Sympathetic magic: The colors of the beads correspond to the different stages of the menstrual cycle, and are a visual cue to prevent undesired pregnancy.

Inversion: Pebbles in a hem resemble babes in a womb, tricking your body into believing you're already pregnant. To prevent redundancy, your body will prevent you from becoming truly pregnant.

TO STOP GALE, HAIL, FIRE, LIGHTNING, FLOOD, AND QUAKE

DON'T UNDERESTIMATE YOUR ABILITY TO WORK WICKED WEATHER magic—in times of peril your magical might is as magnified as folks' physical strength is when a loved one is trapped under a car. Weather-working spells can save your rite, your property—even your life. They depend greatly on Witches' knowledge of Quarter correspondences and their command of the Four Elements. Two effective ways to ward off meteorological disaster are by making Witch's Bottles and working with Quarter altars.

WITCH'S BOTTLES

Avert bad weather and natural disasters in advance by warding the four corners of your property with traditional Witch's Bottles. After sunset during a new Moon, spit into four bottles 3 to 5 inches in height. Then add several handfuls of table salt and as many pins, needles, thumbtacks, nails, glass shards, or other sharps as will fit. Cap and then seal the bottles by dripping black candle wax around the part where their corks or screw tops connect with the glass. Bury each bottle at one of the extreme points that mark the farthest corners of your land.

If one ever works its way back up into view, you're susceptible to that direction's attributes, so rebury it immediately. For example, if the bottle in the East Quarter rises, it portends a tornado or wind damage. If the bottle in the South erupts, it presages a fire or lightning. Should the bottle in the West float to the surface, beware of flood. The North bottle's emergence presages a mudslide or an earthquake.

QUARTER ALTARS

We describe how to create Quarter altars in Spellwork Rules of Thumb, page 258. Having four altars[110] in your home dedicated to the Four Elements is inexpensive magical insurance that can protect you from having to collect on the high-priced mundane variety.

When dangerous weather rages adoors, either appease the offending element at its corresponding altar, or propitiate an element with opposite qualities. For instance, if lightning menaces you, either placate Fire in the South

---

[110] *One in each of the Four Directions (East, South, West, and North). Mind that if you bide in the Southern Hemisphere, your North and South altars should be reversed.*

Quarter, or appeal for calm from its opposite direction, the North Quarter. Either way, the weather will speedily abate and spare your home.

If a howling windstorm such as a hurricane or tornado approaches, offer burning incense to the Air in the East Quarter. Also offer incense to the specific wind itself by name: Eurus blows in from the East, Notus from the South, Zephyrus from the West, and Boreas from the North.

When damaging hailstorms strike, we run adoors and scoop up three sizable hailstones, hurry down to our West altar and offer them to the element Water by dropping them into a silver bowl of water we always keep filled there. The hail promptly abates and is gone by the time the stones finish melting.

To avert wildfire, elicit several elements' aid. First, verbally acknowledge Fire's might and beg its mercy. Then use your Witchy will to compel the wind to blow the flames away from your house. Lastly, conjure an immediate deluge of rain.

A traditional Craft constraint during lightning storms is to avoid sharps and reflections, an in the mnemonic Lady Passion devised: "Hide your shears and cover your mirrors when Zeus appears."

But the following spell boldly challenges the thunderbolt God with a sharp of your own: When lightning looms, run to the highest place in your home, stick a knife into a loaf of bread, and spin the two on the floor. Another way to avert lightning is to hold a pietersite stone in your left hand.

Our three-story covenstead sits atop a hill, so it attracts an inordinate amount of lightning. We've learned to run to our ritual room when thunder threatens and light a red candle or two on our South altar. The fiery bolts don't manifest themselves, and the storm passes swiftly overhead. If you do this, you will feel and practically hear its sulky disappointment in having been denied the opportunity to terrorize your territory.

To stop a flash flood, light a red candle in the South and ask Fire to dry it up, or light a green or brown candle in the North and ask plants or dirt to soak up the dangerous deluge.

To calm a quake, prepare for a temblor in advance. First, determine which is the structurally safest ground floor or basement room where you bide. (So much the better if it's already your basement ritual room.) Set up and dedicate an Earth altar there against the North wall. It doesn't matter how big or small it is—a brick with a green stone atop will suffice. Then if a quake shakes, make your way there if you can, and with your will as well as your hands, hold onto either the corners of the altar or both sides of the floor beneath it. If you can't get there in time, mentally envision yourself doing it.

SPELL VARIATIONS

- To protect your home from lightning damage, suspend coral in your windows.
- To protect yourself from being struck by lightning, wear a malachite or carry a garnet.
- Gypsies insist that a lightning strike leaves behind a garlic smell, so the next time you want to stop a strike, hang cloves of garlic about to fool the flash into believing it's already wreaked havoc in your realm.

SPELL ORIGIN: European, Etruscan, and Slavic magic

SPELL TIMING: as needed, but preferably after dark during a new Moon; bury Witch's Bottles after sunset

INGREDIENTS: several handfuls of table salt, spit, assorted sharps, four closeable bottles, a black candle, and matches; three to five hailstones and a bowl of water on a West altar; a boleen and loaf of bread; a pietersite stone; one or two red candles and matches; a red candle, a South altar, or a green or brown candle and a North altar, and matches; a low area where you bide, such as a basement, and a North altar

  FOR THE VARIATIONS: coral, thread, and tacks; a malachite or garnet; cloves of garlic and hempen hanging string

AMBIANCE: Perform calmly, either adoors or inside.

MAGICAL THEORY:

  ANTIPATHETIC MAGIC: Table salt is a quiet Earth element used to prevent boisterous weather.

  MACROCOSM = MICROCOSM: Calling a wind by its proper (olde) name affords you control over it.

  As you stabilize the Earth altar, so you stabilize the entire Earth.

  LIKE CURES LIKE: The striations of malachite and pietersite resemble lightning, which tricks thunderbolts into assuming you've already been struck. Spit signifies you.

  Sharps oppose violent weather with "sword points" of their own.

DEITIES AND ENTITIES TO INVOKE: Zeus, a Greek thunderbolt God; Jandra, a Slavic God of lightning; the Four Directional Winds: Eurus, Notus, Zephyrus, and Boreas

TO AVERT IMMINENT, LIFE-THREATENING PERIL

SAVE YOURSELF FROM CERTAIN DEATH[111] BY SCATTERING A HANDFUL OR so of white sesame seeds and thrice intoning:

Askei Kataskei
Ero'n Oreo'n
Io'r Mega Samnye'r
Baui Phobantia Semne'

SPELL VARIATION

- To prevent sudden accidental death, carry a piece of rattlesnake root in a purple flannel bag.

SPELL ORIGIN: Egyptian, Etruscan, and Voudon magic
SPELL TIMING: before or during imminent peril
INGREDIENTS: a handful of white sesame seeds
  FOR THE VARIATION: a piece of rattlesnake root in a purple flannel bag
AMBIANCE: calm amidst chaos
MAGICAL THEORY:
  SYMPATHETIC MAGIC: Small scattered seeds confuse big dangers—Death doesn't know what to kill first, so this buys you time to escape.
  MURPHY'S MAGIC: Snakes that have been bitten by another snake in battle crawl away and eat rattlesnake root to survive the poison. Because a rattlesnake bite can kill you, carrying its antidote can magically prevent you from being bitten and, by extension, protect you from other forms of sudden death.
DEITY TO INVOKE: Appeal for help from Aradia, a deified Italian Witch renowned for having cheated death.

[111] PGM, *LXX, 4–19.*

GLOSSARIES

MAGICAL AND MEDICINAL HERBS

Witches use some plants in healing spells because of the magical correspondences they're associated with, and other plants because of the medicinal properties they possess. Sometimes, we choose plants that provide a combination of both virtues.

Generally, you can use any proportion or part of an herb as a spell ingredient to produce a magical effect. Plants' medicinal potency, however, is relative to the density of the part used, and is most concentrated in their root, bulb, stalk, bark, and seeds. Medicinal spells require a specific amount and part of an herb to produce a chemical effect in the body through inhalation, topical absorption, or ingestion.

Before working with any herb, thoroughly familiarize yourself with its magical and medicinal properties. To avoid contact allergies while harvesting, drying, and working with plants, you may elect to wear gloves on your hands and a bandanna over your mouth.

Although Witches sometimes concoct precisely measured potions, we typically prefer to use pinches, handfuls, or equal amounts of herbal ingredients. A pinch is usually anywhere from $1/8$ to $1/4$ of a teaspoon. Contrary to what you might think, a handful doesn't describe the maximum amount you can possibly hold without spilling or grasp without dropping—it's a lesser quantity akin to a heaping palmful. Equal amounts or equal parts of herbs are those needing to be divided into identical portions before mixing. For instance, if a recipe dictates that you use equal parts of two different herbs, you'd measure equal amounts of each to make 100 percent of your brew. If a recipe specifies three different herbs in equal amounts, you'd make each herb $1/3$ of the total mixture; if the formula called for four different herbs, you'd divide them into four equal portions, and so on.

The following is an alphabetized roster of the common and scientific names of the flowers, oils, resins, seeds, and herbal ingredients specified in this book's spells.

Words in parentheses without quotation marks denote the real or primary common name of a plant that is often confused with another name or species.
Words in parentheses with quotation marks indicate secondary common or folk names for a plant.

A

African ginger (black ginger, race ginger)—*Zingiber officinale*

agrimony (sticklewort, cockleburr)—*Agrimonia eupatoria*

ague weed (boneset, antimony)—*Eupatorium perfoliatum*

alfalfa (purple medic)—*Medicago sativa*

all-heal (woundwort)—*Prunella vulgaris*

allspice (pimento)—*Pimenta officinalis*

angelica (American, European garden, or wild species)—*Angelica atropurpurea, A. archangelica,* or *A. sylvestris*

apple—*Pyrus malus*

asafetida (food of the Gods)—*Ferula foetida, F. assa-foetida,* or *F. jaeschikaena*

ash tree—*Fraxinus americana*

aster (sky blue variation)—*Aster azueus*

B

balm of Gilead (balsam poplar buds)—*Populus candicans*

balsam—A name given to various trees that yield an aromatic resin high in benzoic acid, cinnamic acid, or both, or their esters.

bamboo (river cane)—Cold-hardy species include *Phyllostachys rubromarginata, P. viridis, P. vulgaris Houseou, P. vivax,* or *P. vivax Aureocaulis.*

basil—*Ocimum basilicum*

bay (laurel)—*Laurus nobilis*

bayberry (wax myrtle)—*Myrica cerifera*

benzoin resin—*Styrax benzoin*

betony (lousewort, wood betony)—*Stachys officinalis*

bindweed (wild jalap/sweet potato vine)—*Ipomoea pandurata*: For poppet-binding, hand crafts, or construction purposes, you may use any species of strong, pliant vine, such as ivy or honeysuckle. Although a common name for morning glory is bindweed, its stem fragility relegates it to naught

but decorative or other magical purposes.

black candle tobacco—probably *Nicotinana rustica L.* ("wild Aztec"), *Nicotiana attenuata* ("coyote tobacco'), or *Lobelia inflata L. (*"Indian tobacco")—For magical purposes, you may twist any variation of dried tobacco leaf into a cylinder shape with your fingers and burn it as a candle.

bladderwrack—*Fucus vesiculosus L.*

bloodroot—*Sanguinaria canadensis*

bluebell (Hyacinth)—*Hyacinthoides non-scriptus*

buchu—*Barosma betulina*

buckhorn brake (fern)—*Osmunda regalis*

bugloss—probably *Echium vulgare (*viper's bugloss), which both repels serpents and cures snakebite, or *Borago officinalis* (borage)

buttercup—*Ranunculus bulbosus*

C

calendula—*Calendula officinalis*

cascara sagrada (buckthorn, cascara)—*Rhamnus purshinana*

cassia—bark from the evergreen tree *Cinnamomum cassia*

catnip—*Nepeta cataria*

cayenne—*Capsicum frutescens*

chamomile—*Anthemis nobilis* or *Matricaria chamomilla*

chelkbei—possibly *Chelidonium minus* (small celandine, pilewort, or figwort)

chewing john root—see GALANGAL

China rose (radish)—*Rosa roxburghii* or *Raphanus sativus*

cinnamon—*Cinnamomum zeylanicum*

clove—*Caryophyllus aromaticus* or *Syzygium aromaticum*

clover, wild or red species—see TREFOIL

coltsfoot (coughwort, foal's-foot)—*Tussilago farfara*

COMFREY (bruisewort, knitback)—
Symphytum officinale

COPAL RESIN (dammar)—*Agathis dammara*
(pine tree sap)

COSTUS ROOT—*Saussurea lappa*

CYPRESS (cypress pine, bald cypress, China
fir)—*Cupressus callitus, C.
Juniperaceae,* or *C. Taxodiaceae*

D

DAISY, wild—*Bellis perennis;* see also
GOLDEN DAISY

DAMASK ROSE—*Rosa damascena*

DANDELION—*Taraxacum officinale*

DEVIL'S SHOESTRING (hobblebush, cramp
bark, black haw)—*Viburnum alni-
folium, V. opulus,* or *V. prunifolium*

DILL—*Anethum graveolens*

DOVE'S BLOOD INK—possibly refers to a
preparation made from freshly dried
dove's foot or cranesbill *Geranium
maculatum;* available from occult
suppliers

DRAGON'S BLOOD—*Daemomoprops draco*

E

ECHINACEA (purple coneflower)—
Echinacea angustifolia

ELDER, American, black, red, or dwarf
species—To break a fever, use
Sambucus canadensis, S. niger, or
S. racemosa; to treat burns, use
Sambucus ebulus or *S. canadensis.*

ELDERBERRY (American elder) *Sambucus
canadensis*

EUCALYPTUS—*Eucalyptus globulus*

F

FENNEL—*Foeniculum vulgare*

FERN, female, male, buckhorn brake, or
cinnamon species—*Polypodium
vulgare, Dryopteris filixmas, Osmunda
regalis,* or *O. cinnamomea*

FEVERFEW—*Chrysanthemum parthenium*

FEVERWEED—*Gerardia pedicularia*

FRANGIPANI (lei flower)—*Plumeria
frangipani*

FERULA—*F. sumbul* (anti-spasmodic/
nervine), *F. foetida* (incense), or *F. assa-
foetida* and *F. jaeschikaena* (inhibit
embryonic implantation)

G

GALANGAL (CHEWING JOHN ROOT)—*Alpinia
galanga*

GARLIC—*Allium sativum*

GINGER—See AFRICAN and JAMAICAN
GINGER

GOLDEN DAISY (chrysanthemum)—
Chrysanthemum leucanthemum or
Bellis perennis (English daisy, particu-
larly the yellow blossom variety)

GOLDENSEAL—*Hydrastis canadensis*

GRAVELROOT (Queen of the Meadow)—
Eupatorium purpureum

GROUND IVY—*Nepeta hederacea*

GOLD COIN GRASS (Chinese)—*Herba lysi-
machiae*

H

HAZEL (hazel alder, birch, red gum, sweet
gum)—*Alnus serrulata; Betula alnus;
B. serrulata; Hamamelis viginiana L.,*
variety *orbiculata* Nieuland; or
Liquidambar styraciflua L., variety
mexicana Oersted

HEATHER—*Calluna vulgaris*

HELIOTROPE—*Heliotropium peruviana*

HEMP—any variety of *Cannabis sativa*
stalk fibers that have been made into
string or rope

HIGH JOHN THE CONQUEROR ROOT—
Ipomoea jalapa—Legend attributes the
name of this herb to the son of an
African king who was captured as a
slave, but ever resisted subservience.

He displayed trickster-God properties, such as feigning stupidity when he actually knew all, and so on.

I

IRISH MOSS—*Chondrus crispus*

IRONWEED—*Vernonia fasiculata*

IVY—American species *Parthenocissus quinquefolia*

J

JAMAICAN GINGER—*Zingiber officinale*

JEWELWEED—*Impatiens aurea, I. biflora,* or *I. Noli-me-tangere* (European touch-me-not variety)

JEZEBEL ROOT (orchid, fuchsia)—possibly any *Dactylorhiza* species; a species of fuchsia—see also LUCKY HAND ROOT

JUNIPER—*Juniperus communis*

K

KAVA (kava kava root)—*Piper methysticum*

KHUS KHUS—(vertiver)—*Vertiveria zizanioides*

L

LAUREL—see BAY

LAVENDER—*Lavandula vera* or *L. officinalis*

LICORICE—*Glycyrrhiza glabra*

LIGNUM ALOES—*Aquilaria agallocha*

LILAC—*Syringa vulgaris;* an ornamental plant

LINSEED (FLAX)—*Linum usitatissimum*

LOVAGE ROOT—*Levisticum officinale*

LUCKY HAND ROOT (salep root, wild male orchid, saloop, putty root orchid)— any species of *Dactylorhiza* that produces a root resembling a hand with many fingers—see JEZEBEL ROOT

M

MANDRAKE (MANDRAGORA, SATAN'S APPLE)—*Mandragora officinarum,* whose poisonous root resembles a human being and was said to scream when pulled from the ground

MARJORAM (oregano)—*Origanum majorana* or *O. vulgare*

MARSHMALLOW—*Althaea officinalis*

MASTIC—aromatic resin from the mastic tree *Pistacia lentiscus*

MILFOIL—*Achillea millefolium;* also called YARROW

MIMOSA—*Mimosa fragrifolia*

MINT—*Mentha spicata, M. crispa,* or *M. aquatica*—see also PEPPERMINT

MISTLETOE, European or American species—*Viscum album* or *Phoradendron flavescens*

MORNING GLORY (bindweed)—*Ipomea purpurea;* see true BINDWEED species

MUGWORT—*Artemisia vulgaris*

MULLEIN—*Verbascum thapsus, V. thapsi-forme,* or *V. phlomoides*

MUSTARD SEEDS—White mustard seeds from *Brassica hirta* are actually yellow in color. For red mustard seeds, you may use those of either *Armoracia rusticana* (horseradish), *Brassica rapa* (turnip, Chinese cabbage, or Chinese mustard), *B. raphanus* (mustard radish), Russian red kale, or *Alliaria petiolata* (garlic mustard).

MYRRH—*Commiphora myrrha*

MYRTLE—To attract love, plant *Rhodomyrtus tomentosa* (Rose myrtle variety). For lunar incense, use leaves from any variety of the genus *Myrtus,* such as *M. communis.*

N

NARCISSUS (daffodil or jonquil)—*Narcissus princeps, N. jonquilla,* or *N. odorus*

NETTLE, dwarf or stinging species—*Urtica urens* or *U. dioica*

NIGHTSHADE, black, deadly species— *Solanum nigrum*

NUTMEG—*Myristica fragrans*

O

OAK, white or English species—*Quercus alba* or *Q. robur*

OLIVE OIL—*Olea europaea*

ONION—*Allium cepa*

OREGANO (wild marjoram)—*Origanum majorana* or *O. vulgare*

ORRIS ROOT—*Iris florentina*

P

PANSY—*Viola tricolor*

PAPRIKA—*Capsicum annuum L.*

PARSLEY—*Petroselinum sativum*

PASSION FLOWER—*Passiflora incarnata*

PATCHOULI—*Pogostemon patchouli*

PEPPERMINT—*Mentha piperita*

PETUNIA—any species of *Solanaceae petunia*

PINE—*Pinus heterophylla, P. strobus,* or *P. alba*

PIPER LONGUM (long pepper, hirda)—*Terminalia chebula*

POKEWEED BERRIES—*Phytolacca americana*

POPPY (red, garden)—*Papauer rhaeus*

PRIMROSE—*Primula officinalis*

R

RATTLESNAKE ROOT (lion's foot)—*Prenanthes alba*

RED EYEBRIGHT—*Euphrasia officinalis*

RED MUSTARD SEEDS—see MUSTARD SEEDS

RIVER CANE—see BAMBOO

ROSE—*Rosa* species, that is *Rosa* followed by a specific species name, such as *californica, centrifolia, eglanteria, gallica,* or *laevigata,* and so on—any species of hibiscus is a default magical substitute for rose.

ROSEMARY—*Rosmarinus officinalis*

RHUBARB—*Rhubarb officinale* or *Rheum palmatum*

RUE—*Ruta graveolens*

S

SAFFLOWER OIL—*Cathamus tinctorius*

SAFFRON—*Crocus sativus*

SAGE (garden)—*Salvia officinalis*

SALTPETER—Potassium nitrate (KNO_3) forms naturally in warm climates through bacterial action during the decomposition of vegetable refuse and excreta. It is available in bleached, white powdered form from occult suppliers. Saltpeter is flammable, so it is often used as a base for incense.

SANDALWOOD—*Santalum album*

SANICLE (snakeroot)—*Sanicula marilandica* or *S. europaea;* also refers to senega snakeroot (*Polygala senega*)

SASSAFRAS—*Sassafras albidum*

SAVINE—*Juniperas Sabina* or *Sabina cacumina*

SCOTCH BROOM—*Cytisus scoparius*

SESAME (white or black)—To magically unjinx a man's nature or avert imminent peril, use *Sesamum luteum.* For medicinal healing recipes, black sesame (*Sesame indicum*) is the most efficacious variety of this herb species.

SKULLCAP (scullcap)—*Scutellaria lateriflora*

SLIPPERY ELM BARK—*Ulmus fulva*

SNAKEROOT—see SANICLE

SOW THISTLE—*Sonchus oleraceus*

ST. JOHN'S WORT—*Hypericum perforatum*

STAR ANISE—*Illicium anisatum* or *I. verum*

STORAX—aromatic resin obtained from the tree *Liquidambar orientalis*

SWEETGRASS (sweet flag)—*Acorus calamus*

T

TEA TREE OIL—*Melaleuca alterniflora*

THYME—*Thymus vulgaris*

TOBACCO—*Nicotiana tabacum;* a default offering to the Gods.

TORMENTIL—*Tormentilla erecta* or *Potentilla tormentilla*

TREFOIL (wild or red clover)—*Trifolium pratense*

TULIP—To attract love, grow any of the following varieties listed in descending order of magical efficacy: *Tulipa Candida suave rubentibus oris* (blush-colored), *T. Bulbifera* (bulbous stalked, which resembles an erect penis), *T. media sanguinea albis oris* (apple bloom), *T. miniata* (vermillion), or *T. rubra amethistina* (bright red).

TWITCHGRASS—*Agropyron repens*

V

VALERIAN—*Valeriana officinalis* or *V. edulis*

VAVDING—*Embelia ribes*

VERBENA (blue, vervain)—*Verbena officinalis L.* or *V. littoralis*

VERTIVER (khus khus)—*Vertiveria zizanioides*

VERVAIN (blue verbena)—*Verbena hastata*

VIOLET (garden)—*Viola adorata*

W

WAX MYRTLE—see BAYBERRY

WILLOW (white, purple)—For dowsing or divination, use *Salix alba;* to reduce fever, use *S. purpurea.*

WOAD—*Ivatis tinctoria*

Y

YARROW (milfoil)—*Achillea millefolium*

COMMON CRAFT TERMS

Crafters use many olde words and phrases in modern parlance.

A

ASPERGING—see SPURGING

ASPERGILUM—a bough or flowers or similar tool dipped in scented water and flicked around to bless, purify, or cleanse someone or a sacred space

ATHAMÉ—a magical knife, usually double-edged and with a black hilt. Use only to direct magical energy, never to cut or pierce physical objects.

AYENWARD—against the Sun; counter-clockwise (widdershins) in the Northern Hemisphere, clockwise (deosil) in the Southern Hemisphere; opposite of sunwise. Witches move ayenward in circle only to banish or oppose something, and when celebrating the Samhain Sabbat.

B

BANE—anything harmful or potentially so, such as a toxic plant, a malefic person or spirit, or negative influences

BANISH—to magically dismiss, repulse, or nullify negative energy, baneful influences, or unwanted thoughts or occurrences

BESOM—a magic broom traditionally composed of Scotch broom bristles and a willow handle, lashed together with ash bark strips; used by Crafters in prosperity spells, to leap over after being Handfasted, to promote fertility, to clean ritual space, and so on

BLESSED BE!—a traditional Craft blessing said in greeting and when bidding someone farewell

BOLINE—a utility knife with a straight or curved blade and a white hilt. Used to harvest herbs, cut spellwork and handicraft components, bigrave candles, and so forth.

BOOK OF SHADOWS—an olde, sacred, written collection of spells and occult practices traditionally handed down through generations and given to Witches after initiation and elevations. Some Crafters copy the Book of Shadows in their own handwriting. It is often bound and kept wrapped in black silk when not being consulted.

BOON—a request, wish, or favor sought from or granted by a God/dess

BURNING TIMES—centuries of state- and church-sponsored religious persecution of Pagans resulting in forced conversion, property loss, torture, and death by pyre (or other brutal methods) for hundreds of thousands, possibly millions, of people

C

CALLING—summoning the presence or aid of an existing element, elemental, entity, or natural force through words, song, music, or dance

CASTING—delineating a sacred circle prior to doing a working to create a magically protective boundary

CENSER—a fireproof bowl or container, often half-filled with dirt or sand, used for burning resin or incense

CENSING—fumigating with incense. Tools are censed to consecrate them before spellwork, people are often censed to bless them before rites, and areas are censed to bless them or banish negativity.

CHARGING—magically imbuing something with increased power by exposing it to an element, or blessing it with a Craft tool. An Elder or High Priest/ess may "charge," or bid, others to a task, such as keeping a rite secret.

CONE OF POWER—a vortex of magical energy typically raised by fast circle dancing

CONJURING—magically creating a previously non-existent entity or manifestation through spellwork

CORRESPONDENCES—things that have an affinity for, antipathy against, or an interaction with other things in a predictable way based on natural laws and occult rules. The Art of Correspondences is the theory Witches employ to help them select appropriate spell ingredients to cause intended magical effects.

COVEN—a group of no fewer than three, and no more than 13 Witches led by a High Priestess, High Priest, or both, who work with nature to aid humanity

COVENSTEAD—a coven's base; where the coven meets to do spellwork; often a High Priest/ess's home

CRAFT COMMUNITY—all magical folk in the broadest sense, but more commonly, people you circle with or consider allies, such as covenmates; area Witches; Pagans in your town, region, country, or on your continent; folks of like mind on the Internet; and friends you make at gatherings

CROSSING OVER—when a spirit crosses from this world to the afterlife; dying

D

DEOSIL—clockwise (see **SUNWISE**)

DIVINATION—Fortelling future events

DIVINING—using a magical tool, scrying something, or observing omens to intuit future events; includes practices such as chiromancy (reading palms), tasseography (tea leaves), reading tarot cards or runes, and myriad other methods; doing divination

DING-DING DARLING—see POPPET

DOWSING—swinging a pendulum, holding a willow branch split half way down, or using a pair of dowsing rods to psychically determine someone or something's location, such as a missing person, underground water, or a lost object

E

ESBAT—a Craft meeting when spellwork is done, usually during a full or new Moon

F

FAMILIAR—an animal with innate ability to help in spellwork and/or divine the past, present, or future; a pet trained by a Witch to work magic

FETCH—a mentally formed, then magically animated entity used to protect or harass

FOUR ELEMENTS—Fire, Air, Water, Earth; all life-forms require at least one; inherent in everything from the composition of planets and cells, to sub-atomic particles

G

GATHERING—typically, a Sabbat celebration attended by multiple covens, diverse Pagan groups, and many solitary magical practitioners; often involves days of communal camping, workshops, and a main ritual in which all participate

GREEN MAN—a foliate God associated with vegetation or forests who represents the masculine side of nature

GREEN-MANNING—a rite-of-passage ceremony to signify or commemorate a Pagan or Wiccan teenage boy's attainment of maturity, either sexual or magical. The candidate may be sent on a short wilderness quest, perform magical feats as bidden, or start and maintain a ritual fire to prove himself worthy. If he passes his test(s), he's often rewarded with gifts to mark the occasion.

GREENWOODING—a Wiccan word for the mating of a couple in the forest; a natural result of Sabbatic bliss

H

HANDFASTING—an olde method of trial marriage; a Pagan ceremony wherein a couple's hands are bound together symbolizing their commitment. Such unions are considered goodly for a year and a day, when the pair may renew their vows, or part as friends in a Handparting ceremony.

HANDPARTING—a Pagan ceremony wherein a Handfasted couple amicably sever their bond, but vow to remain friends and help each other when in need; often involves cutting or burning the ribbon-wrapped vine that bound their wrists together symbolizing their troth during the original Handfasting rite

L

LADY—an olde term for the Goddess; a term of endearment and respect either appended before a High Priestess's magical name, or used in lieu of it. Coven Oldenwilde's High Priestess's Craft name is Passion, but covenmates may refer to her as Lady Passion, the Lady, Lady, or Milady.

LINEAGE—the Wiccan form of a family tree listing the magical and coven names of your Line's High Priestesses in descending order back to the original Lady who spawned your tradition

(Gardnerian lineage dates from 1071); helpful in tracking the growth of the Craft and exposing posers who claim traditional degrees

LINE—the specific branch of Wiccan tradition into which you were initiated. Coven Oldenwilde is of the California Line of Gardnerian Witchcraft from Great Britain.

M

MAGIC—ancient mystical methods Witches use to intentionally apply spirituality and affect a current or future event

MANIFEST—to attract, create, or materialize something into tangibly appearing through magical work and will. When magical Beings manifest themselves, everyone around can sense, see, or hear them.

MOONBRIGHT—the half of the lunar month when the Moon is full or waxing (bright in the night sky)

MOONDARK—the half of the lunar month when the Moon is new or waning (dark in the night sky)

MOONTIME—the time in the month when women menstruate; the term for the ceremony honoring a newly menstruating Pagan girl; can also refer to when the Moon appears and Witches meet (at night)

MUNDANE—non-magical; anything conventional or ordinary, such as jobs, bills, or birth names

P

PAGAN—a polytheistic nature worshipper; includes Wiccans as well as Hindus, traditional Native Americans, and followers of Yoruba or Voudon. The indigenous religion of every culture is or was originally Pagan.

PENTACLE—a disk of wood or stone, usually with a pentagram and other magical symbols bigraved on it, symbolizing the Element Earth. It magically charges or blesses magical tools, cakes, and such placed atop it.

PENTAGRAM—an ancient occult symbol associated with the archetypal form of the human body; in modern times, an interlaced, five-pointed star of silver, copper, or pewter that Witches wear as an amulet in order to be protected by the powers of the Four Elements and Spirit. The notion that an inverted (point-down) pentagram is Satanic is a Christian fiction, for it's simply the Second Degree symbol, representing the Horned God.

POPPET—also called a ding-ding darling, a poppet is a figure fashioned by hand, typically of wax, cloth, or clay and often filled with herbs, then magically animated. Witches use poppets as microcosmic representations of people needing to be healed, or bound to prevent them from causing harm.

Q

QUINTESSENCE—the fifth element, Spirit, which pervades and animates all

R

RAISING A CONE OF POWER—dancing, chanting, singing, and playing instruments repeatedly around a spellwork circle, and steadily increasing speed until mental focus, emotional will, and physical energy produce a Cone of Power that activates aspect or magnifies its intensity

S

SABBAT—one of eight traditional seasonal Craft celebrations. There is a Sabbat every six to eight weeks throughout the year.

SCRYING—staring intently at something until you see predictive images. Crafters scry reflective, animated, and multi-faceted surfaces, such as sparkling water, flickering flames, and rutilated gemstones.

SHEWSTONE—a stone cut so that you can scry it rather like a crystal ball

SO MOTE IT BE!—May it be thus! An affirmation of intent, often declared at the end of a spell

SPELLCRAFT—See WITCHCRAFT

SPURGING (ASPERGING)—sprinkling consecrated salt water or scented oil on tools, people, or areas, typically with the fingers or a bough, such as a pine or broom branch

STANG—a staff with a forked top representing the Horned God

STREGA—Italian word for *Witch* derived from Latin *strix*, or (wise) owl; *Stregheria* is the term for Italian magical practices

SUMMERLANDS—a beautiful, tranquil netherworld where Wiccans believe people go after earthly death to rest and consider past actions before reincarnating

SUNWISE—in the direction in which the Sun appears to travel; clockwise (deosil) in the Northern Hemisphere, counterclockwise (widdershins) in the Southern Hemisphere; opposite of ayenward. Witches primarily move sunwise in circle.

T

TURNING THE WHEEL OF THE YEAR—magic that Witches have always done at Sabbats to ensure time's seasonal progression; typically involves spellwork, a hand-to-hand circle dance, visualizing turning a huge wheel, and raising a Cone of Power

W

WARD—to place a magical boundary to guard a covenstead, a gathering, premises, or occult meetings

WARLOCK—Contrary to popular opinion, this is not a term for a male Witch. Some Wiccans say it means "oathbreaker." Most likely, it is an olde Scottish word for Witch, from the Norse *vardlokr* (spirit-caller or shaman).

WICCA—the direct modern descendant of the Olde Religion practiced throughout pre-Christian Europe, derived from the Anglo-Saxon word for *Witch*.

WICCAN—a practitioner of Witchcraft. All Wiccans are Pagans, but not all Pagans are Wiccans.

WICCANING—a Pagan rite to bless and protect a newborn, an infant, or a child

WIDDERSHINS—counterclockwise. See AYENWARD.

WITCHCRAFT—a term to denote magical beliefs and occult practices; synonyms include the Craft of the Wise, the Old Ways, the Art Magical, and spellcraft.

WITCH—a descriptive word for magical folk of both sexes. Although a version of it appears in most languages, some attribute the English word's derivation to the German root *wikkjaz*, or "one who wakes the dead" (necromancer). Others think it derives from the old English root word *weik*, "to bend, twist, or wind," describing Witches' ability to warp space and time. Still others claim it comes from *weid*, "to see," describing Witches' seership. *Weid* later spawned the words *wise*, *wit*, and *wizard*.

WORKING—a spell or magical ritual

BIBLIOGRAPHY

PART I

SCOPE

Couliano, Ioan P. *Eros and Magic in the Renaissance*. Trans. Margaret Cook. Chicago: University of Chicago Press, 1987.

Devereaux, Paul. *Secrets of Ancient and Sacred Places*. London: Blandford Press, 1992.

Erler, Mary, and Maryanne Kowaleski, eds. *Women and Power in the Middle Ages*. Athens, Ga.: University of Georgia Press, 1988.

Farrington, Karen. *Punishment & Torture: A Journey Through the Dark Side of Justice*. New York: Sterling Publishing Co., Inc., Hamlyn, 2000.

Frazier, James G. *The Golden Bough: The Roots of Religion and Folklore*. New York: Crown Publishers, Avenel Books, 1981.

Friedman, Richard Elliott. *Who Wrote the Bible?* New York: Harper & Row, 1989.

Gardner, Gerald. *The Meaning of Witchcraft*. London: Aquarian Press, 1959.

Garrett, Susan R. "Light on a Dark Subject and Vice Versa: Magic and Magicians in the New Testament." In *Religion, Science, and Magic*. New York: Oxford University Press, 1992, 142–165.

Glazier, Richard. *Manual of Ornament*. 1899. Reprint, Hertfordshire, England: Wordsworth Editions, 1995.

Greer, Steven M., M.D. *Disclosure: Military and Government Witnesses Reveal the Greatest Secrets in Modern History*. Crozet, Va.: Crossing Point, Inc., 2001.

Jacq, Christian. *L' Enseignement du Sage Ptahhotep*. N.p.: La Maison de Vie, 1993.

Jones, Prudence, and Nigel Pennick. *A History of Pagan Europe*. N.p.: Barnes and Noble Books, 1999.

Kahane, P. P. *Ancient and Classical Art*. New York: Dell, 1967.

Kee, Howard Clark. "Magic and Messiah." *In Religion, Science, and Magic*. New York: Oxford University Press—USA, 1992, 121–141.

Leland, Charles Godfrey. *Etruscan Roman Remains*. Blaine, Wash.: Phoenix Publishing, 1892.

Merchant, Carolyn. *The Death of Nature: Women, Ecology, and the Scientific Revolution*. New York: Harper & Row, 1980.

Michell, John. *At the Center of the World: Polar Symbolism Discovered in Celtic, Norse, and Other Ritualized Landscapes*. London: Thames and Hudson, 1994.

Neumann, Erich. *The Great Mother: An Analysis of the Archetype*. Trans. Ralph Manheim. Princeton, N.J.: Princeton University Press, Bollingen Series, 1955.

Neusner, Jacob, Ernest S. Frerichs, and Paul Virgil McCracken Flesher, eds. *Religion, Science and Magic: In Concert and Conflict*. New York: Oxford University Press, 1989.

Pagels, Elaine. *Adam, Eve, and the Serpent.* New York: Random House, Vintage Books, 1988.
————*The Origin of Satan.* New York: Random House, 1995.
Peterson, Natasha. *Sacred Sites: A Traveler's Guide to North America's Most Powerful, Mystical Landmarks.* Chicago: Contemporary Books, 1988.
Potter, Charles Francis. "Shepherd's Score," *Funk & Wagnalls Standard Dictionary of Folklore, Mythology, and Legend.* Ed. Maria Leach. New York: Harper & Row, 1972, 1006–7.
Ross, Anne. *Everyday Life of the Pagan Celts.* London: Carousel Books, 1972.
Rufus, Anneli S., and Kristan Lawson. *Goddess Sites: Europe—Discover Places Where the Goddess Has Been Celebrated and Worshipped Throughout Time.* New York: HarperCollins, HarperSanFrancisco, 1991.
Tompkins, Peter. *The Magic of Obelisks.* New York: Harper & Row, 1981.
————*Mysteries of the Mexican Pyramid.* New York: Harper & Row, 1976.
————*Secrets of the Great Pyramid.* New York: Harper & Row, 1971.
Turner, Robert. *Elizabethan Magic: The Art and the Magus.* Longmead, Dorset, UK: Element Books, 1989.
Valiente, Doreen. *The Rebirth of Witchcraft.* Blaine, Wash.: Phoenix Publishing, 1989.
Wilczek, Frank. "The Persistence of Ether." *Physics Today*, January 1999.
Wilken, Robert L. *The Christians as the Romans Saw Them.* New Haven: Yale University Press, 1984.
Yates, Frances A. *The Occult Philosophy in the Elizabethan Age.* London: Routledge & Kegan Paul, 1979.
————*The Rosicrucian Enlightenment.* Boston: Shambhala Publications, 1978.

PART II

SKILLS

AS ABOVE, SO BELOW — THE ART OF CORRESPONDENCES

Agrippa, Heinrich C. *Three Books of Occult Philosophy: Written by Henry Cornelius Agrippa of Nettesheim.* 1533. Ed. Donald Tyson. Los Angeles: Llewellyn Publications, 1994.
Cunningham, Scott. *Earth, Air, Fire & Water.* Los Angeles: Llewellyn Publications, 1991.
Whitcomb, Bill. *The Magician's Companion: A Practical & Encyclopedic Guide to Magical & Religious Symbolism.* Los Angeles: Llewellyn Publications, 1993.

WITCHES SCRY OVER SPILT MILK — THE ART OF DIVINATION

Ali, Mohammed, comp. *Telling Fortunes By Cards.* Chicago: Shrewesbury Publishing, 1927.
Buckland, Raymond. *The Fortune-Telling Book: The Encyclopedia of Divination and Soothsaying.* Canton, Mich.: Visible Ink Press, 2004.
Dunwich, Gerina. *A Wiccan's Guide to Prophecy and Divination.* Secaucus, N. J.: Citadel Press, Carol Publishing Group, 1997.
Garen, Nancy. *Tarot Made Easy.* Simon & Schuster, Fireside Books, 1989.
Gettings, Fred. *Fate & Prediction: An Historical Compendium of Astrology, Palmistry & Tarot.* N.p.: Exeter Books, 1980.
Karcher, Stephen. *The Illustrated Encyclopedia of Divination: A Practical Guide to the Systems That*

Can Reveal Your Destiny. Longmead, Dorset, UK: Element Books, 1997.

Leland, Charles G. *Gypsy Sorcery & Fortune-Telling: Illustrated by Incantations, Specimens of Medical Magic, Anecdotes, Tales.* N.p.: Library of the Mystic Arts/Citadel Press, 1891.

Pennick, Nigel. *Games of the Gods: The Origin of Board Games in Magic and Divination.* York Beach, Maine: Red Wheel/Weiser, Weiser Books, 1989.

Skinner, Stephen. *Terrestrial Astrology: Divination by Geomancy.* London: Routledge and Kegan Paul, 1980.

DIVINE NUMBER — THE MAGIC OF COUNTING

Doczi, Gyorgy. *The Power of Limits: Proportional Harmonies in Nature, Art, and Architecture.* Boston: Shambhala Publications, 1981.

Lawlor, Robert. *Sacred Geometry: Philosophy and Practice.* London: Thames and Hudson, 1982.

Plato. *Timaeus and Critias.* Trans. Desmond Lee. London: Penguin UK, 1971.

Schneider, Michael S. *A Beginner's Guide to Constructing the Universe: The Mathematical Archetypes of Nature, Art, and Science.* New York: HarperCollins, 1994.

Waterfield, Robin, trans. *The Theology of Arithmetic: On the Mystical, Mathematical, and Cosmological Symbolism of the First Ten Numbers* (Iamblichus). York Beach, Maine: Red Wheel/Weiser, Phanes Press, 1988.

CHANTS AND CHARMS — THE POWER OF WORDS

Gager, John G., ed. *Curse Tablets and Binding Spells from the Ancient World.* Oxford, England: Oxford University Press, 1992.

Godwin, Joscelyn. *The Mystery of the Seven Vowels: In Theory and Practice.* York Beach, Maine: Red Wheel/Weiser, Phanes Press, 1991.

Graves, Robert. *The White Goddess: A Historical Grammar of Poetic Myth.* New York: Noonday Press, 1948.

Hamilton, Edith and Huntington Cairns, eds. *The Collected Dialogues including the Letters.* Princeton: Princeton University Press, 1985.

Magnus, Margaret. *A Dictionary of English Sound.* 1999. (Available from the author at **www.conknet.com/~mmagnus/LetterPage.html.**)

Martinet, André. *Elements of General Linguistics.* Trans. Elizabeth Palmer. Chicago: University of Chicago Press, 1964.

Paul, Annie Murphy. "Sounds True to Me: Research shows that rhyme has power to influence, as evidenced in political campaigns." *Psychology Today,* Sept./Oct., 1998.

Randall, J. K. "Compose Yourself: A Manual for the Young," Part II, Language Lab, *Perspectives of New Music.* Princeton: Princeton University Press, 1972.

Rheingold, Howard. *They Have a Word for It.* New York: Jeremy P. Tarcher, 1988.

Rossing, Thomas D. *The Science of Sound,* Second Edition. Boston: Addison-Wesley, 1990.

Skeat, Walter W. *A Concise Etymological Dictionary of the English Language.* Seventh printing. New York: Capricorn Books, 1963.

Slawson, Wayne. *Sound Color.* Berkeley, Calif.: University of California Press, 1985.

Touliatos, Diane. "Nonsense Syllables in the Music of the Ancient Greek and Byzantine Traditions," *The Journal of Musicology.* Berkeley, Calif.: University of California Press, 1989.

Townsend, Charles E. *Russian Word-Formation.* Bloomington, Ind.: Slavica Publishers, 1975.

Wadler, Arnold D. *One Language: Source of All Tongues*. N.p.: The American Press for Art and Science, 1948.

Watkins, Calvert. "Indo-European and the Indo-Europeans." *The American Heritage College Dictionary*, Third Edition. Boston: Houghton Mifflin Company, 1993.

SECRET WRITING — LETTERS, GLYPHS, AND RUNES

Goodman, Frederick. *Magic Symbols*. London: Brian Todd Publishing House, 1989.

Jacq, Christian. *Fascinating Hieroglyphs: Discovering, Decoding & Understanding the Ancient Art*. New York: Sterling Publishing Co, Inc., 1998.

Pennick, Nigel. *Magical Alphabets: The Secrets and Significance of Ancient Scripts—Including Runes, Greek, Ogham, Hebrew and Alchemical Alphabets*. York Beach, Maine: Red Wheel/Weiser, Wieser Books, 1992.

Peschel, Lisa. *A Practical Guide to the Runes: Their Uses in Divination and Magick*. Los Angeles: Llewellyn Publications, 1993.

Peterson, James M. *The Enchanted Alphabet: A Guide to Authentic Rune Magic and Divination*. Wellingborough, Northamptonshire, England: Aquarian Press, 1988.

Riva, Anna. *Secrets of Magical Seals: A Modern Grimoire of Amulets, Charms, Symbols & Talismans*. N.p.: International Imports, 1975.

Semaphore Flag Signaling System: **http://www.anbg.gov.au/flags/semaphore.html**

MUSICAL SPELLS — SINGING, PLAYING, AND DRUMMING MAGIC

Boethius, Anicius Manlius Severinus. *De institutione musica* (*Fundamentals of Music*). Trans. Calvin M. Bower, ed. Claude V. Palisca. New Haven: Yale University Press, 1989.

della Porta, Giovanni. *De furtivis literarum notis* (*On the secret notes of letters*). 1563. Reprint, n.p.: n.p., 1602.

d'Olivet, Fabre. *Music Explained as Science and Art and Considered in its Analogical Relations to Religious Mysteries, Ancient Mythology, and History of the World*. 1842. Trans. Joscelyn Godwin. Rochester, Vt.: Inner Traditions, 1987.

Godwin, Joscelyn. *Harmonies of Heaven and Earth*. Rochester, Vt.: Inner Traditions, 1987.

Ultan, Lloyd. *Music Theory: Problems and Practices in the Middle Ages and Renaissance*. Minneapolis: University of Minnesota Press, 1977.

MAGICAL MOVEMENT AND GESTURES

"Carole," *Man, Myth & Magic: The Illustrated Encyclopedia of Mythology, Religion and the Unknown*. Vol. 15. London: Purnell, Inc./BPC Publishing, 1970.

Funk & Wagnalls Standard College Dictionary. Pleasantville, N.Y.: Reader's Digest Association, 1966.

Glory Here: Thomas Morton and the Maypole of Merrymount. N.p.: Pagansword Press, Thomas Morton Alliance Publications, 1992.

Margolin, Malcolm. *The Ohlone Way: Indian Life in the San Francisco–Monterey Bay Area*. Berkeley: Heyday Books, 1978.

Morton, Thomas. *New English Canaan*. 1637. Ed. Jack Dempsey, Digital Scanning, 1999.

Short Description of Gods, Goddesses and Ritual Objects of Buddhism and Hinduism in Nepal. Comp.

Jnan Bahadur Sakya. Kathmandu, Nepal: Handicraft Association of Nepal, 1989.

HANDS-ON SPELLCRAFTING

Budge, E. A. Wallis. *Amulets and Talismans*. London: University Books, 1992.

Camporesi, Piero. *The Magic Harvest: Food, Folklore and Society*. Trans. Joan Hall. Oxford, England: Blackwell Publishing, 1998.

Cunningham, Scott. *The Magic in Food: Legends, Lore and Spellwork*. Los Angeles: Llewellyn Publications, 1993.

González-Wippler, Migene. *The Complete Book of Amulets and Talismans*. Los Angeles: Llewellyn Publications, 1991.

Hartley, Dorothy. *Lost Country Life*. New York: Random House, Pantheon Books, 1979.

Innes, Jocasta. *Food Magic*. New York: Prentice Hall, 1988.

Lehner, Ernst and Johanna Lehner. *Folklore and Odysseys of Food and Medicinal Plants*. New York: Farrar, Straus Giroux, 1973.

Lippman, Deborah and Paul Colin. *How to Make Amulets, Charms, and Talismans: What They Mean and How to Use Them*. N.p.: M Evans and Company, 1985.

Lust, John. *The Herb Book*. New York: Bantam Books, 1974.

Nelson, Felicitas H. *Talismans & Amulets of the World*. New York: Sterling Publishing Co., Inc., 2000.

Telesco, Patricia. *A Kitchen Witch's Cookbook*. Los Angeles: Llewellyn Publications, 1998.

———*Bubble, Bubble, Toil, and Trouble: Mystical Munchies, Prophetic Potions, Sexy Servings, and Other Witchy Dishes*. New York: HarperCollins, HarperSanFrancisco, 2002.

Visser, Margaret. *The Rituals of Dinner: The Origins, Evolution, Eccentricities and Meanings of Table Manners*. Toronto, Ontario, Canada: HarperCollinsPublishers, 1991.

Weiss, Linda. *Kitchen Magic: Now You Eat It, Now You Don't*. Lincolnwood, Ill.: McGraw-Hill, 1994.

HOW TO KNOW YOU'RE DOING SPELLS PROPERLY

Buckland, Raymond. *Buckland's Complete Book of Witchcraft*. Los Angeles: Llewellyn Publications, 1987.

———*The Witch Book: The Encyclopedia of Witchcraft, Wicca, and Neo-paganism*. Canton, Mich.: Visible Ink Press, 2002.

Crowley, Aleister. *Magick in Theory and Practice*. Edison, N.J.: Castle Books, 1991.

Farrar, Janet and Stewart Farrar. *A Witches' Bible Compleat*. New York: Magickal Childe Publishing, 1984.

Fortune, Dion. *Esoteric Orders and Their Work*. Los Angeles: Llewellyn Publications, 1962.

Medici, Marina. *Good Magic*. New York: Simon & Schuster, Fireside Books, 1988.

Valiente, Doreen. *An ABC of Witchcraft*. Blaine, Wash.: Phoenix Publishing, 1973.

PART III

SPELLS

Agrippa, Heinrich Cornelius. *Of Occult Philosophy, or Of Magical Ceremonies: The Fourth Book*. Ca. 1560. Trans. Robert Turner. 1655. Twilit Grotto Esoteric Archives (**http://www.esoteri-carchives.com/agrippa/agrippa4.htm**): Joseph H. Peterson, 2000.

Alibeck the Egyptian. *Grimorium Verum*. Memphis, Egypt: 1517. Trans. Joseph H. Peterson. Twilit Grotto Esoteric Archives (**http://www.esotericarchives.com/solomon/gv_bi.htm**): Joseph H. Peterson, 1999.

Atal, C. K., U. Zutshi, and P.G. Rao. "Scientific evidence on the role of Ayurvedic herbals on bioavailability of drugs," abstract, National Library of Medicine, 1981.

Barrett, Francis. *The Magus*. 1801. Reprint, York Beach, Maine: Red Wheel/Weiser, Weiser Books, 2000.

Betz, Hans Dieter, ed. *Greek Magical Papyri in Translation, Including the Demotic Spells*. Chicago: University of Chicago Press, 1986. Source collections are *Papyri Graecae Magicae (PGM)* and *Papyri Demoticae Magicae (PDM)*. Excerpts from Betz are published online by John Opsopaus as "Ecloga Ex Papyris Magicis" ("Selections from Magical Papyri") at **http://www.hermetic.com/pgm/ecloga-III.html**.

The Boy's Own Toy Maker Illustrating the Art and Science of Practical Mechanism. Racine, Wis.: Johnson Smith & Co., n.d.

Bruno, Giordano. *De Magia*. Ca. 1590. Twilit Grotto Esoteric Archives (**http://www.esoteri-carchives.com/bruno/magia.htm**): Joseph H. Peterson, n.d.

Cunningham, Scott and David Harrington. *Spell Crafts*. Los Angeles: Llewellyn Publications, 1993.

Diagram Group. *The Little Giant Encyclopedia of Spells & Magic*. Ed. Jane Johnson. New York: Sterling Publishing Co., Inc., 1999.

Diagram Group. *The Little Giant Encyclopedia of Superstitions*. New York: Sterling Publishing Co., Inc., 1999.

Dunwich, Gerina. *Candlelight Spells: The Modern Witches' Book of Spellcasting, Feasting and Natural Healing*. New York: Citadel Press/Carol Publishing Group, 1993.

Elworthy, Frederick Thomas. *The Evil Eye: An Account of This Ancient and Widespread Superstition*. 1895. Reprint, New York: Julian Press, 1986.

Ficino, Marcilio. *Liber de Vita (The Book of Life)*. 1489. Trans. Charles Boer. Putnam, Conn.: Spring Publications, Inc., 1980.

Frazier, James. *The Golden Bough: A Study in Comparative Religion*. London: The McMillan Co., 1890.

Gerard, John. *The Herbal, Or General History of Plants*. 1633. Rev. Thomas Johnson. Mineola, N.Y.: Dover Publications, 1975.

Grimassi, Raven. *Ways of the Strega—Italian Witchcraft: Its Lore, Magick and Spells*. Los Angeles: Llewellyn Publications, 1995.

Jordan, Michael. *Encyclopedia of Gods: Over 2,500 Deities of the World*. New York: Facts On File, 1993.

Le Grand Grimoire. 1522. Reprint, Paris: Antonio Venitiana, 1845. Twilit Grotto Esoteric Archives **(http://www.esotericarchives.com/solomon/grand.htm):** Joseph H. Peterson, 1998.

Leland, Charles G. *Aradia: Gospel of the Witches. 1980.* Reprint, Blaine, Wash.: Phoenix Publishing, 1990.

Malbrough, Ray T. *Charms, Spells & Formulas.* Los Angeles: Llewellyn Publications, 1993.

Mathers, S. Liddell MacGregor, trans. *Clavicula Salomonis (The Key of Solomon the King).* York Beach, Maine: Red Wheel/Weiser, Weiser Books, 1972.

Meier, C. A. *Healing Dream and Ritual: Ancient Incubation and Modern Psychotherapy.* Einsiedeln, Switzerland: Daimon Verlag, 1989.

Miller, Patricia Cox. *Dreams in Late Antiquity: Studies in the Imagination of a Culture.* Princeton: Princeton University Press, 1994.

Monaghan, Patricia. *The Book of Goddesses & Heroines.* Los Angeles: Llewellyn Publications, 1993.

Neal, Bill. *Gardener's Latin: Discovering the Origins, Lore & Meaning of Botanical Names.* Chapel Hill, N.C.: Algonquin Books of Chapel Hill, 1992.

Peterson, Joseph H., ed. *Liber Sacratus* (also known as *Liber Juratus,* or *The Sworne Book of Honorius).* Ca. 13th century. Twilit Grotto Esoteric Archives (http://www.esotericarchives.com/ juratus/juratus.htm): Joseph H. Peterson, 1998.

Renee, Janina. *Tarot Spells.* Los Angeles: Llewellyn Publications, 1992.

Tompkins, Peter. *The Secret Life of Nature: Living in Harmony with the Hidden World of Nature Spirits from Fairies to Quarks.* New York: HarperCollins, HarperSanFrancisco, 1997.

Trevelyan, Joanna. *Holistic Home: Creating an Environment for Physical & Spiritual Well-Being.* New York: Sterling Publishing Co., Inc., 1998.

Turner, Robert, trans. *Ars Notoria.* 1657. Twilit Grotto Esoteric Archives **(http://www.eso tericarchives.com/notoria/notoria.htm):** Joseph H. Peterson, 1998.

Wall, Carly. *The Little Giant Encyclopedia of Home Remedies.* Sterling Publishing Co., Inc., 2000.

Watkins, Matthew. *Useful Mathematical & Physical Formulae.* New York: Walker & Company, 2001.

Wilde, Lady. *Irish Cures, Mystic Charms & Superstitions.* New York: Sterling Publishing Co., Inc., 1991.

INDEX

About the Authors

LADY PASSION AND *DIUVEI
> are Third Degree Gardnerian Witches and the High
> Priestess and High Priest of Coven Oldenwilde.

LADY PASSION (DIXIE L. DEERMAN)
> is a grandmother who has practiced Italian *Strega* magic
> for almost 30 years. She is a registered nurse, an herbalist,
> an artist, and a gifted psychic. Among her many magical
> skills on which her townsfolk rely are healing, counsel-
> ing, prognostication, ghost busting, and finding missing
> persons.

*DIUVEI (STEVEN C. RASMUSSEN)
> first discovered the Art Magical while a student of music
> theory at Princeton University and has pursued it in the
> quarter-century since as a professional astrologer,
> computer musicologist, and investigative journalist.

Lady Passion and *Diuvei founded COVEN OLDENWILDE on
> Samhain in 1994. They conduct large, annual, public
> rituals; lecture on Craft topics at universities; teach
> serious Wiccan students; sponsor Pagan covens in prisons
> and on military bases; marry and bury folks; and are
> activists for Wiccan and Pagan religious rights.

They live in Asheville, North Carolina, and may be reached
> through their Web site, www.oldenwilde.org.

Illustration Credits

Art on pp. 25, 197, and 241: *Three Books of Occult Philosophy: The Foundation Book of Western Occultism* by Henry Cornelius Agrippa of Nettesheim, edited and annotated by Donald Tyson © 1993 Llewellyn Worldwide, Ltd., P.O. Box 64383, St. Paul, MN 55164. All rights reserved. Used by permission of the publisher.

Image on p. 67 courtesy of Joseph H. Peterson, esotericarchives.com.

Figures on pp. 97-101 from Giordano Bruno's *Ars Memoraie Part 2*, courtesy of Joseph H. Peterson, esotericarchives.com.

Image on p. 151 © 2005 JupiterImages Corporation.

Image of Greco-Roman jasper amulet depicting Abraxas, p. 278, courtesy of the Kelsey Museum of Archeology, University of Michigan.

Image of Ophiuchus on p. 284 from the *Atlas Coelestis 1753* by John Flamsteed, courtesy of the Istituto di Fisica Generale Applicata (www.brera.unimi.it).

Image on p. 408 excerpted from *The Key of Solomon the King*, translated and edited by S. Liddell MacGregor Mathers, with permission of Red Wheel/Weiser, Boston, MA, and York Beach, ME.